THE ASTROTWINS
2023
HOROSCOPE

Authors: Tali Edut, Ophira Edut
Managing Editor: Lisa M. Sundry
Copy Editors: Amy Anthony, Vanessa Montgomery
Contributing Editors: Matthew Swann, Felicia Bender, Tracy Allen, Kara Nesvig
Research Editor: Stephanie Gailing

Cover Illustration © 2022 by Bodil Jane
Book Design: Rosie Dienhart
Interior Illustrations: Will Dudley

CONTENTS

2023

A Message From The AstroTwins

DEAR READER,

Welcome to the 11th edition of our annual AstroTwins Horoscope guide. In uncertain times, we find solace in all that is predictable and circular. And what fits that bill better than the ever-dependable Sun, moon and stars?

We released our first version of this book in late 2012, with forecasts for the year 2013. That was the last time that the karmic lunar nodes were in Taurus and Scorpio, just as they are now, though in reverse positions. Themes of sustainability, from the environment to the economy, were already in our predictions back then.

The metaphysical masses were counting down to December 21, 2012, the day that the Mayan calendar completed its 5,125-year cycle. Prophecies ranged from the apocolyptic to the enlightened. There was a collective wondering, "What's going to happen next?"

Astrology had not yet seeped into the mainstream the way it has 11 years later. Maybe that's why this books seems to grow in pages every year. More than ever, consulting the "cosmic compass" of our skies has become a widespread way to make sense of these complexifying times.

One of our 2013 headlines was "Water, Water, Everywhere." As we enter the Year of the Water Rabbit (ruled by seafaring Neptune), and Saturn visits oceanic Pisces for the first time since 1996, tapping into the "holographic" realm can change your reality. Visualize the world you wish to live in, even (and especially) when the one you occupy resembles anything but that. We'll meet you there.

Ophi & Tali

THE YEAR OF "WHAT IF...?"

A mystical thing happens while we're planning the cover art for our annual guides. As we sense our way into the year's cosmic lineup, imagery "arrives"before we have concrete understanding of its relevance.

A moonlit medicine ceremony was the subject of our 2020 cover, conceptualized at least half a year before the world plunged into the darkness of the pandemic. In early 2021, we were "feeling aliens for next year," not knowing that the Pentagon would soon release a UFO report and NASA announced formation of a "UFO committee" research group as we write this.

So when Egypt was floated as the 2023 theme, we accepted that there must be a reason why. And thus, we began our astrological dig...

Inquiry led us to a pivotal time in history, approximately 1177 BCE, when a systems-wide civilization crash occurred, known as the Bronze Age Collapse. And it wiped out one of the earliest global trade networks in history, that included as one of its superpowers, (you guessed it) Egypt. Within 100 years, an astounding number of ancient civilizations fell, taking with them a 2,100-year-old economic system.

At the source of this cataclysm was an eerily familiar issue: Climate change.

No, it wasn't greenhouse gasses shifting weather patterns back in 1177 BCE. But there *was* a century-long megadrought waging, which spiraled regions into famine. In turn, this caused mass populations to flee their homelands in the name of survival. (Also a present-day issue and, predictably, a looming one, for hot, dry regions.)

Among the afflicted ancients were the "Sea Peoples," now believed by historians to be the Philistines. Simultaneously refugees *and* raiders, they arrived at major Bronze Age ports, burning cities to the ground and wiping out most of the civilizations who traded the copper ingots and tin used to make this magical metal. At the same time, a series of earthquakes ripped through the Mediterranean zone. This storm of chaotic events decimated a number of ancient groups, including the Hittites, Minoans and Mycenaeans—whose disappearance erased the writing system, Linear B, and plunged the Greeks into a 300-year dark age of illiteracy.

Egypt survived the Sea People's invasions as well as the natural disasters. Under the rulership of Ramses III, they fended off multiple attacks and remained one of the few civilizations standing in the region. Yet this was the beginning of the long, slow finale of the ancient realm. After Ramses III was murdered in a coup in 1155 BCE, Egypt entered an age of decline, was divided in half, and ultimately defeated by Alexander the Great in 332 BCE.

So what does this have to do with 2023's astrology? In a word: Pluto.

Perhaps the most profound astrological event of 2023 arrives this March 23, when the cosmic ruler of death and rebirth changes zodiac signs for the first time since 2008. For the coming two years, Pluto weaves back and forth between iron-fisted, hierarchical Capricorn and innovative, community-focused Aquarius, ready to shake up one system after another.
Pluto made the same shift from Capricorn to Aquarius in 1162 BCE, right smack dab in the middle of Ramses III's reign of Egypt.

And here's another goosebumps-inducing "coincidence," perhaps one that will shine a more hopeful light. Pluto do-si-do'd between Capricorn and

Aquarius from 1777 to 1778, right after the Declaration of Independence was signed. While Pluto was firmly housed in Aquarius (in 1788), the United States Constitution was ratified and remains the world's longest surviving written government charter.

"We The People," as the Constitution begins, could be followed by *so* many sentiments in this current Age of Aquarius. And what if "we the people" could find a way to work together? What if, indeed.

While writing this book, we began so many inquiries with those same two words that we're dubbing 2023 The Year of "What If...?"

"What If...?" is a fork in the road of our mindsets. The inquiry can take us in one of two directions: enervation or innovation. At this present moment, both seem like reasonable paths.

The "What If...?" inquiry can spin us into apocalyptic anxiety. Or it can turn the key in the ignition of our imaginations. We've moved through both fields while preparing your horoscope for 2023.

Like the ancient Egyptians, we've reached a peak moment in humanity. Never before have we had so many resources and information at our fingertips. In 2021, there were 79 zettabytes of data produced in the world. *Zettabytes.* That's 79 trillion gigabytes, in case you're wondering.

Along with our cloud storage capacity, anxiety has been spiking in children and adults since 2020. The pandemic, war, inflation, political fractures, climate change and overall uncertainty about the future—there's no shortage of triggers to flood our bodies with stress hormones.

Paying attention to our thoughts is more important than ever. We're not suggesting an ostrich's approach of burying heads in the sand. But where do we "go" with the current state of the world? Can we take the cold, hard facts and spin the "What if...?" question in an innovative direction? In the year ahead, the planets seem to be asking us to do just that:

As such, Isis was the obvious choice for our "cover model." As the goddess of resurrection, transformation, loyalty and magic, she represents so many themes of 2023. Using her glorious wings, Isis flew to the underworld to deliver fresh air to her husband Osiris. (Who was also her brother...hey, it's mythology.)

We depicted Isis, as she often is in antiquity, wearing the crown of Hathor, who is the goddess of pleasure, fertility, love and motherhood. With its cow horns and sun disc, Hathor's crown represents abundance and the cosmos. With her ability to dive into the shadows and call in the light of the sun, Isis has range. And that's something we could all use this year when the question of "What If...?" invites us to stretch into higher human potential without ignoring the fires burning at our feet.

As an ancient Egyptian proverb tells us, "To have peace there must be strife; both are part of the structure of the world and requirements." While 2023 may deliver both, it is also time for a *restructuring*.

Our hope is that the *2023 Horoscope* will meet you with serendipity as you go through moments of your yearlong journey, whether you're seeking inspiration, comfort or deeper understanding of what loved ones are going through.

And with that, let us send you deeper into the catacombs of this book with an ancient Egyptians salutation of *em hotep,* which means "in peace."

THE *Inner* PLANETS

IN 2023

SUN

MOON

MERCURY

VENUS

MARS

The inner planets are the faster moving heavenly bodies, nearest to the Sun (plus the moon and the Sun itself). United by their rocky cores, they include Mercury, Venus and Mars. Their journey through the zodiac shapes the intimate areas of our lives including family, friendship, love and sex. Because they hit on matters so close to home, astrologers refer to them as the "personal planets." We've tracked their movements for you in the year ahead, to help you make decisions that are close to your heart!

THE SUN

THE SUN IN ASTROLOGY

The Sun is the center of our solar system. It literally gives us life, providing the light, heat and energy that sustains us. Since all other planets revolve around it, we'd say the Sun has earned its well-deserved place as our primary sign in the astrology chart. Your birthday—called your "solar return" in astrospeak—always occurs when the Sun is in your sign.

The Sun doesn't actually orbit anywhere at all. But Western astrology is geocentric, meaning it's calculated from our vantage point down here on Earth. From that perspective, the Sun *does* appear to travel like the other planets. Every 30 days or so, el Sol moves into a new zodiac sign, kicking off a new zodiac "season." This prevailing energy colors the world for all of us. It's as if the Sun slips on a pair of colored glasses—golden yellow for Leo season, smoky amber for Scorpio—and casts its light on us through the mood of that filter.

Planning WITH THE SUN

In our Hotspots section, you can learn how to work with the energy of every Sun sign season. We thought we'd share another one of our favorite ways to plan with el Sol using the three zodiac modalities: cardinal, fixed and mutable. When the Sun travels through one of these positions, it directs our energy accordingly. Should you initiate, hunker down or spread the word? Here's how to know.

THE SUN IN CARDINAL SIGNS

Aries, Cancer, Libra, Capricorn

The cardinal signs start off every season and dovetail with major heavenly events:

Sun in Aries — equinox
Sun in Cancer — solstice
Sun in Libra — equinox
Sun in Capricorn — solstice

During these month-long solar cycles, we should initiate projects, taking on leadership (and ownership) to get them in motion. Map out your ideas, woo supporters and get all hands on deck!

THE SUN IN FIXED SIGNS

Taurus, Leo, Scorpio, Aquarius

Production is underway! The tenacious fixed cycles occur at the middle of each season and help us move from idea to action. You might feel more like a drone than a queen bee during these times, but that's okay. Fixed phases are essential for getting the job done. Stay focused, hustle and pay attention to the bottom line as well as the details.

THE SUN IN MUTABLE SIGNS

Gemini, Virgo, Sagittarius, Pisces

Time to walk your talk! The mutable signs finish each season, helping us bring our work into the world. Time to start buzzing, evangelizing and arousing interest. These solar cycles are highly social and interactive. You might not get much sleep, but hey, the conversations will be
life-changing!

the Sun IN 2023

CAPRICORN
DEC 21, 2022 (4:48PM)
Solstice

AQUARIUS
JAN 20 (3:30AM)

PISCES
FEB 18 (5:34PM)

ARIES
MAR 20 (5:24PM)
Equinox

TAURUS
APR 20 (4:14AM)

GEMINI
MAY 21 (3:09AM)

CANCER
JUN 21 (10:58AM)
Solstice

LEO
JUL 22 (9:50PM)

VIRGO
AUG 23 (5:01AM)

LIBRA
SEP 23 (2:50AM)
Equinox

SCORPIO
OCT 23 (12:21PM)

SAGITTARIUS
NOV 22 (9:03AM)

CAPRICORN
DEC 21 (10:27PM)
Solstice

times listed are Eastern US Time Zone

AKA THE ZODIAC SEASONS

WERE YOU BORN ON A CUSP?

Every year, there's a slight difference in the date and time that the Sun changes signs. If you were born on one of those cusp days, you will have to run a natal chart and include your time of birth to find out your exact Sun sign. Though you may exhibit traits of both zodiac signs, in truth you can only have *one* Sun sign. See our table for the exact minute the Sun changes signs in 2023.

Do your natal chart for free at ASTROSTYLE.COM/BIRTHCHART

SOLAR CONNECTIONS IN 2023

THE DAY OF MIRACLES:
SUN-JUPITER CONJUNCTION IN ARIES
APRIL 11

April 11 is the annual Sun-Jupiter conjunction. In recent years, astrologers have referred to this cosmic event as "The Day of Miracles." Because both celestial bodies beam with such bright promise, our optimism alone can attract abundance! This year, they meet up in fierce, fiery, trailblazing Aries. Got a new initiative to launch? A fresh idea to debut? This could be a rich moment to put yourself out there. No matter what your sign is, lean into some of that Aries entitlement. Hey, this sign knows they deserve the best. And if you believe *you* do, too, this could be the day that you manifest it!

THE MOON

THE MOON IN ASTROLOGY

The moon is the Sun's favorite companion, holding space for all the private matters el Sol doesn't care to shine a light on. These are things like our deepest feelings, secret desires, and the security blankets that we reach for to comfort ourselves. Home and family affairs, how we nurture others and what kind of caretaking we crave are also #MoonMatters. Our society is just starting to truly honor the importance of lunar topics, perhaps because they tend to fall into the archetypally feminine category. As the world grows to respect women's perspectives and issues, the moon's power is being felt more and more!

To find your natal moon sign, cast a free birth chart at:

ASTROSTYLE.COM/BIRTHCHART

THE MOON IN 2023

A wildly experimental year may be in store for us all, at least if the moon has anything to say about it! On January 21, the first new moon of 2023 arrives in eclectic, eccentric Aquarius. This is a huge contrast to years that begin with industrious, traditional Capricorn, which is the only other zodiac sign that can kickstart the year's new moon cycle.

Everything "certain" is up for examination with this new moon. That could lead to some lively debates—and in some cases, time-sucking social media battles. Fortunately, there's a collaborative vibe in years that begin with a new moon in Aquarius—a zodiac sign that wants to give everyone a seat at the table. Where could you open your mind a little wider?

While the moon is emotional, Aquarius is rational, so their dance is an awkward one. Think of the January 21 Aquarius new moon as a day to unite heart and head. That's a theme that everyone could benefit from in 2023!

Planning WITH THE MOON

Each month, we complete a multi-phase moon cycle, as la luna disappears into the darkness of the new moon, then swells into a full moon two weeks later. During the weeks in between, there are quarter moons. While the moon doesn't "go retrograde" like Mercury or the other planets, these waxing and waning spells are just as important to track for planning each month. There are four eclipses in 2023, occurring as two solar (new moon) eclipses and two lunar (full moon) eclipses.

2023 NEW MOONS

New moons occur when la luna is perfectly positioned between the Earth and the Sun. As such, the "backside" of the moon is lit, and it becomes invisible from our view down here. Because everything goes dark, it's as if we have a blank canvas on which to create. In "nothingness" there is a sense of limitless possibilities. That is the gift of the new moon, a great time for setting intentions, making wishes, and taking the first bold step towards a new goal. We may actually start to see the first signs of these lunar requests two weeks later, when the next full moon on the calendar lights up the night skies.

Astro-geek fact: The new moon occurs in the same zodiac sign as the Sun each month.

New Moons

times listed are Eastern US Time Zone

AQUARIUS (1°33)
JAN 21, 3:53PM

PISCES (1°22)
FEB 20, 2:06AM

ARIES #1 OF 2 (0°50)
MAR 21, 1:22PM

ARIES #2 OF 2 (29°50)
APR 20, 12:12AM
HYBRID SOLAR ECLIPSE

TAURUS (28°25)
MAY 19, 11:53AM

GEMINI (26°43)
JUN 18, 12:36AM

CANCER (24°56)
JUL 17, 2:31PM

LEO (23°17)
AUG 16, 5:38AM

VIRGO (21°59)
SEP 14, 9:39PM

LIBRA (21°08)
OCT 14, 1:55PM
ANNULAR SOLAR ECLIPSE

SCORPIO (20°44)
NOV 13, 4:27AM

SAGITTARIUS (20°40)
DEC 12, 6:32PM

2023 FULL MOONS

It's harvest time! During a full moon, you reap the seeds that were sown six months prior during the corresponding new moon. These cosmic manifestation moments can be cause for celebration or major eye-openers. During this lunar phase, the moon is on the exact opposite side of the Earth from the Sun. That explains why it's such a brightly lit spectacle for us to enjoy—and why the full moon is always in the *opposite* sign from the Sun each month. Contradictions stand out in stark reality during full moons, which can stir up intense passion and fierce head-butting. You may realize that you're done with one path and ready to find whatever's next. No matter what, emotions and overall intensity will be amplified. Stay aware of how much energy you're exuding and how people are responding to you. In 2023, there are two full moons in Cancer, which bookend the year on January 6 and December 26 and invite us all to be more emotionally expressive this year.

Full Moons

CANCER #1 OF 2
(16°22)
JAN 6, 6:07PM

LEO (16°41)
FEB 5, 1:28PM

VIRGO (16°40)
MAR 7, 7:40AM

LIBRA (16°07)
APR 6, 12:34AM

SCORPIO (14°58)
MAY 5, 1:33PM
PENUMBRAL LUNAR
ECLIPSE

SAGITTARIUS (13°18)
JUN 3, 11:41PM

CAPRICORN (11°19)
JUL 3, 7:38AM

AQUARIUS (9°16)
AUG 1, 2:31PM

PISCES (7°25)
AUG 30, 9:36PM

ARIES (6°00)
SEP 29, 5:58AM

TAURUS (5°09)
OCT 28, 4:24PM
PARTIAL LUNAR ECLIPSE

GEMINI (4°51)
NOV 27, 4:16AM

CANCER #2 OF 2
(4°58)
DEC 26, 7:33PM

times listed are Eastern US Time Zone

QUARTER MOONS

First Quarter Moon (Waxing)

The first quarter moon comes about a week after each new moon. This marks the halfway point between the new moon and the forthcoming full moon. Since the moon is waxing (growing fuller), it brings a reminder to pick up the pace and make sure that our actions match our words. After all, what's the point of making those new moon wishes if we don't actually *do* something about them? Grab the baton...but no need to burst into a full-on sprint! Since quarter moons are balancers, measured, thoughtful action is key (and haste makes waste). The first quarter moon is a stellar time to map out a plan and take the first few steps.

Third Quarter Moon (Waning)

The third quarter moon comes approximately a week after the full moon, as we are reaping and harvesting, but also winding down to the next new moon. This is a time for sorting the crops. Not every pick is a keeper! During this phase, we might shed a few elements that aren't the right fit. This curating process creates the right setting to help the true gems shine.

Read more on 2023's quarter moons in the Hotspots section.

SOLAR ECLIPSES

Lights out! Solar eclipses take place during a new moon, when the Sun and moon converge at the exact degree in the same zodiac sign on the ecliptic—the plane that the Earth rotates around the Sun. As the moon passes over the Sun from our view, it darkens the sky and, during a total eclipse, changes the appearance of shadows. Eerie or magical (or both!), solar eclipses remind us that all that glitters ain't gold. Look in a new direction during a solar eclipse, because that's where you'll find the magic. This can feel scary at first, especially if you've been tamping down your desires to gain a sense of false control. But change is inevitable, and these momentous new moons push us off the starting block in a big way.

APRIL 20: ARIES HYBRID SOLAR ECLIPSE

OCTOBER 14: LIBRA ANNULAR SOLAR ECLIPSE

In 2023, there are two solar eclipses, which both promise to put on a stunning show in the sky. On April 20, the first solar eclipse to arrive in Aries since 2015 begins a brand-new eclipse series across the Aries-Libra axis. Independence versus partnership, war versus peace: These themes will be major during this new, two-year eclipse series. But the focus starts with you, since this one's in "me first" Aries. But that's not all! The April 20 lunation is an ultra-rare "hybrid" solar eclipse that begins as an annular (ring of fire) eclipse and transitions into a sky-darkening total eclipse along its path.

The second solar eclipse arrives in Libra on October 14—the first one to light up this loving sign since March 2016. Get ready for epiphanies and illuminating insights around relationships also as an annular ring of fire eclipse that reveals the glowing edges of the Sun as it is darkened by the moon.

LUNAR ECLIPSES

Seeing red? Lunar eclipses transpire when the full moon opposes the Sun at the same degree of zodiac sign on the ecliptic. With the Earth sandwiched between these heavenly bodies, el Sol casts a shadow that slowly bleeds across the surface of the moon. (In fact, due to its reddish tint, a total lunar eclipse has earned the nickname of "blood moon.") Lunar eclipses are prime time for doing shadow work and dealing with feelings we've ignored. Buckle up, buttercup! Situations could pivot abruptly or come to a sudden, unceremonious halt. If anything in your life is "eclipsed away," here's our advice: Stop chasing and give it some space. You'll either manifest a better option or circle back to this later—after you've processed the lesson and evolved!

MAY 5: SCORPIO PENUMBRAL LUNAR ECLIPSE
OCTOBER 28: TAURUS PARTIAL LUNAR ECLIPSE

There are two lunar eclipses in 2023, which round out a two-year series that has been burning up the money-minded Taurus-Scorpio axis. From soaring gas prices to inflation to the trend of "quiet quitting," we've shifted the way we think about our fiduciary world.

On May 5, a total lunar eclipse simmers in Scorpio, bringing explosive power struggles. We may uncover nefarious details about people's hidden agendas, criminal activity and scandalous underground activity. Will it be shocking? You'd better believe it. Picking up the pieces could take a while—as it already has since the Russia-Ukraine war escalated near these eclipses last year. A no-nonsense Taurus partial lunar eclipse on October 28 may finally bring some order to the global court. But we'll be forced to deal with everything from world hunger to the global economy—and the weight of that is mighty.

Eclipse DATES & VISIBILITY

APR 20
12:17AM

Hybrid Solar Eclipse in Aries (29°52)
Visible in: Australia, Asia, Philippines. (A partial eclipse will be visible over Indonesia, parts of Australia, Papua New Guinea.)

MAY 5
1:24PM

Penumbral Lunar Eclipse in Scorpio (14°52)
Visible in: Africa, Asia, Australia

OCT 14
2:00PM

Annular Solar Eclipse in Libra (21°10)
Visible in: United States over Oregon, Nevada, Utah, New Mexico, Texas, as well as some parts of California, Idaho, Colorado and Utah; Central America—Mexico, Belize, Honduras, Panama; South America—through Colombia then over the coast of Natal, Brazil over the Atlantic Ocean. (A partial eclipse will be visible over all of the United States, Canada, Alaska, parts of South America, Greenland and western Africa.)

OCT 28
4:15PM

Partial Lunar Eclipse in Taurus (5°03)
Visible in: Americas, Europe, Asia, Africa, Australia

*Visibility as reported by NASA.org

times listed are Eastern US Time Zone

MORE BOOKS
BY THE ASTROTWINS

HOW TO GET ALONG WITH ANYONE (*YES, EVEN THAT PERSON)

Any two zodiac signs CAN be compatible, as long as they understand what makes the other one tick. The AstroTwins simplify the secrets of synastry—the 7 unique energies encoded in the distance between your signs. Take your relationships from difficult to dynamic and start bringing out your best.

SUPERCOUPLE

Unlock the astrology secrets to sizzling attraction and deep connection, and get through the hard stuff fast! Did you know that your relationship has a zodiac sign and chart? The Supercouple system is the ultimate guide to finding true compatibility—by understanding why you came together and what your divine destiny could be!

MOMSTROLOGY

Parenting DOES come with instructions! This ultimate guide to raising your kids AND flourishing as a mom takes you through every season of parenthood, from birth to toddler to school years and leaving the nest. A favorite baby shower gift, featured by *Good Morning America* and a #1 Amazon bestseller.

START READING NOW AT **ASTROSTYLE.COM/BOOKS**

MERCURY

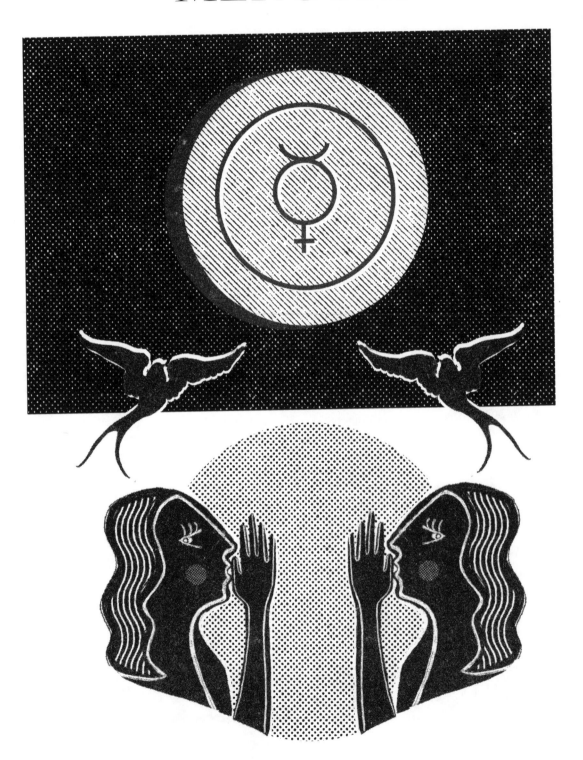

☿

MERCURY IN ASTROLOGY

Messenger Mercury is the ruler of information, communication and our intellectual processes. The closest planet to the Sun, Mercury orbits through each zodiac sign for approximately three weeks. These cycles shape our cultural interests. From the topics we're buzzing about to the ways we communicate, whatever sign Mercury is occupying plays a role. Each year, Mercury turns retrograde for three cycles, appearing to travel backward through the zodiac. During these reverse commutes, it lingers in one or two signs for approximately ten weeks. While the scrambled signals can be agonizing, we have a chance to dive into deeper discourse. People from the past may reappear, like old friends, estranged relatives and exes with unfinished business.

To find your natal Mercury sign, cast a free birth chart at

ASTROSTYLE.COM/BIRTHCHART

Planning WITH MERCURY

Active Mercury loves to help us map our daily schedules and routines. What will you be in the mood for at any given time during the year? If you want to spark up a bold conversation or try an adventurous activity, opt for cycles when Mercury is in a fire sign (Aries, Leo, Sagittarius). Need to hunker down to budget, research or tackle a household repair project? You're most likely to have patience for such mundane things while Mercury is in an earth sign (Taurus, Virgo, Capricorn). There's no better time for networking, hive-minding or collaborating than when Mercury is in a social air sign (Gemini, Libra, Aquarius). Creative brainstorming, processing heavy emotions and connecting to your inner circle of family and friends are best done while Mercury's in a water sign (Cancer, Scorpio, Pisces).

When Mercury turns retrograde three to four times each year, there's no need to panic! But pace yourself during these data-skewing, three-week cycles. Focus on all things with the prefix "re," such as revising, reviewing, redesigning and reconsidering. Pay closer attention to your inner world and get in touch with your thoughts, which signal all your feelings. Is it time to update certain beliefs? Mercury retrograde can help!

Discover how the speedy planet shapes your thoughts, systems and communication style with our pocket course, The Mercury Code!

ASTROSTYLE.COM/MERCURY

SEEING MERCURY *in the sky*

Get a glimpse of winged messenger Mercury in the morning, low in the east before sunrise, on these dates:

JAN 13 – MAR 7
MAY 11 – JUN 24
SEP 14 – OCT 8
Dec 29 – Dec 31

Evening Mercury is visible low in the west after sunset on these dates:

JAN 1 – JAN 2
MAR 26 – APR 23
JUL 9 – AUG 30
NOV 5 – DEC 17

Resource: Llewllyn's 2023 Daily Planetary Guide

MERCURY IN 2023

"Happy Retrograde New Year"? You can say that again...literally! Mercury begins and ends the year in retrograde, bookending the holidays with its notorious signal-scrambling effects.

From December 29, 2022 to January 18, 2023, it's backing up through Capricorn. As we attempt to set our resolutions, the cosmic trickster reminds us of the old adage, "Man plans, god laughs." (Nevermind New Year's Day—we recommend waiting until the January 21 new moon to set yearly intentions in 2023!) In Capricorn, the eldest earth sign and ruler of time-honored wisdom, Mercury puts issues like climate change, health care for the elderly and environmental justice front and center. But will we listen? Hopefully. With Mercury's localized focus, changing systems at the neighborhood level can have a major, worldwide impact.

After January 18, we get a little breathing room from the retrogrades until Mercury reverse commutes through money-minded Taurus from April 21 to May 14. The economy could go through another spin cycle as interest rates and prices fluctuate along with the availability of labor. Don't count your cryptocurrency before it's hatched!

From August 23 to September 15, Mercury will be retrograde in Virgo—a good time to review your day-to-day systems and protect your important data. Cutting corners could have detrimental effects. Take your time and do everything by the books. Virgo rules health but with Mercury in reverse, you could get a false test result or misinformation. Get a second opinion and ideally wait to have any medical procedures. If that's not an option, become an expert on your condition and surgery and ask every question necessary to put your mind at ease.

The final retrograde of the year arrives like an unwelcome Grinch at the holiday festivities. On December 13, the messenger planet U-turns in Capricorn for the second time this year, turning traditions on their ear. (Stay nimble, Dasher and Dancer!) Mercury rules the postal system, so get those packages out early!

Then, on December 23, Mercury backs up one spot in the zodiac, rounding out its retrograde in unfiltered, hotheaded Sagittarius before correcting course on New Year's Day 2024. Not only is this a warning to *not* invite that triggering relative to the tree-trimming, but, since Sagittarius is the ruler of travel, expect long TSA lines, canceled flights and other annoying disruptions to your journeys. Maybe just stay close to home on NYE or ring in 2024 at a nostalgic locale that you've visited in the past.

MERCURY *Retrogrades*

CAPRICORN
DEC 29, 2022 – JAN 18

VIRGO
AUG 23 – SEP 15

TAURUS
APR 21 – MAY 14

CAPRICORN & SAGITTARIUS
DEC 13 – JAN 1, 2024
Moves from Capricorn to Sagittarius on December 23

Mercury THROUGH THE SIGNS IN 2023

times listed are Eastern US Time Zone

CAPRICORN RX
DEC 29, 2022 (4:32AM) – JAN 18

CAPRICORN D
JAN 18 (8:12AM) – FEB 11

AQUARIUS
FEB 11 (6:22AM) – MAR 2

PISCES
MAR 2 (5:52PM) – MAR 19

ARIES
MAR 19 (12:24AM) – APR 3

TAURUS
APR 3 (12:22PM) – APR 21

TAURUS RX
APR 21 (4:35AM) – MAY 14

TAURUS D
MAY 14 (11:17PM) – JUN 11

GEMINI
JUN 11 (6:27AM) – JUN 26

CANCER
JUN 26 (8:24PM) – JUL 11

LEO
JUL 11 (12:11AM) – JUL 28

VIRGO
JUL 28 (5:31PM) – AUG 23

VIRGO RX
AUG 23 (3:59PM) – SEP 15

VIRGO D
SEP 15 (4:21PM) – OCT 4

LIBRA
OCT 4 (8:09PM) – OCT 22

SCORPIO
OCT 22 (2:49PM) – NOV 10

SAGITTARIUS
NOV 10 (1:25AM) – DEC 1

CAPRICORN
DEC 1 (9:31AM) – DEC 13

CAPRICORN RX
DEC 13 (2:09AM) – DEC 23

SAGITTARIUS RX
DEC 23 (1:18AM) – JAN 1, 2024

Rx = retrograde phase
D = resumes direct motion

All other dates indicate
direct motion

MORE BOOKS
BY THE ASTROTWINS

HOW TO GET ALONG WITH ANYONE (*YES, EVEN THAT PERSON)

Any two zodiac signs CAN be compatible, as long as they understand what makes the other one tick. The AstroTwins simplify the secrets of synastry—the 7 unique energies encoded in the distance between your signs. Take your relationships from difficult to dynamic and start bringing out your best.

SUPERCOUPLE

Unlock the astrology secrets to sizzling attraction and deep connection, and get through the hard stuff fast! Did you know that your relationship has a zodiac sign and chart? The Supercouple system is the ultimate guide to finding true compatibility—by understanding why you came together and what your divine destiny could be!

MOMSTROLOGY

Parenting DOES come with instructions! This ultimate guide to raising your kids AND flourishing as a mom takes you through every season of parenthood, from birth to toddler to school years and leaving the nest. A favorite baby shower gift, featured by *Good Morning America* and a #1 Amazon bestseller.

START READING NOW AT ASTROSTYLE.COM/BOOKS

VENUS

♀

VENUS IN ASTROLOGY

Venus is the planet of love, beauty and luxury, lending its decadent energy to every zodiac sign for three to five weeks each year. Who will we fall for...and how? Venus sets the seductive vibe, determining whether we'll take the world by storm as a power couple (Capricorn) or conduct a relationship entirely by Instagram (Aquarius). Leos Jennifer Lopez and Ben Affleck revived their PDA-fueled "Bennifer" portmanteau when Venus visited their exhibitionistic, unbridled sign in 2021. When Venus returned to Leo in August 2022 they tied the knot at their lavish Georgia nuptials!

To find your natal Venus sign, cast a free birth chart at

ASTROSTYLE.COM/BIRTHCHART

Planning WITH VENUS

Know when to set the right mood—and how—with the power of Venus. Boredom is the enemy when this planet sashays through a fire sign (Aries, Leo, Sagittarius). Invite your love interest on a spontaneous adventure packed with surprises. Introduce yourself to someone who intrigues you. Then show that you can be equally dependable when Venus moves through responsible earth signs (Taurus, Virgo, Capricorn). Cook meals together, run errands for each other and make life more pleasant and easy all around. Give the nice ones a chance to woo you!

When Venus cruises through air signs (Gemini, Libra, Aquarius), get out for some play dates! Make plans with other couples or let friends fix you up for meet-cutes. Draw the drapes and cuddle up for those intimate water sign Venus cycles (Cancer, Scorpio, Pisces). When you're not luxuriating in bed, you might even meet each other's parents and BFFs or co-host a dinner party. Seduce with your sensitivity.

SEEING VENUS *in the sky*

Want to get a glimpse of the radiant love planet? Check out evening star Venus, *Hesperus*, from January 1 to August 8 before she moves too close to the Sun for us to observe.

Morning star Venus, *Phosphorus*, reappears from August 18 to December 31 before moving in sync with the Sun and disappearing from view.

Resource: Llewllyn's 2023 Daily Planetary Guide

VENUS IN 2023

Venus begins the year in Capricorn but switches to Aquarius on January 2, quickly turning the tide in a frisky, experimental direction. This could be the year that you rewrite the rules on relationships with a progressive flourish that suits 2023 you.

VENUS RETROGRADE IN LEO
JULY 22 - SEPTEMBER 3

Happy news for all the die-hard romantics out there. The love planet will linger in Leo for an extra-long time—from June 5 to October 8! That's four times longer than Venus' usual visit to a sign, which lasts around four weeks. Spring fever could spill over into the most passionate summer lovin' anyone has felt in years!

Caveat: The reason for this protracted Venus in Leo transit is the dreaded "r" word. From July 22 to September 3, Venus will be retrograde, a cycle that comes around every 18 months. (Better renew those vows Jen and Ben...)

During this backspin, Venus changes from evening star (visible at dusk) to morning star (visible right before dawn). The ancients thought Venus was two separate planets and thus has two Greek names: *Phosphorus*, "the bringer of light" for her morning star cycle, and *Hesperus*, "the star of the evening," for her evening phase.

Love could imitate art while Venus retrogrades through Leo from July 22 to September 3—but this may not be a "midsummer night's dream." In the sign of the fiery, dramatic lion, affairs of the heart could feel more like an immersive theater performance. Or maybe a three-ring circus!

Passion or provocation? This six-week phase will be quite the storied one. Venus retrogrades are not always easy. They can exhume ghosts of relationships past...or provoke sudden ghostings just when connections are heating up. Long-lost lovers may reunite but struggle to find their footing when it's time to produce an actual "sequel."

Our advice? Enjoy the dopamine rush of attraction but wait until Venus corrects course on September 3 before doing any future planning. And if you're already otherwise engaged when that old flame hits you up on Snapchat? Keep lines as clear as possible and just remember that it will all shake out by autumn. Remember that "new love energy" can be intoxicating—but with Venus in reverse, it can also screen out someone's toxic traits.

When Venus backstrokes through scene-stealing Leo, we'll all want attention in megadoses. But when our friends, family and lovers can't give it, look out! Tantrums can get reality-show ugly. Plus, who is going to play the role of the cheering supporter? The big challenge this summer is remembering that love is a two-way street. Nothing wrong with wanting to be cherished and adored, but if you treat anyone like the on-demand president of your personal fan club, things could take a nasty turn. Remember to step back and share the limelight! Helping others shine is so rewarding.

In the middle of the retrograde, Venus disappears from view as it makes an inferior conjunction to the Sun. This year, the rebirth of Venus happens on August 18, which might bring a major perspective shift around love! If you've been perpetually single, you may be inspired to put yourself out on the apps again. In fashion-forward Leo, beauty-queen Venus can inspire you to revamp your style or set up a sexy photo shoot. Start with mood boards, then shop for 'fits and hire your snapper *after* the retrograde. (Or get it all going in early June!)

What's absolutely verboten during Venus retrograde? (Or should be...) Cosmetic surgeries, drastic makeovers, tattoos or any changes to your look that are hard to undo. Everyone loves a fringe of bangs...until it's time to grow them out.

Got wedding plans during Venus retrograde? No need to call off the caterers and elope to Vegas. But it wouldn't hurt to squeeze in one extra therapy session before the nuptials, *juuuuuust* to be sure you've worked out all those final knots and fears. We recommend a vow renewal on your first anniversary. Thankfully, Venus will NOT be retrograde a year after your wedding since its backspins only take place every 18 months. Our dear friend, astrologer Susan Miller, recommends going to city hall for a pre-wedding wedding before the retrograde. She's definitely onto something there!

Ultimately, these cycles help us recalibrate our settings so that we can make better choices in the future. But those lessons won't be a starlit stroll in the park. Fortunately, bravehearted Venus in Leo will do anything for love (yes, even *that*). Should Cupid give you lemons, you could work through the pain with your partner then turn it all into a visual album like Beyoncé. No relationship is perfect! The summer could bring some uncomfortable (or downright agonizing) tests for couples. But if you are both committed and willing to push through, you can create a lasting sense of security.

Even if everything's copacetic on the surface, check in: Could you be doing more to support each other's creative expression and joy? Venus in pleasure-centric Leo believes that happiness is a birthright. But if the work-play balance is lopsided between you and your boo, resentment could blow up fast. Find ways that you can both let your hair down, whether one of you is pinch-hitting at home while the other gets a much-needed salon treatment or you're slipping off for a decadent weekend baecation together.

Should your romance be on the rocks, Venus retrograde could snap the last thread. Maybe you start with a trial separation, however, since feelings *can* reverse once Venus corrects course on September 3. Whatever the case, you'd be wise to get everything out on the table before July 22. It helps that Venus lingers in Leo until October 8, giving everyone a chance to process the retrograde's grueling lessons.

VENUS CONNECTIONS IN 2023

VENUS-MARS-TRINE
JAN 9

While Venus connects to many planets in 2023, we always like to note her special dates with dance-partner Mars. On January 9, the cosmic co-pilots fly high in a heady air trine. Venus will be in experimental Aquarius while Mars is retrograde in Gemini. Conversations about the state of your union get provocative and exploratory. With these open-minded signs at play, you could solve an age-old conflict with a willingness to open your minds.

VENUS-MARS-SQUARE
FEB 4

Love languages collide! The second of the year's two Venus-Mars aspects happens a month later, but it's not smooth sailing. Venus in watery, sensitive Pisces locks horns with Mars who is now moving direct through Gemini. What one of you considers "words of affirmation" could land as insensitive and superficial to the other. Meanwhile, acts of service can feel more like painful sacrifices. Our advice? Don't try to "twin" each other (a Mars in Gemini pitfall). Just give people room to *be*. Rather than arguing, try these magic words: "I can see how you would feel that way."

Due to Venus' proximity to the Sun, your natal Venus sign will never be farther than two signs away from your natal Sun sign. Find out what sign Venus was in when you were born with our cosmic calculator. Want to learn more? Discover how the sultry planet shapes your seductive powers, style and spending habits with our pocket course, The Venus Code!

ASTROSTYLE.COM/VENUS

Venus THROUGH THE SIGNS

CAPRICORN
DEC 9, 2022

AQUARIUS
JAN 2, 9:09PM

PISCES
JAN 26, 9:33PM

ARIES
FEB 20, 2:56AM

TAURUS
MAR 16, 6:34PM

GEMINI
APR 11, 12:47AM

CANCER
MAY 7, 10:25AM

LEO
JUN 5, 9:46AM

LEO RX
JUL 22, 9:33PM

LEO D
SEP 3, 9:20PM

VIRGO
OCT 8, 9:11PM

LIBRA
NOV 8, 4:30AM

SCORPIO
DEC 4, 1:51PM

SAGITTARIUS
DEC 29, 3:34PM

Rx = retrograde phase
D = resumes direct motion

times listed are Eastern US Time Zone

♀

MARS

MARS IN ASTROLOGY

Mars is the last of the personal inner planets—the planets before Jupiter which are closest to the Sun. This might explain its protective, and sometimes combative, stance. Like a celestial sentry, Mars readies us to fight for what we hold dear. The red planet hangs out in a zodiac sign for approximately eight weeks, directing the global temperament and fighting style. Will we march peacefully, topple statues or sweet-talk the opposition? Tactics change depending on the sign Mars occupies. Lusty Mars is the forthright companion to seductive Venus and can bring out the "cosmic cave(wo)man" in us all. Our raw desire will be on display during certain Mars cycles, while other zodiac signs provoke a more discreet style of pursuit.

Mars pivots retrograde every couple years, which prolongs its passage through a particular area of the zodiac. Often, these backspins keep the red planet locked and loaded in one sign for seven months—rather than the usual seven weeks. Mars will be retrograde briefly, until January 12, 2023, finishing out a reverse commute that began on October 30, 2022.

Planning WITH MARS

Where there's smoke there's fire, so why not build upon that heat? Daring, energetic Mars provides exothermic momentum throughout the year. While in fire signs (Aries, Leo, Sagittarius), Mars gives you the gumption to take a risk and initiate the action. Travel, play sports or get an entrepreneurial venture in motion. You may hit the gas too quickly, but at least stuck energy is moving! When the red planet is grounded in earth signs (Taurus, Virgo, Capricorn) get pumped about your routines. There's no better time to kick off a fitness regimen or take on an ambitious project at work. You'll stick it out and see results. While in air signs (Gemini, Libra, Aquarius), Mars makes you a networking wizard. You'll have the courage to slide into DMs and get into the VIP room. Just slow down long enough to make meaningful connections. When Mars plunges into the water signs (Cancer, Scorpio, Pisces), it brings its passion to our personal interactions. Starting a family, moving in together, getting engaged—you'll have the courage to take those "next steps." While things get a lot sultrier, the intensity levels can go nuclear. Careful not to overload yourself (or anyone else) with all those feelings!

Find out what sign Mars was in when you were born with our cosmic calculator. Want to learn more? Harness the red planet's fiercely ambitious and passion-stoking powers in our pocket course, The Mars Code!

ASTROSTYLE.COM/MARS

MARS IN 2023

Firebrand Mars will be a cranky voice in the chorus for the first twelve days of the year. Maybe a hoarse one too! In curious, contrarian Gemini, Mars loves to stir up trouble and start debates. Many of us are already exhausted by all the polarizing, disinformation and other data-skewing hype that's been raging for the past few years with Mars in dualistic, fast-talking Gemini for an extended *seven-month* circuit, which started August 20, 2022 and lasts until March 25, 2023.

It certainly doesn't help that the red planet's been retrograde since October 30, 2022! But happy news arrives on January 12 when Mars makes a positive pivot and resumes direct motion. We'll get a chance to decipher fact from fiction in Q1 of 2023. Digging our way through the data and figuring out who deserves forgiveness (and to whom we need to extend an apology)? That could take a minute. Fortunately, Mars hovers in Gemini until March 25, setting the stage for healing, but direct, communication.

SEEING MARS *in the sky*

Mars won't be visible in the morning sky in 2023, but if you're heading out for an evening of carousing, the red planet will be a visible wingperson between January 1 and September 30. Oh, behave!

Resource: Llewllyn's 2023 Daily Planetary Guide

MARS CONNECTIONS IN 2023

MARS-NEPTUNE SQUARE

MAR 14

Passive or aggressive? Three times in 2022, combative Mars locked horns with compassionate Neptune as the two spun into a tense 90-degree square. Hurtful words turned into epic emotional battles for some people, while others seethed in silence. On March 14, 2023, they're at it again for a final showdown. It's hard to know who to trust during these suspicion-provoking aspects. Deceit may even come from a so-called ally. By the same token, try not to run away with your fears! The stories you tell yourself may be far from the truth.

MARS-NEPTUNE TRINE

MAY 15

When Mars *finally* moves on to Cancer on March 25, it dances into a far happier formation with Neptune—and their exact trine on May 15 can help you hug it out or toughen your shell (and your boundaries!) so a certain someone can no longer get under your skin.

MARS IN SCORPIO OPPOSITE JUPITER IN TAURUS

OCT 28

Face-off! This combustible day comes with an active trigger warning. As hotheaded Mars locks horns with know-it-all Jupiter, no one's backing down from their righteous stance. Since Mars is in secretive Scorpio, you may not see an offensive coming. Stay on guard for passive-aggressive behavior, a warning that something bigger may be brewing. Normally Jupiter in Taurus would favor candid conversation, but approaching the "enemy" directly could inflame the conflict. Be watchful and strategic, keeping classified information in the vault.

Mars THROUGH THE SIGNS

Times listed are when Mars transit begins, Eastern US Time Zone

GEMINI
AUG 20, 2022

GEMINI RX
OCT 30, 2022

GEMINI D
JAN 12, 3:56PM

CANCER
MAR 25, 7:45AM

LEO
MAY 20, 11:31AM

VIRGO
JUL 11, 12:11AM

LIBRA
AUG 27, 9:20AM

SCORPIO
OCT 12, 12:04AM

SAGITTARIUS
NOV 24, 5:15AM

Rx = retrograde phase
D = resumes direct motion

THE LUNAR NODES

THE LUNAR NODES IN ASTROLOGY

What's the next step in the evolution of the human race? What patterns must we break to collectively heal? The lunar nodes hold the keys to our destiny and ultimate life lessons. In astrology, life purpose is encoded in the North Node and South Node of the moon. The North Node represents our karmic paths and the lessons we came here to learn—or the "language" we are learning to speak. The South Node reveals the challenges and gifts we bring in from previous lifetimes.

Sitting directly opposite each other in the chart, the lunar nodes aren't planets, but rather mathematical points that fall in two opposite zodiac signs. They're determined by the points where the moon's orbit crosses the ecliptic—the apparent path the Sun makes around the earth. (We say "apparent" because, in reality, the earth is revolving around the Sun...but from our vantage point on the planet, it appears that the Sun is moving.) Generally, they fall in the same signs that the eclipses are in when you're born.

The nodes change signs every 18 to 19 months. Unlike the planets, they move backward through the zodiac, underscoring the idea that transformation is as much about reflecting and "unlearning" as it is about chasing new discoveries. People born within your same lunar node set (in the same or opposite configuration) are part of a shared soul group. You incarnated with them to learn the same lessons and might be each other's greatest allies and teachers in this lifetime.

To find your natal nodes, cast a free birth chart at

ASTROSTYLE.COM/BIRTHCHART

THE LUNAR NODES IN 2023

In 2023, the lunar nodes split their time between two pairs of signs. The year begins with the destiny-driven North Node in Taurus and the soul-searching South Node in Scorpio, putting the emphasis on the labor market, the economy and reproductive rights. This is the final third of a cycle that began on January 18, 2022.

On July 17, the North Node slips back into autonomous Aries while the South Node calls partnership-powered Libra its home. Relationships plunge into a new evolutionary cycle as we work to balance our desire for autonomy with the necessity of interdependence. Aries is the sign of war while Libra rules peace. Can we fight the good fight without destroying each other in the process? This 18-month cycle is sure to bring some collective awakenings around personal power—and the power of love.

Nodes THROUGH THE SIGNS

**NORTH NODE IN TAURUS &
SOUTH NODE IN SCORPIO**
JAN 18, 2022 - JUL 17, 2023

**NORTH NODE IN ARIES &
SOUTH NODE IN LIBRA**
JUL 17, 2023 - JAN 11, 2025

Dates listed are when transit begins, Eastern US Time Zone

NORTH NODE IN TAURUS

JAN 18, 2022 - JUL 17, 2023

There's a popular saying that we are "spiritual beings having a human experience." Yes, we have bodies, but what animates us with life? COVID plunged the world into an existential crisis that reshaped priorities broadly. Rather than going through the motions of modern life, we began to question every action, from the hours spent toiling at work to the people we shared our precious time with. A new way of life has been emerging—slowly and chaotically.

Fast forward to January 18, 2022, when the lunar nodes began their 18-month odyssey across the Taurus-Scorpio axis. Terrestrial Taurus traffics in the physical world while mystical Scorpio lives in the metaphysical realm. One might argue that, in fact, our collective grasp on the truth is more slippery than ever. And yet our material-world matters like public health, money and natural resources (food, water, shelter) are in dire need of attention.

The North Node is like a beacon, pointing us toward the next collective evolution. Its tour through rooted Taurus has been nothing short of unmooring. In many ways, it pulled the rug out from under our feet and placed it on an upper level that we are still climbing to reach. Will we ascend to this higher ground before the cycle ends this July 17?

Much of that depends upon how we grapple with the karmic South Node. In Scorpio, the sign of money, power, sex, reproduction and death, it's going to be a heavy lift. As autocrats tighten their iron grips and idealogues force their religious beliefs into broad-based legislation (often through Scorpionic private donor funds), it can feel like "too much to handle" some days. Buckle up. We have our work cut out for us while this transit continues until July 17.

Market Corrections and Karmic Connections

Financial matters and power dynamics will continue to be a huge plotline in 2023, coloring both our personal lives and global headlines. Taurus and Scorpio are the "money signs" of the zodiac. Taurus rules our daily bread, the income earned by our hustle and grind. Scorpio governs the money we can't "see," like the long-term investments tucked in 401Ks, stocks and bonds.

Since this nodal cycle began on January 18, 2022, both the labor market and the financial market have been in wild flux. As we enter 2023, nerve wracking headlines about inflation, a recession and plummeting markets may all be part of the "karmic correction" these nodes have in store.

The gold rush of cryptocurrency and NFTs that was celebrated in 2021 took a swift downturn shortly after the investment-focused South Node moved from Sagittarius (the sign of the gambler) into Scorpio on January 18, 2022. This isn't actually surprising. Scorpio plays the long game with money, but it can also reveal scandals and devastating schemes, for example, the $8 billion implosion of crypto bro Sam Bankman-Fried's FTX exchange that threw the market into flux in late 2022.

But does that spell doom for all coins? With this nodal cycle continuing until July 17, we'd say, no. It may still be worth your while to open a digital wallet and learn all you can about the blockchain. A "buy low, sell high" scenario is not beyond the range of possibilities, particularly with longstanding holdouts such as Bitcoin and Ethereum.

Calling all angel investors! In 2023, we may also see wealth managers and individuals alike flow funds into promising startups, which could suddenly feel less risky in this market. That's good news for all the bright innovators out there. Get your pitch decks ready!

You'd Better Work?

Industrious Taurus rules our daily earnings, and it's no secret that labor shortages have been a huge issue in recent years. This nodal cycle began on the heels of The Great Resignation, when 11.5 million people quit their jobs between April and June of 2021. Worker scarcities continue to plague every industry, from healthcare to education to farming and airlines, causing burnout among the ranks. Global supply chains are also in crisis—the cause for 2022's perilous shortage of baby formula.

Herein lies the opportunity for another correction. Workers are now in a stronger position to negotiate favorable terms like flexible hours, shorter shifts and better benefits. Stricter immigration laws may also ease up, allowing foreign workers back in to help cover the gap.

The metric of kindness in workplace culture has become a key to retaining employees. When Kim Kardashian, clad in a couture leather bandage dress, told Variety that "nobody wants to work anymore" she only had half the story straight. A sense of purpose is integral to our happiness as humans, and a safe, non-toxic work environment can supply that. Will the Taurus North Node give rise to compassionate companies? With apps like Glassdoor allowing employees to privately rate their workplaces, no one's getting away with their old tricks.

Under (Leo) CEO Satya Nadella, Microsoft was ranked the number one company to work for in 2022 with IBM and Google right behind. The primary reason? Flexible work arrangements. Of course, that's a whole lot easier to manage when the team is doing computer work. Still, we maintain that you don't have to be a tech company to tap into the magic of this Taurus North Node cycle. Companies that care about and invest in their workers, foster inclusivity, encourage input and creativity and give employees a sense of ownership are likely to fare well in 2023, even if they are unable to pay top dollar.

Okay Google, Encrypt My Data

But there's a Catch-22 to the remote workforce: data security issues. With offsite employees parsing through sensitive materials on coffeeshop wifi networks or their home routers (generally non-VPN and often shared with roommates, kids and neighbors), it's tough to keep any company data confidential.

While the South Node skulks through secretive Scorpio, hackers, spies and other hidden forces continue to outpace the cybersecurity capabilities at many organizations. It's not just office communications that are getting breached. Supply chains have been under threat, particularly from ransomware attackers who can shut down an entire portion of an industry with their digital piracy.

You might wonder why anyone ever logs into a network, uses social media or shares documents to the cloud (which has its own landmine of security issues). For what it's worth, Facebook, a known data-mining offender, was founded by Taurus Mark Zuckerberg during the 2004 Scorpio South Node transit.

The Taurus North Node would be fine if we all just went back to the analog way of life. But can we turn back the clock? Even the earthy #CottageCore movement, still a top interiors trend in 2022, relies on TikTok for sharing tips and inspo. We doubt your toile wallpaper and gathered wildflower bouquets will be going offline anytime soon. Still, we predict that enhanced security measures will become an even bigger concern for both individuals and companies alike in 2023. Working from home could go through another evolution with stricter logging, VPN requirements or other regulations.

Let's Talk About Sex

Sex is back on the menu during this nodal cycle, with Taurus-on-Taurus couple Megan Fox and Machine Gun Kelly winning the award for Most Widely Instagrammed PDA. Even Scorpio Rachel Dolezal has an Only Fans page now. The ex-NAACP president, fired for impersonating a Black woman, is now posting paeans to Rihanna's Fenty lingerie. For a monthly fee, subscribers can "see how my sensual side pairs with my creative spirit through intimate images inspired by color, light, and lingerie on the weekends." While we can't personally report on how this tagline comes together, it has the aesthetically oriented Taurus North Node's fingerprints all over it.

During the 1995 Taurus-Scorpio nodal cycle, Match.com entered the scene, the longest-running dating site that now owns Tinder and Hinge. (The North Node was in Scorpio then, but the resonance was similar.) The free-spirited "Summer of Love" went down during this nodal transit in 1967, which also brought then-controversial miniskirts into fashion. Bikinis gained popularity during the prior Scorpio South Node in 1947. (So daring!)

My Body, My Choice...Right?

Scorpio rules the reproductive system and the karmic South Node's position has brought the shocking overturn of Roe v. Wade, the historic ruling which protects a woman's constitutional right to an abortion. This devastating decision goes beyond morality and ethics; it puts women's health and lives in jeopardy.

Yet, true to the fluctuating tides of this nodal cycle, abortion was a key ballot item that cost U.S. Republicans the "red wave" of seats they were expecting in the U.S. midterm elections in 2022. California, Vermont and Michigan enshrined abortion rights in their state constitutions, protecting reproductive freedom, but they are in the minority. Because abortion is criminalized with steep fines and loss of medical license in other states, options are limited to at-home abortions using the five-pill regimen of Mifepristone and Misoprostol. Sites like PlanC.com direct women to finding safe abortion pills, but for how long will this remain legal? The fight is hardly over, especially with a Supreme Court and state legislations stacked with judges who oppose abortion, even in the case of rape and incest. While the South Node remains in Scorpio until July 17, we will grapple with the weight of these consequences.

Meanwhile, transgender rights remain under constant fire. As the Biden administration works to reinstate Title IX protections tossed out by Trump's secretary of education Betsy DeVos—and make changes that combat sexual discrimination in schools by incorporating language that includes sexual orientation and gender identity for LGBTQI+ students— states including Ohio and Virginia are attempting to block these measures.

Florida Governor Ron DeSantis has banned Medicaid coverage of transgender procedures and is currently at work to ban all gender-affirming health care for minors, despite evidence showing the dire impact this will have on the mental health of trans children. This grappling match is bound to continue as the nodes wind down their tour though body-based Taurus and Scorpio, the sign that governs sexual identity.

The Phoenix in the Ashes

In Western culture, death is still largely a taboo topic, or one most people would rather avoid unless it's 100% necessary to discuss. Yet our mortality has loomed large since the pandemic began—and with apocalyptic warnings of a climate crisis and threats of nuclear warfare, it's an ever-present guest in the collective psyche.

Enter the Scorpio South Node. When the karmic point traverses the sign of death, rebirth and transformation, we may find spiritual solace in facing this undeniable inevitability head on. The first cryogenically preserved man, Dr. James H. Bedford, was frozen during the 1967 Scorpio-Taurus nodal phase.

Books on reincarnation are worth a read this year. (Among our favorites are Between Death and Life by Dolores Cannon and Many Lives, Many Masters by Scorpio Brian Weiss.) Soul retrievals, channeling and past life regressions can help us make peace with the eternal aspects of our being.

O, Give Me a Home

Real estate, which falls under investment-minded Scorpio's domain, has been a hot commodity during this nodal cycle. Although the housing market appears to be cooling as interest rates rise, there is still a reported housing shortage in the United States as we enter 2023. A similar housing shortage took place during the Taurus-Scorpio nodal cycle of 1948. Cheap, prefab post-war housing was built, tailored for young couples wishing to start a family. (Hello, Baby Boom.)

And it's not just buyers who are getting hit. In 2022, rent increased at the fastest rate since 1986, making housing inaccessible for many working folks. Shelter, which is a basic necessity, has now become an unattainable luxury, forcing families to crowd together in tight spaces or live in their cars or on the streets.

Will this nodal cycle help us to reimagine the concept of home? This same nodal cycle in 1909-10 brought us the Israeli kibbutzim, communal settlements where members were given housing, worked together to farm the land and, at times, produce a particular commodity for an industry.

While moving to a farm commune might seem out of step for many folks in 2023, refurbished buildings with shared resources like daycare or cafeterias might be a solution. Zoning for ADUs (Additional Dwelling Units) has been expanding in recent years, allowing people to build small "mother-in-laws" and tiny homes in their backyards. For many people, this additional source of income has allowed them to keep food on the table while also serving the growing population needs in their areas.

The green building movement is also getting a burst from the Taurus North Node. In the Bronx, two affordable housing buildings are currently switching from fossil fuel heat to SHARC technology, which captures wastewater and repurposes it for heating and cooling. We anticipate more regenerative construction strategies will emerge in 2023.

NORTH NODE IN ARIES

JUL 17, 2023 - JAN 11, 2025

Coming in Hot

When the lunar North Node positions itself in Aries this July 17, we can expect lots of groundbreaking and trailblazing innovations to arrive. Aries is the first sign of the zodiac and originality ranks high as a "must-have" quality under the Ram's watch.

Historically, this nodal cycle has dovetailed with major discoveries, including the dwarf planet Eris—which was actually transiting through Aries when discovered on January 5, 2005. Originally considered a tenth planet, Eris was named after the goddess of discourse and strife, fitting for anything that falls under the reign of in-your-face Aries.

Speaking of faces, during this same transit in November 2005, surgeons in France carried out the first human face transplant on Isabelle Dinoire. This is especially significant since Aries rules the head and face.

Faster, Pussycat!

Got a need for speed? Everything accelerates when speed-demon Aries takes the wheel of the North Node. In summer 2023, New Zealand automaker Rodin will unleash its FZERO hypercar, the world's fastest road vehicle to date! With a lightweight four-liter V10 twin-turbo engine, the FZERO can hit a top speed near 224 MPH, zipping past Formula One automobiles.

Speaking of F1, the first ever Formula One race took place when the North Node hit the gas in Aries in 1950. Hot Wheels, the toy collector cars, were introduced to the market during the subsequent transit in 1968. Even cartoons pick up the pace during this nodal cycle. In 1949, Warner Bros. released its Fast and Furry-ous cartoon with the iconic, nonstop chase scenes between Wile E. Coyote and the Road Runner.

Internet Famous

Attention, attention! Everyone's a star when the North Node is in Aries— so if you thought the TikTok rage would bottom out soon, guess again. YouTube was registered as an official domain during the 2005 transit, a groundbreaking disruption to Hollywood's roped-off accessibility to video. For Gen Z and younger, YouTubers are legit celebrities, holding as much sway as (if not more than) big-name actors.

This same cycle brought us Twitter, launched in March 2006 under the outspoken Aries North Node. The cacophony of opinions has gone beyond fever pitch. Now under ownership of megabillionaire Elon Musk, the Tweetstorms are already brewing well in advance of July 17.

Marriage Equality Milestones

Across the zodiac wheel, the murky South Node will be slipping back through partnership-oriented Libra, serving challenges to committed couples from July 17 to January 11, 2025. Just as the Scorpio South Node put reproductive rights in jeopardy, fears are looming that the conservative U.S. Supreme Court will come for same-sex couples next.

This is not unfounded! In the wake of Roe's overturn, Justice Clarence Thomas wrote a concurring opinion that the courts might reverse decisions such as 2015's Obergfell vs Hodges (ruled while the North Node was in Libra in 2015). This landmark civil rights ruling has guaranteed same-sex couples the right to marry in all 50 states, under protection of the Fourteenth

Amendment. At time of writing, the Respect for Marriage Act, which upholds marriage equality for the LGBTQ community, has passed the House but awaits vote by the Senate.

If history repeats itself, we have good reason to remain hopeful about the future of marriage equality. The Gay Rights Bill was signed into effect by New York City Mayor Ed Koch during this circuit in 1986. The first legal same-sex marriage ceremony to be held in the United States occurred on February 12, 2004, another year the South Node was moving through Scorpio and Libra.

Interracial marriage rights have tracked through Libra South Node cycles in significant ways. The first recorded interracial marriage took place during the 1614 transit when indigenous Pocahontas wed tobacco planter John Rolfe.

In 1948, while the South Node wove back through Scorpio and Libra, the California Supreme Court struck down anti-miscegenation laws in the historic Perez v. Sharp case. But it took until the next Scorpio-to-Libra South Node transition in 1967 for the U.S. Supreme Court to legalize interracial marriages in all 50 states according to a unanimous ruling in Loving v. Virginia.

Big Bangs

The term "Big Bang" was coined on a radio broadcast during a prior North-Node-in-Aries transit in 1949. That's not surprising since combative Aries loves anything that goes boom or pop. That same year brought us the first TV Western series, Hopalong Cassidy, about a fictional gunslinger by that name.

It's no secret that U.S. gun laws are the most lax of any major nation—and not surprisingly, gun violence here is more rampant than any other place in the world. The Gun Control Act of 1968 was signed into law by Lyndon B. Johnson, but don't let the name fool you. This legislation generally prohibits interstate commerce of firearms between individuals, but doesn't do much to prevent weapons from getting into the hands of the average citizen.

Active shooter crimes have been on the rise since 2017, elevating fear at schools, worship centers and public places. With gun-slinging civilians showing up at polling sites during the U.S. midterm elections—not to mention at Capitol buildings, we wouldn't be surprised to see a legislative battle heat up again after July 17.

Other explosive devices are also tied to this transit. The Soviet Union tested its first atomic bomb in August 1949. The following year, Truman ordered development of the hydrogen bomb. In frightening resonance, the Chernobyl Disaster occurred while the North Node was in Aries on April 26, 1986. A failed experiment at the Soviet nuclear power plant (located in current-day Ukraine) caused a devastating explosion that contaminated millions of acres of forest and caused deformations, long-term health effects and other environmental impacts that are felt to this day.

Chernobyl hit the headlines again in 2022 when Russian soldiers invaded Ukraine and took temporary occupation of the dangerous exclusion zone.

Ukraine's Zaporizhzhia Nuclear Power Station—among the 10 largest nuclear power plants on the globe—has been under Russian command (but Ukrainian operation) since March 2022.

War and Peace

Aries is the sign of war while Libra reigns over peace. Before this nodal passage has even begun, global powers are breaking and forming alliances in deeply fracturing ways, such as providing weapons or reducing oil production. BRICS, an acronym for Brazil, Russia, India, China, South Africa was once a concept drummed up by a Goldman-Sachs economist for nations with the fastest-growing emerging markets. Since 2009, these government leaders have met annually for formal summits. At time of writing, Saudi Arabia is being considered for inclusion, a move that would be consequential to the United States.

Prior Aries-Libra nodal transits have coincided with actual wars as well as anti-war revolts and uprisings. The Korean War began during this cycle in 1950, the same year the International Police Association formed—and the Stasi secret police were founded in East Germany.

Troubles in North Ireland began while the North Node was in Aries in October 1968. That same year, support for the Vietnam War crumbled with news of the My Lai massacre of around 500 unarmed Vietnamese civilians by a U.S. platoon. In eerie resonance, the movie Platoon, starring Charlie Sheen, won Best Picture at the Oscars when the North Node returned to Aries in 1987.

Meanwhile in France, the Paris Student Riots erupted in May 1968, marking a cultural and sexual revolution along with a political one. A student-led rebellion, partially in response to the Vietnam War and also against the entrenched patriarchal leadership of Charles De Gaulle, was soon joined by factory workers. After weeks of student-police clashes, De Gaulle ultimately resigned and the women's movement and sexual revolution were ushered into France, along with better labor conditions. As patriarchal and religious policies continue to tighten the noose around women's reproductive rights in the United States, we can't help but wonder if the second half of 2023 will resemble Paris in 1968.

Justice Leagues

The scales of Justice can swing wildly while the South Node transits through Libra. Notably, the Civil Rights Act of 1968 (which expanded upon prior acts) established the Fair Housing Act, prohibiting discrimination in the sale, rental or financing of housing based on race, religion, national origin, sex, handicap and family status. In 1967 Thurgood Marshall was the first African-American to be appointed Supreme Court Justice. Sadly, this period also brought the assassinations of civil rights movement leader MLK, and also RFK (Bobby Kennedy), a powerful political voice in the fight against racism and poverty.

The UN Human Rights Council was established during the 2006 Libra South Node phase, again illuminating the way in which the intense schisms between peace and war can occur during this nodal cycle. With radical (and radicalizing) political factions causing deep divides around the globe, it's easy to imagine many of the ideologically charged scenarios becoming inflamed and pushed to explosive limits in 2023. ✳

THE *Outer*
PLANETS
IN 2023

JUPITER
SATURN
URANUS
NEPTUNE
PLUTO

The outer planets include the gas giants—Jupiter, Saturn, Uranus and Neptune—plus icy, rocky Pluto. Due to their slower-moving orbit through the zodiac, they shape larger trends. Since outer planet lessons take more time to work through, they shift the trajectory of your life in a major way that's not always obvious at first. We've mapped out their movements in 2023 to help you plan your long-term goals.

JUPITER

JUPITER IN ASTROLOGY

Wise, wild Jupiter is the galactic gambler, global nomad and eternal seeker. The fastest spinning planet in the solar system, developments happen rapidly in this planet's path. Jupiter's job is to push us out of our comfort zones and into uncharted territory—even if that means leaping before we look! The point is that we jump, as far as Jupiter's concerned. If at first we don't succeed, Jupiter wants us to try, try again.

Regardless of which zodiac sign Jupiter is orbiting through at any given time, there are bound to be exciting developments. Higher learning and philosophy fall under its reign. Here's where we collectively expand and elevate to the next level of human development! But how much is too much? Like a giant cosmic spotlight, Jupiter exposes flaws in the machinery and might even reveal a scandal. Issues of global importance are also spotlighted under Jupiter's watch and often dominate the headline news.

To find your natal Jupiter sign, cast a free birth chart at

ASTROSTYLE.COM/BIRTHCHART

JUPITER IN 2023

In 2023, the red-spotted planet splits its time between a pair of zodiac signs: high-octane, self-serving Aries and slow-jamming, tactile Taurus. Until May 16, Jupiter in Aries provides supersonic momentum for new initiatives.

This is Jupiter's second pass through the Ram's realm. From May 10 to October 28, 2022, the red-spotted planet charged through Aries, creating a fiery worldwide climate that brought an economy-toppling war and some of the bravest fighters in recent history.

When Jupiter heads into Taurus on May 16, it cools its jets (and hopefully its jetfighters). This cautiously optimistic cycle, which lasts until May 25, 2024, calls for measured, sustainable growth and longevity.

4

Jupiter THROUGH THE SIGNS

ARIES
DEC 20, 2022, 9:32AM

TAURUS D
DEC 30, 9:40PM

TAURUS
MAY 16, 2023, 1:20PM

GEMINI
MAY 25, 2024

TAURUS RX
SEP 4, 10:10AM

Times listed are when Jupiter transit begins, Eastern US Time Zone

JUPITER IN ARIES
DEC 20, 2022 — MAY 16, 2023

Breaking into a New Beat

Blaze those trails! Expansive Jupiter in innovative Aries is a time for limitless possibilities. Take those "wouldn't it be crazy if..." ideas for a test run. Let things get messy. That's how many great discoveries are made!

Although the Jazz Age wasn't going full throttle until the 1920s, the style began evolving out of ragtime in 1916-17, while Jupiter was weaving between Aries and Taurus. The swinging, rhythmic Down Home Rag was recorded twice during that period, once by the instrumental quartet the Versatile Four, and again by the original composer Wilbur Sweatman.

Whatever your medium, tap the originating powers of Jupiter in Aries for a creative breakthrough. The trick? Letting yourself experiment wildly and make "mistakes." When Jupiter cycled through Aries in 1975, DJ Grand Wizzard Theodore invented the record scratch by sheer accident. As the story goes, he tried to hold a spinning record in place so he could hear his mom talking—a happy "slip-up" that brought an essential element to the art of deejaying.

Feeling the Friction

Jupiter in Aries periods are often marked by friction, both in our personal lives and across international borders. Amplifier Jupiter charges up Aries' combative nature and can make every sentiment come out sounding like fighting words.

During the 1917 Jupiter in Aries cycle, the United States was preparing to join then-allied Britain, France and Russia to fight World War I. The start of World War II happened in 1939, during another Jupiter in Aries transit.

In our *2022 Horoscope* guide, we predicted that violence may escalate while zealous Jupiter ran its midyear combat mission through Aries, from May 10 to October 28, 2022. While we wish that wasn't the case, alas the aggressive side of Aries emerged. Russia escalated its attacks on Ukraine, forcing world powers to act with concerted strategy in order to avoid a nuclear fallout—or a full-on World War III.

We aren't trying to scare you here! But we'd be remiss if we painted a falsely optimistic picture of this current Jupiter in Aries cycle. With the United States so harshly divided, fears of a Civil War are not completely unfounded, especially as citizens polarize over everything from election results to gun laws to reproductive freedom.

♃

Personal Safety Requirements

Considering the easy access to automatic weapons and "ghost guns" (untraceable, Lego-like assembly weapons), personal safety concerns may mount in the first part of 2023. With militant factions forming around the world, ideological and religious disagreements have already escalated into rogue violence.

During the 2022 Jupiter in Aries cycle, a gut-wrenching shooting at a Uvalde, Texas, elementary school killed 19 children and two adults. During the 1999 Jupiter in Aries cycle, the tragic Columbine High School massacre took place. Unfortunately, we could go on with the count of such tragedies as of this writing.

A small bit of justice was served in October 2022, a Connecticut jury fined far-right radio host Alex Jones nearly $1 billion in compensatory damages to be paid to eight families of 2012's Sandy Hook Elementary shooting victims. For a decade, Jones has baselessly insisted that the grieving Sandy Hook parents were "crisis actors." Grieving families have been ceaselessly harassed by his followers, compounding their agony since 2012.

Fighting the Good Fight

Sometimes, it's necessary to fight back, especially when justice is being infringed upon. As principled Jupiter in Aries sounds the clarion call for personal power, "going to battle" may seem like the only option. We've certainly seen that with the indefatigable courage of Ukraine's soldiers and civilian fighters.

Dystopian frustration often evolves into a full-scale uprising during Jupiter in Aries. That's been the case in Iran since September 2022, when a 22-year-old Mahsa Amini, died while in custody of the country's brutal morality police. Amini was arrested for allegedly wearing her headscarf (hijab) too loosely. When news of her death broke, Iran's first women-led uprising exploded. In public demonstrations, brave women have been burning their hijabs and cutting their hair, facing death, arrest and abuse. In an interesting resonance, the Arab Spring escalated during Jupiter's 2011 transit through Aries.

A word to the wise: While Jupiter blazes through hotheaded Aries until May 16, make sure the cause you're fighting for is grounded in facts. In some cases, what looks like a revolution might simply be a distraction that leads you further afield. Angry, disenfranchised masses may be easily manipulated by narcissistic extremists who are preying on their emotions. Practice self-defense, an Aries protective measure, by always thinking for yourself.

Holding Space for Peace

While it may be a study in contrast, Jupiter in Aries underscores the need for peace. The first worldwide meditation occurred on August 16-17, 1987, during the Harmonic Convergence. As seven planets (in fire signs, including Jupiter at 29° Aries) assembled into a harmonious Grand Trine, people gathered at energy centers from Mount Shasta to the pyramids of Egypt to send up a collective "Om!"

Anything that soothes the psyche is worth trying when Jupiter's blazing a fiery trail through Aries. Transcendental Meditation, which originated in India in the mid-1950s with Maharishi Mahesh Yogi, gained mass popularity while Jupiter was in Aries in 1975-76.

If there's friction in your household or among the people you gather with regularly, do your part to deescalate the drama. Prevention is even smarter: How can you dial down stress in your environment? Skilled mediators and counselors can help restore peace when no one is willing to declare a ceasefire.

If you must be a warrior, how about being a "love warrior," appropriately the title of Aries Glennon Doyle's book. Or a "freedom fighter" who doesn't need to take up arms, unless you're (safely) encircling someone in a hug?

While Jupiter blazed in Aries in 1987, Britain's Order of the Garter—the most exclusive and prestigious level of knighthood—opened to women for the first time in history. That's more reason to aim for the honorable side of Aries instead of the hot-headed one.

JUPITER IN TAURUS

MAY 16, 2023 – MAY 25, 2024

Mighty Aphrodite

With reproductive freedoms under fire in the United States, it's not a stretch to predict that women's rights will be a hot topic for 2023. And outspoken Jupiter provides a global megaphone for the movement. Taurus is one of the two zodiac signs (along with Libra) that is ruled by the planet—and female deity—Venus. But how might this play out in our polarized times?

While Jupiter toured Taurus in 1988, Pakistan's Benazir Bhutto became the first female prime minister of a Muslim country. In 2023, we may see more women getting involved in government, especially on a state and local level. But that's no guarantee they will represent an agenda that jibes with the modern-day, multifaceted woman. At time of writing, Sweden, a country that once led the way in gender equality, released a statement that it is ditching its "feminist foreign policy."

Will historical apron strings lasso women back to the kitchen and nursery? Jupiter in Taurus could amplify the conservative outcry for women to fall back into "traditional" roles as wives and mothers—and seductresses. To wit, the first Miss Universe pageant was held while Jupiter was in Taurus in 1952, putting women on display as objects of beauty. During Jupiter's 1940 spin through Taurus, Daisy Duck joined Donald, wooing and cooing with the flounce of her tail feathers—moves cartoonists may have cribbed from international spy Mata Hari who introduced her exotic dance act while Jupiter was in Taurus in 1905.

While Mata Hari may have batted her lashes in the name of espionage, we're not suggesting that women will woo their way to equality in 2023.

Taurus rules the throat—and Jupiter here can help people "speak truth to power." Women's health and reproductive justice will no doubt be a huge part of 2023's conversation. It's worth noting that while Jupiter orbited through Taurus in 1916, Margaret Sanger opened the first U.S. birth control clinic, a forerunner of Planned Parenthood.

Big Buck Energy

With a recession looming, Jupiter's arrival in money-minded Taurus may provide a buffer—at least for those who play their cards right. Happy-go-lucky Jupiter is the galactic gambler: Some of the biggest fortunes were made while this planet passed through Taurus. (Talk about a new spin on a "Bull market.") Fun fact: Las Vegas was founded during a Jupiter in Taurus transit on May 5, 1905!

John D. Rockefeller became the world's first billionaire during the 1916 Jupiter in Taurus cycle. During the 2012 circuit, Apple claimed a value of $600 billion, making it the world's largest company by market capitalization. While most of us aren't playing such a high-stakes game, we can still capitalize on this potential. Expansive Jupiter in Taurus can help everyday people grow their fortunes and increase their earnings, perhaps in the same self-made way that brought Rockefeller his wealth.

Hedge Your Bets

Watch out! Spending can creep up in equal proportion to earning. Historically, there have been some major financing deals happening while Jupiter dealt hands in Taurus. In 1940, FDR asked Congress for a jaw-dropping credit of approximately $900 million dollars to finance the construction of approximately 50,000 airplanes per year. In 2012, the Guggenheim Partners made the largest purchase of a sports franchise up to that date, buying the LA Dodgers for $2.1 billion. (Higher prices have been paid for a team since—and we wonder what this upcoming Jupiter in Taurus cycle will bring!)

What might get tricky after May 16: Knowing the difference between a "calculated risk" and a straight-up gamble. When Jupiter trekked into Taurus in February 2000, Internet start-up funding was flowing like wine at a Roman orgy. (And signature cocktails were flowing freely at the open bars of nightly launch parties in dot-com hub cities!) Less than a month later, on March 10, 2000, NASDAQ peaked at 5132.52. This event signaled the beginning of the end of the dot-com boom. Before Jupiter moved on to Gemini, an astounding number of these overfunded-yet-underwhelming ventures shut down leaving investors in the red.

It's a cautionary tale for us all in the era of blockchain bros and Silicon Valley start-ups that are a far cry from safe bets. Not that this has ever stopped humans from spinning the proverbial roulette wheel in the hopes of an epic payout. While Jupiter in Taurus is sure to make some folks rich, it could also bring more crushing losses and a not-altogether-unfounded fear of investing in general.

♃

A Rise in Anti-Capitalism

In salt-of-the-earth Taurus, righteous Jupiter will sound a loud, and possibly artistic, cry for economic reform. And we could use it! With housing rates skyrocketing for the past few years and inflation driving up the cost of everything from food to fuel, life has been a struggle for the everyday citizen.

Yes, the rich often get richer while Jupiter is in Taurus. But these cycles also correspond to anti-capitalist movements. The late 1999 protests against the World Trade Organization (WTO) in Seattle, WA, that resulted in destruction of downtown shops and violent confrontations between activists and police happened while Jupiter was weaving between Aries and Taurus. During that same circuit, Microsoft chairman Bill Gates—already one of the world's wealthiest humans—stepped down as CEO amidst an antitrust investigation.

Fast-forward to Montreal 2012, as over 200,000 people marched against government tuition hikes and in favor of free access to college education. To date, this is the largest protest in Quebec's history. And way back in 1928 Berlin, Jupiter in Taurus brought us Berthold Brecht's *Threepenny Opera*, a scorching critique of capitalism performed as a musical.

Public demonstrations have been the norm in recent years. But in 2023, people may rally around a focused demand for everyday survival: affordable housing, free education or deep cuts in medical expenses, like the hearing aids that are now available over the counter, saving primarily elderly folks on a fixed income thousands of dollars.

Build It Up

Taurus is associated with construction, and while no-limits Jupiter is zoned here, buildings tend to get bigger and more majestic. Some of the world's tallest structures opened while Jupiter was in Taurus. 1976 brought us the CN Tower in Toronto, then the highest free-standing land structure. Not to be outdone, the Petronas Towers officially opened in Kuala Lumpur as the world's tallest building of 1999. In 2012, the then-unfinished One World Trade Center surpassed The Empire State Building as NYC's most soaring structure.

Architecture continues to trend up with high-rise buildings continuing their popularity. By 2050, 68% of the world's population will live in urban areas, according to a UN report. Mixed-use properties that create community and reduce strain on utilities only make sense in our ever-changing world.

Build It Green

Jupiter in earthy Taurus can also help us live in greater attunement with nature. With interest rates hiked, 2023's builds may be less about "buying new" and more about making our homes greener with things like solar panels and water efficiency systems. Turning your front yard into a permaculture garden could be the new "fix and flip" trend.

Of course, if you're a card-carrying solarpunk, this way of life is nothing new. For those with skills in the sustainable living department: Time to set up that YouTube channel and show people what regenerative design is all about. But beware the dreaded "greenwashing"! Jupiter is prone to hyperbole. In mid 2023, we may see a rise in the trend of corporate marketers leaning into environmentally friendly buzzwords without actually doing anything impactful to address the issues.

Make Love...and Art!

If financial lulls are "good" for anything, perhaps it's a reminder that the best things in life are free. As Jupiter free-ranges through romantic, artistic Taurus, it might just spark a renaissance. That's another nod to Mata Hari's first exotic dance. Will burlesque storm TikTok as 2023's top trend?

Nerdy Jupiter in Taurus could also make art appreciators out of us all. The 1st Academy Awards were held during the 1929 transit, as a 15-minute ceremony at the Hollywood Roosevelt Hotel. Fast forward to 1953, when the 25th Academy Awards marked the first time the ceremony was broadcast on TV—also under Jupiter in Taurus. In 2023, we might see new genres emerge—or perhaps a degenderizing in the awards process itself.

If you're inspired to make art, break out the paints and easel. And by the way, making NFTs *could* still be a worthy pursuit. Although 2022 was hardly a heyday for the medium, once Jupiter heads back into Taurus on May 16, there could be a new wave of interest, especially as generative A.I. apps like Midjourney and Stable Diffusion allow users to create digital video and images from mere strings of text.

Will we see digital dealers make a fortune again? If Jupiter in Taurus repeats itself, perhaps. On May 8, 2012, Mark Rothko's 1961 color-field painting *Orange, Red, Yellow* was sold at Christie's for $86 million, a record price for post-war contemporary art at public auction.

JUPITER CONNECTIONS IN 2023

JUPITER-CHIRON MEETUP
MARCH 12

Chiron, the "wounded healer" comet, has been on an eight-year trek through Aries since April 2018, forcing the world to reckon with our anger, violence and unwillingness to compromise. When is it smart to take a stand and when is a "my way or the highway" attitude verging on narcissism? When Jupiter catches up to Chiron on March 12, it could be like a lit match in a powder keg—or an invitation to "go high" and deal with conflict constructively.

SUN-JUPITER MEETUP IN ARIES, THE "DAY OF MIRACLES"
APRIL 11

When a planet makes an exact connection, or conjunction, to the Sun, it gets a solar charge of bright, bountiful energy. In recent years, astrologers have started calling the once-per-year Sun-Jupiter conjunction "The Day of Miracles" as a nod to Jupiter's beneficent, abundant influence. It certainly can't hurt to schedule this day for bold action, especially near 6:07PM ET, the peak of their merger. Auditions, presentations and proposals could all go exceedingly well, as long as you don't overshoot your mark.

JUPITER

JUPITER-PLUTO SQUARE

MAY 17

Massive power struggle: incoming! As pioneering Jupiter in Taurus locks into a challenging square with powermonger Pluto in Aquarius, intense forces pull us in dueling directions. On the one hand, there's a current sweeping us toward major change, demanding that we try a radically new way of doing things. An equally strong force will resist these new attempts: If it ain't broke, why fix it? When these two dominant planets sit down at the negotiating table, compromise won't be comfortable—or easy to find. Do your part by at least hearing the other party's desires, even if they sound more like demands (and unreasonable ones at that).

JUPITER-SATURN SEXTILE

JUN 19

It's always a good day when the planet of expansion (Jupiter) and the planet of structure (Saturn) play nicely with each other. Jupiter in Taurus brings the excitement and sensuality while Saturn in Pisces brings a dose of sobering sensibility. We won't just figure out *what* needs to be done, but we'll also see *how* to do it. Discuss your dream scenario, then put a solid plan in place for achieving the next steps.

MARS OPPOSITE JUPITER

OCT 28

Face-off! This combustible day comes with an active trigger warning. As hotheaded Mars locks horns with know-it-all Jupiter in Taurus, no one's backing down from their righteous stance. Since Mars is in secretive Scorpio, stay on guard for passive-aggressive behavior, a warning that something bigger may be brewing. Be watchful and strategic and keep classified information in the vault.

SEEING JUPITER *in the sky*

MORNING   APR 26 - NOV 3

EVENING   JAN 1 - MAR 29
NOV 3 - DEC 31

JUPITER RETROGRADE

SEP 4 - DEC 30

Jupiter turns retrograde annually, napping in low-power mode for four months. In 2023, the backspin takes place from September 4 to December 30, backing up through Taurus the entire time. As exciting as Jupiter's developments are, they can also be exhausting! The retrograde timeouts may come as a blessed relief, giving us a window to integrate all the rapid changes the red-spotted planet has us striving to achieve.

Let's be honest: Some of our gambling instincts do need to be tamed. While in reverse, Jupiter slows our rapid expansion before the sprawl becomes too stressful. This is a great time to go back to the drawing board to review goals, reconfigure plans, refine our efforts and make sure we are set up with all the right resources before we go back to the "build site."

ARE YOU HAVING A JUPITER RETURN?

People born with Jupiter at 1°-29° Aries or Taurus (0°-15°) will have an exact Jupiter Return this year. This happens when the red-spotted planet transits across the same sign (and degree) it was in when you were born. These year-long phases, which happen every 12-13 years, are marked by abundance, expansion and game-changing growth! Wanderlust may strike, leading you on a peripatetic quest to another corner of the world. Cross-cultural relations may give your life new dimension. Discovering your faith and doing spiritual work can inform an entrepreneurial or media venture. Follow this scholarly planet's prompting and enroll in schooling or an experiential self-development program. No matter the direction you choose, it's time to expand!

♃

Want to learn more? Discover how to unlock growth, good fortune and abundance in your chart with our pocket course, The Jupiter Code!

ASTROSTYLE.COM/JUPITER

SATURN

SATURN IN ASTROLOGY

Where have we become excessive? When is enough just...enough? The whistleblowing planet of integrity reveals where we need to set better boundaries. As a slower-moving outer planet, Saturn shapes longer trends. The ringed planet lurks in a single zodiac sign for 2.5 to 3 years and orbits through the entire zodiac in 29.5 years.

Taskmaster Saturn applauds perseverance and shines a light on where you need to keep on pushing. This is the planet that rules structured Capricorn, the zodiac's Sea Goat (a "WTF?!" creature if ever there were). With its mermaid tail and two front legs, the Capricorn Goat makes an unwavering ascent to the top of the mountain for the win. Before Uranus was discovered by telescope in 1781, Saturn was also considered the sole ruler of futuristic, otherworldly Aquarius. Since then, Saturn has been sharing the distinction as "co-ruler" of the Water Bearer's realm with side-spinning, rebel Uranus—an uncanny match! Maybe that's why there's so much hidden magic to Saturn's process. One minute, you feel like Sisyphus rolling an interminable boulder up the hill. Then, your hustle yields a breakthrough and you're living the dream!

To find your natal Saturn sign, cast a free birth chart at

ASTROSTYLE.COM/BIRTHCHART

ħ

SATURN IN 2023

What happens when the planet of visibility tucks into the zodiac sign of invisibility? We're about to find out starting March 7, as clear-eyed Saturn is enveloped in Pisces' fog. This three-year cycle, which lasts until February 13, 2026, will melt tangible reality into virtual reality like the clock in Salvador Dalí's *The Persistence of Memory*.

We already have the technology to create this mind-boggling effect, thanks to Saturn's three-year pass through geeky Aquarius. But will we utilize these developments for the good of humanity? That remains to be seen as the ringed taskmaster paddles into Piscean seas for the first time since May 21, 1993 to April 7, 1996.

ħ

Saturn THROUGH THE SIGNS

AQUARIUS
MAR 21 - JUL 1, 2020
DEC 17, 2020

PISCES
MAR 7, 2023, 8:35AM

PISCES RX
JUN 17, 1:27PM

PISCES D
NOV 4, 3:03AM

ARIES
FEB 13, 2026

Times listed are when Jupiter transit begins, Eastern US Time Zone

Blasting Out of Saturn in Aquarius

As 2023 dawns, we have nine weeks left of restrictive Saturn's tour through communal Aquarius. Not ironically, this transit began on March 21, 2020, ten days after COVID was declared a pandemic and cities began locking down. "Social distancing" is the epitome of a Saturn-in-Aquarius concept. Saturn restricts whatever it touches, forcing new structures to emerge. And so it has for our societal interactions ever since.

Aquarius rules communities and scientific developments. With Saturn here, the world scrambled to set up remote offices, "Zoom school" kids and shelter in place—all while waiting in agony for a vaccine to be approved. We watched helplessly while loved ones gasped for breath as Saturn cycled through this air sign—the result of an airborne disease spread through droplets. (Aquarius is the sign of the Water Bearer.) We'll stop there... We know you lived through it and hopefully won't have to *relive* anything like it again in your lifetime.

While it's hard to call anything pandemic-related a "silver lining," society has shifted in undeniably Aquarian directions since March 21, 2020. As companies shuttered their offices, many realized that remote work (or hybrid remote-office work) allowed greater efficiency and employee satisfaction. "Digital nomad" has become a new lifestyle category, turning sleepy resort towns into micro Silicon Valleys—for better and for worse. We're all experts on Zoom, staying connected across the miles like never before.

Space travel took new leaps with Saturn in cosmonaut Aquarius. Billionaires Elon Musk, Richard Branson and Jeff Bezos all launched civilian-bound rockets into orbit; Branson and Bezos even buckled in for a ride. But Saturn in Aquarius brought a grave misuse of science, too. We've watched Russia fire military rockets into Ukraine during authoritarian Saturn's circuit of Aquarius, destroying entire cities and infrastructures of the once-thriving nation and casting a looming threat of nuclear warfare.

This situation has also shown the world that an unstoppable underdog *can* stand up to bully. The unfathomable courage, togetherness and stalwart "staying power" of Ukranians (young and elderly)—led by Aquarius President Zelensky—is exemplary of Saturn's backbone combined with the unifying energy of Aquarius.

Technology: Unbound

Paradox #1: Saturn is the boundary-hound of the skies while Pisces is the boundary dissolver. So how will we navigate this bizarre dichotomy? The seams are already fraying in the tech world as Saturn winds down its tour of Aquarius.

As of this writing, Elon Musk—a Saturn-in-Aquarius technocrat if ever there were—has added Twitter to his toy chest and is wreaking havoc across the platform with mass firings, bargain-basement blue checks and bizarre tweetstorms. Fears that he will tank Twitter are not unfounded, and the consequences could be dire on a historical level. The end of the platform would wipe out a vast public archive of firsthand global news reporting. Should these 16-years be erased from digital memory, the "truth" could be revamped by spin doctors to cast doubt and denial, the shadow of Saturn in Pisces.

Speaking of technocrats, Jeff Bezos founded Amazon in July 1994 during the prior Saturn-in-Pisces circuit. Since then, he's become one of the ten richest people on planet Earth. But as Amazon approaches its "Saturn return" (its first sweep back into Pisces since the company's inception), the tide has turned. In October 2022, the company reported gloomy Q4 projections, which sent stock prices tumbling as much as 21%, wiping multiple eight figures from Bezos' net worth.

His billionaire buddies Mark Zuckerberg, Changpeng Zhao and Elon Musk are not faring any better. Meta, Binance and Tesla have reported massive losses in 2022. What's the message? We'll borrow a line from late-Pisces Steve Jobs and suggest that these Silicon Valley giants try to "think different."

Idealistic Aquarius is fundamentally a "power to the people" sign. But with restrictive Saturn here, true wealth has remained in the hands of the same crew, notably with Aquarius-ruled tech founders Elon Musk, Jeff Bezos and Bill Gates holding steady at the top of the pyramid.

Once Saturn heads into Pisces on March 7, these digital overlords may not receive the same level of planetary protection as they did when the galactic guru was logged in to Aquarius. We're already seeing this as Pluto is edging out of patriarchal Capricorn. We may see some new kids on the blockchain in 2023. Yet who will rise to power under can't-stop-won't-stop Saturn in Pisces? From pop stars to cult leaders to political prisoners, if history repeats itself, this shift could send us into tumultuous waters.

Worship Me

With pious Saturn in reverent Pisces, we are predicting a schism. Religious rule makers from age-old traditions will strengthen their hold in power. Simultaneously, spiritual groups centered in neo-esoteric practices will formalize into religions or possibly cults. What will 2023's version of Scientology be? (Started by Pisces L. Ron Hubbard, FWIW.) Will sanctimonious Supreme Court justices continue to blur the lines between church and state? Bombshells may be dropped across the spectrum.

Noteworthy religious moments have blossomed while Saturn was in Pisces. In 1965, Pope Paul VI declared that Jews are not collectively responsible for the death of Jesus Christ—a historical moment for the Catholic Church. In 1966, Kwanzaa was celebrated for the first time under the leadership of activist Maulana Karenga, honoring seven principles

ħ

(*Nguzo Saba* in Swahili) of African culture.

Pisces is symbolized by two fish swimming in opposite directions. One might be thought of as a shark, ready to defend its waters and attack at the first scent of blood. The other is more like a trout, easily baited on the hook of a charismatic figure, subverting its power and slipping into idolization.

Indeed, some notorious cult activity has happened under Saturn in Pisces' watch. In March 1995, members of the doomsday sect "Aum Shinrikyo" carried out the Tokyo subway sarin attack, which killed 14 people and injured over a thousand. To date, this remains the deadliest terrorist attack in Japanese history.

Piscean paranoia and delusion reached a fever pitch elsewhere in 1995. Weeks after the Tokyo attacks, Tejano popstar Selena was murdered by her very own fan club president, Yolanda Saldívar, a shocking loss that was felt around the world.

Victims and Martyrs

Here's one way that Saturn and Pisces collide: Neither one is a stranger to sacrifice. Saturn holds out for the big win while Pisces wants to absorb the suffering of others. Together, they can strengthen the resolve we put behind our ideals. As we step into 2023, the clock seems to be turning back on many human rights as autocratic forces grow in power. Other planets transiting through Pisces might allow us to bury our heads in the sand, but not Saturn. The ringed realist puts ugly truths in our faces and demands that we deal.

Some of the world's most legendary martyrs have performed heroic acts under Saturn in Pisces' watch. In 1906, Gandhi organized his first campaign of *satyagraha*, meaning mass civil disobedience, protesting restricted rights of Indians in South Africa.

In 1964, Nelson Mandela delivered his *I Am Prepared to Die* speech at a key anti-apartheid event, the Rivonia Trial. In his words, "I have cherished the ideal of a democratic and free society in which all persons live together in harmony and with equal opportunities. It is an ideal which I hope to live for and to achieve. But if needs be, it is an ideal for which I am prepared to die."

Will we make the same sacrifices for our beliefs over the coming three years? If Saturn in Pisces has a say in it, yes. During this same transit in 1965, late civil rights activist and Congressman John Lewis (a Pisces) risked his life in the "Bloody Sunday" march through Selma, Alabama, that ended in violent attacks from police and the Ku Klux Klan on the peaceful protestors. The attacks were televised, evoking national civil rights action that ultimately led to Congress passing the Voting Rights Act on August 6, 1965.

Nearly 60 years later, voter suppression and gerrymandering have slowly but surely created a new form of racial disparity around U.S. elections. Disempowerment, the shadow of Saturn in Pisces, may bring an uprising in the years ahead. To wit, while Saturn was winding through its tour of Pisces in 1965, the Watts Riots broke out in Los Angeles. In October 1966, Bobby Seale and Huey P. Newton founded the Black Panther Party with an ideology of Black nationalism, socialism and armed self-defense, particularly against police brutality.

Delusions of Grandeur

With Saturn heading out of anti-establishmentarian Aquarius and into Pisces, a sign with a slippery grasp on reality, we need to be extremely mindful of both fringe groups and dominating leaders that seem to be touting the next world-changing ideal. Unchecked, this Saturn cycle could make "going Q" look relatively tame.

To wit, in April 1995, anti-government extremists Timothy McVeigh and Terry Nichols bombed the Oklahoma City Federal Building, killing 168 people and wounding 680. While we pray that insurrectionists don't go full-on terrorist in 2023, there's reason to be vigilant, especially as gun-toting civilians become more and more emboldened to show up at places like, oh, voter polling booths or on the steps of a state capitol building.

During this transit in 1966, the Chinese Communist Party issued the "May 16 Notice," marking the beginning of the violent and chaotic Cultural Revolution. Mao Zedong (AKA Chairman Mao) rallied school-aged youth as his rebel army to "purge remnants of capitalist and traditional elements from Chinese society." The personality cult, which lasted ten years, led to the killing of 1.5 million people. Millions more were imprisoned, tortured, humiliated and left in ruin.

China's current leader Xi Jinping began his precedent-breaking third term in 2022. While his ideals and approach are different, his strict "zero COVID" policy, crackdowns on Hong Kong (remember the 2019 Umbrella Movement?) and authoritarian rulership style have chilling echoes as we enter Saturn in Pisces.

Mind Over Matter

Pisces is the sign that rules fantasy, and even dour Saturn can't stop us from escaping into our imaginations as stressful headlines loom. But this pragmatic planet *can* help us work with unseen forces to manifest material-world results.

While Saturn toured Pisces in March 1937, Napoleon Hill's then-groundbreaking self-help book, *Think and Grow Rich*, was published, making a case that mindset and wealth are inextricably linked. Hill wrote of creating a cabinet of "invisible counselors." Each night before drifting off to sleep, he imagined himself as Chairman at a table of great historical figures who he would ask to "impress upon my subconscious mind" the answers to whatever question he posed.

Are these the types of ethereal guides who appear while CEO Saturn drifts through the Pisces dream field? If so, we might summon late marine biologist and conservationist Rachel Carson. She advanced the global environmental movement with studies and books including *The Sea Around Us* (1951) and was born with Saturn in Pisces during its prior tour, in 1907.

We'll add Pisces Albert Einstein to the cabinet while we're at it. While Saturn trekked through his sign in 1905, he submitted a series of groundbreaking papers. One on the particle theory of light became the foundation of modern physics. Another paper established the theory of special relativity and the famous equation of $E=mc2$. Scientists call 1905 Einstein's *annus mirabilis*, his year of miracles. Will Saturn's three-year circuit bring more divine breakthroughs in science—perhaps ones around green energy, carbon capture and water purification? Here's hoping.

Water, Water Everywhere

Speaking of $H2O$, once Saturn plunges into Pisces this March 7, the water crisis that brought record droughts, intense floods, wildfires and hurricanes in 2022 could grow even more serious. The United States West is already reeling from 2022's megadrought and if suppressive Saturn has a say, we anticipate strict water rationing in 2023.

But it's not just farmland crops and household drinking and bathing supplies that are affected. The Hoover Dam, which was constructed while Saturn was in Pisces in 1936, powers hydroelectricity for much of the Southwest. As both Lake Mead and the Hoover Dam recede perilously close to a "dead pool" tipping point, considerations are being made for alternate power, which, at the moment, seems limited to fossil fuels. That would be a huge setback in the already-beleaguered global efforts to reduce greenhouse gasses and, in turn, keep ocean temperatures from elevating past the point of no return.

Will Saturn in Pisces bring a reckoning from sea god Neptune? Turning the tide on environmental damage seems more and more like a distant dream. But that's not to say collective efforts and civic plans could not produce a miracle. Conservation, in fact, is one of infrastructure-builder Saturn's favorite words. We'll continue to hold out for hope that Saturn in Pisces can engineer a water-saving plan that hasn't yet been considered. If Saturn in Aquarius could send civilians to suborbital space...well, why not?

While Saturn in Aquarius may have suppressed global cooperation, Saturn in Pisces may dissolve hostile boundaries out of sheer survival. A ray of hope: In October 2022, long-warring nations Israel and Lebanon negotiated a permanent maritime boundary along a formerly disputed stretch of the Mediterranean Sea. Since, Israel has begun extracting natural gas, a cleaner fossil fuel than coal, from the Karish Field. Lebanon will begin exploring its natural gas resources in its now-legally determined waters. Yes, it's a small step in a time when giant leaps are needed. But after March 7, we may see more treaties of its kind emerge in the name of saving the planet.

Fantasies Become Realities

Will life in the metaverse become the new normal? Some might argue that it already is, as the Internet becomes more immersive and interactive by the day. Apple's mixed reality headset due to launch in January 2023 and Meta and Sony are introducing updated versions—the Meta Quest 3 and Sony PlayStation VR 2, respectively.

And there's no telling *where* this will go when the planet of reality (Saturn) weaves through the sign of fantasy (Pisces). During this same transit lasting from 1935-38, the world's first regular TV program was transmitted from Berlin, Germany and Walt Disney premiered the world's first feature-length film, *Snow White and the Seven Dwarfs*, at LA's Carthay Circle Theater, on December 21, 1937. Both events were considered groundbreaking in their time.

I Want a New Drug

Speaking of, er, augmented reality, Saturn's tours through reality-bending Pisces have brought both legislation and developments in the world of drugs, spirits and pharmaceuticals. Eerie fact: Pisces Kurt Cobain, whose addictions haunted his daily life, was born with Saturn in Pisces in 1967 and died shortly after the planet returned here in 1994.

In 2021, a six-week clinical study revealed that psilocybin was a faster treatment for depression than the serotonin reuptake inhibitor, escitalopram, which is marketed as Lexapro. Psilocybin mushrooms are now legalized for therapeutic use in Oregon and decriminalized in a handful of U.S. cities including Denver, Oakland and Washington, D.C. Ketamine, also classified as a psychedelic, is currently legalized for medical use in all 50 U.S. states.

Enterprising Saturn also rules "big pharma." We may see corporatization of psychedelics in a similar vein to legalized marijuana. No matter whose pockets are lined, there's no denying that Saturn in Pisces has converged with groundbreaking developments in medicine, including the origins of the BCG vaccine for tuberculosis in 1906. The first broadly effective antibiotic, Prontosil, was discovered and clinically developed in 1935. During Saturn's 1995 pass through Pisces, the FDA approved Saquinavir, the first protease inhibitor to treat HIV and AIDS. As we grapple with new strains of COVID, here's hoping this passage brings another medical miracle.

ħ

Alas, there's already a Saturnian plot twist at play as the planet moves from Aquarius to Pisces. In late 2022, social media was abuzz with celebrity revelations that the Type 2 diabetes drug, semaglutide, was already in popular use for weight loss. As word gets out, there is fear that the treatment will not only be harder for diabetics to access, but that prices will increase due to the beauty industry's demand.

SATURN CONNECTIONS IN 2023

ANNUAL SUN-SATURN CONJUNCTION
FEB 16

The lifegiving Sun joins up with sobering Saturn in a once-yearly meeting of the minds. This is a day when diligent efforts could *finally* pay off or attract the hard-earned respect of an industry leader. Give credit where it's due, then accept kudos with grace. As the ringed taskmaster merges with el Sol, your buoyant hopes and optimistic plans could get a harsh reality check. Watch for heavy moods under this annual "downer day." Instead of getting discouraged, go back to the drawing board, mutter some chants- or prayers-of-choice (or just take a deep breath), and put a solid plan in place.

MARS-SATURN OPPOSITION
JUL 20

We'd never suggest you give up a dream, even when obstacles are showing up left, right and center. But when vigilant Mars in Virgo faces off with censuring Saturn in Pisces, you may be forced to pull the emergency brake to avoid veering off course. Plant your feet as you hatch your lofty plans. Use the slower pace to ground your vision with market tests, solid research or a rebalanced budget. Call up a trusted mentor and seek advice from seasoned pros. Once you circle back on the details, success will be yours for the launching!

MARS-SATURN SQUARE
NOV 25

Though you want to drop your guard and keep things friendly, don't! A smooth talker might dangle an offer that SEEMS to be an incredible opportunity. But with sober Saturn in fantasy-driven Pisces squaring Mars in optimistic Sagittarius, you'll need to give yourself one reality check after another. Get all the facts, and if this person is selling more promises than data, don't be shy about uttering an unyielding "No, thank-you!" This could be an energy vampire looking for a free ride.

ℏ

SEEING SATURN *in the sky*

MORNING	MAR 6 - AUG 27
EVENING	JAN 1 - JAN 30
	AUG 27 - DEC 31

SATURN RETROGRADE

JUN 17 - NOV 4

Saturn turns retrograde annually for approximately four and a half months. These backspins may stall progress and shuttle you back to the drawing board to ensure that you're developing plans on a stable foundation—and with proper levels of integrity. While Saturn's in reverse, relying on empirical data is more important than ever. Knowing where boundaries lie is equally essential, and you could learn some tough lessons by dropping your guard during a retrograde. Read the directions and don the safety gear—before you make a move.

Lessons around time-management and authority tend to arise during Saturn's backspin. These forced timeouts can be a hidden blessing, provided you're willing to take the medicine. Sign up for a management training class, learn how to use project management software, whip your calendar into shape. With Saturn in spiritual, subconscious Pisces in 2023, this is a powerful year for exploring your faith or healing from past triggers and traumas. No, this isn't the sexiest stuff, but think of it this way: When your inner world is in order, navigating the external world gets a whole lot easier.

ħ

Want to learn more? Discover where you'll gain leadership, status and long-term success with our pocket course, The Saturn Code!

ASTROSTYLE.COM/SATURN

ARE YOU IN YOUR SATURN RETURN?

Every 29.5 years (approximately) comes the Saturn return, a maturing rite of passage marking Saturn's homecoming to the sign it was in when you were born. The first return happens between ages 27-30, depending on Saturn's degree in your chart and is generally the first intro to adulting. The second return occurs between ages 56-60—and the third in one's early 80s. The planet's heavy-hitting energy will make itself known, bringing opportunities to quickly grow up and even take on powerful roles of authority.

Everyone born with Saturn in Aquarius or Pisces will feel the impact of this cosmic rite of passage. In 2023, Saturn will travel between 22°25' Aquarius to 7°13' Pisces. Those with Saturn falling between those degrees will have their exact Saturn return at some time in 2023, which may feel like its peak intensity. Get ready for some eye-opening lessons in adulting. You may be called to play a more active leadership role this year. Expect to hit some speed bumps around personal identity. Redefining yourself may feel like an act of rebellion and liberation rolled into one. Either way, a newer, truer you is emerging. Status-conscious Saturn can bring up "what will the neighbors think?" worries while also helping you build a stronger backbone when it comes to sticking up for your values.

ħ

Use our cosmic calculator to find out if you are currently in your Saturn return:

ASTROSTYLE.COM/COSMIC-CALCULATORS/SATURN-RETURN

URANUS

URANUS IN ASTROLOGY

Uranus takes 84 years to cycle through the zodiac, visiting each sign for approximately seven years. Because of its longer span, it's considered a generational planet, shaping the mindset of an entire age group. Since Uranus governs society and collective consciousness, its transits shape mass culture.

Technology and scientific developments are directed by Uranus, we'll see great innovations in the areas ruled by each zodiac sign it passes through. As the planet of societal interactions, Uranus directs everything from cultural trends to humanitarian efforts. The ruler of communal, innovative Aquarius, this side-spinning planet wants us to "get weird" in the most delightful ways! On the flipside, its disruptive influence can lead to dystopian thinking. Either way, it's here to help us embrace change—the only true constant in life.

To find your natal Uranus sign, cast a free birth chart at

ASTROSTYLE.COM/BIRTHCHART

URANUS IN 2023

On May 15, 2018, innovative Uranus, the planet of revolution, technology and rebellion, moved from firebrand Aries into conservative Taurus, entering the Bull's pen for the first time since 1942. Unconventional Uranus pushes for radical evolution and progress, while nostalgic Taurus upholds time-tested traditions, resisting change at every turn. Definitely a mismatch!

Uranus in Taurus is never a comfortable transit. While Uranus is future-driven, Taurus is recalcitrant and conservative. According to the principle of "essential dignities" in astrology, Uranus is in "fall" in Taurus—a weakened position since the energies are an awkward pairing. It's a simple energetic mismatch: Uranus governs the future while Taurus clings to the past.

In 2023, we've made it past the halfway point of Uranus' current journey through Taurus and now have a clear-eyed view of its impact on the world. Taurus' astrological rulership includes money, work, material objects, security, farming, the food supply, the arts and music. From cashless transactions to green energy to "quiet quitting," Uranus has already given these realms an extreme makeover. The convergence of Uranian AR metaverse and Taurean sensory reality has changed the way we use our everyday products. And we have an ongoing microchip shortage to show for it.

With machine-learning, smart devices, edge computing and other technologies doing the thinking for us, Uranian developments seem to be far outpacing the abilities of our Taurus-ruled physical capacities.

Progress at a Price?

Until 2026, we are tasked with resolving this planetary paradox: Can we create much-needed progress without erasing timeless traditions that still hold value and utility?

Take, for example, the statues of historical figures that were toppled and names removed from public spaces (parks, schools, buildings) in 2020-21. Many of these men owned slaves or committed acts that would be considered heinous human rights crimes today. The storming of the U.S. Capitol and insurrection of January 6, 2021 was another vivid example.

Progress has met backlash and unexpected curveballs along the way—particularly in 2022 as the eye-opening lunar North Node joined Uranus in moralistic Taurus last January 18. Florida passed its Parental Rights in Education Act (AKA the "Don't Say Gay" Bill) in March of 2022, prohibiting teachers from kindergarten to third grade from discussing gender identity and sexual orientation. In June 2022, the U.S. Supreme Court reversed *Roe v. Wade*, ending a half-century constitutional right to abortion—a decision that has created a reproductive justice crisis.

Upsetting issues have cropped up within nonprofits, notably ones that have been spotlighted during Uranus in Taurus. In 2022, Planned Parenthood was sued by a former employee for racial discrimination while Black Lives Matter Grassroots has taken executives of Black Lives Matter Global Network Foundation to court over alleged misappropriation of donated funds.

Progress without process simply creates chaos and division on Uranus in Taurus' watch. But who is the regulator and who sets the rules? Distrust of "the system" is a hallmark of this transit. And when it dovetails with a global pandemic and climate crisis, getting populations to work together is (and has been) nothing short of an obstacle course.

Labor Pains

Uranus in Taurus has disrupted the labor cycle, for better *and* for worse. After 2020's work-from-home mandates, 11 million U.S. workers quit their jobs between April and June 2021, a trend now widely known as "The Great Resignation." Burnout and unhappiness were cited as key reasons for people leaving their corporate gigs. In 2022, "quiet quitting" was the phenomenon *du jour*, a trend of fed up workers refusing to go above and beyond for their jobs, all while remaining on the payroll.

On a mental health level, this is a win for humankind. But markets and supply chains are now struggling from a shortage of workers. As profits decrease and inflation rises, we are facing another crisis in 2023: Finding jobs that pay a living wage given the current cost of everything from food to fuel. Cost-of-living data assembled by a team at MIT found that even a $15 minimum wage would not be enough for an average U.S. family of four to afford their basic expenses.

For the past few years, companies have been unrolling a flexible, hybrid workforce model, building teams comprised of both in-office and remote workers. But as A.I. replaces human labor, our relationship with money could also go through a massive shift. Will there be enough jobs that people are qualified for or even capable of doing?

The entire concept of a workforce is in flux, reshaping itself alongside technology during this Uranus cycle. Models like a UBI—Universal Basic Income—that guarantee citizens enough money for their survival—may soon be more of a necessity than an ideal.

Economic Makeovers Afoot

With stock prices trending up in 2018, Uranus in Taurus started out as a bull market, but switched to a bear in March 2020 with the advent of the pandemic. The downward cycle has continued with inflation and the burst of the housing bubble. Fears of a recession loom in 2023.

The U.S. spent the entire last Uranus in Taurus transit climbing out of the Great Depression, which ended in 1941, right as Uranus departed from Taurus. FDR also signed the U.S. Social Security act, providing unemployment compensation and pensions for the elderly.

Tighten up your belts, because 2023 is likely to be a lean year for many. Ongoing supply chain kinks and international trade struggles will continue forcing prices upwards on everything from goods to airline tickets. Those who are flush with resources may be in search of creative places to grow their funds as both the stock and bond markets plummet to lows we haven't seen in decades. (Of course, bear markets *are* times when savvy investors can "buy low.") Money may move into angel investments, for example, which could help grow small businesses—something grassroots Uranus in Taurus can definitely stand behind!

Decentralized Currency

Taurus rules money, and since technological Uranus landed here in 2018, dollars have gone digital. Cashless technology has made it easy to pay with the tap of a smartphone or the scan of a QR code—and now, the palm of your hand. Mobile apps like PayPal allow transactions to take place in cryptocurrency.

As Bitcoin reached its all-time high of around $68,789.63 in 2021, it became evident that the technology of money would be disrupted by the innovation of cryptocurrency and blockchains. Stories of surprise Bitcoin millionaires stormed the Interwebs. And just as surprisingly, many institutional investors joined the blockchain revolution—some enthusiastically and others with grudging reluctance. Blackrock, the world's largest asset manager, invested nearly $400 million in Bitcoin mining companies. As of February

2021, MicroStrategy invested $2.171 billion, adding 90,000 Bitcoins to the company's balance sheet under CEO Michael Saylor's direction. In August 2021, JP Morgan CEO Jamie Dimon, a one-time Bitcoin skeptic who called the digital currency a fraud in 2017, quietly backpedaled and gave wealth management clients access to six newly created cryptocurrency funds.

Countries began purchasing for their treasuries, too. In 2021, El Salvador became the first nation in the world to buy Bitcoin and make the digital currency legal tender, doubtless initiating a domino effect of Bitcoin acquisition by other countries.

Of course, Uranus is a destabilizer and crypto has certainly gone through annual highs and lows. As of this writing, the market is embroiled in chaos and a house-of-cards collapse of many coins, due to the FTX scandal. Is this a "correction" or the writing on the wall of crypto's doom? Ask 100 analysts and you'll get 100 different opinions. If Uranus in Taurus has anything to do with it, we'll see more rising and falling before 2026.

But here's what makes Bitcoin—and all cryptocurrency—so Uranian: decentralization. Unlike banks, which issue physical currency from a central authority, Bitcoin is entirely a virtual currency that operates on an observable, decentralized network, accessible to anyone with an internet connection. There is no central bank—or head banker—controlling Bitcoin with opaque accounting and questionable monetary policies. Transactions take place on a public database called a distributed ledger, which greatly reduces—or eliminates—the burden of a fee-charging middleman (in this case, the banks) to process, validate and authenticate transactions.

Because cryptocurrencies like Bitcoin have been created with limited and/ or controlled supply capped by mathematical algorithms, they are more resistant to manipulation that erodes their purchasing power. Regardless of your risk appetite, technology has now reached an inarguable point of no return, disrupting, even toppling, our most deeply entrenched institutions of banking and "money."

The Rise of Populism and Dictatorship

The worst manifestations of Uranus in Taurus can be bigotry, stubbornness and warmongering. Adolf Hitler, a Taurus, seized power just as Uranus was ending its last transit of Aries, and retained his dictatorial grip through the 1930s while Uranus was in Taurus. Mussolini also came into power during the last Uranus in Taurus transit, spreading fascism.

Fast forward to Uranus in Taurus, 2018 to 2026, and we've seen a steep rise in authoritarian rulers with iron-fisted ambitions. Putin's attack on Ukraine—and his "no limits" partnership with China and the country's third-time president Xi Jinping—has left the world on edge with fears of nuclear attacks, the overtaking of Taiwan and a possible World War III.

In "modern" nations globally, extremist politicians are not only on the rise, but winning races based on lies and propaganda spread through social media, slanted news outlets, populist rallies and cyber hacking. In the past couple years, Uranus in Taurus has provoked violent disruptors, many using technology to mobilize and plot public acts of terrorism or to spread messages of hate. With proud election deniers in Secretary of State roles, which oversee voting in the U.S....well, here's reason to be hawkishly concerned about history repeating itself.

From NFTs to Generative A.I.

Uranus in sensory Taurus is busy altering the way we interact with the physical and digital worlds. Under the Bull's cultured influence, fine art, literature and dance have blended with artificial intelligence, decentralization, and open-source software...to name a few things.

The craze for NFT art, also known as "crypto art," took hold in early 2021, when Christie's auction house sold a digital collage by artist Mike Winkelmann (AKA Beeple) for a jaw-dropping $69 million! The 41-year-old Wisconsin illustrator sparked an accidental frenzy when his piece, "Everydays: the First 5,000 Days," became the third-most expensive work ever sold by a living artist at an auction, carving out a $400 million-plus market by the end of 2021's first quarter.

Lo-fi CryptoPunks NFTs, which were originally free, have garnered staggering sums. Top sales ranged between $4.35 and $23.58 million! Meanwhile games such as CryptoKitties allowed players to collect, "breed" and trade virtual kittens.

So what makes these pieces, many of which are hackneyed and amateurish, so valuable? Digital rights. While most of these works can all be right-clicked and downloaded right to your desktop, an NFT purchase confers verified ownership of the piece. Essentially, it's like the difference between owning an original Van Gogh versus an Ikea print of "Starry Night." While the NFT bubble has burst since its inception, the craze is not over. With tech-savvy Uranus in "It's mine!" Taurus, the price of possession, whether virtual or real, has taken on a life of its own.

Need a break from all the NFT hype? Make way for Generative A.I. This form of artificial intelligence doesn't merely give you nifty things to collect. It forms a creative partnership between humans and machines, taking a snippet of text and transforming it into a computer-generated image, video, meme or...oh, the future possibilities!

Companies like OpenAI, DALL-E, Midjourney and Stable Diffusion have blown open the doors on this market. A user may choose a string of text like, "Frida Kahlo meets Afrofuturist dreamscape," and the software creates a visual mashup that can be co-edited and even shared in community galleries. Programs like Midjourney aren't a household name, but they amassed over 3 million members on Discord in 2022.

The same principle applies for other types of generative AI. Copywriting apps like Jasper can build entire keyword-friendly, SEO-ready blog posts based on a few prompts. While the final output still requires a human editor and fact checker, it puts together a solid draft.

Sounds incredible, right? Well... Renegade Uranus' fingerprints are already smudging up a few of these unregulated technologies. Stable Diffusion, one of the most buzzed-about generative A.I. apps, is becoming a fast-favorite among indie artists. The reason? Its open-source code and *laissez-faire* regulations. The platform is already being used to create violent memes, pornography (much with nonconsensual images) and other "art" that violates privacy and copyrights.

Still, Stable Diffusion's founder and CEO, Emad Mostaque, is resolute about the company's policies, and raised $101 million dollars in funding to prove it. As he told the *New York Times*, "We trust the people and we trust the community." Bold words while Uranus in money-hungry Taurus is playing celestial CTO of the world.

Farming and Food Technology

Taurus is an earth sign that governs sustenance and self-sufficiency. Farming and the food supply are already going through mega transitions with disruptive Uranus here. Can we implement solutions to global hunger—ones that don't involve factory farms and genetically modified seeds? At this writing, 3D "printed" food is already a legitimate thing with machines mixing together edible ingredients and heating them with lasers.

Food growers are turning to AgTech (agricultural technology) as an essential strategy. Drones now "walk the fields" to scout, map and survey the acreage. Their advanced cameras are equipped with sensors that can detect everything from moisture content to the health of plants. On the ground, internet-based sensors can provide data about soil quality, report on pest control and monitor the health and whereabouts of farm animals.

A movement has been evolving in recent years called "Drawdown," which focuses on *reversing* climate change instead of mitigating the impacts. Emphasized in the plans are solutions like permaculture and regenerative agriculture, both which aim to heal land that's been damaged by things like monocropping and deforestation. Other strategies include reducing food waste and education and family planning which empower women to make their own choices regarding childbearing.

Want to learn more? Find out where you need freedom, innovation and adventure with our pocket course, The Uranus Code!

ASTROSTYLE.COM/URANUS

URANUS CONNECTIONS IN 2023

In 2023, Uranus is not making any out-of-the-ordinary connections to other planets, which merits a sigh of relief. One day to circle is May 9,2023, when Uranus makes its annual conjunction to the Sun, a peak moment for innovation, scientific developments and both civil rights work and civil disobedience.

URANUS RETROGRADE

JANUARY 1-22 (SINCE AUGUST 24, 2022)
AUGUST 28, 2023 TO JANUARY 27, 2024

Uranus has an annual retrograde cycle that lasts for approximately five months each year. During these spells, progress can slow to a grinding halt. Technology, which is ruled by Uranus, can break down and classified information stored online can be subject to security breaches. The best way to deal? Strengthen your passwords, then step back to reconnect to the analog world. With the metaphysical planet snoozing, developing mindfulness practices can help you stay alert and aware. Get conscious about your every move—and your impact! Your interest in community work and activism may blossom in the process.

NEPTUNE

NEPTUNE IN ASTROLOGY

Because of its distance from the Sun, Neptune has a huge orbit to make. It takes 165 years to circle el Sol, spending an average of 15 years in each one of the zodiac signs. Each of these cycles shapes a generation, directing the music that moves us, the spiritual ideologies that resonate, the way we live out our dreams.

As the planet of unconditional love (and unconditional everything!), Neptune suspends logic. It allows us to truly dream as if anything were possible. Sometimes the visions are pure bliss; other times, they descend into nightmares. Limitlessness is the name of Neptune's game—and that includes *all* of it.

If romance requires a level of illusion, Neptune is the rose-tinted, soft-filter lens that lets us view the world in this way. As the ruler of watery, mutable Pisces, this planet pulls us under the sea where everything looks blurry and dark. A tumble down the rabbit hole might seem like a trip to Wonderland, but easy does it! Following Neptune's cues can spiral us into delusion and denial, as well as some dangerous addictions.

Through its trials, Neptune teaches us how to set boundaries. But first, it dissolves them, creating lessons in compassion and codependence alike. Does it all sound like a head trip? Yep, that's fantasy-agent Neptune. Try to enjoy the pretty colors while you spin this cosmic kaleidoscope.

To find your natal Neptune sign, cast a free birth chart at

ASTROSTYLE.COM/BIRTHCHART

NEPTUNE IN 2023

Let the spiritual awakening commence! ...Or shall we say, continue?
Neptune is deep into its 15-year transit through its home sign of Pisces,
an epic cycle that spans from February 3, 2011 until January 27, 2026. This
cycle only occurs every 165 years, a banner time for art, spirituality and the
emergence of esoteric information. Pisces is ruled by two fish swimming in
opposite directions. With limitless Neptune sailing through these waters,
we're ascending to new heights *and* achieving depth records. The highs
and lows have been dizzying at times, bringing out the best and worst of
humanity.

Water Is Life

Neptune is the god of the seas, and we've been doing damage to ours for
years. Denial ain't "just a river" anymore, it's an increasingly polluted
system of oceans that we must heal. In eerie synchronicity, the Tōhoku
earthquake and tsunami, which devastated areas of Japan and set off
explosions in the Fukushima nuclear plant, happened March 11, 2011, just
one month after the watery planet moved into Pisces for the first time in
165 years.

During Neptune's transit through Pisces, "Water is life" became the
rallying cry for activists of the Standing Rock Sioux tribe and the "Water
Protectors" who joined the demonstrations to block the construction of
the Dakota Access Pipeline in 2016-17.

The distribution of fresh, clean water to places that don't have easy access
to wells has become a prominent human rights topic. At the time of this
writing, the CDC reports that 2 billion people around the globe lack access
to safely managed drinking water at home. Climate change has brought

hurricanes and floods to some regions and extreme heat and drought to others. Meanwhile, polar ice caps continue to melt and rising temperatures are turning Antarctica green.

While collectively we all *know* that oceans are warming to critical temperatures. We see evidence of it through alarming coastal flooding, land loss and devastating hurricanes like 2022's Ian. Plastic waste is washing up on shores after being ingested by fish. The environmental violations are more than enough to drown in.

Yet, the shadow expression of Neptune in Pisces has brought out climate change deniers, many who are well-funded enough to manipulate public perspectives. Sadly, with so many politicians influenced by fossil-fuel companies and other environmentally damaging corporations, changing legislation around water pollution remains a deeply challenging goal.

On March 7, 2023, structured, suppressive Saturn will join Neptune in Pisces—a journey that lasts for three years. Saturn is a hardcore realist, demanding restrictions and sacrifices be made in the name of change. Waterways in the American West have been reaching critical lows, a trend that's been happening for 20 years. If Lake Mead and Lake Powell reach "dead pool" status, there won't be a strong enough current to power hydroelectricity, nor will there be enough water for agricultural irrigation. This aridification trend is happening globally as temperatures rise. In the summer of 2022, a drought caused parts of China's Yangtze River to dip to critical lows, affecting hydropower.

While Neptune and Saturn won't make an exact connection in Pisces, they remain in together in the Fish's waters until January of 2026. (Then both team up in Aries again after February 13, 2026.) As Saturn evaporates Neptune's fog, it exposes the flaws in our worldwide system. What washes up might not be pretty (like those bodies found in Lake Mead) but it will expedite the implementation of solutions that, we hope, are not too late to turn the tide on this crisis.

Spiritual or Religious?

During Neptune's previous transit through Pisces (1847-1862), the Spiritualist movement was thriving in the United States, Britain and France. Centered in a belief that the departed could communicate with the living, seances and "sittings" brought mediumship into the mainstream. (Hello, spirit guides?) Connecting to ancestors has been a longtime practice for indigenous cultures around the world. But the Spiritualist Movement marked Western society's first open embrace of the esoteric realm since the Salem Witch trials—which, incidentally, occurred while Neptune was in Pisces from 1692-93.

These metaphysical practices became a new sort of religion for many people who were disenfranchised by the iron grip of the church. Spiritualists were also active in the abolitionist and suffragist movements, true to the conscious, compassionate nature of Neptune in Pisces.

Neptune in Pisces cycles have brought a mix of both religious and spiritual developments. Buddhism was introduced to China during the Neptune in Pisces transit of 47-61ADE, expanding into Japan when Neptune cycled back to home base from 538 to 552ADE.

In 2011, Neptune's re-entry into Pisces dovetailed with the end of a 5,126-year cycle of the Mayan calendar. Despite widespread Armageddon hype, the world didn't end on December 21, 2012. But the date did mark a symbolic "end of the world as we know it." Intuitive practices, like tarot, channeling, and other divinations have been on the rise ever since. A 2017 Pew study found that 44% of Americans identified as "SBNR" (Spiritual but Not Religious).

Astrology may very well be the "neo-Spiritualism" of Neptune's 2011-2026 cycle. The groundswell of interest has grown into a global obsession that reporters have compared to a modern-day religion. (Trust us, we've been interviewed for these articles!)

CGI seance, anyone? With this Neptune in Pisces cycle happening against the backdrop of technology, artificial intelligence now allows people to have simulated conversations with departed loved ones. Through machine learning, a bot is able to capture mannerisms, personality traits and voice inflections by "studying" photos, recorded messages and videos of the "revived" person.

Altered States

Reality? We'd rather escape its harshness while Neptune cycles through Pisces. It's little surprise that psychedelic healing has been gaining popularity since 2011.

Ayahuasca ceremonies, while still held as underground events, have gained notable popularity in recent years. These guided, hours-long journeys can yield deep trances, prophetic visions, out-of-body experiences and profound illumination—grounded by Indigenous drumming and melodies. Meanwhile ketamine and psilocybin are being legalized as therapeutic treatments.

Sadly, Neptune in Pisces also brought the opioid crisis, a shadow of the healthcare industry, which is ruled in part by this planet. The deadliest drug crisis in U.S. history has been attributed to misinformation from pharmaceutical companies who assured the medical community that use of prescription oxycontin, fentanyl and other potent pain relievers would not lead to addiction. This is an example of the illusory, deceptive nature of Neptune in Pisces. Declared a public health crisis in 2017, opioid use continues to destroy lives around the world.

Ψ

Grappling with Grief and Trauma

Neptune in Pisces forces us to confront our pain, but it expands our ability to process subconscious triggers and ancient emotional blocks. This watery, compassionate cycle has opened up dialogues about empathy, highly sensitive people and *fluidity* in every arena.

The concept of "trauma-bonding" arose during this cycle. This attachment style confuses pain and passion for true love, making it hard for victims to leave their abusers. Given that Neptune is known for blurring boundaries and also rules imprisonment (including the psychological kind), it's no surprise that we're recognizing these subconscious traps.

Collectively, the pandemic has forced us to look mortality squarely in the eye. Neptune and Pisces are both associated with the dreamlike passage from life to death. Fear and panic of this "great unknown" are perhaps driving the bizarre behaviors that have been on bolder display since 2020.

Coronavirus, which has proven to spread through respiratory droplets, is a watery Neptune-in-Pisces disease. And with this transit provoking fears of the invisible "boogeyman," paranoia and fear around vaccines are equally in line with this cosmic phenomenon. Rising anxiety and depression are another outcome of the pandemic, creating more conversations about mental health as we step into 2023.

Artistic Renaissance

The arts are blessed by this Neptune transit, which has brought fascinating developments in the Pisces-ruled areas of dance, film and music. Legendary Pisces masters include Michelangelo, Nina Simone and Alexander McQueen, all who exemplify the imaginative energy of both planet and sign.

Got goosebumps? This subconscious-activating Neptune in Pisces cycle brought us a bizarre new art-form, ASMR (Autonomous Sensory Meridian Response). Sounds like whispering, blowing into a microphone and crinkling paper are meant to bring a low-grade euphoria, stimulating a tingling sensation that travels from the scalp to the spine and across the skin.

The point of this exercise is to bring about relaxation—a nod to the meditative mojo of Neptune in Pisces. ASMR videos are their own genre of performance art. Nod off to sleep with an endorphin-and-oxytocin-releasing YouTube of a simulated massage, or the "Dark & Relaxing Tapping & Scratching" video which has over 16 million views to date!

Want to learn more? Invite fantasy, creativity and divine support into your life with our pocket course, The Neptune Code!

ASTROSTYLE.COM/NEPTUNE

Ψ

NEPTUNE CONNECTIONS IN 2023

NEPTUNE-MARS SQUARE
MARCH 14

Neptune, the god of the seas goes to battle with Mars, the god of war on March 14, as the planets lock into a challenging, 90-degree square. Battles may erupt over religious and political ideologies, further dividing the public. As righteous anger takes the helm, this could be one of the most befuddling and mind-bending moments of the year! On a positive note, the Mars-Neptune square can soften hardcore stances. Simultaneously, the "softies" out there may be forced to strengthen their backbones. Can we be tough and tender at once? This final square can bring the best of both worlds.

NEPTUNE RETROGRADE
JUNE 30 - DECEMBER 6

Like the other outer planets, Neptune goes retrograde annually, for about five months. These periods can be deeply introspective times—but ones that require extra reality checks! You may feel like retreating or escaping from the world, which can be a healing process or one that lures you back to a destructive habit. "Just this once" can become famous last words when Neptune's in reverse. Set up support systems so you don't give in to toxic temptations that lure you away from your best life. With Neptune intensifying its boundary-dissolving effect in its home sign of Pisces, that goes double!

MORE BOOKS BY THE ASTROTWINS

HOW TO GET ALONG WITH ANYONE (*YES, EVEN THAT PERSON)

Any two zodiac signs CAN be compatible, as long as they understand what makes the other one tick. The AstroTwins simplify the secrets of synastry—the 7 unique energies encoded in the distance between your signs. Take your relationships from difficult to dynamic and start bringing out your best.

SUPERCOUPLE

Unlock the astrology secrets to sizzling attraction and deep connection, and get through the hard stuff fast! Did you know that your relationship has a zodiac sign and chart? The Supercouple system is the ultimate guide to finding true compatibility—by understanding why you came together and what your divine destiny could be!

MOMSTROLOGY

Parenting DOES come with instructions! This ultimate guide to raising your kids AND flourishing as a mom takes you through every season of parenthood, from birth to toddler to school years and leaving the nest.A favorite baby shower gift, featured by *Good Morning America* and a #1 Amazon bestseller.

START READING NOW AT **ASTROSTYLE.COM/BOOKS**

PLUTO

PLUTO IN ASTROLOGY

What skeletons are rattling in the closet? Where do we go "unconscious," unable to see our role in a crisis? As the cosmic ruler of the underworld, Pluto's impulse is to conceal. Projection is one of this planet's favorite defense mechanisms. Whenever and wherever you're pointing the finger, Pluto is probably at play.

Because of its distance from the Sun, Pluto has a long, inconsistent orbit, taking approximately 248 years to make one full journey around el Sol. This means Pluto will hover in a single sign for 12-21 years. As a result, it is one of the planets that shapes generational trends. Pluto can be a destroyer, tearing down what is begging to evolve, forcing us to rebuild from the ashes. As a result, great innovations have been born during these cycles. But they are generally accompanied by grief, crisis and loss as we release the outmoded past. Pluto's extended cycles often begin with a massive, headline-generating event, but end with breakthroughs that transform an entire industry. Wealth may change hands as a result, resonant with Pluto's penchant for power plays.

To find your natal Pluto sign, cast a free birth chart at

ASTROSTYLE.COM/BIRTHCHART

PLUTO IN 2023

Farewell capitalism, hello technototalitarianism? From March 23 to June 11, Pluto darts out of corporate Capricorn and into anarchistic Aquarius for the first of two warm-up laps before it settles into Aquarius from November 19, 2024 to January 19, 2044. This is the mighty dwarf planet's first sign swap since 2008! So yes, this is a very big deal.

In mythology, Pluto rules the underworld, so there can also be a dark aspect to its dealings. It can bring out perverse or hidden scandals, showing us the shadow side of whatever it affects. But in the wake of all that, space is created for something new and improved to be born, much like a phoenix rising from the ashes.

While this year's Pluto-in-Aquarius prequel may be more of a rumble than a thunderclap, it's our astrological duty to prepare you for the oncoming storm of a transformation. Remind yourself that humans are supremely adaptable...because we'll need to be as 2023 unfolds.

Pluto in Capricorn: A Retrospective

Pluto transits come in like a wrecking ball, tearing down entire systems and clearing the foundation for emerging technologies. To wit, weeks after Pluto settled into Capricorn in 2008, the largest ever single-day stock market crash followed suit. Then, after a slew of financial bailouts and mortgage lending mishaps, the demise of the Lehman Brothers, Fannie Mae and Freddie Mac ensued, and fiscal giant Merrill Lynch imploded. Bernie Madoff was arrested in December 2008 after his financially devastating Ponzi scheme was discovered.

In early 2009, the first non-Caucasian male U.S. President, Barack Obama, was inaugurated and a new economic stimulus plan was born. Markets slowly began to re-stabilize and the first block of Bitcoin, an innovative digital currency, debuted. Yet, the wealth gap widened. The Occupy Wall Street Movement of 2011 pointed to the deep divisions between the wealthiest one percent and the rest of the U.S. population.

In 2016—the halfway point of Pluto's transit through Capricorn—the U.S. almost broke the patriarchal spell by electing Hillary Clinton to be the first female president. Instead, a shocking turn of events vaulted Donald Trump into the role of Commander-in-Chief. From the gaslighting and hypnotic control he has over his base to the elusive tax returns and subsequent theft of classified documents, scandalous Pluto's fingerprints are everywhere.

A Rise in Authoritarian Rulership

Since 2008, autocrats have unleashed a Plutonian wrath on their citizens—not to mention the world at large—with Vladimir Putin as the current poster icon for crimes against humanity. His unrelenting destruction of Ukraine paired with his control of natural resources has plunged the worldwide economy into darkness and despair.

But let's not forget the lineup of others who have flaunted their wrath during this Pluto cycle. North Korea's dictator Capricorn Kim Jong-un has a long report card of human rights violations, considered among the worst in the world by watchdog organizations like Amnesty International. Syrian president Bashar al-Assad has committed atrocious war crimes during the ongoing civil war, which began in 2011. Allegations include gassing citizens and bombing hospitals and schools. In Hong Kong, pro-democracy citizens have watched with horror as freedom was stripped away by mainland China's Communist Leader Xi Jinping, recently elected for an unprecedented third term. With the Taliban reclaiming Afghanistan and Iran beating citizens to death for participating in women's rights protests, this Pluto cycle is ending on a grim note.

Still, there are rays of Aquarian transformation peeking through. In October 2022, Brazil elected (Pluto-ruled Scorpio) Luiz Inácio Lula da Silva, AKA Lula, to power. The former trade unionist has pledged to tackle the climate crisis and get the country to zero deforestation—the diametrically opposite policy of his predecessor Jair Bolsonaro. Given that the Amazon contains 25% of the world's terrestrial biodiversity and is crucial to carbon capture and water release, this change of power has the potential to save the planet... if Plutonian politics and greed don't get in the way.

Democracy in Crisis and the United States' Pluto Return

Three times in 2022, the United States "celebrated" its Pluto return, a seismic cycle that only comes around every 248 years. What does that mean exactly? When the "land of the free, home of the brave" declared itself independent on July 4, 1776, subterranean Pluto was parked at 27°33 Capricorn. Because of Pluto's long orbit, it took until 2022 for the planet to make its way through the zodiac and return to 27°33 Capricorn. In 2022, the United States had three exact Pluto returns on February 21-22, July 11 and finally on December 28, 2022.

And oh, have we ever felt it! From the Supreme Court's overturn of Roe v. Wade (Pluto rules reproduction) to skyrocketing inflation to a monkeypox outbreak and devastating droughts and hurricanes, powers both within and beyond our control have been at play.

During Pluto's last visit to Capricorn from 1762-1778, America's Revolutionary War began and the U.S. Declaration of Independence was drafted and signed. Two and a half centuries later, one might argue that the country hasn't been so divided since the Civil War. Democracy has definitely been in peril in this age of election deniers—a key ballot item that fortunately, landed on the liberated side of history with the 2022 U.S. midterm election results. As the cosmic transformer weaves in and out of innovative Aquarius in 2023-24, the fight to uphold egalitarian ideals is sadly far from over.

Water Bearer: Take the Wheel

What might happen when metamorphic Pluto embarks on its 21-year journey through Aquarius, the sign that rules democracy, community, populism, science, innovation and technology? We wouldn't exactly call these energies an "easy match." But it's important to remember that Pluto is not simply destructive, it's also regenerative. As the planet overseeing alchemy, reproduction and hidden resources, Pluto's brutal teardowns can reveal buried treasures.

Pluto's past two circuits provide evidence of this. During its 1995 to 2008 tour through Sagittarius—the sign that rules publishing and global communications—print magazines shuttered and the telecommunications industry was devastated. And then...we got hi-speed Internet, smart phones, print-on-demand and blogging. Capricorn-ruled financial institutes were the first to be felled by Pluto in 2008, but the blockchain emerged, putting power back in the people's hands with decentralized currency.

So WTF is Pluto gonna do next? In space-age Aquarius, this next chapter could be torn right out of a sci-fi novel. Whether that creates a utopian or dystopian effect, mad scientists will certainly come out and play. These cycles have brought incredible developments from the metric system to the cotton gin, shoelaces, bifocals and the first-ever vaccine. Make this your new mantra as of March 23: *Le geek c'est chic!*

Chips Ahoy!

In case you haven't heard, there's a chip shortage going on. No, we're not talking about those "once you pop, you can't stop" Pringles. Semiconductor chips have been in greater demand than supply in recent years, bottlenecking production of everything from PCs to electric vehicles.

Tied to this conundrum are many factors. Trade wars between China and the United States. A drought in Taiwan, where 90% of the world's most advanced chips are produced. A winter storm in Texas that took out the electric grid and halted U.S. production.

So dire is this that in summer 2022, the U.S. Congress passed the CHIPS Act to provide 280 billion dollars of funding for domestic manufacturing and research of semiconductors. An important start, but this won't be an overnight process.

With dark overlord Pluto edging into technology-driven Aquarius, it gets more intense. Xi Jinping, the General Secretary of the Chinese Communist Party, is intent on "reunification" of China and independently governed Taiwan. After China's crackdowns on Hong Kong, there is reason to be concerned. Given dependency on Taiwan's chips, it would be difficult for the U.S. to stay out of this conflict. Although Biden and Xi held a three-hour meeting at the G20 Summit in the fall of 2022, the "understanding" they reached may need more hashing out in 2023.

As powermonger Pluto weaves between corporate Capricorn and futuristic Aquarius, a technology war between global superpowers certainly tracks as the first swing of the celestial sledgehammer. But knowing what we do about Pluto's past transits, we must also ask: How *will* the phoenix rise from these ashes?

Maybe we humans will just have to live without all those digital consumer goods. We survived without iPads for complete eras. And hey, aren't all those carbon-belching factories heating the oceans and killing our survival?

Sure...yet subterranean Pluto is never satisfied with a simple (or surface-level) solution. This is the planet whose transits left us with game-changing advances like fiber optic cables and crypto-mining, after all. We're more likely to see carbon-capture technology accelerate in unprecedented, planet-saving directions, with current solutions going out like rotary phones, dial-up modems and paying with cash.

Sharing Economy to Circular Economy

Pluto in Capricorn brought us shared economy models like WeWork and Uber that changed the landscape for professionals and laborers. But the old-school power pyramid of Uber and cult-leader grandiosity of WeWork CEO Adam Neumann make them ineligible to qualify for "Aquarian" status. For the Water Bearer, sharing ain't just caring. It's more like "owning is dethroning." Will a cooperative model be embraced? And can humans, with our survival instincts, actually fight the urge to dominate each other and be the kid with the most toys?

We may find out while Pluto marches through egalitarian Aquarius until 2044. Perhaps the success of such experiments hinges on our ability to embrace one of Aquarius' greatest qualities: Its communion of individuality and teamwork. The co-ops of the world will be doomed to failure if they demand uniformity on Pluto in Aquarius' watch. Instead, they must play to the strengths of the people involved.

A possible Pluto in Aquarius scenario: Communities may form their own microsocieties where each person contributes a unique (but necessary!) skill that benefits everyone. These collectives will hinge upon the high-vibe idealism of Aquarius. Members must uphold their integrity, keeping promises and self-monitoring behavior. Does that sound like a pipedream? It might just be. But who's to say? If the people involved have a clear sense of ownership and profit from their actions, they may have ample motivation to contribute.

Perhaps more immediately attainable is the concept of the circular economy, which pairs well with Pluto's regenerative qualities. In this model, consumers would no longer buy products like refrigerators, air conditioners or washer-dryers. Instead, they would take out a service agreement with a company like GE. When the appliance becomes outdated or breaks down, GE would provide a replacement model. But rather than dumping that old fridge into a landfill, GE would recycle and repurpose the parts for the next generation of appliances, a huge win for the environment.

This is already happening with cell phone companies. Many are buying back old model phones at time of contract renewal, offering customers a discount on their upgrades. While this certainly benefits the Apples and AT&Ts of the world, it's also a step toward sustainability that we are certain to see more of over the coming 21 years.

Thought leaders are also exploring new avenues for "cradle to cradle" design, which is a fancy way of saying, "we make products that can be 100% recycled or returned to the earth at the end of their life." From compostable sporks to potato-starch wrappers, we've already gotten this party started. Where will Pluto in Aquarius take us next?

Reproductive Care Goes Underground

Pluto, the planet associated with reproduction, also rules the underground. Given the state of reproductive justice in the U.S., its transit through tech-savvy Aquarius is timely. At time of writing, abortion pills ordered from the Internet are still accessible to people in all 50 states. No surprise, medications like mifepristone are now being targeted by conservative lawmakers who are on a path to criminalize these transactions.

In States where abortion has not been enshrined, reproductive care could find its way to the oh-so-Pluto-in-Aquarius darknet. The anonymity of this "secret Internet" is a double-edged sword. While it may allow some women the ability to find pregnancy blockers or abortion providers, it leaves a dangerous opening for antiabortion extremists to deceive patients and medical care providers alike. The patriarchy and religious right versus women's bodies? This is sure to be one of the primary fights in years ahead—and cause for revolution—as Pluto weaves between Capricorn and Aquarius in 2023 and 2024.

Battery Life

"Renewable energy" is basically another way of saying "Pluto in Aquarius." As this regenerative planet pulses through the sign represented by two waves of energy, we eagerly await developments in this realm. Aquarius is an air sign, which bodes well for wind and solar—which capture the sun's rays from the ether.

And here's a statistic that the outbound Pluto in Capricorn cycle can get behind. A 2022 Oxford University study showed that switching to renewable energy could actually save companies trillions in their budget. That's a 180 from prior estimations claiming the switchover would be cost prohibitive.

Pluto does rule things that are underground. Mined assets that are used for energy may switch from fossil fuels to uranium and plutonium if we are able to utilize nuclear power in a safer way. That may be necessary for the transitional cycle as we figure out how to power all the plants making turbines and solar panels. (Until we can ideally power them with turbines and solar panels, that is.)

Batteries for electric vehicles are getting huge cash infusions as we enter 2023, but that's not all! Battery manufacturing hubs are being built (or refurbished from older plants) all across the United States, bringing production close to home for U.S. automakers like Ford and Chevrolet. Both

U.S. and foreign companies are getting involved, funding factories in the States. That's good news for the supply chain, and also the oceans, which won't be taxed by more freighters carrying essential cargo overseas. Perhaps this really will be a green initiative.

There are more eco-conscious ways to put the pedal to the metal than investing in an F-150 Lightning. In 2022, Denver started an e-bike rebate program, handing out vouchers to residents that could be cashed in for an immediate discount when they bought an electric bike at a local retailer. The program is part of the city's initiative to get the city to net zero emissions by 2040. And it's been wildly popular! By Q4 of 2022, $4.1 million in vouchers has been cashed in, setting the stage for the program to run again in 2023.

A "More Perfect" Union?

While Pluto took its 1778-1798 orbit through Aquarius, 39 delegates dipped quills in ink to sign the United States Constitution. And so it began with this preamble: *We the People of the United States, in Order to form a more perfect Union, establish Justice, insure domestic Tranquility, provide for the common defense, promote the general Welfare, and secure the Blessings of Liberty to ourselves and our Posterity, do ordain and establish this Constitution for the United States of America.*

Fast forward to 2023, Pluto's first journey back into Aquarius since. That "more perfect union" is so divided that the term "Constitutional crisis" has become a favorite of nightly newscasters on both sides of the aisle. Secessionists talk (and write books) about "Texit," envisioning the Lone Star state being truly...alone. In the Pacific Northwest, dreams of breaking off into Cascadia are nothing new; in fact, they've become a board game!

The American Revolution was still going on when Pluto moved into

Aquarius back in the 18th century. The French Revolution broke out during this cycle from 1789 to 1799, as did the Irish Rebellion against British rule. Two centuries prior, while Pluto was in Aquarius, the Church of England historically broke away from the Roman Catholic Church and their papal authority. Known as the English Reformation, this event, led by Henry VIII, transformed Christianity. Sadly, that same Pluto transit brought the deadly Roman and Portuguese Inquisitions.

Is unity beyond our reach? Are we really that different? If social media threads tell the story, divisions are so deep that we might as well be aliens to each other. For the record, we're not ruling out that possibility! With Pluto in otherworldly Aquarius, we may discover that our roots date back to Pleiades and Atlantis or that "lizard people" are...a thing.

Might we all get along, though? For all their utopian ideals, that's not something our "founding fathers" put to the test. The first Constitution wasn't exactly a diversity-and-inclusivity initiative. Seam-ripping Pluto won't let us stand on ceremony. Far from it. Perhaps we'll end this cycle with a revised edition, one that includes women and considers every person 100% human, rather than three-fifths—as all those who were "not free" were reduced to in the original Constitution.

♇

Spacing Out

If you need to get away from it all, consider outer space. Virgin Galactic is gearing up to offer commercial space flights in 2023. Space X already launched over 30 times in 2022 with plans to ramp up its cadence in 2023. Astronaut fashion is certain to be trending in years to come. Excuse me, is that an Aviator Nation spacesuit you're wearing?

Can't handle the g-force? Set up your telescope and be a "space appreciator." While Pluto toured Aquarius in the late 1700s, Caroline Herschel and her brother William, both musicians turned astronomers and telescope makers, made history.

Caroline Herschel was the first woman to discover a comet. Over the course of her career, she discovered eight of them and three nebulae, to boot. She was also the first woman to receive a salary as a scientist, to hold a government position in England, to publish findings in the scientific journal Philosophical Transactions of the Royal Society, to be awarded a Gold Medal of the Royal Astronomical Society and to be named an Honorary Member of the Royal Astronomical Society. Two years after Pluto entered Aquarius, in 1781, she facilitated her brother's accidental discovery of the planet Uranus—which became the astrological ruler of Aquarius along with Saturn!

Of course, the lens swings both ways. Telescopic technology is now being used for high-res, hyperspectral satellites that unfold when they reach their desired coordinates in space and beam images down to Earth. Although purportedly developed for ag-tech and military defense, this could be Secret Agent Pluto's Aquarian Age way of spying on us all—or really making it necessary to build those underground bunkers!

PLUTO CONNECTIONS IN 2023

JUPITER-PLUTO SQUARE
MAY 17

Massive power struggle: incoming! As pioneering Jupiter in Taurus locks into a challenging square with powermonger Pluto in Aquarius, intense forces pull us in dueling directions. On the one hand, there's a current sweeping us toward major change, demanding that we try a radically new way of doing things. An equally strong force will resist these new attempts: If it ain't broke, why fix it? When these two dominant planets sit down at the negotiating table, compromise won't be comfortable—or easy to find. Do your part by at least hearing the other party's desires, even if they sound more like demands (and unreasonable ones at that).

PLUTO RETROGRADE

MAY 1 - OCTOBER 10

Like its fellow outer planets, Pluto spends approximately five months of each year retrograde. During these times, we will often feel relief from the planet's intensity. Retrogrades are times for introspection, and deep-diving Pluto's backspin can bring penetrating insights. Progress may be put on hold as we process everything from pain to grief to revenge fantasies. For the first year since 2009, Pluto's retrograde takes place in two signs. The dwarf planet spins back through Aquarius from May 1 to June 11, then slips back into Capricorn for the remainder of its retrograde, until October 10. We could find ourselves reeling from technological developments, ones that may cause a reordering of world powers. On a personal note, we should expect changes in our communities as people align themselves around divergent ideals and politics. Finding consensus could be like herding cats. The challenge is to use these backpedals to get realigned, even if that means playing in separate sandboxes—without turning anyone else's sandbox into a litterbox.

2023

ARIES

♈

WHAT'S IN THE STARS FOR

ARIES

Brand new you! The first half of 2023 is all about reinventing yourself, as you kick off a new 12-year chapter of your life. Out with the old: Refresh everything from your image and style to what you do for a living. Money is a big focus in the second half of the year. You could get a nice pay bump, but be careful not to spend it all in one place. Stay open to unexpected work opportunities, possibly a job with travel or relocation. From July onward, you'll feel an urgent need to follow your calling. A key relationship will need to be renegotiated so you have room to "do you." Making sacrifices for your sweetie or taking one for the team is great to a point, but not at the expense of your own dreams. Be mindful of the friends you invite into your circle this spring and summer; not all of them will have pure intentions, no matter how they advertise themselves.

ARIES WILL BE LUCKY WITH:
Independent pursuits, solo stardom, money and work

ARIES WILL BE CHALLENGED WITH:
Healing from past wounds, setting healthy boundaries in your relationships

LOVE

Soulmate or bust? High-stakes, high-intensity loving is on deck for Rams while the karmic South Node rolls through Scorpio until July 17. On May 5, the Scorpio lunar eclipse could cement a long-term bond or break it apart (at least for this lifetime). Whatever you decide, you won't be at a loss for summer lovin'! Ardent Venus sashays through Leo from June 5 to October 8, serving peak romantic experiences and passionate playtime. While Venus is retrograde from July 22 to September 3, you could reconnect to "the one that got away" or *finally* sort out drama with your plus-one. Peaceful balance is restored once the karmic lunar South Node shifts into Libra on July 17 and helps you negotiate your needs. That sweet serenity could lead you straight down the aisle before January 11, 2025.

CAREER & MONEY

Get ready for prime time! Maximizer Jupiter blazes a trail through Aries until May 16 increasing your visibility. That's not all! The destiny-driven North Node will visit Aries for the first time in nearly two decades from July 17 to January 11, 2025. Rich career opportunities are available all year, whether you're expanding your role within an organization or entering a cutting-edge field. Move ahead decisively, but don't rush through formalities. Jupiter can bring overnight success but it can also sweep you into raw deals. Spend conservatively and make a budget for legal counsel if contracts are involved. Get ready for a cash influx when Jupiter heads into money-earning Taurus for a year on May 16!

WELLNESS

Ready, set, de-stress! Heavy-hitting Saturn moves into Pisces on March 7, starting a three-year-journey through your twelfth house of subconscious healing and detoxification. Aries already have a finely tuned nervous system, but you'll be ultra-sensitive to triggers that rattle your anxiety. An elimination diet can help you identify foods that may be fueling that fire. Start with obvious stimulants like caffeine and sugar, then move through inflammatories like wheat and dairy to see how your body—and mental health!—respond. Edgier Aries may find support through plant-based microdosing. When Jupiter heads into tactile Taurus, incorporate bodywork and try somatic therapy that combines psychological and physical healing.

FRIENDS & FAMILY

2023 is bookended by a pair of full moons in family-focused Cancer, putting cherished bonds in the spotlight. A child or an older relative may require more care, which could shift matters under your roof. Some Aries may be ready for a total relocation, which could feel both blessedly overdue *and* bittersweet. With transformational Pluto weaving between dutiful Capricorn and experimental Aquarius, you'll need to strike a balance between supporting your peeps and exploring new friendships. Get involved in groups centered around altruism and activism.

♈

JUPITER IN ARIES
Follow Your Bliss

Jupiter in Aries

December 20, 2022
to May 16, 2023

Set out for parts unknown, Aries. It's your year to explore new ground as adventurous Jupiter begins 2023 in your sign for the second of two circuits. You started hosting the beneficent planet on December 20, 2022 and will be in its good graces until May 16, 2023. Pump up the volume on your passions and go full-on in your pursuit of pleasure.

When Jupiter arrived in Aries last year (from May 10 to October 28), it launched a new 12-year chapter of your life. A lot of Rams will do a complete reboot in 2023. In your pioneering first house, this transit ushers in fresh starts, originality and experimentation. You got a small taste of this exciting reset when the red-spotted planet toured Aries from May 10 to October 28, 2022. Once again, you'll be catapulted out of your comfort zone like a heat-seeking missile. No one can say for sure where you'll wind up. The journey *is* the adventure now. Plus, you'll be flying too high to worry about the destination.

Even if you're one of those rare *cautious* Rams, you'd be smart to give yourself plenty of leeway. The thing is, it would be inconceivable to map out your ultimate goals in early 2023, because you're just getting started. That said, you may have clues from whatever you revved up between May 10 and October 28, 2022, during Jupiter's first sprint through Aries. You could also scroll back to a little over a decade ago on your timeline. The supersizer planet toured Aries from June 6, 2010 to June 4, 2011. Do you spot similar themes of reinvention happening now?

ARIES

With Jupiter in your groundbreaking first house of new beginnings and solo ventures, your personal pursuits are front and center in 2023. Whether you take off on a trip by yourself, sign up for teacher training or start private lessons with a vocal coach, the point is to try, try again with no agenda. Learning can be fun if you stop trying to race to the head of the class on the first day. Get your feet wet and adopt a playful attitude.

Early in 2023, allow yourself to brainstorm, even if that means detouring off the main road to explore some side streets. You might decide to take a huge gamble. If you do, pay no attention to the Debbie Downers. Heed the words of Audrey Hepburn who said, "Nothing is impossible. The word itself says, 'I'm possible.'" You may find a way to turn one of your big ideas into a moneymaker. If you can review the year on December 31, 2023, and say that you prioritized happiness over suffering (and hopefully crossed a slew of items off your bucket list), Jupiter's lessons were well learned.

Did you know that people form an opinion within seven seconds of meeting you? Visuals are worth their weight in gold during this Jupiter cycle, since the first house rules first impressions. Invest in headshots and, if relevant, a videographer. Think about hiring hair and makeup professionals for your shoots. Launch a polished, well-designed website. Write in the first-person voice, so your visitors feel like they're having a conversation with you over coffee.

If you're a "solopreneur," this autonomous Jupiter phase is ideal for building buzz through social media, public relations and a message that shines the spotlight on you. What's your singular niche or brand story? Jupiter in your trailblazing first house encourages you to stand out—or step out of the shadows—as the heart and soul of your mission. Play up your uniqueness and be your edgy, pioneering self. As you'd expect, that will get people noticing...and talking!

For instance, maybe you're a health coach who needs to differentiate yourself in a crowded market. How best can you show off your personality and underscore your expertise? Do you specialize in a certain school of

ϒ

thought or demographic? Do you have hobbies that you could integrate into your practice, like vegan cooking or wildcrafting, or something that would make your bio memorable? For example, if you love the outdoors, maybe you'll take your clients on a virtual hiking series that not only inspires them to explore local trails but teaches them how to forage the area's edible herbs and medicinal plants.

Courageous Jupiter in your sign can make you somewhat of an outlier (or an outlaw!) this year. Look to genre-busting Aries Montero Lamar Hill—AKA Lil' Nas X—for some Ram-strong inspiration. His first hit, *Old Town Road*, topped the country music charts and went viral through TikTok's #YeehawChallenge with the help of the performer's savvy social media skills. In a short time, this Aries became an icon for the LGBTQIA community, smashing through homophobia with his loud, proud music videos.

You're invited to take the same brave approach in your love life. If you're dating, lean into your quirks and humor instead of making chitchat or standing back and observing. Rather than bending yourself into a pretzel, relationships should grow to accommodate *your* needs this year. You could be starting a fresh career chapter, globetrotting, and dedicating yourself to an all-consuming new interest. People may need to adjust along with your growth in 2023.

To be clear, Aries: When Jupiter tours your sign every 12-13 years, you are the *star*, not the sidekick. And while that doesn't give you permission to treat people like your minions, you might embrace the term "diva" like Aries Mariah Carey, enjoying more unapologetic grandeur in your life. (Wearing stilettos in your plunge-pool-sized bathtub, as Carey once did on camera, remains optional.) Bottom line: Don't miss out on this chance to express your big energy.

Since the first house rules appearances, you could drastically change your look like dying your hair turquoise or finally getting that full-sleeve tattoo. A word of warning: Jupiter is the "too much is never enough" planet, but once it ends its circuit, you may be left with a heavenly hangover. Avoid impulsive decisions like, say, shaving your head at 3AM after getting home from a party. While you may swear by a #NoRegrets policy, you could push the outer limits this year.

Not that you can be swayed. Jupiter gives swagger, and it can make any sign a little arrogant when it tours the "me"-centric first house. (Your new favorite subject: Yourself!) Be careful not to let your self-confidence become self-absorption. It's fantastic to feel so proud of your achievements, and even to do some self-promotion. Just don't treat your crew like the studio audience of The Aries Show.

No-filters Jupiter can turn even the most subdued Ram into a motor-mouth. There's an impulse to report every minute detail—from a lunchtime "table read" of your email chain with a coworker to a rambling recount of the entitled sales associate who ignored you at a shoe store when you were ready to drop a paycheck on a pair of Loubs. Ask yourself this key question: *How does sharing this help people*? Your story could change someone's life or it could bore them to tears. It's all in the angle from which you approach it.

Jupiter rules publishing, broadcasting and public speaking. Maybe your experiences contain inspiring life lessons. What's the message for your audience? Curate those personal tales and you might have material for a memoir or a motivational TED-style talk. Even shy Rams could get bitten by the performance bug in 2023. If you're truly passionate about something, you'll hardly even notice when the cameras are rolling.

♈

JUPITER IN TAURUS
Seeking security

Jupiter in Taurus

May 16, 2023 to
May 25, 2024

Jupiter Retrograde

September 4 to
December 30, 2023

Okay, Aries...you've given an Oscar-worthy performance while Jupiter toured your sign. And there's no two ways about it: You deserve kudos for all the risks you've taken and the ways you've grown. What happens next? From May 16, 2023 to May 25, 2024, Jupiter ambles through Taurus, highlighting your stable second house. So, on the heels of five months of adventure and discovery, you'll segue into a building phase. As your attention shifts to money and security, examine the crazy ideas you've cooked up, and choose one or two winners. How can you develop them into a lucrative and rewarding venture? With Jupiter in this hardworking zone, you're ready to put your shoulder to the wheel. Fortunately, you should have loads of opportunities to do precisely that!

See ya, glass ceilings and wage gaps! Abundant Jupiter wants to compensate you generously for your work. This phase could bring a pay raise, a promotion, or a cream-of-the-crop client list. Since Jupiter governs long-distance travel, you might become a frequent flier for work, collaborate with people over Zoom or even relocate to a tony new zip code to pursue a plum opportunity. Keep an open mind! An offer across state, country or global lines could be too incredible to turn down.

♈

If you're a little dazed from the buzz of Jupiter in Aries, you'll embrace this chance to line up your priorities and adopt a sound plan of action. There's a lot to do! But first, streamline. What is most important to you? Getting clear on that is crucial now, as you'll want to design your life around what you truly value. For instance, if you thrive on the stimulation of hustle culture, moving to a sedate bedroom community in suburbia won't cut it. Start looking into a possible lifestyle change toward the middle of 2023.

In love, Jupiter's journey through traditional Taurus could attract a passionate but steady partner. Unattached? someone you might have swiped left on for being too predictable may now seem totally ideal. Rams may swap their arm candy for someone who is great on paper *and* in real life—even if they aren't scroll-stoppers on your Instagram feed.

Coupled Aries, break out the warming massage oils and scented votives. Jupiter in your tasteful and tactile second house invites you to get sensual. Level up your date planning. How about a couple's spa weekend, a whiskey tasting or a private event where you create your own fragrance?

Since "quality over quantity" is Jupiter in Taurus' mantra, use the second half of the year to simplify—and that includes your budget, schedule and routines. After a whirlwind first half of 2023, you'll relish the chance to amble at your own pace. While it might not be your usual M.O. as a fiery Ram, after May 16, the best things emerge from a slow and steady approach. Plant the seeds and lay the groundwork, then patiently await the most bountiful harvest you've had in years!

♈

MARS IN GEMINI
Use your words

Mars in Gemini

August 20, 2022 to
March 25, 2023

Mars Retrograde

October 30, 2022
to January 12, 2023

Cat got your tongue, Aries? That "feline" might actually be your ruling planet Mars, who's been retrograde in Gemini and your third house of communication since October 30, 2022. Holding back isn't really your fiery sign's style, but with Mars in the time-out chair for the latter part of last year, you've been hesitant to speak freely.

Good news! The galactic gag order lifts January 12, 2023, as your red-hot ruler resumes direct motion and barrels through Gemini until the early part of Aries season, on March 25, 2023. Shortly after you write down those New Year's resolutions, you may go on a "sharing spree," vocalizing all the bottled-up thoughts that have been brewing in that brilliant head of yours.

A bit of advice? Choose appropriate sounding boards! Even while transiting in direct motion, Mars can be rash and brash. And while in Gemini until March 25, you run the risk of offloading to the wrong person—a gossipy type who smiles in your face then burns you with your own tea behind your back. Keep lines clean with coworkers, too. You've got a lot on your mind as 2023 ignites, but don't confuse an office chair for a therapist's couch (no matter how comfy it is).

Do, however, find healthy outlets for your unbridled thoughts to outflow. Since Gemini rules your third house of local activity, good friends could be a short walk from your front door in early 2023. Bundle up and go mingle IRL. Bold Mars helps you take the initiative to get out and circulate. Is an astrologer hosting a new moon circle? Is there a memoir writing class being taught at the local community college? A business incubator group (maybe at a local coworking space) could be the perfect hotspot for venturesome Rams.

In total, Mars is moving through Gemini for seven whole *months*, since its transit there began on August 20, 2022. Conversations you initiated at the end of last summer could pick up steam. Since the third house rules platonic partnerships, you could formalize a tag team effort in Q1 of this year. Lawyer up and make it contractual, even if you're working on a one-time project. Doing so is the best insurance policy for a happy ending to this story—or the runway for a future of continued collaboration.

Whether pairing up or remaining a one-Ram show, early 2023 is an optimal time for any communications-related project. Start pricing out podcasting mics and webcams because your desk may soon double as a recording studio. If there's a book rattling around inside you, get those words onto a page. Or like many Aries, shop yourself around as a public speaker and move the crowds with your motivating stories of triumph over obstacles!

♈

SATURN IN PISCES
Stepping back and setting limits

Saturn in Pisces

March 7, 2023 to
February 13, 2026

Saturn Retrograde

June 17 to
November 4, 2023

Come out, come out, wherever you are! Hide and Seek could be your new favorite game starting March 7, 2023, when boundary-hound Saturn retreats into Pisces and your solitary, spiritual twelfth house until February 13, 2026. This circuit, which only comes around every 29.5 years, is like a three-year artist's residence. Your imagination is stirred and you're channeling all sorts of divine inspiration. Industrious Saturn's presence makes this an opportune period for honing your creative gifts and turning them into something tangible.

But there's a catch: Buttoned-up Saturn is painfully ill at ease in the flowy, bohemian twelfth house. This planet favors limits, regulations, systems and prestige. Meanwhile, the twelfth house is immeasurable, ethereal, unshackled and dreamy. It is indeed a riddle wrapped in a mystery inside an enigma!

Figuring out how to balance these paradoxical energies might throw you off-balance temporarily, but once you get your bearings...watch out, world! Mastering the magical could turn into your 2023 mission. Since Saturn is the solar system's most diligent planet, wherever it's orbiting, you'll readily put your nose to the grindstone. During the next three years, you might start some type of creative or spiritual training or go full "woo-woo" and become certified as an animal communicator, art therapist or sacred medicine practitioner.

Pragmatic Saturn reminds you that no matter how enlightened you become, you still need to put food on the table. There's nothing "un-spiritual" about receiving compensation for your sacred services, so if you're ready to monetize your healing or artistic gifts, hang the shingle. Money is a fair exchange for all the hours, work and love you devote to your calling. (A calling that, incidentally, you won't have time for if you refuse to charge then have to work a "real job" to cover your bills.)

With slow-moving Saturn in the frame, there's no need to rush. Keep moving forward with whatever you choose to pursue or study. Don't waste this chance to explore the rich landscape of your soul! At the same time, don't push yourself *too* hard. Maintaining firm boundaries between work and downtime is another important lesson for 2023. With Saturn dozing in a house that rules dreams, you'll require more sleep than usual between now and February 13, 2026. Orderly Saturn advocates going to bed and waking up at set times. Sync your schedule with your circadian rhythms!

Reflective Saturn in Pisces may seem oppressive sometimes, as buried emotions get unearthed, prodding you to feel, heal and deal. You're probably inclined to muscle through, but professional help would enable you to fully process any trauma, shame or grief that has been dwelling in your subconscious since childhood. The side effects could manifest in your body, showing up as chronic knee aches, for instance, a Saturn-ruled area. The bones, teeth and skin are also governed by the ringed planet, so any issues there could be tied to unprocessed emotional issues.

But there's good news! With Saturn in your twelfth house, you're able to do the profound internal work that vanquishes your demons once and for all. Even Rams who had an idyllic childhood may face obstacles that stand in the way of your happiness. The twelfth house governs your subconscious, and beyond traditional talk therapy, you might explore other treatment modalities such as inner child work, NLP (neuro-linguistic programming) or voice dialogue to access hard-to-reach corners of your psyche. If you're grappling with addiction, this Saturn circuit can facilitate powerful recovery. Your hard work—supervised by professionals and practitioners who you've thoroughly screened—can uncover blocks you didn't know existed. Spiritual modalities like radiant heart therapy or Reiki can also help you to heal issues buried in your subconscious.

Saturn's journey through your twelfth house provides yet another benefit. You can use this time to break unhealthy patterns of people-pleasing and codependence. No more giving 'til it hurts. That won't work in 2023. Rams who have been sacrificing essential desires could uncover a wellspring of resentment. You can't keep living out other people's dreams—or setting yours to the side to play Best Supporting Castmate. While concrete Saturn meshes its powers with numinous Pisces, you're called to bring your personal vision into form over the next three years. Once the success-striving planet shifts into Aries on February 13, 2026, the work you put in could bring serious clout!

Because the twelfth house is the last wedge of the zodiac wheel, it's the domain of endings and closure. Letting go of a once-cherished situation may be inevitable. If something that used to lift your spirits now leaves you drained, Saturn can help you to plot an exit strategy that permits graceful release. Grieve and ritualize the goodbye process. While emotions will be tender, unknotting the once-binding ties is the way to keep going and growing, Aries.

♈

PLUTO IN AQUARIUS

A new era in teamwork

Pluto in Capricorn
Janury 1, 2023
to March 23, 2023

June 11, 2023 to
January 20, 2024

Pluto in Aquarius
March 23 to
June 11, 2023

Pluto Retrograde
May 1 to
October 10, 2023

In 2023, even the most indie-spirited Aries gets by with a little help from your (VIP) friends. You may need to call in some favors near March 23, when powerhouse Pluto weaves out of Capricorn (your tenth house of status) and into Aquarius (your eleventh house of teams) for the first of three loops. The question is: Who actually has your back, Ram? Surprising developments may emerge. Keep your mind—and your eagle eyes—wide open while Pluto passes through Aquarius until June 11. Hidden figures could step forward on your behalf while a trusted ally may go rogue. Act quickly upon suspicions if something feels off.

Although this is a quick trip, Pluto's pop-in to Aquarius is a *huge* deal! The alchemical dwarf planet only changes zodiac signs every 12-21 years. And it's been orbiting through Capricorn since January 2008, creating all kinds of intensified developments for your career path. You've been at the top, the bottom and everywhere in between, reimagining your goals and diving deep to figure out what a meaningful path looks like. Many Aries dabbled in the "woo" or worked with people to uncover the depths of their unconscious. Or perhaps you found yourself in a field where you could exude sexy originality. Mystical Pluto in Capricorn was a solid time to become a coder or to learn a precise technique that only a rare few have access to. Anything "elite" is now synonymous with "Aries."

ARIES

When Pluto spins into Aquarius from March 23 to June 11 this year, it will mark its first visit back to the Water Bearer's realm since 1778-1798! You've never experienced this cycle before, Aries, so you're on new ground here. While Pluto orbits Aquarius until 2044, it's not so much about *what* you do as it is about *who* you're doing it with. Intense encounters are ahead—with disruptors, thought leaders and straight-up rebels.

Plutonian shifts are not for the faint of heart. During this first pass into Aquarius, be super mindful of the company you keep. The charismatic influencers who hold you in their thrall may have self-serving, even nefarious, intentions. If your savvy sign was ever in danger of joining a cult, 2023 would be the year. We kid...kind of? But maybe be ultra-cautious before joining any new organizations in the first half of the year. Allow yourself to dabble and explore with one eyebrow raised.

Are you interested in a career pivot? After all the lessons Pluto has served since 2008, you may be more than ready to tackle a new challenge. Just don't throw the baby out with the bathwater! While it's tempting to not-so-quietly quit your current industry, you might find renewed purpose studying a modern approach to your subject of mastery: green energy, trauma-informed therapies, communal economic models...

Pluto lives on the edge, so there may be an element of danger involved in new pursuits. This suits your daredevil sign well but it's important to be aware of what you're getting yourself into! That goes for your social life, too. Whether you're mingling casually or considering a membership package to a club, the company you keep can make or break you while Pluto's in Aquarius. Questionable characters won't be easy to spot immediately, so run thorough background checks.

And don't give *your* power away. You're about to earn an astrological MBA from having Pluto in Capricorn and your ambitious tenth house since 2008! Seize the chance to position yourself as a leader. Where have you gained solid expertise since 2008? This is a place to focus and really make sure you promote your gifts. Fellow Aries Lady Gaga's entire career to date has spanned the transit of Pluto through Capricorn, beginning with the 2009 release of *The Fame Monster* and evolving from The Haus of Gaga to *The House of Gucci*, with award-winning roles in *A Star Is Born* and a Super Bowl performance along the way. No matter how public your own professional journey has been, Pluto in Aquarius helps you expand your online presence and share your message. Get testimonials and create case studies to show social proof of your capabilities.

While you do, hire an attorney who can help you protect your intellectual property! Competitors are hungry and swirling in 2023 and you don't want open-ended technology giving them a doorway into your data. You may soon know more than you ever wanted to about encryption, VPNs and digital wallets. That doesn't mean you'll have a breach, but treat your ideas and information like the gold they are!

Ultimately, 2023 is a transitional year for Pluto. In 2024, the metamorphic dwarf planet pings Capricorn for two more cycles before finally settling into Aquarius on November 19 for the rest of its twenty-year cycle. When it comes to your career path, you may feel as if you're being guided; however, you should not rush to act upon instinct. For every rung you ascend, there will be politics to navigate, new technology to learn and an opportunity to embrace a more communal approach. Get your bearings before bounding ahead. Steady is the head that wears the crown in 2023!

♈

VENUS RETROGRADE IN LEO
Lights, camera, Aries

Venus in Leo

June 5 to
October 8, 2023

Venus Retrograde

July 22 to
September 3, 2023

From June 5 to October 8, Venus rolls out a long red carpet and struts through Leo, giving juice to your fifth house of glamour, fame and unbridled self-expression. Gucci shades may be your 24/7 fashion staple, as you protect your eyes from incessant camera flashes and attempt to go incognito. (Good luck with that.) Fortunately, Aries, you feel right at home in the spotlight. And during this passage, you'll have zero problems soaking up the attention and publicizing your work!

If one of your trailblazing projects is ready for a big reveal, put it out there before mid-July. There's a reason for Venus' longer-than-usual passage through Leo, and it's definitely complicated. From July 22 to September 3, la love planet pivots retrograde—a cycle that comes around every 18 months, when Venus ends her time as an evening star, goes dark, then rises again in pre-dawn as a morning star. This cosmic costume change can throw everyone off their game for six weeks, so it's a better phase for developing plans behind the scenes.

Your fifth house may play the fame game, but it also rules fertility. If you're trying to expand your fam, Venus in Leo is an optimal time to get busy or stock up on pregnancy tests. Of course, if you're not planning to birth an Aries mini-me, protect yourself accordingly! Venus in Leo is a hot and heavy match that sets you up for all kinds of romantic heat and intrigue, but during the retrograde, you are also susceptible to getting burned. Faces from your past may pop up and tempt you with "what ifs" aplenty. Unless you think this could be a Bennifer 2.0 situation, it's wiser to leave the past in the past and use this six-week retrograde as a chance to process any lingering pain and clear the decks for what's to come.

Alas, the backspin may throw a wrench in even your best-laid love life plans. Internal check: Have you been pushing an agenda that your other half is not fully aligned with? That wouldn't be unlike your headstrong sign. But

> *As you reignite personal passions, you'll take the obvious pressure off your partner to fill any holes in your soul.*

forgetting that love is a two-way street will come back to haunt you between July 22 and September 3. Venus may send you back to the drawing board to redo plans in partnership instead of as a one-Aries show. Agonizing as this may sound, it could be one of the greatest creative moments you've had with your boo in quite a long time.

If you're paired up, Venus' retrograde through dramatic Leo could rock the boat unceremoniously, dredging up old grudges that you swore were cast out to sea long ago. And check your own boundaries, Ram! Flirty DMs with a cute coworker might not be as innocent as you insist. But they could be an important warning flag that you need to put some work into reviving the magic with your significant other. You're not the first person in history to feel bored, neglected or complacent in a long-term relationship. But rather than sneaking around to get your thrills, have the uncomfortable conversations with your partner to figure out how you can reroute the ship to steamier shores...together!

By "together," Aries, we also mean agreeing to do more things separately, too. The truth is, you might be feeling a little bored with your own self-development. As Venus paddles back through Leo and your ultra-creative fifth house, you have a golden opportunity to reconnect to your own imagination. Pick up a dormant project that you were once so obsessed with that you lost track of time. Sign up for that dance workshop or get the band back together. As you reignite personal passions, you'll take the obvious pressure off your partner to fill any holes in your soul. Better still? When Venus resumes direct motion on September 3, you may have enough finished works to book a gig, submit to a group gallery show or shop a screenplay.

Even while retrograde, Venus keeps you at the center of attention while in Leo. Keep yourself looking fabulous with regular pampering sessions: blowouts, manicures and massages are all fair game during Venus retrograde in Leo. And so is growing out your gray and going makeup-free if that's your chosen "lewk." But press pause on any body modifications like piercings and tattoos during the July 22 to September 3 backspin. Radical hair chops or anything else that might bring a whiff of potential regret should also be off the menu until the planet of beauty is back to her senses later in September. Meanwhile, get the mood boards and lookbooks going!

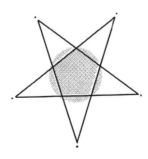

♈

NORTH NODE IN ARIES
Destiny Calling!

> **Lunar North Node in Aries**
>
> July 17, 2023
> to January 11, 2025

You were put on Earth to do great things, Ram! And in 2023, you're poised to achieve something that's "peak Aries." This July 17, the fateful lunar North Node returns to your sign for the first time since June 2006. During this 18-month cycle, the world thrums at *your* vibrational frequency. It's a "call to action" to step into your authority and pursue your next epic passion.

The lunar nodes are not planets, but special points in the sky that are associated with your spiritual evolution. Every 18.5 years, the fateful North Node soars through Aries, marking one of *the* most auspicious periods of self-discovery and personal growth. Prepare to make massive strides during this cycle, which lasts until January 11, 2025. When the North Node traveled here last from November 2004 to June 2006, one Aries we know broke a long cycle of underearning and accepted his first job as an engineer for a large tech company.

Significant developments like these may be coming your way after July 17. Just don't expect this process to be a cakewalk. We call the North Node the "Zone of Miracles" because, invariably, magic *will* arise. But first, this cosmic cycle pulls you so far out of your comfort zone that you feel like you're trekking on foreign soil with only a temporary visa. In this new "environment," you can't help but discover new parts of yourself. You'll fumble through awkward learning curves and an identity crisis (or three).

Activities that brought you joy for years may no longer hold sway. Certain relationships will require redefining. Rough, but what can you do? The call to explore what *you* are capable of is too loud to ignore!

Our recommendation? Start setting aside funds for personal growth. (Or look into work-study programs and scholarships.) This nodal cycle isn't exactly boot camp, but it's definitely a soul-enriching journey. Since group settings can overwhelm your mentally sensitive sign, don't force yourself to be a joiner. A private coach or trainer may be your best "sherpa" through all the changes that lie ahead. Growth can be scary, even for an adventurer like you. When self-doubt creeps in, you want a champion in your corner, reminding you to keep on keeping on.

Are there gaps in your skill set? You have a couple obvious choices, Aries: Do the training yourself or team up with people whose expertise can fill in where you leave off. DIY-ing comes naturally to your independent sign, but it may not be the most effective route. Want to evolve? Your methodology looks a lot less scrappy mid-2023 as you embrace a director's role instead of being so hands-on.

On the other side of your chart, the North Node's polar opposite, the lunar South Node, shifts into Libra and your relationship realm. Your closest connections are ready for their own revolution between July 17, 2023 and January 11, 2025. The South Node is associated with karma, past lives and comfort zones that are perhaps a bit *too* cozy. If you sacrificed any passions to please a partner, look out! The abandoned parts of your soul come roaring back, demanding attention.

Even the healthiest relationships could fluctuate during this 18-month nodal cycle. Try not to freak out when that happens, Aries. As you step in a new direction, your "dance partners" have to adjust along with you. Libra is the sign of balance and with the South Node here, do your level best to keep everyone calm. The most effective approach? Engage them in your process. Grant the people closest to you "insider access" so that they can keep track of your accelerated growth and (hello!) support you along the way! This also helps *them* feel less like a rug is being pulled out from under them when you suddenly announce a desire to study abroad for a semester or relocate the family to the opposite coast.

That said, you still need a semblance of autonomy while the North Node is in your sign. Sometimes, you'll need to go dark so you can keep the focus solely on *your* development. But this can be unmooring for anyone who is accustomed to checking in with you regularly—or having you around 24/7. While we're not suggesting you pull a disappearing act, gently extricate yourself from codependent dynamics. Rather than babying people, encourage them to do their own self-discovery work. Trust that they'll find their flight paths, even if it takes a minute for them to remember they have wings.

While relationships are more of the cherry on top of the sundae after July 17, the karmic Libra South Node *can* bring a twin flame reunion. No matter your relationship status, encounters like these can shake up your universe. Some people believe the explosive intensity between twin flames makes it hard to sustain these connections for long. But for adrenaline-junkie Aries, all that heat, passion and immediacy can feel like a fantasy come true. Whether you choose to act upon it or quietly enjoy the "tempting, but not gonna go there" vibes, you may be up for a few soul-evolving lessons together in this lifetime.

What you *don't* want to do is let relationship drama distract you from your personal path—or worse, derail you! The North Node only blesses you with its beacon-like powers every 18.5 years. So carve out ample space for solo initiatives. Call it your path, your purpose, a true calling...whatever the case, the North Node in Aries gives you massive shine when you're ready to put your work out in the world!

ECLIPSES IN 2023
Solo stardom and dynamic duets

Hybrid Solar Eclipse in Aries (new moon)

April 20 at 12:17AM

Penumbral Lunar Eclipse in Scorpio (full moon)

May 5 at 1:24PM

Annular Solar Eclipse in Libra (new moon)

October 14 at 2:00PM

Partial Lunar Eclipse in Taurus (full moon)

October 28 at 4:15PM

*times in eastern time

APRIL 20:
HYBRID SOLAR ECLIPSE IN ARIES
29°52, 12:17AM ET

Hello, dynamo! The first eclipse in Aries since 2015 arrives with the new moon and brings a major power surge this April 20. Even more special? It's an ultra-rare hybrid solar eclipse, meaning it begins as an annular "ring of fire" eclipse and transforms into a total solar eclipse for part of its path. Metaphorically, where can you shine your light into dark spaces, Aries? You're no stranger to being the lone wolf, self-starter and igniter of trends. As this eclipse series wages on for the next two years, stepping into your power as a leader could feel like a calling. Simultaneously, you'll discover new passions, slumbering talents and even a fresh life direction. Forget about waiting for others' permission or validation. This exciting quest is all about celebrating your independence.

ᛘ

MAY 5: LUNAR ECLIPSE IN SCORPIO
PENUMBRAL LUNAR ECLIPSE, 14°52, 1:24PM ET

Letting go can be liberating, Aries, and today's lunar eclipse in Scorpio and your eighth house of transformations helps you do just that. Is a financial obligation pointing you away from the profit zone and down into debt? Time to disentangle yourself. On the flip side, investment capital could flow in for one of your genius ideas as someone could step forth to put dollars behind your dreams. (Make sure you retain majority ownership!) On a personal note, this eclipse brings sexy back in a major way. A relationship could hit a milestone moment as the rubber meets the road. You might just put a ring on it—or set yourself free from a bad romance.

OCTOBER 14: SOLAR ECLIPSE IN LIBRA
ANNULAR SOLAR ECLIPSE 21°10, 2:00PM ET

Relationships are full of their fair share of surprises and October 14 is no exception to that rule. With another annular "ring of fire" solar eclipse, this time in Libra and your seventh house of partnerships, feelings you didn't even know you had could come to light. Someone you adore could express a reciprocal love: hello, mutual admiration society! Or, you may suddenly become aware of something that is missing from a particular connection. If you've been waiting for the right moment to bring up a "state of our union" discussion, this eclipse brings the cue. That said, sudden movements could bring regret, so mull over the right way to approach the topic so you don't burn bridges in the process. Pro tip: Ditch the assumptions and accusations and lean into diplomatic Libra's strategy of asking questions and seeking to understand.

♈

OCTOBER 28: LUNAR ECLIPSE IN TAURUS
PARTIAL LUNAR ECLIPSE 5°03, 4:15PM ET

"Making it rain" won't be a worthy enough financial forecast for you this October 28. You're ready for a full-on downpour! As the final lunar eclipse in Taurus (of a two-year series) reveals unexpected openings on the work front, you want *in* to a bigger league. Lucky you, Aries: Over the coming two weeks, you could be offered a job opportunity, come up with a breakthrough business idea, or connect with the client of your dreams. Carpe diem! Start putting your ambitious plans in motion today and you'll reap the rewards.

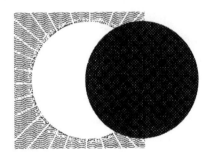

MORE BOOKS
BY THE ASTROTWINS

HOW TO GET ALONG WITH ANYONE (*YES, EVEN THAT PERSON)

Any two zodiac signs CAN be compatible, as long as they understand what makes the other one tick. The AstroTwins simplify the secrets of synastry—the 7 unique energies encoded in the distance between your signs. Take your relationships from difficult to dynamic and start bringing out your best.

SUPERCOUPLE

Unlock the astrology secrets to sizzling attraction and deep connection, and get through the hard stuff fast! Did you know that your relationship has a zodiac sign and chart? The Supercouple system is the ultimate guide to finding true compatibility—by understanding why you came together and what your divine destiny could be!

MOMSTROLOGY

Parenting DOES come with instructions! This ultimate guide to raising your kids AND flourishing as a mom takes you through every season of parenthood, from birth to toddler to school years and leaving the nest. A favorite baby shower gift, featured by *Good Morning America* and a #1 Amazon bestseller.

START READING NOW AT ASTROSTYLE.COM/BOOKS

2023

—

TAURUS

TAURUS

Say what? Your zodiac sign is famous for consistency, but the only constant in your 2023 is change! Repeat after us, Taurus: Change is good. And it's lucky—especially in the second half of this year, when a fresh 12-year chapter of your life begins anew. In the first few months of 2023, push yourself to (lovingly) release people and situations that are no longer a fit. Distance yourself from draining friendships and energy vampires. Your reward? Sweet success. If your career's been moving at a slower pace for the past few years, get ready for professional liftoff this spring! A surprising supporter could emerge to champion your work and open doors. (Where did THEY come from?) Keep everything on the up-and-up and avoid any shortcuts or shady schemes. The temptation to gamble will be strong in 2023, but this is ultimately a marathon, not a sprint.

TAURUS WILL BE LUCKY WITH:
Embracing a total life makeover, taking calculated risks

TAURUS WILL BE CHALLENGED WITH:
Curbing your impulses, letting go of people and possessions you've outgrown

LOVE

Where's the balance between "me" and "we"? That's the question as the North Node hovers in Taurus until July 17. If you've been hyperextending yourself in relationships, rein that in. In 2023, developing your own interests makes you highly attractive—and it might be the "warning shot" your S.O. needs to step up their game. Meanwhile, the karmic South Node in Scorpio could connect you to a meant-to-be mate. Has a relationship been rocky? The May 5 lunar eclipse delivers a critical "choose or lose" moment. If it's all green flags, you'll enjoy a sentimental summer while your ruler, romantic Venus, gets cozy in Leo from June 5 to October 8. Cohabitation or other home matters could be on the table, but brace for speedbumps while Venus is retrograde from July 22 to September 3.

CAREER & MONEY

With so much fresh-start energy swirling around, Bulls might not be sure which direction to charge in first! Not only is renegade Uranus electrifying your sign all year, but on May 16, horizon-expanding Jupiter bounds into Taurus for the first time in a decade. Comfort zone—what's that? With the galactic gambler pouring Miracle-Gro on your life until May 25, 2024, seize any opportunity to travel, learn and experiment with new income models. You've already been stretching since the lunar North Node landed in Taurus on January 18, 2022. Good news! You'll have that destiny-driven fuel in your tanks until July 17. Your dedicated exploration could bring a rich manifestation with the Taurus full moon on October 28—the final lunar eclipse in a trio that began on November 19, 2021. And as powerhouse Pluto weaves in and out of your career zone starting March 23, you're heading back into boss mode for a fresh, 21-year cycle!

WELLNESS

Get your glow on! When robust Jupiter lands in your sign on May 16, it kicks off a yearlong cycle of vitality. But don't wait until spring to clean up your eating, detox your habits, hydrate and sweat (then hydrate and sweat again). Hit that in the first half of 2023 so you can be ready to enjoy a sporty, active summer. Jupiter can drive up indulgence, so make it your goal to be a "healthy hedonist" with treats that do your body good. And when the South Node backs into Libra on July 17, you'll need a pleasurable routine that keeps you inspired. Try core-based workouts and anxiety-busting meditations.

FRIENDS & FAMILY

Family reunion time! Your ruling star Venus sashays through Leo, showering your fourth house of kin with sentimental vibes from June 5 to October 8. Reconnect with relatives or "chosen family" to celebrate your bond. Head's up: Venus spins retrograde from July 22 to September 3 which could throw a wrench in planning or arouse some old feuds. Try to schedule any big events before or after those dates. With Saturn heading into your community zone for three years this March 7, you'll be judged by the company you keep. Join an elite networking group, apply for that country club or take on a board member position for a community organization!

℧

JUPITER IN ARIES
Pace yourself and find peace

Jupiter in Aries

December 20, 2022
to May 16, 2023

New Year's challenge: Master the fine art of surrender. Sounds nice, right? Except "surrender" can be counterintuitive to your, ahem, bullheaded nature. But do your best to lean back. For the first five months of the year, free-spirited Jupiter drifts through Aries and your twelfth house of cathartic release. This mystical, reflective phase only rolls around every 12-13 years. While life won't come to a standstill, you may learn to appreciate the unhurried, peaceful pace of this twelfth house transit.

Regardless, prepare to experience a less temporal side of life. Because this is the second of two Jupiter-in-Aries tours, you already had a sneak preview from May 10 to October 28, 2022. And ever since Jupiter returned to the Ram's realm on December 20, 2022, you may have been feeling out of step with the rest of civilization, asking yourself why everyone is running around like chickens with their heads cut off. On the other hand, you might have the typical response to this Jupiter circuit and try to swim upstream to force an outcome...until the pointlessness dawns on you. The universe has a grand plan, but you won't be able to wrap your head around it until you let go of your fixed idea about the way things *should* go.

Here's the good news, Taurus. As soon as you stop fighting the current and decide to go with the flow, a blissful feeling overtakes you. Take the path of *least* resistance now! Fortunately, stillness is a Taurus forte when you're being the "sleeping Bull" rather than the charging one. You may or may not go meditate on a mountaintop, but spending more time in nature—particularly near water—can be profoundly healing during this period.

Since merit badges aren't handed out for busy work, stop and question your habitual behavior. Are you acting with intention or passing the time to stave off ennui or anxiety? Jupiter has a custom-made package of wisdom and insight to deliver in 2023. If you're scurrying about, you won't be in a position to accept these offerings. Look at speedbumps as opportunities, rather than setbacks. Until May 16, embrace the Taoist concept of *wei wu wei*—which translates to "doing by not doing." This philosophy of non-action keeps you from filling up the void with Sturm und Drang. Silence will permit something deeper to emerge.

With Jupiter in your somnolent twelfth house, you may feel low-energy or a lot more tired than normal. Rather than pushing through with caffeine and grit, honor your body's need for rest. Jupiter was in Aries from January 17, 2010 until June 4, 2011. What was happening then? Were you wrapping up one chapter of your life in anticipation of another? You may identify a recurring theme of transition or letting go.

To maximize this, think of 2023's Jupiter-in-Aries cycle like a celestial sabbatical. Even if you can't escape from everyday life, guard your off-time like a hawk. Warning: Jupiter is the planetary voyager, but in your selfless twelfth house, guilt trips could impede the spiritual journeys that your soul is longing for. Set firm limits, like, *I'm only willing to discuss this once or twice at the very most*. Resist the temptation to fix other people's feelings when they don't like your choices. It's your life to live, Taurus, not theirs!

Putting yourself first is actually a form of self-care while Jupiter rolls through Aries and your sacrificial twelfth house. When you set firm boundaries, you'll swiftly find out who's on Team Bull and who's lurking around, waiting to suck you dry. Sayonara, energy vampires! You may do some housecleaning of your inner circle in early 2023.

♉

Tauruses are known for making up your minds and tenaciously sticking to your beliefs. But early this year, you may have more questions than answers. Try to become an open channel. Your inner guidance system is finely tuned with Jupiter in your realm of spirituality and the subconscious. And since your dreams will be vivid and prophetic, your bed is sacred space. Keep a journal on the nightstand to record nocturnal symbols and messages. There's definitely a meaning in there, even if it isn't directly obvious.

Jupiter rules travel and education, and some Bulls will join a spiritual center or study a healing modality. This is an excellent year for a wellness retreat—ideally near water—or a volunteer vacation, where you travel to a place where you'll help a community in need. For artists and healers, Jupiter in Aries can inspire a renaissance. Think of yourself as being "in the studio" or a teacher-in-training. Welcome in the muse. Summon your guides. Ask those guardian angels for help, and their handiwork will appear.

With the twelfth house's emphasis on healing and forgiveness, Jupiter in Aries lets you unpack old baggage. It can feel sad to release the memories or the hope you've invested. But there are "moths" in those garments: grudges, resentments, anger you've clung to forever. Call it divine decluttering. You won't want any of that old stuff back once you make room for new experiences to flow your way.

Do you need to mourn a loss, Taurus? Aspects of your life may come to a close while Jupiter tours Aries until May 16, and you'll need to process any bottled-up emotions. Seek healthy outlets so you don't fall down the slippery slope of the twelfth house and resort to toxic vices and self-sabotaging habits. Traditional talk therapy is often helpful for your sign, but with broad-minded Jupiter in the frame, you could be drawn to other modalities: past-life regression hypnosis, crystal bowl sound healing, shamanic energy work—all things "woo" can be invaluable tools for resetting the deeper realms of your mind.

Got a bad habit to break? We all have addictions—if not to alcohol, food and cigarettes, then certainly to the demands of modern life. Jupiter in Aries could be conducive to recovery or to changing habits that don't feed your soul.

As for your love life, this Jupiter in Aries circuit could bring a soulmate—or someone who seems to have that potential, at least. Don't rush to label things, though. With Jupiter in your fanciful twelfth house, you're apt to don rose-colored specs or fall for a suave lovebomber.

For some Bulls, this transit could hasten a long-overdue breakup, which will clear the path for a much better connection. But there's no fast-forwarding past the healing process, which entails self-reflection and inner work. The goal is to break a regressive pattern, not reflexively repeat it with the next available candidate. History is doomed to repeat itself until you exhume the ghosts of your romantic (and childhood) past.

Career-wise you could be quite busy, but you may slip out of the public eye and perfect your formula offstage. Develop your vision "in the lab," then plan the big reveal for when Jupiter enters your sign on May 16. In the meantime, stay tucked away in the chrysalis!

There will be moments when Jupiter in Aries tests your patience and maybe brings you to your knees. You'll need to remind yourself that this is all temporary and transitional. It may be challenging to keep the faith, but clarity lies ahead. Even if you have a few dark nights of the soul when you wonder if you'll feel hopelessly lost forever, some of your richest spiritual and emotional development can occur now. Let people support you, from friends and family to departed ancestors and your "guides." Maybe somebody else has a better plan. Welcome their contributions. You don't have to do this all by yourself!

JUPITER IN TAURUS
Blasting into orbit

Jupiter in Taurus

May 16, 2023 to
May 25, 2024

Jupiter Retrograde

September 4 to
December 30, 2023

Look who's getting their groove back! (Yes, you!) On May 16, Jupiter makes its long-awaited arrival in Taurus, blazing a trail through your first house of self-expression and identity until May 25, 2024! This is absolutely a reason to celebrate! A brand-new 12-year chapter of your life has officially launched—one that's chock-full of novel experiences and epic reinventions. You haven't had this much rocket fuel in your cosmic tanks in over a decade!

The last time Jupiter blessed your sign was June 4, 2011 to June 11, 2012. It would be worth your while to scroll back through your social media timelines—and reread those old journals—to refresh your memory. What did you have cooking then? You might pick up where you left off, breathe new life into a talent or put a 2.0 upgrade on whatever you've been developing over the last decade-plus.

At first, Jupiter's entrance into Taurus might feel disorienting. When a planet moves from the shadowy twelfth house into the supersonic first, it's like coming out of a dark cave and having the bright sun blast into your eyes. The light is dazzling, but you can't make out any specifics. You only know that a new day has dawned.

And so it has, Bull! If the first half of 2023 makes you feel as if you're drifting—or doing a lot of "hurry up and wait"—the second half of the year has a totally different command: focus and pursue. While Jupiter in Aries calls for you to release and surrender, Jupiter in Taurus does an empowered about-face. Switch to make-it-happen mode. It won't be long before you make up any "lost time" from early 2023.

If you weathered rough patches, it may be hard for you to trust that things are actually getting better. We know that Jupiter in Aries may have pulled you into a scary undertow, but there were vital lessons to soak up. The faster you shake off the victim mindset, the better. We're not advocating ignoring your feelings, of course. Instead, try reframing them as inestimable learning experiences. For example, if Jupiter in Aries had you waving the white flag and conceding "I feel stuck," Jupiter in Taurus helps you proceed to "I'm ready to manifest the help I need."

With your can-do first house highlighted, you could feel infused with hope and optimism. The cloak of invisibility you wore in early 2023 magically transforms into a technicolor dreamcoat—which is basically your superhero costume while the red-spotted planet soars through your sign until May 25, 2024.

Get used to the glaring spotlight tracking your every move! The second half of 2023 is peak season for Taurus performers and influencers. Whether you're shooting an indie short or making six figures as a YouTube star, bountiful Jupiter opens a treasure trove to Bulls who brave the public eye. "Healthy, wealthy and wise" is music to Jupiter's ears. If you've figured out a formula for achieving any (or all) of this triad of #Goals, "edutainer" Jupiter might fire you up to craft a patented formula—one that helps others *and* puts money in the bank. That's a win-win any Taurus can get behind.

No matter where your compass is pointed, buckle up! As Jupiter charges through your first house of new beginnings, enthusiasm and initiative, all that pent-up energy shifts from potential to kinetic. Before you know it, the sacrifices and struggles you endured will pay off handsomely. (And finally

♉

make sense!) If you've been cooking up a project behind the scenes, Jupiter in Taurus is the perfect time to hit the gas on development, or if it's ready, stage a buzzworthy launch.

Not sure what's next? That's 100% fine, Taurus! You're at the trailhead of a fresh, 12-year cycle. Give yourself permission to experiment with untested ideas and novel opportunities, even if you don't put the pedal to the metal right away. Don't pressure yourself to figure it all out. Turn to a fresh page and set a few larger-than-life intentions. Or commit to crossing a couple high-key items off your bucket list before next May. Just be sure to take time between each milestone to integrate the progress!

One thing to remember about Jupiter is that it magnifies everything it touches. Keep your intentions sharp and pure, Bull, because the universe is ready to make your every wish its command. As Bob Marley famously said, "Complaints are like prayers to the devil." We're not suggesting you suppress your feelings, but watch how you frame things, Taurus. During this yearlong Jupiter cycle, if you can't "keep it positive," you definitely want to keep it proactive.

MARS IN GEMINI
Pursue the shiny things

Mars in Gemini

August 20, 2022 to
March 25, 2023

Mars Retrograde

October 30, 2022 to
January 12, 2023

Have resumé, will travel! Your money moves could lead you in all sorts of fascinating directions in the first quarter of 2023. On January 12, action planet Mars snaps out of its ten-week retrograde and gets you back on your feet. Better still? Mars powers forward through Gemini and your second house of income and security until March 25, 2023. Talk about adding some muscle to your hustle!

There's a good chance you've been blowing all over the place—and possibly blowing time and money—since Mars turned retrograde on October 30, 2022. Are you exhausted yet? Fortunately, Taurus, the stability you crave is within your grasp in early 2023. You may have to skip a few shindigs and burn the midnight oil, but it'll be well worth it. With excitable Mars providing a strong tailwind, there will be plenty of speed and intensity behind all your efforts.

The true key to success in early 2023? Pursue opportunities that light you up, but be directional about your takeoff and landing. How you begin a mission will determine its outcome entirely. Before you start pushing launch buttons, get all your ducks in a row and operate from a platform of integrity. Cutting corners could get you canceled.

Simultaneously, clarify your destination. Is it time to hit pause on the side hustle and get a full-time job? A steady paycheck could bring major relief in

2023. Even the "quiet quitters" among you could have a mindset shift and find some juice in the job by spearheading an initiative. If you can't map out the 10-year plan, how about 10 months from January 12, or 10 weeks? Short-term wins will bolster your confidence. Look back to August 20, 2022, when Mars first moved into Gemini for this prolonged, seven-month journey. Plans that got cooking late summer could pick up steam again—and in 2023, you may be able to take them all the way to the bank.

Once you do start pulling in more cash, be mindful, Bull. With "see it, want it" Mars revving in this luxe-loving chart sector, you can burn as fast as you earn. Loosen your belt a notch or two, but keep it snug. You have a plum opportunity to create a cushion for yourself (ahhhhh, breathing room!) so you can be ready when a big-ticket item is up for purchase...all while contributing to your retirement savings, naturally.

How's the climate at your workplace? Retrograde Mars may have ratcheted up tension with coworkers since October 30, 2022. But with the planetary provocateur back in direct motion, you'll see which battles are worth fighting. If you were passed over unfairly for a promotion or have a conflict over intellectual property, talk to an attorney to find out your rights. But when it comes to personality clashes, Mars' direct turn brings a swift reminder of the importance of being professional. When you are engaging with difficult people or handling delicate situations, remember to listen more than you talk, and to keep your comments positive—never defensive or dismissive. And always use "I language" instead of the accusatory "you." For example, "I'm feeling the need for more structure with our workflow" will yield better results than, "You're always rescheduling our meetings!" Your deft handling of a difficult situation will not go unnoticed!

SATURN IN PISCES
Team Taurus 2.0

Saturn in Pisces

March 7, 2023 to
February 13, 2026

Saturn Retrograde

June 17 to
November 4, 2023

Where's your soul squad at, Bull? On March 7, 2023, ambitious Saturn arrives in Pisces, visiting your communal eleventh house for the first time in 29.5 years and activating your *esprit de corps*. You're no longer keen to call the shots alone. You'd rather snuff out the torch and try a non-hierarchical model based on trust and agreement. As utopian as a "leaderless" organization might sound, if you're teaming up with the right people, you could make a success of this concept while Saturn splashes through Pisces' enlightened waters until February 13, 2026.

Even if you pass the baton to others in the group, keep your eye on the ball! Everything is interconnected when Saturn architects its way through your eleventh house of teamwork. And thanks to Saturn's substantial prestige, the weight of your personal decisions will impact everyone around you. Watch what happens: When your halo slips, your team starts slacking. But when you hold yourself to unimpeachable standards, your crew crushes it. People will be your mirrors this year—and although that's a lot of responsibility to bear, you'll wield plenty of power in the bargain!

That said, being a role model won't prevent you from becoming a "renegade Bull" at times this year. The eleventh house has an edgy, progressive vibe, so planets passing through it can trigger a rebellious impulse. (Yes, even uptight Saturn.) There's a part of you that wants to overthrow the status quo, march

ඊ

against corruption and injustice and put the worst offenders on blast in scathing Twitter posts.

But is that advisable? Yes and no. Stern Saturn won't leave you lots of latitude to do things according to the Raging Bull Rulebook, no matter how much you want to lay down the law...or should we say, break it. The end doesn't justify the means while responsible Saturn is in the picture. Anger (no matter how righteous) and aggressive behavior could put off potential supporters. By riling yourself up, you might give opponents an easy win.

Do you really want to make change happen? Follow Saturn's edict. The prudent planet favors experience, integrity and authority. Operate strategically, like a five-star general rather than a rogue warrior. Map out your complete game plan *before* you rally the troops. Work out all the Saturnian points, including a timeline and budget. With an airtight plan, you can turn that idealistic vision into a reality like the manifesting magician you were born to be. Plus, you'll be the last one standing, because who has more stamina than the mighty Bull?

Wherever you channel your prodigious energy in 2023, putting together the right crew is vital to your success. Instead of wowing the masses with your brilliant moves, empower people to do things for themselves. After showing them the ropes, step back and let them keep learning on the job, even if that means watching them beat their wings in struggle. Offer calm guidance along the way, but ultimately, try instilling your trust in them so they believe in themselves.

If you could use support for your own missions, join a mastermind group where you can interact with people whose impressive credentials can be verified. And don't overlook your own contacts list, which is a goldmine in its own right. Someone who can fill your exact need might be just an email or a DM away. But before you start reaching out for favors, make sure you've earned their allegiance. How can you prove your value? Volunteer for one of *their* projects and show them what you've got! It won't take long to turn this into a win-win, whether you're helping to organize a fundraiser or pitching in on a marketing campaign. Better still? Saturn can give this connection legs so it grows from mutual backscratching into a long-term collaboration.

Since the eleventh house governs technology, you could finally redesign your website, get cracking on your idea for an app or create a digital product that offers the perfect lifehack. If one of your "strange" hobbies is evolving into a lucrative gig, that's just the type of venture that can flourish this year. Your instructional videos could turn you into a household name and bring in advertising money as you build a big audience. Talk trademarks or patents with an IP attorney; mint a gallery of NFTs! A few years down the road, your "kooky idea" could be an in-demand invention that major manufacturers are clamoring for. Or maybe your proprietary methodology will become standard protocol around the world. Who knows? If your gut is telling you that this could be big, CYA by investing in protection from the get-go. A $750 legal fee will seem like a drop in the bucket compared to your future wealth. Show the world how it's done!

While Saturn is lodged in your tech zone, don't be surprised if you form a solid relationship with an online contact. If someone inspires you, DM them with praise and a pitch, Taurus. From fashion influencers to industry bloggers to potential entrepreneurial partners, start pinging them! Leave thought-provoking comments on other people's posts. They'll get a conversation going that could easily lead to all sorts of opportunities— including biz collabs for YOU.

PLUTO IN AQUARIUS
Living in a material world

Pluto in Capricorn
Janury 1, 2023
to March 23, 2023

June 11, 2023 to
January 20, 2024

Pluto in Aquarius
March 23 to
June 11, 2023

Pluto Retrograde
May 1 to
October 10, 2023

Are you ready to feel like...a *Taurus* again? As the first of the zodiac's three earth signs, you are here to navigate the material world in a grounded, practical way. But ever since space-cadet Uranus invaded your sign in May 2018, you've been on a hovercraft ride to unknown destinations. Getting your hooves on terra firma? Ha! Your head's been far too high in the clouds for that!

And let's talk about metamorphic Pluto, which has been on a spiritual pilgrimage in Capricorn and your worldly, adventurous ninth house since January 2008. That long slow roll only comes around once in your lifetime. And it has *not* made it any easier for you to get into the sensual, but sensible, rhythm your sign prefers. But my how you've grown! Over the past fifteen years, you've fire walked through trials of the spirit to get to the state you're in today. Since 2008, Taurus George Clooney went from notorious bachelor to devoted husband; Lizzo changed the body image game. Adele gave us 19, 21, 25 and 30.

Fun as it's been, you're an achiever at heart. You like to have results in your hot little hands, things you can touch, wave around and put on display. Yet since 2008 (and definitely 2018), you've spent more time in the "conceptual" world than you normally care to.

While Pluto's journey through Capricorn had its excruciating arcs, it transformed you forever. Take notes because that odyssey is coming to a close on March 23, 2023, when the dwarf planet marches on to Aquarius for the first time since 1798! Your perspective is so wise and worldly now, Taurus. Anyone who dares to call a Bull myopic can be swiftly disabused of *that* notion. If you don't have the passport stamps through ancient runes, mountain peaks and multinational hub cities to prove it, you have other game-changing experiences under your belt.

But back to those material world strategies, Bull. As Pluto rises into Aquarius, it climbs to the very top of your solar chart and activates your tenth house of career ambition until 2044! For the first time in over two *centuries*, your sign is receiving the professional blessings of the planetary wealth agent. It's a privilege, albeit a heavy-handed one.

The lofty ideals that you learned from Pluto in Capricorn may inform your mission statement in this next stage of the game. But they won't be a substitute for the tangible, actionable results you are about to produce while Pluto traverses Aquarius these next twenty years. The tenth house goal-getting zone is where your innate planning skills have a chance to shine. While that might sound like a lot of responsibility to other zodiac signs, to you, it spells sweet relief!

So yes, Taurus, starting this March 23, you *will* feel more like the charging Bull going after the target again. (As opposed to the gentle steer wandering through the verdant pasture.) It's exciting, edgy, even a little "dangerous" for you since you may need to take a gamble on an opportunity that feels a little bit out of your league.

But relax, there's no need to race to the tailor to get fitted for a power suit. This year, Pluto only visits Aquarius for a brief preview spell, from March 23 to June 11. Your evolution from nomad to mogul won't happen overnight. Pluto is weaving back and forth between Capricorn and Aquarius a couple more times before plowing ahead through Aquarius from November 19, 2024 to January 19, 2044.

♉

Pluto is slow-moving, strategic and super secretive. Over the next couple decades, your career path may involve working with highly classified intel. Either that or you'll be privy to conversations that only take place among the VIPs. The tenth house is the corporate zone of the wheel, so enterprising Bulls may find a home within an established company that appreciates your unique strategic abilities.

Developing a business? Your ideas are worth their weight in gold and will be ready for monetization (perhaps in cryptocurrency investments) as Pluto moves into progressive Aquarius. Keep developing your genius in 2023 while also polishing up your professional image and establishing your credibility. You may need to trade in some of your free-spirited roaming for an anchored approach before the year is out. At the very least, try showing up at the office regularly...and not in yoga pants, k?

Do you need to raise your prestige level? Work with an executive coach, consultants and others who can help you elevate your profile. A resumé-builder job may be part of the journey to establishing credibility—or perhaps you'll spearhead an initiative during this transition. Just be sure to keep your eye on a goal that slowly but surely brings security to your life while also helping you make a name for yourself!

On a personal note, Pluto's shift into Aquarius brings back your traditional side...with a twist! While the tenth house is all about customs and legacies, Aquarius is a game-changing disruptor. You've grown and stretched mightily in recent years: What wisdom do you want to keep in your arsenal? After all that exploring, you could spearhead diversity and inclusivity initiatives that don't just offer people seats at the table but reset the table itself!

VENUS RETROGRADE
Cherished bonds deepen

ɞ

Venus in Leo

June 5 to
October 8, 2023

Venus Retrograde

July 22 to
September 3, 2023

Ready to take a long, soulful meander down Memory Lane? The waves of nostalgia are sure to wash over you from June 5 to October 8 as your ruling planet Venus lounges in Leo and your fourth house of family and roots. Direct your attention toward happier times and this extended, four-month journey will warm your heart. But this transit *does* come with a trigger alert! From July 22 to September 3, Venus slips into retrograde, which could arouse some sleeping dragons filed under "family secrets" or "intergenerational trauma."

If it's been awhile since you texted your childhood bestie or paid a visit to the friend who held your hand (and your hair back) during your, er, experimental halcyon years, what are you waiting for? There's no time like the present to strengthen those bonds and, in the process, reconnect to the younger, more innocent parts of yourself. And during the retrograde, journeys like these can dig up all sorts of warm and fuzzy feelings for a long-lost friend you fell out with or a relative you've gone through a rough patch with.

If you're single and looking, drop your bullish nature and allow potential partners to discover the real you. A tough hide and strong façade are fine when you need to protect your heart, but don't fence yourself in and end up going stag forever. In open-hearted Leo, Venus reminds you that sharing your feelings is the *true* access to intimacy. When you're in touch with yourself, you're more open to connecting with others—and thus, more likely to create the deeper connections required to form a legit relationship.

Have you been locked in a family feud? Venus wants to patch things up and choose happiness. Lean on the love planet from June 5 to October 8. Ideally, you'll want to extend olive branches *before* the retrograde begins on July 22. But you also shouldn't rush a reunion or shove issues away for later, which could make them insurmountable. Advance slowly to re-establish trust and allow for authentic communication. You'll need to be open to things you may not want to hear, Taurus! So if you flood yourself with an all-night conversation (instead of stretching out talks over a series of meetings), you could flip from peaceful steer into a raging bull. That's as good a reason to pace yourself as any!

Sharing your space? Because this love-heavy retrograde is happening in your home-and-family zone, cohabitation could get catastrophic if you don't set some ground rules. Even the most possessive Bull needs breathing room. So how can you enjoy an RDA of alone time while still prioritizing your family and romantic relationships? Close quarters might send you in search of a coworking space or studio rental. Can you bring your easel outside or write poetry on the patio? It's also a great time to make a few simple tweaks to your surroundings, like new art, splurge-worthy bedding or a pretty rug. Notice we didn't say "renovate the bathroom," okay? This is not the time to start ripping out built-ins or refinishing your cabinets. Save that for after September 3 to avoid a kitchen DIY gone very, very wrong.

NORTH NODE IN TAURUS
Coming into your own

> **Lunar North Node in Taurus**
>
> January 18, 2022 to to July 17, 2023

Your extended date with destiny wages on in 2023, as the lunar North Node rounds out its final six and a half months in Taurus. Since this cycle began on January 18, 2022, you've had some seismic shifts to contend with. Maybe they've been external, like a move to an entirely new zip code or a radical change in relationship status. Or perhaps you've transformed internally, breaking out of a limiting belief system (e.g., "I can't handle that alone.") or making lifestyle changes in the name of vibrant good health.

Whatever the case, Bull, keep on stretching! The North Node only journeys through your sign every 18.5 years and when it does, the universe is definitely vibing at *your* frequency. Until July 17, 2023, you're poised to make a very different kind of mark on the world than you have in the past.

Got a passion project in the works? Put the pedal to the metal before July 17. While the world is thrumming to your BPM, you'll be in perfect step with the shot-callers and innovators. (You're even a little ahead of the curve!) Funds may come available in surprising ways, allowing you to retain controlling ownership *and* keep the R&D going.

But there is an asterisk here! Since May 2018 (and until April 2026), wrench-throwing Uranus has been in Taurus, making it hard for routine-loving Bulls to feel grounded and secure. For every lofty goal you've aspired to,

Uranus lobbed a curveball your way. While the North Node calls you onto higher ground, getting there has felt like ascending a mountain during an earthquake. The climb may still be too precarious to take without support.

Surprise! That's the hidden "blessing" of this nodal passage. While the North Node transits through Taurus, its companion—the lunar South Node—is parked in your opposite sign of Scorpio, serving up karmic relationship lessons right and left.

If you're accustomed to stubbornly forging ahead on your own, the South Node may have stopped you in your tracks since January 18, 2022. From health challenges to lacking resources, circumstances forced you to get humble and ask for help. Take note of your discoveries, Taurus. Not only are you learning who you can depend on, but you're also getting a master class in collaboration *without* manipulation, overfunctioning or Faustian bargains. Who knew that negotiating could be so...straightforward?

If you're not sure where you're heading, take the pressure off yourself to arrive at a destination, Taurus. For some Bulls, the only goal for the rest of this North Node cycle should be to "come into your own," as you define it. When you stop planning, the breakthrough may arrive, the soulmate could appear, the next best step could present itself. Are you willing to let go of some control? That alone may be the most miraculous step you take in 2023!

NORTH NODE IN ARIES
Healing body and soul

**Lunar North
Node in Aries**

July 17, 2023
to January 11, 2025

Your focus shifts on July 17 as the North Node leaves your sign and moves on to Aries, weaving a soulful pathway through your twelfth house of dreams, spirituality and subconscious healing, until January 11, 2025. While you won't host the lunar North Node again for nearly two more decades, you'll be ready to say goodbye. Change is exhilarating—but it can also be exhausting to do *that* much self-development all at once. Midsummer, you can switch off and enjoy a celestial sabbatical lounging in the proverbial pasture like a serene steer.

Peace may not come right away, however. When the North Node paddles back through your twelfth house every 18.5 years, it sends you on a healing journey. Time to do that shadow work, Taurus! Luckily, the North Node in courageous Aries gives you the guts to face down your demons between July 17, 2023 and January 11, 2025. This can be a profound cycle of transformation *if* you're willing to "do the work." Begin by examining past traumas (go deeper), then connect the dots to current triggers. From there, practice bringing awareness to your own unproductive reactions and responses. You know, Taurus, the ones that keep causing breakdowns at work and in your personal relationships.

One of the hardest parts of this process for you may lie in allowing certain emotions to arise. Fear and anxiety can be hard for even the most die-hard self-development junkie to sit with. Since the twelfth house rules the subconscious realm, hypnotherapy and EMDR may be especially effective modalities, allowing you to get into a relaxed state before you tackle those tough nuts. Start a meditation or breathwork practice—there's literally no better time. Besides healing fractured neural pathways, divine downloads will flow during these sessions. All the ideas you spun up while the North Node was in Taurus earlier in the year could transmute into works of art after July 17.

Need some guidance? Since Aries rules your twelfth house of mentors, helpful people will be miraculously accessible between now and January 11, 2025. From agents to therapists to influencers who take a shining to you, it might feel like there's an angel on your shoulder, guiding you through this exploration of your deepest feelings.

That might sound like a tall order (and we're not gonna lie, it kind of is). Remember that you don't have to achieve this newfound awareness overnight! Across the wheel from the Aries North Node is the patient, gentle Libra South Node in your process-driven sixth house. Lather, rinse, repeat? Suddenly that doesn't sound like such a bad idea. Repetition is what makes the lessons stick, after all. By doing, reading or practicing the same thing over and over again, you'll start discovering nuances within nuances. And that's when the epiphanies arise!

With the Libra South Node's creative influence, add beauty to the process by ritualizing your routines. How can you make a mundane moment feel more like a special occasion? For example, play music while chopping ingredients for your dinner, then serve every meal on the best plates you have. Listen to a business podcast while folding laundry or doing a puzzle, which can help make the information stick. If you usually slam down coffee and dash out the door, try waking up a little earlier so you can meditate, sip your joe and write in a handmade journal.

♉

Head's up to the charging Bull! While you may be fine moving at a supersonic pace *before* July 17, you won't be able to stomach stressful situations in the second half of 2023. The sixth house is the domain of healthy habits and savvy systems. How can you work smarter, not harder? Maybe you scale back your hours or take a temporary pay cut to work a "bridge job" as you go in search of a path that brings fulfillment without destroying your sanity.

Before you tender your resignation, however, would changing things like your workflow, time- and people-management and scheduling software make a difference? Service providers live in the sixth house and with the karmic South Node here (in partnership-powered Libra, no less), hiring a virtual assistant or outsourcing a few aspects of your job could turn things around miraculously. Bonus: It's easier to set boundaries when you're not constantly putting out fires or having a work crisis.

We all have healing gifts to offer the world, and yours will come to light during this nodal cycle. With your house of service alight, give back through a volunteer effort, monthly donation or even starting your own support circle for people who are dealing with the same pain that you are. There's something so humbling about this, and you'll resonate with this expression: "Before enlightenment, chop wood and carry water. After enlightenment, chop wood and carry water."

♉

ECLIPSES IN 2023
Balancing "me" and "we"

Hybrid Solar Eclipse in Aries (new moon)

April 20 at 12:17AM

Penumbral Lunar Eclipse in Scorpio (full moon)

May 5 at 1:24PM

Annular Solar Eclipse in Libra (new moon)

October 14 at 2:00PM

Partial Lunar Eclipse in Taurus (full moon)

October 28 at 4:15PM

times in eastern time

APRIL 20:
SOLAR ECLIPSE IN ARIES
HYBRID SOLAR ECLIPSE 29°52,
12:17AM ET

If you're struggling to find answers, there's only one thing to do during this solar eclipse in your spiritual twelfth house: stop looking! Counterintuitive as it seems, the solution may appear the moment you relax your mind and create the space for new thoughts to arise. This is a rare and special hybrid solar eclipse, meaning it begins as an annular "ring of fire" eclipse then shifts into a total eclipse as the moon blocks out the Sun completely. Metaphorically, you may see the light of promise in a situation that you were ready to ditch for good. Before you close the door completely, Bull, make sure you aren't stubbornly barricading yourself from future opportunities. How can you devise an exit strategy that leaves room for powerful possibilities to arise down the road? Take your time! Since this is the first eclipse in a new Aries-Libra series, you have two whole years to map it out.

MAY 5: LUNAR ECLIPSE IN SCORPIO
PENUMBRAL LUNAR ECLIPSE, 14°52, 1:24PM ET

Should you stay or should you go? The rubber meets the road under the intensity of the year's only lunar (full moon) eclipse in Scorpio. A decision must be made: Will you become a formal duo or go your separate ways? Use the next couple weeks to make your final choice. Single? Today's eclipse could reveal a shockingly unexpected (but kind of perfect) candidate for a portmanteau. Yes, things CAN develop fast under the light of the eclipse. Just don't get hung up on "knowing" exactly what you want. If you're willing to be open, the universe may deliver something even better than what you pictured.

OCTOBER 14: SOLAR ECLIPSE IN LIBRA
ANNULAR SOLAR ECLIPSE 21°10, 2:00PM ET

The first Libra eclipse in nearly a decade arrives as an annular "ring of fire" solar eclipse, activating your sixth house of healthy living. Follow this burst of "fall fitness" momentum. This is the day to lace up the cross-trainers or sign up for a few private sessions with an instructor who can demonstrate proper postures and help you tailor a nutritional plan for your body type. This eclipse could bring sudden changes at the workplace, too. Someone in the office could take leave, opening up a new position that has your name written all over it. Don't ignore any nagging aches and pains. Early detection is the way to nip those beasts in the bud.

OCTOBER 28: LUNAR ECLIPSE IN TAURUS
PARTIAL LUNAR ECLIPSE 5°03, 4:15PM ET

You're ready to soar, Taurus! October 28 marks the final lunar (full moon) eclipse in a two-year series, that's been activating your sign and first house of self-expression since November 2021. The personal growth and change you've implemented since then hasn't been an easy ride, but guess what? If you did the soul-searching and took action on your dreams, that inner and outer work could bring a huge victory in the coming days. Stop resisting and let the next chapter of life take hold. You may feel unmoored temporarily, but you WILL regain your footing. And stay alert! Eclipses reveal hidden opportunities, but you have to jump on them quickly. An exciting challenge may appear—one that has your name written all over it!

MORE BOOKS
BY THE ASTROTWINS

HOW TO GET ALONG WITH ANYONE (*YES, EVEN THAT PERSON)

Any two zodiac signs CAN be compatible, as long as they understand what makes the other one tick. The AstroTwins simplify the secrets of synastry—the 7 unique energies encoded in the distance between your signs. Take your relationships from difficult to dynamic and start bringing out your best.

SUPERCOUPLE

Unlock the astrology secrets to sizzling attraction and deep connection, and get through the hard stuff fast! Did you know that your relationship has a zodiac sign and chart? The Supercouple system is the ultimate guide to finding true compatibility—by understanding why you came together and what your divine destiny could be!

MOMSTROLOGY

Parenting DOES come with instructions! This ultimate guide to raising your kids AND flourishing as a mom takes you through every season of parenthood, from birth to toddler to school years and leaving the nest.A favorite baby shower gift, featured by *Good Morning America* and a #1 Amazon bestseller.

START READING NOW AT **ASTROSTYLE.COM/BOOKS**

2023

GEMINI

GEMINI

♊

What do you want to be known for, Gemini? In 2023, leadership is calling—but don't expect to take any shortcuts. Are your skills up to par? Level up! Over the next couple years, you can establish yourself as a heavy hitter or an expert in your field, as long as you're willing to put in the time. Need credentials or additional training? Pay the dues now and it will pay dividends later. Friends in your network can open doors, especially in the first half of the year, when your social butterfly wings will shimmer. In the second part of 2023, cultivate your artistic and spiritual gifts and release what no longer serves you. You're preparing for a new 12-year chapter in 2024. This is a time to "sort the crops" and decide what you'll bring into the next decade-plus of your life. Stay curious and humble, as life could serve important lessons in unexpected packages.

GEMINI WILL BE LUCKY WITH:
Networking, creative and spiritual pursuits

GEMINI WILL BE CHALLENGED WITH:
Patience around your career growth, releasing the past

LOVE

You'll be hotter than a boiler room in early 2023, thanks to lusty Mars powering forward through Gemini from January 12 to March 25. Mingle with new crowds, swipe liberally and experiment to your heart's content. Twins could add some new toys to the arsenal or push the romantic envelope in exhilarating ways while bawdy Jupiter hangs out in Aries until May 16. You'll have your hands full of admirers while Venus swings through your coquettish third house from June 5 to October 8. Attached? Fill up the cultural calendar with playdates to keep your attention from wandering—a definite risk while Venus spins retrograde from July 22 to September 3. When the South Node settles into Libra and your fifth house of romance and fertility from July 17 to January 11, 2025, it's peak season for attracting a soulmate or taking a big next step with your meant-to-be mate.

CAREER & MONEY

Professional growth opportunities are incoming when industrious Saturn sets up shop in Pisces and your tenth house of career on March 7. This three-year cycle is all about establishing yourself as a pro, building credibility and longevity. First step? Get a worthy goal in your crosshairs. With go-getter Mars in Gemini until March 25, you'll have fuel in your tanks to explore different work arrangements or make a bold pitch. These leaps can move the needle, but since Saturn plays the long game, there will be dues to pay. Stay on your grind while the South Node lingers in your industrious sixth house until July 17. This is prime time to train yourself and learn the ropes of a new system. And if you exceed expectations? The May 5 lunar eclipse could bring a job offer—even a position created especially for you!

WELLNESS

Healing is an inside job for Geminis in 2023, as the North Node and Jupiter travel through Taurus and your twelfth house of subconscious triggers and release. Are you trying to digest a situation that is too hard to swallow? Start putting up boundaries—and making an exit strategy, perhaps—or your body may start "admonishing" you with lowered energy. Yin practices that soothe your parasympathetic nervous system—like yoga and meditation—will be as (if not more) impactful as high-impact cardio. Talk therapy is also beneficial for your verbal processing style. If your energy is sluggish, try an elimination diet and put a focus on gut health and hydration. Pay special attention to your feet, wearing shoes that support your ankles and arches.

FRIENDS & FAMILY

You're back in your social element in 2023! Get out and explore new groups while expansive Jupiter zooms through Aries and your outgoing eleventh house until May 16. Once the fateful North Node swings into Aries on July 17, you'll be ready to fill out the official membership papers. From activism to team sports, give your varied interests airtime and watch your popularity soar. But don't forget your oldest, dearest pals. While Venus is retrograde from July 22 to September 3, a reunion trip could be epic!

JUPITER IN ARIES
Casting for your dream team

Ⅱ

Jupiter in Aries
December 20, 2022
to May 16, 2023

Gemini a-go-go! After a driven and ambitious 2022, it's time to loosen up and have some well-earned fun! For the first half of 2023, until May 16, Jupiter blasts through Aries and your eleventh house of friendship, collaboration and technology. Attracting great people has always been a superpower for your outgoing sign. But with expansive Jupiter in Aries, clout will be chasing *you*! Skip the popularity contests and form your dream team. Working with other innovative movers and shakers will lift you all higher together.

If you were *really* on your grind last year, your entertainment budget may be flush with resources. You have plenty of achievements to be proud of, Gemini, but in 2023, Jupiter reminds you that there's more to life than work, work, work. As you raise your shoulder from the wheel, look beyond the usual suspects for your social fix. With your offbeat eleventh house aglow, you'll keep company with fascinating people whose genius ideas inspire your own visionary explorations. Groundbreaking moments will happen out of the office, while hanging with your soul squad and relishing the adventures life has to offer.

You already had a sample of Jupiter in Aries last year, when the red-spotted planet zipped through Aries from May 10 to October 28, 2022. Connections you cultivated then could develop in exciting directions in the first part of 2023. You won't get much alone time before May 16, but you'll have an embarrassment of riches when it comes to meeting amazing people. Whether you're spearheading a philanthropic venture, joining a climbing club or starting

Ⅱ

a book club, become a keen participant in all your social squads. (By midyear, you may have VIP-shopper status at the wine store and cheese counter.)

Since global Jupiter attracts collaborators from around the world, corralling everyone in the same room won't be necessary! But you might need to upgrade your Zoom plan. With expansive Jupiter here, guest lists will multiply! But a Gemini cannot live on screentime alone, so make sure to feed your IRL schedule with plenty of "multi-player games." Gathering in a shared space could take on many forms, from arranging a coworking office to creating a co-living residence with a curated circle.

While philosophical Jupiter travels through your progressive, idealistic eleventh house, you move beyond rigid thinking. No surprise it was a Gemini—humanist poet, Walt Whitman—who said, "I contain multitudes." And so you do! While Jupiter is in Aries, stay out of any echo chambers. Distance yourself from people who cling to ignorance or espouse narrow perspectives. Jupiter in Aries doesn't back down from a challenge, and for Geminis that might look like drilling down deeper on a difficult subject as you raise awareness in your crew. Screen a documentary for a diverse pool of friends and host an open dialogue. Get tickets to a town hall or do a motivational workshop with friends. It's a lot more enlightening than sitting around discussing the latest tea.

If you've dreamed of giving van life a whirl, a Sprinter may soon be in your future. Your bohemian side takes the wheel while Jupiter is in Aries for the first five months of the year. Or maybe you'll get your fix through festival hopping or champion a social justice cause. Activism could be a major part of 2023 while Jupiter in Aries awakens your humanitarian side. Some Twins may run for political office or spearhead an out-of-the-box initiative within the company that employs you.

Even if you hit the open road, keep your devices charged up and handy. With Jupiter in your tech-savvy eleventh house, you'll thrive in the digital sphere. An online pursuit could draw financial backers, or, thanks to Jupiter's global influence, you might join forces with far-flung collaborators. ("Siri, find me a designer in Lisbon!") Inventors and scientists flourish during this Jupiter phase. Maybe you'll trademark an invention that becomes the ubiquitous "helpmate" in everyone's home. Stranger things have happened when supersizer Jupiter storms the eleventh house.

Gemini media mavens, pick your platform! This is the year to use Instagram, YouTube, TikTok, or your personal website—to launch a startup. Since Jupiter rules teaching and publishing, an instructive product, like a webinar or digital download, may offer big returns. You could sign up for online courses to polish your own skills or take advantage of any educational credits offered by your employer and become certified in branding, performance marketing, or social media management.

The eleventh house rules casual connections, and you'll gravitate to a lighthearted wavelength. As far as your love life goes, this Jupiter phase tends toward the platonic end of the spectrum. Couples might like mingling with mutual friends versus sneaking off for intimate dates. With liberated Jupiter driving your social life, you shouldn't think twice about pursuing your own interests. Forward-thinking Twins could test non-traditional arrangements, from dating several people at once to trying an open relationship. Or, you'll experiment within a monogamous bond. Time to write the script of your own erotic "Toy Story"? Your bedroom could be, er, buzzing with activity by the time your birthday rolls around.

If you're single and dating, shift your focus to assembling a circle of good friends. You could meet your next great love through a mutual acquaintance. The groups you join this year could provide interesting prospects. But take your time and build a solid friendship first. That person who shares your fascination for old movies or collecting comic books might turn out to be your soulmate-in-waiting. But "testing those waters" could also completely disrupt the peace of this posse. Unless you're fairly certain there's a future, it's probably to everyone's benefit that you keep this in the flirting-only zone.

JUPITER IN TAURUS
Reflect and release

Ⅱ

Jupiter in Taurus

May 16, 2023 to
May 25, 2024

Jupiter Retrograde

September 4 to
December 30, 2023

Relocate the party outfits to the back of the closet on May 16—or at least pull some beachy casuals to the front hangers. After a wild kickoff to 2023, Jupiter slips into Taurus and your twelfth house of closure, catharsis and release. This is a blessed chance to "rest and digest" after a whirlwind of socializing and exciting experiences that stretched you past your comfort zone.

With the red-spotted planet bedded down in your peaceful twelfth house from May 16, 2023 to May 25, 2024, you could pull a U-turn and suddenly go MIA on the very scene you reigned over earlier this year. Try not to leave people hanging, even if you've discovered a greener, serener pasture off the grid. Since you don't want to burn bridges, be honest about the fact that you're taking a break to replenish your reserves. Besides, you'll still enjoy inspiring company at times while Jupiter is in Taurus...just in smaller doses.

Taking your foot off the gas gives you a much-needed chance to reflect and process. What do you want to carry into the next phase of your life—and what needs to go the way of skinny jeans? Jupiter will soar into Gemini on May 25, 2024, handing you the keys to a brand-new adventure, the likes of which you haven't had since Jupiter's *last* cycle through your sign from June 11, 2012 to June 25, 2013. Which means that until mid-2024, you can gently clear the decks and create room for the new.

Step one: Consider what no longer serves you, whether that's a relationship, a belief or a behavior. Some Geminis could be at the end of a chapter, or maybe you're in the liminal space of a transition. For instance, perhaps you're just finishing grad school and don't have a toehold yet in the industry you hope to enter. While Jupiter is ambling through steady Taurus after May 16, you can observe and get your bearings.

It can be helpful to think of Jupiter in Taurus like a celestial sabbatical. The only footnote? With your subconscious mind getting stimulated by excitable Jupiter, your resting state is bound to be active. Make space for divine downloads during meditation, yoga and waterside quiet time. How about a beachside vacation where you can tick off all the boxes? Count Jupiter in!

In fact, you'll be channeling the muse frequently after May 16! Brush nothing off, Gemini, even if it comes to you in a befuddling dream. Great works of art, music and writing can be produced during this yearlong Jupiter transit. The trick is to *not* let self-doubt creep in during your process! Should you hit such a wall, this is a perfect time for spiritual exploration, therapy or immersing yourself in a healing modality.

It's not uncommon to attract a soulmate or have a "meant-to-be" pregnancy while Jupiter is in this esoteric zone. In part, that may be due to the easy flow this cycle can bring. "Surrender" is one of Jupiter's favorite keywords when it's traveling through the twelfth house. But that can be especially difficult for restless Geminis. All humans labor under the delusion that we're in control—or that, with enough determination and drive, there's nothing we can't accomplish. As much as that might hold true at times, those "fail-safe" strategies could leave you spinning your wheels when Jupiter swims through these murky depths.

Jupiter in the twelfth house has a sacred plan, and it will show you the blueprints as soon as you quit resisting. Humbling as this can be, you'll draw in miracles when you finally stop swimming against the tide.

MARS IN GEMINI
Pursue a personal passion

Ⅱ

> **Mars in Gemini**
> August 20, 2022 to
> March 25, 2023
>
> **Mars Retrograde**
> October 30, 2022
> to January 12, 2023

Pick up the pace, Gemini! Not that you'll have much choice. On January 12, 2023, action planet Mars snaps out of a 10-week retrograde and powers forward in *your* sign, firing up your trailblazing first house until March 25. Stalled, delayed or abandoned personal projects take off at warp speed again. Buckle up so you don't get whiplash from this sudden acceleration.

Fortunately, Gemini, your "twin engines" thrive on the supersonic velocity that Mars delivers when it visits your sign every other year. This Mars circuit's been a rare one! Normally the red planet visits you for seven weeks, but thanks to its mid-cycle retrograde, you're hosting it for seven *months*—from August 20, 2022 to March 25, 2023. Although Mars may not have the clearest sense of direction, stuck energy is definitely moving. And now that the temperamental retrograde is in your rearview mirror, you can hit the gas without fear of crashing into yet another wall.

The question is: What's next for you? And how fast *can* you get there? This is no time for playing small, but you also don't want to lock yourself into any commitments prematurely. Some Geminis would do well to devote yourselves to the pursuit of adventure until March 25. Always wanted to do a stint as a seasonal surf or ski instructor? (Ah, the roving roster of guests to meet and maybe hook up with!) Dreamed of training with a tantric master who offers application-only masterclasses in Kauai? Tour the Western states with your band (and a van)? Mars in Gemini *is* the time to throw caution to the wind and write an exciting entry in your autobiography.

What's "too much" for most people is just an average day for you, Gemini. If you had a choice, your mercurial air sign would rather be overwhelmed than bored. While there will be arrangements to coordinate and manage, your goddess-given charm will attract plenty of supportive friends who help you bring your wilder notions to life.

If you've been eager to make any epic life changes, intrepid and risk-taking Mars accelerates the timeline. Shortly after the New Year, you may be moving across the country for a job, relationship or temporary home swap. Saying goodbye is always bittersweet, but making space for the *new you* holds far greater weight than any sentimental attachments.

No need to be completely impulsive with your moves, however. Combative Mars might convince you that it's faster to completely blow up a situation, walk away and start over from scratch. While that's possible, it's not your only option! Don't push people out of your life just because you "need space" or "aren't feeling it anymore." The best use of Mars in Gemini is to be forthright about your desire to explore new parts of your personality. Friends (and lovers!) will be your biggest cheerleaders if you give them a chance to support you!

SATURN IN PISCES
If you build it, they will come

Ⅱ

Saturn in Pisces

March 7, 2023 to
February 13, 2026

Saturn Retrograde

June 17 to
November 4, 2023

Compile the CAD drawings and hire the contractor! It's time to build, Gemini, whether it's your professional reputation or an actual brick-and-mortar structure. On March 7, 2023, structured Saturn climbs to Pisces and the peak of your chart, raising the stakes in your tenth house of success until February 13, 2026. This potent manifestation cycle only rolls around every 29.5 years, rewarding on-your-grind ambition with honors, respect and authority.

Have you put in your 10,000 hours—or at least your first 100? Since Saturn is associated with time, your level of expertise will come under scrutiny. There's no cutting corners where the planet of integrity is concerned, but in 2023, even if you're still a junior associate, this could be the year you rise through the ranks. If you've earned your status as a role model, people will seek you out for expert advice. Ready to start a business? Maybe you've always wanted to plan wellness retreats or to open your own independent bookstore. Whatever the dream, Saturn can help you figure out how to turn it into a reality, one step at a time. Don't ponder; start investigating until you crack the code.

If you've had your shoulder to the wheel trying to accomplish a goal, you could climb the ladder, rung by rung, or become preeminent in your field over the coming few years. Just know that with rules-bound Saturn at the helm, you'll have to do this the hard way. Get ready to burn the candle at both ends and pay your dues. Sweat equity is required for one last push to the finish line. The silver lining? Organized Saturn enables you to streamline your efforts. Rather than scattering your energy to the winds, put your nose to the grindstone and stay laser-focused.

You don't have to do the heavy lifting alone though, Twin! The tenth house happens to be the "executive suite" of the chart, and Saturn is putting you through your paces as a leader between now and February 2026. Strive to get better at delegating, supervising and project managing rather than just jumping in to DIY.

Late nights at the office may be inevitable, but they shouldn't be your new normal. An exhausted Gemini is a ball of nervous energy. If work worries are causing you to toss and turn in the wee hours or you're pulling all-nighters to meet deadlines, that's your cue to recruit support. Lucky for you, this Saturn cycle makes it easier to home in on savvy coaches, experienced mentors and even wise elders in your personal circle who can offer guidance.

Not sure what's next? Structured Saturn enables you to craft a solid plan for the future. Envision where you'd like to be much further down the road, say, in seven years when Saturn wraps up this new quarter of its full 29.5 year cycle. There's always more to learn, but simply moving steadily in your desired direction allows you to build momentum that carries you toward the destination of your dreams.

Mastery and public relations are part of the tenth house's domain, and Saturn in Pisces can help you to polish your image with the stylish flair a Gemini is known for. Anything from presentation materials to social media profiles deserves a sleek revamping. Your image matters more than a little with Saturn here, which won't come as a shock to your media-savvy sign. Luckily, "dress for success" no longer means donning a dull uniform. Invest in sophisticated pieces that suit your body to a T and add a dash of personality with statement accessories.

Since Saturn in Pisces will form a stressful square (90-degree angle) to your Gemini Sun, you could encounter some speed bumps and experience extra growing pains. At some point before February 2026, you might even have a professional identity crisis. This can either push you onto a new path or strengthen your resolve to push through and make your mark in the world. You could clash with management while strict Saturn travels through laid-back Pisces and even leave a job because you can't stand the corporate code. Or you may exit your industry in pursuit of a fresh field. The company you work for might undergo restructuring or a changing of the guard that catalyzes your new trajectory.

This square is associated with stress-related injuries, so try to minimize strain on your joints. Good posture makes a difference, Gemini! Invest in an ergonomic office chair or standing desk, a better mattress for your body type and sleeping position or orthotic inserts for your shoes. Saturn rules the bones and teeth, so you could realize that you're grinding your pearly whites while you sleep. Get a night guard for starters, but find ways to dial down anxiety as well.

Men and fathers fall under the rubric of the tenth house, so you may experience a tough but necessary evolution in your relationship with your dad, brother, son or another important male-identified person in your life. If you want to strengthen your bond, start making a consistent effort to build the relationship. Arrange weekly phone calls, or plan Sunday dinners once a month. Ask open-ended questions instead of making small talk or giving unsolicited advice.

Try following relationship expert Alison Armstrong's "30-Second Rule." After researching men's behavior and communication patterns, she concluded that men are like deep wells. "When you ask them a question, they consider it seriously and 'go to the well' for the answer," she writes. "If you wait and give him a chance to draw up another bucket, you will get to hear what is beneath the surface."

Whether you buy into Armstrong's theory or not, it's a good example of the type of patience that Saturn rewards. Who among us has absolutely flawless listening skills that leave no room for improvement? It's worth exploring, right? Notice what develops if you resist the impulse to fill a pregnant pause. You could learn more about a special guy in your life.

PLUTO IN AQUARIUS
Wisdom and wonder

♊

Pluto in Capricorn
Janury 1, 2023
to March 23, 2023

June 11, 2023 to
January 20, 2024

Pluto in Aquarius
March 23 to
June 11, 2023

Pluto Retrograde
May 1 to
October 10, 2023

Rise and shine, Gemini! Or at the very least, begin adjusting your eyes to the light. From March 23 to June 11, 2023, subterranean Pluto makes its first major move since 2008, lifting out of Capricorn and the crucible of your eighth house. For this brief spell, Pluto darts through Aquarius and your ninth house, luring you out of your meditation cave and onto higher ground.

Disorienting? You better believe it. Although Pluto's 2023 circuit through Aquarius happens in a blink, there's no way you'll miss it. This game-changing shift won't simply be palpable. It's literally like going from night to day. Consider it a prelude of what's to come. On November 19, 2024, Pluto moves back into Aquarius full-time, sending you on an adventurous nineteen-year trek that lasts until January 19, 2044.

Since January 2008, Pluto has been right at home in the shadowy depths of your Capricorn-ruled, solar eighth house—literally the sector of the zodiac wheel this planet rules. And what a transformational journey it's been! Both Pluto and the eighth house reign over highly intense and classified matters: shadow work, death, sex, secrets, reproduction, marriage and divorce, hidden wealth, scandals, regenerative transformation. Geminis have been through the ringer since 2008. (You have the battle scars to prove it!)

We don't mean to scare you. In fact, we should give you a medal for surviving this $#!%. Pluto in the eighth house made you feel like Darth Vader flying around in his Super Star Destroyer, unsure of whether to use the force or give yourself over to the dark side. Because Pluto stays in a single sign for 12-21 years, many people will never experience the dwarf planet occupying their metamorphic eighth house. And while it sounds frightening (and definitely was on some days!) this cycle has been the ultimate test of your spiritual strength!

It's also kept many Geminis under the radar (or on edge), like Angelina Jolie, who married and divorced Brad Pitt, birthed twins Knox and Vivienne, underwent a double mastectomy and oophorectomy to prevent both breast and ovarian cancer, for which she is genetically at high risk. Her most noteworthy Hollywood credentials since 2008? Playing Maleficent, a queen who turned evil after the betrayal of her true love—a Plutonian character to the core!

We're happy to report that what's ahead for your sign looks *so* much brighter! But you may need to do a little trauma-informed healing before you can fully accept (and even understand!) the far-more-positive energy that is heading your way. Go in slowly! Plutonian shifts don't bring overnight results; in fact, they often begin with a breakdown. After all that you've been through since late 2008, you need a bit of recovery time. That's what this last lap of Pluto in Capricorn can provide, so invest in any support you need in 2023.

Life becomes more bountiful once Pluto rises to Aquarius, allowing you to take whatever wealth you've generated over the past two decades and turn it into something that grows and expands. But first, who can you trust? As you step into the light of Pluto in Aquarius, you may experience "stranger danger," feeling uncertain about who really has your best interests at heart. You're wise to take your time here, Twin. Even while basking in the hopeful aura of Aquarius and your ninth house, Pluto can be a shady figure. This year and next, you'll probably meet a few snake oil salespeople. Promising situations will reveal themselves as "too good to be true." Even when fielding legitimate offers, vet everything with *extreme* care. And get yourself a damn good lawyer (agent and manager) if money, time or intellectual property are involved.

Here's the raw data: The truth will *not* be self-evident—or evident in any way—as Pluto adjusts to its new station in your ninth house of wisdom, philosophy and higher learning. Beware! Ideologies that *seem* to make sense could lead you down a scary path. Take a hard pass on any group that spins up hate in the name of "revolution." Unless your focus is on freedom and justice (ninth house ideals) that bring equality to *all* (Aquarian ideals), you could be an unwitting pawn in a manipulative villain's game.

There's one surefire way to know: Follow the money! Who is profiting from this? Unless the answer is something along the lines of, "the people who are suffering and marginalized," you can be assured that you're on a slippery slope.

On the subject of money, wealth-agent Pluto could bring a large lump sum your way as it closes its tour of Capricorn. This may come from an inheritance, settlement, royalty check or the sale of property. Some Geminis may choose to leave an industry that you know, in the depths of your soul, you've outgrown.

As Pluto shifts into Aquarius, your entrepreneurial side can slowly take the wheel. How can you create a career path that brings freedom, creativity and allows you to shine in your natural expression of truth? Don't rush to answer that! After all, Pluto hangs out in Aquarius until 2043. Just begin a visionary exploration of what life *could* look like if you were your own boss—or created a role with tons of autonomy within an existing company, like Director of New Ventures or Social Media Lead. Already there? Cast a wider net because you're about to enter a profound growth cycle.

Erotic energy shift: incoming? Pluto in Capricorn has been serving its own brand of sex magick since 2008, however, that intensity was *a lot* for your normally free-flowing sign. Jealousy, obsession, possessiveness, ugh! Are you ready to be freed from those grips? In "live and let live" Aquarius, Pluto is far more enlightened about relationship rules. Over the coming twenty years, you could make a clear pivot away from a "property" mindset with partnerships and move to a model that's a lot more...open.

We're not saying you'll ditch monogamy (though you could) or decide that you're happier living in your own space (but you might). What *will* be the likely case is that Pluto's tour through your ninth house replaces your "us against the world" mindset with a desire to *explore* the world with your partner, traveling, learning and being students of life. That's good news for goodwill ambassador Angelina Jolie and her global family! In fact, we predict that her Gemini lookalike kid, Shiloh Jolie-Pitt, whose impressive dance skills made a splash on YouTube in 2022, could become quite influential during this forthcoming Pluto-in-Aquarius cycle.

No doubt, Gemini, Pluto's shift portends a transitional time ahead. And it *will* make you feel like a phoenix rising from the ashes. But with the knowledge that's about to pour into your cup between March 23, 2023 and January 19, 2044, you will be brimming with inspiration. With your media-savvy ninth house getting beamed by potent Pluto, you could influence the world as a podcaster, published author, teacher or leader of a brand new school of thought!

VENUS RETROGRADE

A case of the butterflies

Ⅱ

Venus in Leo

June 5 to
October 8, 2023

Venus Retrograde

July 22 to
September 3, 2023

No one delivers an award-winning monologue better than you Gemini, but how are those "audience appreciation" skills? If you've forgotten that communication is a two-way street, grab a mirror and take a good look at your reflection. From June 5 to October 8, Venus takes off on a prolonged journey through Leo and your third house of interactivity and cooperation. Consider this an invitation to evaluate the ways you show up for—and stand with—the people you love.

There's no doubt that you care! When people pass your loyalty tests, you'll scratch their backs until you've filed your nails to the tip. But are you supplying the attention they crave; the feedback that *they* find helpful? You may discover that your well-intentioned words have been falling on recalcitrant ears. What's a talkative Twin to do? From June 5 to October 8, save your breath and sharpen your listening skills. That's how you discover people's deepest quirks and truest preferences. (The ones they've been telling you, albeit subliminally, all along!) And as for friends who treat you like their personal, unpaid therapist? Close your books and stop the spoonfeeding. Asking the right questions is how to help them drum up their own solutions. And TBH, those are the ones that tend to stick best.

During this four-month cycle, fair-minded Venus in Leo craves a "kumbaya" vibe to your friendships and collaborations, but that might be a lofty goal from July 22 to September 3 when Venus rolls back into retrograde. Discussions could get heated, teeth could be gritted and smiles could be faked all in the name of keeping the peace. Here's where your Gemini duality threatens to kick in. You could go along with the phony BS and slowly watch these relationships disintegrate. Or, you could summon the courage to face the tough conversations, knowing that they are the clearest path to true intimacy.

Here's a silver lining: This time Venus is *not* going retrograde in your sign. The last Venus retrograde took place in Gemini, from May 13 to June 25, 2020. If you look back to that period—right smack dab in the early days of the pandemic—you might get clues about where you need to clear the air in 2023. But this time around, you don't have to work through them on your own. Get into dialogue and let others support you with mapping out solutions. You'll be amazed by what you can resolve when you invite others to give you feedback.

Be fair warned, Twin: Tensions are bound to rise, even if you're intent on having a healthy discussion to settle issues. What you *can* be responsible for? Being clear and confident about your needs and setting boundaries with folks who consistently overstep, like your pushy coworker, nosy neighbor or even your S.O. And of course, call a timeout when talks shift in a combative direction. Take everything in small bites while Venus is retrograde, including getting to know new people and reuniting with old friends.

Because Venus in Leo will be charging up your platonic third house, single Gems could start getting butterflies for a pal who suddenly seems worthy of pursuing. But how *sure* are you, actually? Venus retrograde can easily make a mess of complicated feelings between July 22 and September 3. If you can, keep your crush in check until the fall (or when you can sustain the feeling of certainty for more than 72 hours).

On the other hand, you may decide to friendzone a crush who seems too good to be true. They could be hiding a partner at home and making you their dirty little secret or pulling the wool over your enthusiastic eyes, only to disappoint you later. The way to find out for sure is to give it time. Our advice? Keep it in your pants and develop a solid connection during the full four-month Venus in Leo cycle. By October 8, you'll know for sure if those flags are red or green.

If you're coupled up, this is a time for easy companionship, not jump-your-bones, can't-live-without-you passion. And that's okay! Use this laid-back period to deepen your intellectual connection and strengthen the friendship aspect of your bond. When things are less than sizzling in the bedroom, this camaraderie will get you through the dry spells.

Geminis are known for being outspoken and blunt, but is that always the most effective form of communication? A softer approach may be best, especially in sticky situations. As the old adage says, you catch more flies with honey! In fact, you might even go on your own version of a "silent retreat" between July 22 and September 3, to tune in to the brilliance of your inner voice. Regular meditation is great for any mentally active Gemini, but during Venus retrograde, these quiet spells could bring epic creative downloads. When you emerge, you may have notes for a screenplay, themes for a podcast or the napkin sketches for your future sustainable yoga wear line! Just get in tune with your mind.

NORTH NODE IN ARIES
Gaining clout

Ⅱ

**Lunar North
Node in Aries**

July 17, 2023
to January 11, 2025

Cooperative Geminis know that the strength of a mission relies on its teamwork *and* its leadership—two areas of life that get an epic burst of momentum this July 17. As the lunar North Node heads into Aries until January 11, 2025, it charges up your *esprit de corps* in your collaborative, progressive eleventh house.

If you practically felt invisible in early 2023, suddenly, everyone's jockeying for a piece of your time. Hello, popularity boost! Your presence adds street cred to any organization, whether it's your quirky, clever charm that sets everyone at ease or the out-of-left-field strategic genius you provide that makes everything you touch truly original. To put it in marketing-speak: You're a value-add.

So where will you invest your precious time and energy? The company you keep can make or break you during this 18.5-month cycle. Keep stricter control over your social direction, even if that means evicting every troublemaker and energy vampire from your inner circle. *Do* leave room for spontaneous combustions of magic with fascinating strangers. After July 17, you could meet anywhere from an industry convention to an adjacent bar stool. At times you'll feel like a casting agent, who is "auditioning" people via friendly banter. Hey, you never know who might be a contender for the Gemini Supergroup!

If you've already assembled your own "League of Legends," hit the gas on joint ventures after July 17. Don't settle for the status quo. The Gemini mind is nimble: While others are stuck on Version 1.0, you're already devising strategies to expand and improve the game. These are worth bringing to the table and workshopping with your squad. Ignore the grumbling that may arise. That's just people's natural resistance to change. Your can-do spirit has the power to pull everyone out of a rut.

The eleventh house is the technology sector and when it's stoked by the innovative Aries North Node, you could find your peeps in a virtual world. Got an idea for an app, membership site or another cutting edge product? Begin spec-ing it out mid-2023. If it has legs, move into the development phase. Align with industry disruptors and you'll tap into a whole new world of inventive possibilities. And you can take them to the bank when the North Node lunges into your career zone on January 11, 2025.

Happily ensconced at a 9-to-5 job? The Aries North Node inspires you to be more "intrapreneurial," supplying your gifts to not only motivate others but to bring an entire project onto a new frontier. Provide data to back up your playful assertions and people are likely to fall in step with whatever you're making, doing or offering. That's the kind of foresight the world could use more of!

But forget about blending into the background! While joining groups comes naturally to a Twin, you're not always eager to step into the captain's role—or really stand out in the crowd beyond a certain point. The commitment, the responsibilities, the ATTENTION...oof! It's a lot for your free-spirited sign to manage.

Alas, there's no ducking the limelight this July 17, when directly across the zodiac wheel, the karmic *South* Node settles onto the throne of Libra and your regal, romantic fifth house. Ascend! Fame is calling and you are ready to greet it...with a level of ease that might even shock you. Check your front-facing materials. Do you have headshots, a reel, an online presence? Polish them up then start promoting yourself strategically. Make it easy for people to not only discover you but experience you. The path to the mainstage is surprisingly seamless—and downright serendipitous with the South Node in your fifth house.

GEMINI

Brace yourself: In Libra, the sign of judgment, the South Node can trigger your "what will other people think of me" fears. Let's be honest, Gemini: You like to be liked! But no matter how hard you try to win folks over, you can't stop anyone from labeling you. The human brain is designed to form opinions; it's a survival mechanism. Rather than spin yourself up with social anxiety, do things that fortify your inner strength and bolster your confidence. Then, you can show the world what a Gemini looks like when you're dialed up to 11!

Do you own a brand? Give everything a mid-year design review, making sure that photos and graphics are both edgy and sophisticated—and that all your pages and feeds have a consistent look and feel. It's rare to find a Gemini who fears speaking in public, but there's always room for improvement. Working with a performance coach can put the final polish on your presentation. From acting to motivational coaching to broadcasting on YouTube, your role as a public figure may take off at a gallop.

Romantically, there's a "meant to be" quality to events that happen under the Libra South Node. Libra is the sign of beauty, harmony and lasting romance. It's hard to hold a Gemini's attention, but between July 17, 2023 and January 11, 2025, Geminis could find far more than a fleeting situationship. Both you and "the one that got away" may finally be at a level of maturity to discuss a real relationship, or move your union to a more official status.

Coupled Twins could actualize a long-held dream that's only lived (up 'til now) on their Pinterest boards. Why yes, you should show bae the ethical diamond engagement baubles, three-bedroom Tudors and dichromatic hexagon backsplash tiles you so carefully curated. This fertile South Node cycle could bring a walk down the aisle, an addition to the family or another co-created project that puts your (and your band's) name on the map.

If you've reached the end of your shared journey, this 18-month cycle will be tide turning. You just can't fake it where the South Node is concerned. But here's some good news: The fair and gentle energy of the Libra South Node *can* support a "conscious uncoupling," a term invented by author Kathryn

Woodward Thomas and popularized by Libra Gwyneth Paltrow during her amicable split from (Pisces) Coldplay frontman Chris Martin.

It's not always easy for a Gemini to remain friends after a divorce or a business breakup. When hurt, you don't always have the best emotional control. You can get petty, catty and mean—and it's hard to walk back on that if you've run a smear campaign on an ex. But in 2023, you have an option to sidestep the drama, especially since the Aries North Node is rising high in your progressive, experimental eleventh house. A split doesn't have to create a chasm. Remake the rules so they suit *your* unique situation.

Of course, you can't keep it "all love" with toxic people like narcissists and gaslighters—or folks who aren't ready to be responsible for their trauma and addiction. In cases like these, you may find the strength to set a firm boundary.

Then there are folks with whom the initial magic *has* run its course, but you still like leaning on each other for support. You may have no choice if children or co-ownership of a thriving company is part of the package. Keep things as harmonious as you can. The concept of "relationship anarchy" applies broadly for Twins in 2023. Buck against convention and roll your eyes at "what the neighbors have to say." Their judgment speaks volumes about them—*not* you. And, you never know: As you proudly live life by your own design, they might follow suit.

ECLIPSES IN 2023
Shifting alliances

Hybrid Solar Eclipse in Aries (new moon)

April 20 at 12:17AM

Penumbral Lunar Eclipse in Scorpio (full moon)

May 5 at 1:24PM

Annular Solar Eclipse in Libra (new moon)

October 14 at 2:00PM

Partial Lunar Eclipse in Taurus (full moon)

October 28 at 4:15PM

times in eastern time

APRIL 20:
SOLAR ECLIPSE IN ARIES
HYBRID SOLAR ECLIPSE 29°52, 12:17AM ET

New you, new crew? Your desire for stimulating interactivity heats up as the solar (new moon) eclipse lands in Aries and your eleventh house of friendship and groups—the first in this zodiac sign since 2015. It's also an ultra-rare hybrid eclipse, beginning as a "ring of fire" annular eclipse and moving into totality for part of its journey. While you may be ready to revamp your entire social structure, don't throw out the babies with the bathwater. Some members of the Gemini Squad can evolve with you, even if you've fully outgrown others. If you've been hovering on the periphery of a like-minded entourage, step in as a card-carrying member. (Commit, Gemini...you can do it!) Eclipses bring sudden developments and this one governs your technology zone. The two weeks following this eclipse could bring a fateful connection. Slide into those DMs, Tweet your needs—your social network will come through for you.

MAY 5: LUNAR ECLIPSE IN SCORPIO
PENUMBRAL LUNAR ECLIPSE, 14°52, 1:24PM ET

Old habits die hard, but it's time to stick a fork in one of them, Gemini. The year's only lunar (full moon) eclipse in Scorpio and your house of healthy living helps you face down a toxic vice for good. Still refusing to budge? Uh-oh. Don't provoke a mini crisis in your life by ignoring the problem! Your work is also governed by this eclipse. A project you've been laboring away at since the solar eclipse in Scorpio on October 25, 2022, could hit a high note, bringing a fresh wave of prosperity your way. Ready to change jobs or try for a new position at your current gig? Keep your antennas up for opportunity over the coming two weeks.

OCTOBER 14: SOLAR ECLIPSE IN LIBRA
ANNULAR SOLAR ECLIPSE 21°10, 2:00PM ET

O l'amour! When the new moon in Libra arrives as an annular "ring of fire" solar eclipse, it electrifies your fifth house of passion, glamour and romance. You could tap into a host of hidden desires or discover that someone's catching feelings for *you*. But none of that endless deliberating allowed! Eclipses only offer a brief, rare window of opportunity. If this is something you want to pursue, you'll need to act upon it. Can't get past the uncertainty? Put it on the back burner. Coupled Gems could get a burst of momentum to leap toward the next step—which might involve picking out engagement rings or baby names.

OCTOBER 28: LUNAR ECLIPSE IN TAURUS
PARTIAL LUNAR ECLIPSE 5°03, 4:15PM ET

Support is all around you as the October 28 lunar eclipse arrives in your twelfth house of healing and "earth angels." The only issue standing in the way? Your own resistance to receiving help. Sometimes, Gemini, the most efficient way to get things done is to simply surrender and allow the vast power of the universe to do the heavy lifting. Take the pressure off yourself to have all the answers. With your spiritually introspective twelfth house getting spotlighted by this full moon, the very message you need to hear could arrive the minute you stop pushing and forcing. If you need a sounding board in "the real world," enlist a mentor, therapist, healer or coach to help you put your feelings into words—and from there, you'll know exactly what action to take.

2023

—

CANCER

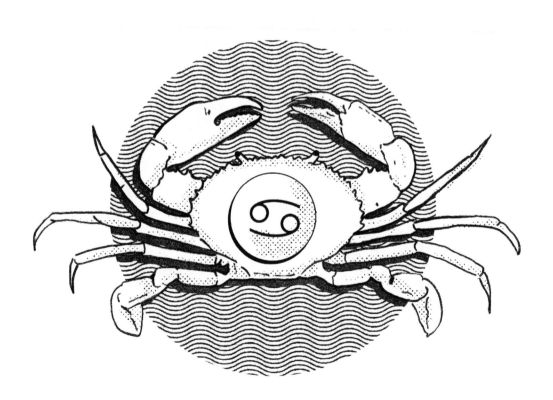

CANCER

No more hiding in that shell, Cancer—the Crab's out of the bag! The 2023 stars show you coming into your own, rising up as an inspiring leader and innovator. No need to stand in the spotlight's harsh glare (unless you want to, of course). You could lead a team to victory and shine in the role of superconnector, working behind the scenes. Got a yearning to start your own business, teach or return to school? The next couple years support a slow-and-steady path toward these dreams. In the second half of 2023, balancing your personal and professional pursuits could take extra negotiating. If you're the typical caretaking Cancer, it's time to move away from being the world's maternal figure and to start setting firm, healthy boundaries. Aim to empower, not enable. You may need to do some deep inner work, as doing so could drive up some shadowy old fears about abandonment, trust and belonging.

CANCER WILL BE LUCKY WITH:
Career, teamwork

CANCER WILL BE CHALLENGED WITH:
Travel, work-life balance

LOVE

Soul-stirring romance is on the agenda while the South Node hovers in Scorpio and your passionate fifth house until July 17. Get proactive about creating magic by picking up tickets to shows and exhibits and planning vacations. The May 5 lunar eclipse could bring a milestone moment that's worth sharing in a teary social media tribute. For some Cancers, it's the love affair with yourself that feels richest this year, but don't wall off your heart! Pluto's brief visit to Aquarius (March 23 to June 11) is the beginning of its 20-year trek through your sultry, spiritual eighth house. As much as you love your alone time, the urge to merge is heating up, too. A lovely, romantic summer's in store while Venus luxuriates in Leo from June 5 to October 8. Spoil your partner (and yourself!), but watch your cash flow. Divergent financial perspectives could become a sticking point while Venus is retrograde from July 22 to September 3.

CAREER & MONEY

It's a great big year for your career, Cancer! Expansive Jupiter in Aries heats up your tenth house of success until May 16—and the March 21 solar eclipse in Aries could bring an exciting new role. The fate-fueling North Node picks up the baton on July 17, bringing 18 months of professional growth. Exciting? Absolutely, but make space for a learning curve. The best balance? Don't bite off more than you can chew, but don't play it *so* safe that you stunt your growth. On March 7, slow and steady Saturn heads into Pisces and your enterprising ninth house. This three-year cycle can support Cancers who want to open a business, develop online courses or write a book. (Take your time with these initiatives!) A 20-year wealth building cycle begins with Pluto's shift into Aquarius from March 23 to June 11. You may choose to sell off certain assets to open up funding for others.

THE ASTROTWINS

WELLNESS

With limited time for fitness this year, you'll have to rely on lifehacks. Join a gym right near the office or invest in a treadmill desk. If you've been self-soothing with sweets or other unhealthy substances, Saturn's shift into Pisces can help you curb excess. Athletic Cancers could get serious about sports training, working with a coach or joining a league. The connection between food and mood becomes sharply evident when the karmic South Node heads into Libra for 18 months on July 17. Dietary changes may be necessary to reduce inflammation, rebalance hormones or curb food allergies.

FRIENDS & FAMILY

So many friends, so little time! Your popularity is set to soar once boundless Jupiter heads into Taurus and your eleventh house of community this May 16. And with the lunar North Node in this zone until July 17, you're keen to spread your wings and find kindred spirits both virtually and IRL. Family obligations could get a bit heavier after July 17 once the South Node settles into Libra. While your duty-bound sign would never shirk such responsibilities, don't fall into the martyr role. With a bit of ingenuity, you can support your loved ones while also taking care of yourself.

JUPITER IN ARIES
Taking the wheel

Jupiter in Aries

December 20, 2022
to May 16, 2023

Who runs the world? You might be the one raising your hand for the job in the first half of 2023, Cancer. With courageous Jupiter barreling through Aries and your tenth house of success until May 16, your leadership skills come to the fore. Stop pretending to be mother hen when you're vying for the top dog role. While some folks may be threatened by your ambition, this is no time for playing small.

Jupiter only visits this part of your chart every 12-13 years, which means this could be your luckiest professional period in more than a decade. While in Aries, the "planet of plenty" throws open doors (and windows!) of opportunity. And with entrepreneurial Jupiter calling the shots, you *don't* have to join the rat race in order to succeed. Under this venturesome influence, you might become your own boss before the year is through. That said, if there were ever a time to take a well-paying corporate job, 2023 is it.

Cancers already got a taste of this energy in 2022, when Jupiter made its first of two passes through Aries. What spun up for you last year, between May 10 and October 28? You may see recurring themes now. With Jupiter back in Aries as of December 20, 2022, you can pick up the reins again. Maybe you already set off on a new career course last year. Since Jupiter rules risk-taking and expansion, you could feel like you've already outgrown that professional path early in the new year. Keep forging ahead with your can't-stop-won't-stop grit. The ceiling cannot hold a Cancer in 2023!

Now for a paradox you'll need to navigate: Indie-spirited Jupiter doesn't like being reined in, but the tenth house rules goals and plans. Luckily, Crabs know how to proceed with caution, testing the waters before sailing full steam ahead. In 2023, a solid structure can, ironically, be the very thing that sets you free. Take time to map out as much of your future trajectory as you possibly can. While every project requires pivots along the way, a clear

66

Stop pretending to be mother hen when you're vying for the top dog role.

99

sense of where you'd like to end up can help you get there faster.

The only downside of this transit? While in Aries, Jupiter forms a challenging, 90-degree square to your Cancer Sun. With all this rapid expansion, you could face a few tough hurdles and suffer from growing pains. The bumps and bruises will be worth it, as long as you learn the lessons and apply them properly.

Either way, fresh frontiers have your name written all over them in 2023. With adventurous Jupiter in the driver's seat of your success, you don't have to rush to commit to an entirely new industry. (Although you might!) If you're still making a name for yourself, take on shorter-term projects that allow you to build credibility in your field, and eventually, climb to a higher rung on the ladder. If you're doing a 180 from doula to database administrator, say, you might need to keep a foot in both camps for a while. Or perhaps you'll proceed like a true crab by scuttling sideways, which is much easier and faster for your namesake animal than rushing forward.

Happily employed? Surprising evolutions could happen at your current job before May 16. For example, the company gets bought and decides to restructure. Adapt quickly if you love it there! Write up your job description and present it to the new managers. Pitch a pilot program. Wise, daring Jupiter in your professional realm could put you several steps ahead of the game. Don't be shy about getting discourse going at the office. Chutzpah will pay off in the first half of 2023!

Even if nothing's changing, seize opportunities to branch out, especially if doing so involves greater responsibility. Jupiter in Aries opens the window wide and invites you to show how capable you are. For some Cancers, your best strategy might be to adopt the role of "intrapreneur"—a person who assumes an entrepreneurial role within a large organization.

The tenth house sits at the top of the chart, and visionary Jupiter at its summit has you asking substantial questions, such as: *How do I want to be seen in the world? What kind of legacy do I want to leave behind?* If you've mastered a skill, "edutainer" Jupiter encourages you to create a platform for sharing your experience. Spring for headshots, web developers and sleek business materials to present the most polished image possible. If you're already a seasoned pro in your industry, you might be invited to speak in public. But don't just bide your time until the calls come in. Fire up the camera and start livestreaming.

Still a rookie? Working with a veteran can boost your odds of success, since the tenth house governs mentors. With fortunate Jupiter in this corporate province, your career could involve work with an established business or a publicly traded company. (Negotiate stock options if possible!) Having copious Jupiter in your corner could even land you in the middle of a bidding war. A word of warning: The jobs on offer might call for you to travel or relocate, which your homebody sign may oppose at first...until the courage of the red-spotted planet kicks in. Even if you're not the power suit type, you may shock yourself by weighing a full-time position with an impressive salary and benefits.

The way you handle authority can also shift before May 16. Maybe you complain a lot on social media about the government's inaction on issues you care about but don't show up to protests because you don't like crowds. Or you're the disgruntled employee who always moans to coworkers about management being too set in their ways. This year, if you don't like the way things are being run, Jupiter dares you to act on your beliefs. Who knows? Maybe you'll run for public office or befriend a decision-maker. Once you have their ear, give your input on how to do something better. Since Jupiter rules higher education, you might investigate formal management training. Even a helpful person like you could benefit from learning how to interact with people from a whole new angle.

The trick to getting the most out of the Jupiter-in-Aries circuit? Blending the right portions of freedom and responsibility. You'll want more assurances and long-range plans—but not so many that you feel fenced in. Be smart with your time and money management. You could finish this phase on higher ground, toasting to one of your most successful years ever!

JUPITER IN TAURUS
Feed your head

Jupiter in Taurus

May 16, 2023 to
May 25, 2024

Jupiter Retrograde

September 4 to
December 30, 2023

All for one and one for all! The bounds of your social circle start to stretch beginning May 16, when plentiful Jupiter blasts into Taurus, activating your eleventh house of friendship, groups and technology until May 25, 2024. Caretaking Cancers have a knack for cultivating a family of friends. During this yearlong cycle, you're on a quest to gather your squad under one umbrella. Virtual or IRL; it's your choice. The goal is to connect the amazing people you know, then step aside and let your community blossom. Friends may form independent bonds with each other—and for a change, this makes you feel excited (not threatened).

Teamwork truly does make the dream work while Jupiter is in Taurus, so sprinkle some of the responsibility around to lighten your load. Exciting collabs and inspiring people could enter your sphere between May 16, 2023 and May 25, 2024. Flex your superconnector muscles and pull people together for a compelling venture. During this yearlong transit, nothing feels sweeter than taking a bow together as an ensemble cast!

Simultaneously, obsolete friendships may fall by the wayside. Don't abandon your ride-or-dies, of course, but do note who you're spending the most time with. Empathizing with each other is one thing, Cancer. But these cathartic chats should lift your spirits, not drag you down like a crab in a barrel. Optimistic, uplifting Jupiter could reveal a few energy vampires who have crept into your circle. Or maybe you'll realize that they've been draining you for years. Cut off their supply so *you* can fly free. They'll either come to their senses or find another sucker. The good news is, it won't be your problem anymore.

With enterprising Jupiter traipsing through acquisitional Taurus, you can extend your social media reach. If you've already created a buzz, shop yourself around more assertively. There's no reason you can't earn influencer income or get hired as a thought leader who speaks at conferences. People want to hear your visionary ideas!

Got an idea for an app or an invention in development? With Jupiter in this wired-up zone of your chart, the second half of 2023 offers a smart window to invest in developing reputable tech. Or, if you have a full-fledged product ready and waiting, go all in with a new marketing effort. Don't assume people heard loud and clear the first time around. Think of different ways you can address a problem for them in the 2023 climate.

The super-social second half of 2023 might feel like a never-ending party—for better and for worse. You'll relish any chance to network and let off steam as long as you don't sacrifice the alone time every Cancer needs in order to recharge. True friends will understand your need to slip off for periodic retreats, but make sure you check in regularly.

MARS IN GEMINI
Clear your field

Mars in Gemini

August 20, 2022 to
March 25, 2023

Mars Retrograde

October 30, 2022
to January 12, 2023

Poetry in motion? Make that your "new year, new you" status for 2023, Cancer! On January 12, go-getter Mars snaps out of a 10-week retrograde and powers forward through Gemini and your divinely inspired twelfth house. While this won't do much to support a firmer grasp on reality, that's more than okay! Your imagination will produce some insanely creative gems while the red planet rolls through Gemini until March 25, 2023. Drop any judgment or self-criticism and just make art for art's sake. Inspired visions could arrive in your sleep—and then keep you awake half the night turning them into an oil painting, acoustic single or the clincher scene in your screenplay. Relax your mind and be an open vessel. You'll be amazed by what flows out of you.

Normally, Mars spends seven weeks in a sign, but because of its biennial retrograde cycle, it's been in Gemini since August 20, 2022, and, in total, sticks around here for seven *months*. During this time, you're more internally focused than usual—and ever since Mars turned retrograde on October 30, 2022, possibly more sensitive and reactive...but also more tuned in to higher dimensions. Any healing, forgiveness or transformation you're hoping for could come through under this transit. And once Mars turns direct on January 12, you'll be ready to take action to bring forth change in your most meaningful relationships.

For some Cancers, getting the wheels off the ground has been a challenge since August 2022. There were lots of loose ends to tie up and emotions to process—possibly grief from a breakup or the loss of a loved one. It doesn't help that your energy levels have not been at their peak. With accelerator Mars sinking into the cosmic quicksand of the twelfth house, you may have bursts of momentum followed by spells of fatigue.

66

With Mars in this esoteric realm,

you might have unprecedented

results with hypnotherapy, shamanic

or energetic healing work.

99

What does this all add up to? A major life detox that kicks off in January 2023. When agitator Mars visits your twelfth house of transitions every two years, it forces you to deal with anything you've been sweeping under the rug. This can get particularly explosive for Cancers who insist that they "can't deal with" anything stressful or "negative." But the unprocessed sediment in your psyche (buried fears *and* desires) can churn up anxiety. And certain processed food in your diet may cause inflammation, low energy and other undesirable effects.

So what's a Crab to do? Summon the warrior planet's courage and shine a light on all those monsters under the metaphoric bed. Start working with your incredible somatic therapist again, the one who knows how to move stuck energy out of your mind *and* your body. Have a doctor test you for food allergies to see if you're struggling with any forms of digestion (the twelfth house rules elimination). With go-getter Mars in this esoteric realm, you might have unprecedented results with hypnotherapy, shamanic or energetic healing work.

But the opposite can also be true: If you've been working in those areas but still feel stuck, this might be the time to switch gears and try a traditional route, perhaps with cognitive-behavioral therapy (since Gemini is the communicator and mentalist of the zodiac).

Do you need to cut the cord of an unhealthy bond? Toxic frenemies, cruel bosses, bad romances—don't spend 2023 trying to figure out *why* you're stuck in this dynamic. First, use that Martian strength to extricate yourself from the relationship itself, or at least take a notable break.

That empty space will feel scary and surreal at times, but you'll get through it. When Mars is in your sacrificial twelfth house (as it has been since August 20, 2022) you can fall into what therapists call "repetition compulsion." Translation? You compulsively put yourself in situations that feel like a repeat of a past trauma, hoping to slay the dragon and get a different outcome. Alas, this slippery slope usually pulls people straight back into a compromised position. So break away first and *then* focus on breaking free from any psychological imprisonment you're caged in.

For other Cancers, the olive branch looks mighty appealing come January 12. Finally! You may be ready to accept one that's been dangled for a while. Do *you* need to initiate amends? Brave Mars helps you extend the first gesture.

Emotions will need to be metabolized as you move through the forgiveness process. Reminder: healing can be body-based, too! From lap swims to yoga classes, active Mars can help you find a 2023 fitness modality that's as spiritual as it is physical. Follow up with other detoxifying practices like salt baths (and sound baths!) to sweating it out in the infrared sauna.

Pay attention to signs and serendipities, especially where metaphysical matters are concerned.

Your own healing gifts have probably come to light with Mars in Gemini since last August. (Hands-on healing perhaps, since Gemini rules the hands and arms.) After January 12, they'll develop at an accelerated pace. You might even sign up for training to get certified in a modality. Whether you pursue it professionally or just tuck it into your arsenal of skills you use to support your friends is your call.

Pay attention to signs and serendipities, especially where metaphysical matters are concerned. If you keep hearing about the same spiritual book or reader multiple times, follow the thread. Before March 25, it could lead you on a fantastic voyage!

2023 HOROSCOPE GUIDE   235

SATURN IN PISCES

Knowledge is power

Saturn in Pisces

March 7, 2023 to
February 13, 2026

Saturn Retrograde

June 17 to
November 4, 2023

Ready to roam far from home sweet home? Cancers like to hunker down and make their nests as cozy as possible, but in 2023, you could flip the script and forego domestic tranquility in a quest to broaden your horizons. You might become a world traveler or a traveler of the mind, and you have disciplined Saturn to thank for this.

On March 7, 2023, the cosmic coach drifts into imaginative Pisces, waking up your ninth house of higher learning and global exploration until February 13, 2026. Saturn only tours each part of your chart every 29.5 years, and its visits really pack a punch! Wherever the taskmaster planet hangs out will be an area of life that feels a bit like boot camp. You need to set an early alarm, put yourself through your paces and power through in order to reap the benefits. Fortunately, you'll be plenty motivated to rise to the challenge!

Saturn's journey through the ninth house is one of its most rewarding cycles. Although Saturn is limiting by nature, the ninth house rules expansion. Despite that contradiction, you're prepared to embrace this planetary push—even if it forces you to switch into beast mode.

As astrologers, we have seen the positive results of Saturn's ascent into the ninth house for our clients (in either the natal chart or the solar one, as described here). And it's often a welcome relief after the past two Saturn circuits through your seventh house of relationships (December 2017 to

December 2020) and your eighth house of intense, binding entanglements (December 2020-March 2023). You've been paying your dues—emotionally, financially, karmically—and you'll finally see the light at the end of the tunnel.

While you'll still work hard during Saturn's tour of Pisces, it won't feel like a never-ending series of tests from the universe. You might even discover that those hard knocks of the past several years built real character *and* know-how. Over the next three years, you could be tapped to teach something that you learned in the trenches. Put together a curriculum or record live

You've been paying your dues—emotionally, financially, karmically—and you'll finally see the light at the end of the tunnel.

demonstrations on YouTube. This could turn into a steady source of income. Get going on your lesson plans! Maybe you have a TED talk burgeoning inside you or personal wisdom to impart in a memoir. Deliberate Saturn will support your development efforts.

The ninth house rules diversity and inclusivity. This year, Cancers will feel a powerful pull to establish greater equity in the world. Whatever your purview—music, dance, art, or engineering the mechanics behind it all—your quest will resonate with kindred spirits around the globe. And wherever you're located, Saturn's tour of Pisces will awaken your pursuit of knowledge, truth and enlightenment. Since the ninth house oversees higher education—and Saturn cares about credentials—you might make one of your self-taught skills "legit" with formal training. Is there a degree program out there that sounds tailor-made for you? Enrolling in university classes—even part-time—can position you for professional ascendance in March 2023, when Saturn moves into your tenth house of career.

With Saturn in this athletic arena, you're inspired to take better care of your body. If your job is sedentary, switch to a standing desk, or make frequent movement a priority. Pushing yourself (without going to extremes) can lead to greater flexibility and muscle tone while the "personal trainer" planet is parked here in 2023. Saturn favors a regimen, and you can draw motivation from a sense of community. You might join a 30-day challenge, for example, to kickstart your personal fitness campaign.

Are you ready to relocate? With your ninth house of global expansion under Saturn's watch, you may widen your search parameters further than expected, dropping anchor in another state or continent! Wherever you land, expect to stay a while. Serious Saturn plants deep roots, even while in the nomadic ninth house. If this new area doesn't become your future primary residence, it may serve as a vacation home or an area that you return to frequently to do business.

PLUTO IN AQUARIUS
Double your pleasure

Pluto in Capricorn
Janury 1, 2023
to March 23, 2023

June 11, 2023 to
January 20, 2024

Pluto in Aquarius
March 23 to
June 11, 2023

Pluto Retrograde
May 1 to
October 10, 2023

Power to your partnerships, Cancer! But will they be fueled by the clean energy of love and affinity or a nuclear blast of vengeance? Keep a clear watch over your motives between March 23 and June 11, 2023. For the first time since 2008, magnetic, mysterious Pluto is changing signs, heading into Aquarius and the stormy seas of your eighth house. While its 2023 visit here is brief, its impact will be felt. Take notes! Pluto returns to Aquarius on November 19, 2024, and stays there for a solid nineteen years, until January 19, 2044.

There's no denying the intensity of *any* planet passing through your eighth house, Cancer. (And TBH, you should be used to it by now, having had both bountiful Jupiter and strict Saturn do time in this zone between March 2020 and March 2023.) Pluto, however, is right at home in the eighth house. Both share traits with Scorpio, the eighth sign of the zodiac, known to swing between sexy extremes and take on life-or-death situations like a phoenix ready to rise from the ashes.

While Pluto, the Darth Vader of astrology, is not exactly a welcome guest, at least it's at home in your eighth house. So how will you "use the force," Cancer? Will you turn to the dark side or reprise your Jedi knighthood like Anakin Skywalker? (Vader's former identity...to keep this *Star Wars* metaphor rolling.) That sounds dramatic, but it's real. Whenever Pluto changes signs, the shifts can be seismic.

Since January 25, 2008, Pluto has been purging through Capricorn and your seventh house—a segment of the chart wheel that, much like the eighth house, is also focused on relationships. The difference? The seventh house is all about peace, love and harmony. It's the wedding and honeymoon season. The phase when co-creation feels like a magical discovery of each other's hidden gifts. For many Cancers, the past fifteen years have brought delightful opportunities to bond, perhaps with people who were formerly off your radar. We're not saying that it hasn't been intense at times! Pluto pulls no punches, even in a pleasant zone like the seventh house.

Since Capricorn is your opposite sign, your mates have been your mirrors since 2008. There's nothing quite like an intimate relationship to reflect both your greatness *and* your "areas in need of improvement." But with transformational Pluto guiding this mission, you've also been willing to do the inner work and grow through the healing salve of love.

Or, like Cancer Khloe Kardashian, perhaps you struck a deal that wasn't perfect, but helped you get certain needs met. The *Good American* fashion mogul's desire to become a mother—and challenges with conception—was an ongoing thread on *Keeping Up with the Kardashians*. After giving birth to True in 2018, her second child with Tristan Thompson was born by surrogate in 2022, despite his record of cheating. Although the two are rarely on speaking terms, they have negotiated a co-parenting plan.

The eighth house is the place where partnerships take on a permanent status—or go up in flames. It's "all or nothing" here. Rock-solid with bae? The two of you may take on a trial by fire together, battling a dragon and growing closer in the process. But if, like Cancer Gisele Bundchen, you find yourself needing more time from your partner, you may find yourself taking more drastic measures to get your point across once Pluto enters Aquarius.

In other words, Pluto in Aquarius *could* bring a make-it-or-break-it moment to certain partnerships. Will you get married or divorced? Merge and acquire or break away as an independent venture? All sorts of unions will be affected by this Pluto circuit. You simply won't be able to settle for *not* living on your edge. If you're willing to take the plunge into deeper waters—and your "other half" is, too—Pluto in Aquarius could bring wealth beyond your dreams, the kind that leaves a legacy for future generations.

Let's talk about the scintillating parts of this Pluto passage as well. The eighth house is the tantric zone of the zodiac wheel, where mind, body and soul merge. There is no shortage of Crabs who have been sex symbols for at least part of their careers: Pamela Anderson, Tom Cruise, Ariana Grande, Saweetie. But Pluto in the eighth house arouses a deeper brand of sex magick, the kind that's about creating a compelling connection that's so profound, it's spiritual! In experimental Aquarius, Pluto could lure you to a play party or find you setting up a special sex room in your abode.

Reproductive health comes under Pluto's magnifying glass. As the dwarf planet weaves back and forth between Capricorn and Aquarius, you may feel a sudden desire (or lack thereof) to improve your sex life. If you're over 40, balancing your hormones may be the key to reawakening that erotic fire. Hoping to conceive? Pluto in the eighth house could necessitate some extra measures to boost fertility.

Darker subject matter, like death and the afterlife, could be on your mind. Not because you're literally dying, Cancer, but because Pluto and the eighth house govern the unconscious and the underworld. Who *are* you...beyond your physical form? And who are you when you are in a body? Pluto in Aquarius could evoke a profound exploration of both your psychic field and the power you hold in your physical form. Cancers may uncover hidden gifts as mediums and channels. Already there? While Pluto tours Aquarius, people may seek you out for readings and advice. Perhaps you'll hang your shingle and offer these services for a fee; or make your client list more exclusive so you can work with the VIP leaders that Pluto reigns over.

CANCER

What you want to do in 2023 is let go of anything that sucks your life force energy! You need to feel sexy and alive, Cancer, not weighed down by the burden of responsibility. Even if you don't leave a relationship, you may need to let everyone in your field know that there is a new sheriff in town. And this Cancer cop is putting everyone under arrest who breaches your right to *not* play caretaker to their demands!

Give your finances a review this year, too. Wealth-agent Pluto will support you in building a portfolio of investments over the next twenty years. But first, do you need to disentangle yourself from anyone? Those unsigned contracts (divorce papers, maybe?) or handshake deals could become the bane of your existence in 2024. Don't wait until things get complicated. Liberate yourself from bad deals and protect your property (intellectual and otherwise) with the support of a lawyer.

By the same token, Pluto's move into your eighth house can bring great abundance through shared investments. Happily coupled—for business or pleasure? Between March 23 and June 11, start setting up everything from your wills to trusts for your children to estate planning guidelines. Even if you're at ground zero of this journey, the path to financial security begins in 3, 2, 1...

VENUS RETROGRADE
Sensuality and sensibility

Venus in Leo

June 5 to
October 8, 2023

Venus Retrograde

July 22 to
September 3, 2023

Watch out for curveballs from your past, Cancer! From July 22 to September 3, Venus spins retrograde in Leo, and dredges up feelings for people you swore you were so over. This is a common occurrence when the love planet backflips every 18 months. And truth be told, reconnecting with a former flame may feel like a safer bet for your nostalgic sign. But here's the problem: When Venus pivots into reverse, hindsight is anything *but* 20-20.

It goes without saying that you should exercise caution during this retrograde, Cancer. And with the love planet backstroking through your slow-and-steady second house, keep things at a simmer instead of high heat. That goes for existing relationships and new situationships, too! As a water sign, you can never fully shut off your emotional valves—nor should you! But dialing down the intensity will be your mission this summer. (No, it's not always personal.) And it might take a meditation practice, yoga retreat and support circle to nail this empowering new skill.

But let's back up our timeline a little. Venus actually struts into Leo on June 5, providing a solid buffer period to buckle up and prepare for any big bumps in the road during the retrograde. Are there people to clear the air with? Names and accounts to block? Don't leave this up to chance. The retrograde officially ends on September 3, but Venus will continue to pal around with the Lion until October 8. That's a blessing for soft, introspective Cancers who may need some extra time to get your bearings after the dust settles.

Before Venus spins into retrograde on July 22, get your serotonin surging! Romance is a proven booster, whether you have a plus-one or are creating a romantic atmosphere for yourself. Turn up your favorite music, light the candles and indulge your most sensual cravings. Zero judgments if you hit up your FWB for some feel-good, no-strings-attached action. If you're dating someone more seriously, you'd be wise to clarify expectations before Venus retrograde muddles everything up.

Physically, serotonin is actually produced in the gut. Nourishment is already a critical factor for your sign, which rules the chest and stomach. You might talk to your doctor about supplements like L-Tryptophan, which the body converts into serotonin. No one knows better than a Cancer that there's a connection between food and mood! Natural serotonin boosters include salmon, eggs, spinach and seeds, so if you're not allergic to this fare, add it to your plate.

Of course, once the retrograde shift happens on July 22, everyone's gonna feel it. If you're not in a grounded place, it could cause you to dig in your Crab claws unceremoniously. Alas, clinging could make a promising partner run far away and fast, the exact opposite of what you're hoping for. When you're feeling vulnerable and afraid of being abandoned, call your therapist or a levelheaded friend to talk you down from the ledge. Even if you *do* have a legitimate reason to be upset, you want to speak from a place of power, not insecurity. And that means remembering *your* value in the relationship!

The good news is, Leo is the ruler of your second house of self-worth. If you tend to fold instead of standing up for yourself during conflicts, you could find your fight while Venus is on this extended tour through the lion's den. Take the chance to practice being assertive and speaking up. Crawling back into your shell won't solve anything. Has it ever?

Protecting yourself also means being mindful of your money. Where is all your cash going? If you're blowing more than you're saving, and splurging left and right, take a step back and figure out what's really going on. Retail therapy can be soothing for Cancers who have a special connection to color, creativity and style. But make a shopping budget instead of spending on a whim. That way you can actually *enjoy* the treasures you accumulate. Venus and Leo in your second house of financial wellness will play the role of celestial Suze Orman and get you back on track.

Precious Crab, you may not be able to predict what other people will do, but you *can* control yourself and your reactions. Do what it takes to be your best self: go for long walks, hide Instagram or Tinder if you need to, drink lots of water and remember to breathe. Consider these routines and rituals like a new coat of armor that will have you coming out fiercer than ever when Venus does its post-retrograde lap through Leo from September 3 to October 8!

NORTH NODE IN ARIES
Stepping up to the plate

**Lunar North
Node in Aries**

July 17, 2023
to January 11, 2025

There's a time to lead and a time to follow, Cancer. And when the North Node shifts into Aries this July 17, it ascends to the top of your chart, illuminating your take-charge tenth house until January 11, 2025. Step up to the plate, Crab! As one of the zodiac's four initiating cardinal signs (the signs that begin every season), it's your destiny to reign with a wise and nurturing hand.

Taking responsibility comes naturally to you, Cancer, but you aren't 100% comfortable being the final word on matters. Sensitive as *you* are to every emotional ripple, you may worry that people will misread your requests as demands—or worse (though likely), project their mommy and daddy issues onto you and resent your authority. And guess what? You simply cannot prevent this from happening. When the North Node ascends to your tenth house every 18.5 years, you need to keep your eye on a totally different ball, namely the direction in which you're going to steer the ship.

Opportunities to shine begin popping up everywhere mid-summer. Rise to the occasion and you'll experience some of the most profoundly meaningful moments of your professional life! With your prestigious tenth house getting charged up, these opportunities could elevate you to a new status in your industry. Since this is new terrain, you may feel the urge to scurry back to comfort here and there. Try not to! While it *can* be lonely at the top, it doesn't have to be. That said, you may need to bond with a different peer group who understands this newfound role you are stepping into. Coaches, agents, managers and mentors may become your go-to advisers.

Discernment is essential, however, so you may be saying more "no's" than "yesses" after July 17. While it's flattering to be invited as the guest speaker at every event, avoid spreading yourself paper thin. It can help to make a criteria checklist for assessing offers. Unless they tick all the boxes, take a pass or negotiate a counteroffer.

If you're still getting started on your path, you *do* want to say yes to anything that leads you closer to your personal Promised Land. Making coffee runs on the set of an independent film, for example, isn't just grunt work worthy of eyerolls in the age of the Great Resignation. A few months of hustle could give

66

You may be saying

more "no's"

than "yesses"

after July 17

99

you the birds eye view into the industry. You'll learn what it takes to set up a scene, get the right equipment and manage the org chart of your own future production. Moreover, there's no better way to get your ballet slipper in the door and build a database of connections who may hook you up for future gigs.

Manifestation involves acting as if you have already achieved the goal. This technique can be wildly successful for Cancers, thanks to your potent emotional range. It's been said that the craft of acting isn't so much about becoming a character, but rather finding that character *within* yourself in a place where it already exists. Dress, speak and live the role you'd like to play, Cancer. You could cast yourself into an entirely new lifestyle in the second half of the year.

The last time the North Node visited Aries was between November 30, 2004 and June 19, 2006. Whatever you were spearheading then could give clues about what's to come in 2023. Yes, even if you were setting up a lemonade stand (enterprising!) or trying out for the lead in the school play (Cancers can come out of left field like that). Pursue what you want with determination, because luck is on your side during this success-boosting cycle.

So what about work-life balance? Without proper "shell time," a Crab can get ornery! You're in luck, Cancer, because while the North Node is in Aries, its counterpart, the karmic South Node, will be flowing through gentle, harmonizing Libra and your domestic fourth house. The rooted fourth house sits at the base of the zodiac wheel and shares similar properties to Cancer (the fourth sign). Get ready to feel more anchored in home and family affairs than you have in a while!

On a literal level, it may be time to switch things up at the Crab Castle. Survey your abode. Is it time to make some changes? Maybe you'll build a covered porch so you can sip coffee and read books while the rain patters down. Would redoing the master bedroom sanctify your sleep? Price out possibilities and see what you can create.

Are you ready to relocate to an area that better suits your lifestyle? Cancers may leave a sleepy, bedroom community for an apartment in the heart of the city or invest in a vacation cottage on a lake. Other Crabs may redo the roster of folks living under your roof. Perhaps you'll make space to care for an aging parent or blend families with a partner. Kids may move out for college or move back in after undergrad—or you could head to a different zip code where the school district offers the level of education you want for your little ones.

Priceless bonding moments will be plentiful while the South Node is in Libra, but this comes with an asterisk. If you burn yourself out "being there" for everyone, you won't have fuel in your tanks to pursue the ambitions offered by the North Node in Aries. A key lesson of this nodal cycle: Finding a way to support others *without* making sacrifices to your own serenity.

Crucial to that process? Pumping up your self-care. Libra energy is all about aesthetic balance. And you'll want to feel that way wherever you live! That includes the four walls that house you *and* the way you feel in your own body. With regards to both, it's not size that matters—it's a sense of personal safety and ease. Without ample privacy, you may find yourself leaving home more than staying or dissociating from your feelings in an effort to manage the moods of the people around you. Whether it's a room or the entire house, you need a place to retreat and recharge alone—and more than usual after July 17.

Food has always been a comfort for Cancers, so how about reinventing your favorite recipes with healthy ingredients? (Or better yet, finding one of the hundreds of amazing cookbooks that have already done the job?) Monthly massage, acupuncture and energy healing is not a luxury now; it's a necessity. Whenever possible, incorporate calming rituals into your workflow, like rubbing essential oils only on your wrists and temples, adjusting the lighting of the room and listening to music while you move through the day. Exercise builds energy, but what motivates you to get your heartrate up? This is a great year to set up a home fitness plan, but also bring in support from a trainer once or twice a week.

Security alert! Along with revving up your nesting instincts, the Libra South Node helps you build your nest egg. The rallying cry of "location, location, location!" may shift to "saving, saving, saving!" especially if your shelter (and food!) costs have been zapping most of your earnings. Financial planning could be a driving factor regarding choices after July 17. The South Node in Libra balancing act helps create a lifestyle you love that fits your economic plan *and* offers enough creature comforts to keep a Cancer creatively inspired. Fortunately, the Aries North Node is revving up your earning power. Keep forging ahead and watch the funds appear!

ECLIPSES IN 2023
Raising the stakes

Hybrid Solar Eclipse in Aries (new moon)

April 20 at 12:17AM

Penumbral Lunar Eclipse in Scorpio (full moon)

May 5 at 1:24PM

Annular Solar Eclipse in Libra (new moon)

October 14 at 2:00PM

Partial Lunar Eclipse in Taurus (full moon)

October 28 at 4:15PM

times in eastern time

APRIL 20:
SOLAR ECLIPSE IN ARIES
HYBRID SOLAR ECLIPSE
29º52, 12:17AM ET

What's next for your career? Illuminating insights roll in as the year's only new moon in Aries arrives as a rare hybrid solar eclipse. This is the first eclipse to land in your professional zone since 2015 and for some Crabs, it could bring a shakeup, along with exciting developments that you need to move on at lightning speed. For others, this tide-turner can bring the realization that you're ready to move on up the ladder or make some life-enhancing shifts to the *way* you do your work. Be it an impressive new title, a job that lets you travel abroad, a WFH gig or the start of your own business, you'll develop in this direction quickly during this series of Aries eclipses which last until March 2025.

MAY 5: LUNAR ECLIPSE IN SCORPIO
PENUMBRAL LUNAR ECLIPSE, 14°52, 1:24PM ET

The sparks could erupt in a full-on fireworks display as today's lunar (full moon) eclipse arrives in sexy Scorpio and sets it off in your fifth house of true romance. At last! Someone worthy of your precious heart could be revealed—or maybe you'll get clarity around "next steps" with the person you've already given it to. With so much fertile energy afoot, you might catch a case of baby fever or get to work on your creative brainchild. Have you been caught in a bad romance? Today's eclipse hands you the keys to those self-imposed shackles and commands you to break free. With the extreme energy of this eclipse, forget about trying to be friends with anyone who torments you so. Moving on means cutting ties—at least while your heart is healing.

OCTOBER 14: SOLAR ECLIPSE IN LIBRA
ANNULAR SOLAR ECLIPSE 21°10, 2:00PM ET

Hygge season could bring some heavenly surprises as the year's second annual "ring of fire" eclipse arrives in Libra and your fourth house of roots. Ready to make some changes to your living situation? Stay open to possibilities that weren't on your radar, like a dreamy listing that's in a part of town you never considered before—or a roommate suddenly moving out. Remain fluid, as only a water sign can. Happily nested? You might welcome a new household member, pet, or partner to your quarters. The interior decorator bug could bite, but are you ready for an outright renovation? Start pricing it out: If you're going to do it, you might as well do it right.

OCTOBER 28: LUNAR ECLIPSE IN TAURUS
PARTIAL LUNAR ECLIPSE 5°03, 4:15PM ET

Summon your soul squad! As an electrifying lunar (full moon) eclipse in Taurus lands in your collaborative eleventh house, you'll need all (capable!) hands on deck this October 28. This is the third and final Taurus lunar eclipse in a two-year series, so you may be toasting a milestone for a project you've worked on for a while. Is it time for an encore or are you ready to move on? If you know you've outgrown this particular affiliation, the eclipse will hasten your departure. Do your best to not burn bridges as you go—but no guilt about making your exit, Cancer! Since the eleventh house rules activism, you might get involved in a project that benefits society or changes the cultural landscape. Wherever you are playing, check any ego at the door and show what a team player you can truly be.

MORE BOOKS
BY THE ASTROTWINS

HOW TO GET ALONG WITH ANYONE (*YES, EVEN THAT PERSON)

Any two zodiac signs CAN be compatible, as long as they understand what makes the other one tick. The AstroTwins simplify the secrets of synastry—the 7 unique energies encoded in the distance between your signs. Take your relationships from difficult to dynamic and start bringing out your best.

SUPERCOUPLE

Unlock the astrology secrets to sizzling attraction and deep connection, and get through the hard stuff fast! Did you know that your relationship has a zodiac sign and chart? The Supercouple system is the ultimate guide to finding true compatibility—by understanding why you came together and what your divine destiny could be!

MOMSTROLOGY

Parenting DOES come with instructions! This ultimate guide to raising your kids AND flourishing as a mom takes you through every season of parenthood, from birth to toddler to school years and leaving the nest. A favorite baby shower gift, featured by *Good Morning America* and a #1 Amazon bestseller.

START READING NOW AT ASTROSTYLE.COM/BOOKS

2023

—

LEO

WHAT'S IN THE STARS FOR

LEO

Give me shelter...or give me freedom? In 2023, you'll yearn to spread your wings, so let your adventurous Leo spirit roam free. You've been cultivating some big ideas, and in the second half of the year especially, you might be ready to take one to prime time. An exciting new career opportunity could be in the making, but you may need more support from loved ones to pull this off. Old issues around power, trust and control could arise. Sort through those before leaping into any financial entanglements or binding relationships. While you're a mighty force of nature, you can't do other people's emotional work for them. Instead of micromanaging, focus on your own interests. Cultivate a new hobby, start a podcast, draft a few chapters of your memoir. Worldly adventures are calling in this year, too. Pack your bags, whether you go solo or take your favorite plus-one along for your royal escapades.

LEO WILL BE LUCKY WITH:
Career, travel

LEO WILL BE CHALLENGED WITH:
Emotional growth, relationship dynamics

LOVE

Passion without action? No, thank you! Serious Saturn plunges into Pisces on March 7, activating your eighth house of soulful sexuality and permanent bonding for three years. You want wholehearted commitment, but here's a curveball: Your relationship needs could spin in a totally new direction, thanks to Pluto's preview pass into Aquarius (March 23 to June 11), an evolution that will continue for 21 years. What's a lion to do? Slow down, appreciate the moment and put one bejeweled paw in front of the other. Love planet Venus *will* spend four rare months in Leo, from June 5 to October 8. During that time, you'll have more fawning admirers than perhaps you know what to do with. Brace yourself: Venus spins retrograde from July 22 to September 3. Unresolved issues could rear up and you might get tangled up with an ex. Confusion may not dissipate until after October 8, so go easy on yourself—and everyone around you.

CAREER & MONEY

You're on a growth trajectory in 2023! With expansive Jupiter in Aries parked in the ivory tower of your ninth house until May 16, you could train with a master or enroll in a degree program. On July 17, the fate-fueling North Node shifts into Aries for 18 months, further stoking your quest for knowledge. Think: Global expansion, from wooing remote clients to giving the digital nomad life a whirl. Make sure your passport is up to date! On May 16, worldly Jupiter ascends into Taurus for a year, elevating you to a prestigious new role in your career. But be careful not to take on too much debt in the process. With conservative Saturn in your investment zone for three years, pay down what you owe and park your funds in safer bets.

WELLNESS

Are you eating enough "good mood" foods, Leo? You may want to load up your diet with fatty fish, fermented products, dark chocolate, berries and raw almonds—all proven to shore up happiness. The karmic South Node in Scorpio turns your focus to nutrition until July 17. And with prickly Pluto weaving in and out of Capricorn and your digestion-focused sixth house all year, you have even more incentive to get the flora and microbiomes balanced in your gut. Focus further south, too. Structured Saturn moves into your eighth house, which rules reproductive organs. Depending on your age, you may need to change your birth control methods or get hormone levels tested. A healthy sex life does wonders for mood, too, and serious Saturn could bring someone who's more than ready to be a regular, er, "buddy workout" partner.

FRIENDS & FAMILY

Oh, the weight of obligation! Leos adore their pride, but with the heavy, karmic South Node stirring the pot in your fourth house of kin until July 17 (and since January 2021), family can feel like your least favorite f-word at times. With freebird Jupiter in your independent ninth house until May 16, you'll go crazy if you don't carve out space for yourself to travel and explore personal passions. That might mean kids, parents and relatives have to step up and support *you* for a change. Train them to fend for themselves (they *can* handle it) and stop saddling yourself with the role of entertainment director. When the South Node wings into Libra on July 17, you could connect to an incredible friend group—or one life-changing bestie!

JUPITER IN ARIES

Everything is elevated

Jupiter in Aries

December 20, 2022
to May 16, 2023

Get growing! Leos are poised for major expansion as horizon-broadening Jupiter careens through Aries and your ninth house of travel, higher learning and entrepreneurship until May 16. Cast a wide net and interface with people across the globe. As worldly Jupiter plays cruise director, cross-cultural connections catch fire. Your friends circle could become a lot more diverse in the first half of the year. Maybe you'll put down stakes in another zip code (or country code) or give the digital nomad life a whirl.

If you can't travel in the physical sense, take yourself on a journey of the mind. Before May 16, you could delve into a mesmerizing course of study or apply to grad school. Have you mastered a subject? Document your unique methodology so you can share it with the world. This could be your year to write a how-to guide, film an online course or share your knowledge through a live, monthly mastermind group.

Jupiter is the natural ruler of the ninth house, which means you're getting a double dose of its "elevate everything!" energy. Even more serendipitous? In Aries, Jupiter forms a flowing 120° trine to your Sun in Leo. This revitalizing transit releases a torrent of passion. Don't be surprised if you feel more glamorous and optimistic than you have in years!

You already got a taste of this in 2022, when adventurous Jupiter powered up Aries from May 10 to October 28. As the red-spotted planet takes its second of two laps through the Ram's realm, you will feel your good luck returning! But mighty Jupiter serves a potent brew, maximizing every detail, including the flaws! A supposedly golden opportunity that you've been pursuing may also come with a hidden clause. But here's the deal: Jupiter in your truth-telling ninth house will expose everything that's in need of repair. Your job, Leo, is to decide whether to walk away or take the time to fix them. Whatever you do, don't sweep issues under the rug! They'll only get "bigger, stronger and faster" under Jupiter's accelerating influence.

The saying "know thyself" should become your guiding mantra, as philosophical Jupiter in Aries sends you on a path of self-discovery. Explore beyond your comfort zone, Lion, and seek master teachers and spiritual guides who can lead you through this journey. Create time for personal growth and self-development, which is fertile terrain in 2023. Learn to express yourself authentically instead of chasing praise or a shiny gold star. As you muster the courage to speak your truth, your relationships grow more and more intimate.

And get moving! Jupiter in the ninth house supersizes your energy. You might start playing volleyball for the first time since 9th grade or take tennis lessons at a club. Leos may be ready for higher-intensity workouts while sporty Jupiter travels through Aries, your fellow fire sign. Competitive ones, too! You'll love being on the winning team—or grabbing that gold medal for an individual victory.

Your appetite could also increase in the first part of 2023, for everything from food to sex to luxury vacations. While we'd never suggest you deprive yourself, a little discipline can go a long way to keep you from overdoing it. Responsible indulgence is the ideal state. But you may need some friendly reminders to take "all things in moderation" when your excessive streak kicks in.

Got a clever concept for a startup? Shoot your shot, Leo! Entrepreneurial Jupiter in Aries could turn your side hustle into a thriving business before May 16. Don't paint yourself into a corner if you're still in the preliminary stages. Instead, devour all the knowledge you can. Attend conferences and industry events. Soak up the stories of entrepreneurs who did it their way instead of following the usual scripts. Thanks to Jupiter's global influence, you might even develop an international audience. Just the excuse you needed to book an epic trip!

JUPITER IN TAURUS
In the winner's circle

Jupiter in Taurus

May 16, 2023 to
May 25, 2024

Jupiter Retrograde

September 4 to
December 30, 2023

Success! After Jupiter's exciting trek through Aries, you're poised to make some power moves. And lucky for you, the planets got the memo. Your most auspicious professional period in over a decade could arrive May 16, when Jupiter begins its tour of Taurus and rises into your goal-driven tenth house until May 25, 2024.

No more walking around town in a messy bun and leggings. Power-dressing is *de riguer* during this yearlong Jupiter cycle—which only comes around every 12-13 years. Pull out the chic blazers and wide-legged trousers—or whatever your industry's "uniform" happens to be.

The tenth house is the sphere of ambition, authority and status. It's located at the very peak of the chart like a planetary penthouse—and with Jupiter in Taurus, you have an express elevator to the top. With a little effort, you'll find yourself in the winner's circle, surrounded by power players. With forthright Jupiter here, you may have a golden opportunity to pitch your big ideas, and a mentor or seasoned pro in your field could give you a leg up before the end of 2023.

Here's a paradox you'll need to reconcile between May 16, 2023 and May 25, 2024: Jupiter is a proponent of freedom, and the tenth house rules structure. So how can you combine these dueling desires? Get creative! For example, if you're employed at an established company, you might find a spot in their "new ventures" department or a position that involves travel or a flexible schedule. Jupiter's transit through your tenth house is perfect timing for "intrapraneurship"—being entrepreneurial within an existing company. Do you own a business? Become a regular at stimulating conferences and leadership summits, where you can build your network and polish your executive skills.

Of course, you might actually *want* to settle into the executive suites while Jupiter spends this 12-month circuit in the corporate sector (AKA the tenth house) of your solar chart. A too-good-to-pass-up offer may roll in, like a leadership post with an impressive title and benefits to match. With worldly Jupiter involved, relocation could come with the deal. You might receive public honors or long-overdue recognition if you're a veteran in your industry.

There is one hitch: While in Taurus, Jupiter forms a tense, 90-degree square to your Leo Sun. Growing pains and obstacles could be part and parcel of all your rapid expansion. It will be worth it to take your lumps, as long as you also take the lessons—and apply them well!

Although we don't like to genderize astrology, the tenth house is traditionally associated with fathers and men. For you, this might translate to the parent who had the most authority when you were growing up. Or it could represent role models who led by example without a lot of handholding. Your relationship with this type of person could evolve, maybe in challenging ways at times. If you've been trapped in an uneven parent-child dynamic that no longer suits, candid Jupiter can open up conversations about new ways to relate to each other as adults.

One thing's for sure: Your loftiest aspirations get a massive boost while Jupiter is in Taurus. You'll need to prioritize so you can achieve your sky-high aims—not an easy feat for your FOMO-fueled sign. But if you want to hit peak achievement levels, you simply cannot say "yes" to everything. This is a time to slate in what matters most to you. By not scattering your energy, you'll make unparalleled progress toward your goals. Stay zeroed in on your main objectives. Jupiter hasn't visited Taurus since January 2011, and you don't want to squander the opportunity it brings!

MARS IN GEMINI
Stronger together

Mars in Gemini

August 20, 2022 to
March 25, 2023

Mars Retrograde

October 30, 2022
to January 12, 2023

There's that pep in your step, Leo! In early 2023, you'll reclaim your role as Chief Motivating Officer of your crew. The proverbial pom-poms are back in your grasp starting January 12, 2023, when go-getter Mars wraps a frustrating, 10-week retrograde in Gemini and your collaborative eleventh house.

When the "Action Jackson" of the solar system hits snooze every other year, initiatives can stall. But these forced timeouts are crucial review periods. Are you effectively utilizing your resources (time, money, tech) or have you been leaking energy on going-nowhere people and projects? (Or maybe a mix of both?) Hopefully you've given that some serious thought since October 30, 2022.

Whatever the case, simply start looking forward again beginning January 12. As Mars shifts back into drive, team initiatives take off at a galloping pace. Better still? The red planet powers forward through Gemini until March 25, 2023, pumping you up with enthusiasm and *esprit de corps*. Typically, you like to keep an open door policy for your squad. Hey, you never know where people's hidden talents lie. But not in 2023! Crucial to your success this year is a new layer of discernment. If certain people have consistently let you down, stop inviting them to play. You need competent collaborators in 2023, not lazy benchwarmers who only show up for the glory. Start casting elsewhere for your dream team!

Or Leo, do you need to get honest about a few of your control issues? Perhaps you've been overfunctioning, not trusting others to pull their weight—and not giving them a chance to "fail faster." It may be your leadership style that could use an upgrade. What if you wrote up a training manual or SOP (Standard Operating Procedure) document that others could use to orient themselves along the way. Maybe you enlist a second-in-command to manage the troops? Letting go, even a little, could do wonders to open up hours on your schedule and even boost profits and productivity.

Before spinning retrograde on October 30, 2022, Mars moved into Gemini on August 20, 2022. What had you pumped up late summer into mid-fall of last year? That mission could pick up steam in Q1 of 2023. Reassemble your star-studded squad and bring any interested luminaries back into the fold. Re-pitch them on your idea, if necessary, making sure to deliver an airtight presentation. Get a firm commitment from anyone who wants a spot on Team Lion. Spell out requirements and don't sugarcoat them. The right people for your crew will embrace the challenge and rise to it!

Already part of a dreamy ensemble cast? Utilize the 2023 Martian power surge for goal setting. The eleventh house rules hopes and dreams. When daring Mars visits this zone of your chart every couple years, you're at your innovative best. Guide discussions: What if there were no box to think inside of at all? Start there, then whittle down with reality checks.

A note of caution here. Whether retrograde or direct, Mars can be rash, speeding past important details like, say, protecting your rights. If valuable ideas or intellectual property are involved, get people to sign nondisclosure agreements or detailed contacts. Loyalty and integrity may be YOUR stock in trade, but don't assume that others share your high-minded values. Plus, ambiguity has been known to breed contempt. Clear agreements are the secret to long-term success—especially if you're teaming up with friends.

Since the eleventh house is also your tech zone, this progressive Mars cycle helps you radar in on apps, devices and software that can take your work to the next level. Do you own a business? This may be the year that you develop a membership model where customers pay a monthly subscription fee to access certain content or services. Growing a virtual community takes time, but with red-hot Mars in this popularity-boosting zone, Q1 of 2023 is the perfect time to explore initiatives like these. Leo entertainers, the virtual stage is yours! With activating Mars in articulate, creative Gemini, you might become an overnight TikTok or YouTube sensation or an Instagram influencer.

Your activist humanitarian side may get a second wind once Mars turns direct on January 12. Use your innate gifts to mobilize people and spread the word about a cause that's close to your magnanimous heart. The early part of the year is also an ideal time to update your online presence, from your professional profile to your online dating photos and bio. Whatever 2023 Leo looks like, you're ready to be showcased and seen everywhere!

SATURN IN PISCES
Control and soul

Saturn in Pisces

March 7, 2023 to
February 13, 2026

Saturn Retrograde

June 17 to
November 4, 2023

Money, power, sex—and a whopping dose of alchemical magic! These substantial themes will percolate throughout 2023, as karmic Saturn travels through Pisces and your transformational eighth house. The ringed planet takes the helm on March 7 and lingers here until February 13, 2026, teaching a masterclass in the regenerative power of letting go and allowing things to be reborn.

Where will your first deep dive take place? The eighth house governs the life cycle from birth to death to reincarnation, as well as the realm of metaphysics. Your world could look remarkably different by the end of 2023, *if* you're willing to immerse yourself in the process and "do the work" (Saturn's favorite mantra). Heads up: You may have to let go of something precious that you've outgrown. Get clear about where you'd like to make seismic shifts. With methodical Saturn guiding the operative, you can dismantle outmoded frameworks bit by bit rather than smashing them with a wrecking ball. Aim for deconstruction rather than destruction. Your reward will be a lasting inside-out change that puts you on a more empowered path.

Early in the year, take an honest inventory of your relationships, both personal and professional. A once-flourishing partnership may now feel like a drain on your spirit. Whether you're leaking money or sapping your strength taking care of others, limits-loving Saturn demands that you set firm boundaries. Has your dreamy lover or dream client started treating you like their personal assistant? No more! A complete 180 may be necessary to rebalance these depleting dynamics.

The eighth house is one of the chart's financial zones, overseeing the "big money" funds that come in lump sums: tax returns, inheritance, royalties, grants. With the planet of adulting here, you'll be extra interested in long-term security. It's time to build (or begin building) a sound investment portfolio, boost contributions to your retirement accounts, or otherwise set yourself up for a wealthier life—as you define it. Teaming up with talented experts can result in mutual gain.

Have you checked your credit score lately, Leo? Debt can be paid off while savvy Saturn spins through this zone. Taking the first look is the hardest part, but trust us, you'll eventually be glad you did. Saturn's trip through the eighth house only occurs every 29.5 years, and it's a prime window for establishing financial freedom.

If you need to fill the coffers, look beyond the nine-to-five grind. Creative Leos might earn a larger one-time payment, like an advance on a book or a record deal. You might receive a signing bonus or a performance-based one if you put in the blood, sweat and tears. But don't devote all your time to working harder rather than smarter! Look for ways to earn passive income (on the up and up!), such as rental income, affiliate or direct sales. Maybe you'll create a downloadable product, like a class that you only have to record once but can sell for years to come. Between now and 2026, you could see a major surge in your net worth by funneling funds into a diverse portfolio of investments, like real estate or index funds that yield compounding interest.

Sharing resources and merging assets could augment your affluence during this Saturn circuit, especially with boundless Pisces ruling this chart sector. Be strategic about networking with industry movers and shakers. Spend time with friends who are money savvy. You'll soak up their prosperity prowess before you know it, Leo! Bear in mind, however, that slowpoke Saturn espouses a marathon over a sprint. You're not just switching up your behavior; you're transforming lifelong habits.

Now let's get to the sexy stuff: Since the eighth house is the domain of perma-bonding, one or two key relationships could be locked and loaded before the year is up. This is the district where "two become one," and due to Saturn's staying power, you could stumble upon that ultra-rare unicorn who is not only seductive AF but also comes equipped with a secure attachment style. While

66

One or two

key relationships

could be locked and loaded

before the year is up

99

loyal Lions play the long game in love, you sometimes take your time settling down. No-nonsense Saturn can provide the discernment you need to radar in on an appropriate life partner, someone who will stand by you through thick and thin.

Nevertheless, you may want to brace yourself: Even the most intoxicatingly erotic encounter can set off your alarm bells if you long for nightly spooning (and then some) but start to feel suffocated when people are in your personal space 24/7. Once again, setting limits is essential. Enduring the discomfort of such conversations is better than burning bridges with someone you love and then feeling the pangs of regret. Honor your desire for alone time *before* your bubble is "invaded." That way, you won't set up false expectations that freak you out to the point where you're scanning for the nearest exit.

Since the eighth house is about trust and intimacy, the slightest whiff of betrayal now can send you into a spiral. If you met your mate when they were already spoken for, you could get scared that they'll cheat on you or leave you. Prior infidelities (perhaps your own) must be reckoned with, but this doesn't have to turn into full-blown karmic justice. Plenty of couples endure scandals like lies or cheating and come out stronger on the other side, once they've both done the emotional heavy lifting. Breaches of trust don't have to mean "the end" if both parties are committed to working through the problem. These experiences can lead to greater character-strengthening and trust-building than you ever thought possible.

We're fans of modern-love expert Esther Perel's book *The State of Affairs,* in which she takes an unflinching look at why people stray. Her theory is that we're trying to reconnect with a lost part of ourselves through an infatuation. For a passionate soul like you, Leo, it's easy to forget where you begin and your lover ends. If you've lost touch with your sensuality or neglected your creative hobbies, reclaim "me time." Relationships flourish when you attend to your personal needs.

Your reproductive system should be given special attention now, regardless of #FertilityGoals. For instance, you might need to find different birth control that doesn't give you headaches or make you nauseous. For female Leos, strengthening your pelvic floor muscles with exercises like Kegels, squats and bridges can benefit you in a variety of ways, from better bladder control to more enjoyable sex through ages and stages. Hoping for a pregnancy in 2023? Saturn in the eighth house can delay fertility plans, but IVF treatments might be part of this year's forecast. With this in mind, you may choose to change some habits accordingly, perhaps saving up for out-of-pocket costs so you're ready when the time is right.

PLUTO IN AQUARIUS
Reconfiguring relationships

Pluto in Capricorn
Janury 1, 2023
to March 23, 2023

June 11, 2023 to
January 20, 2024

Pluto in Aquarius
March 23 to
June 11, 2023

Pluto Retrograde
May 1 to
October 10, 2023

𝒮

Relationship health check! How satisfying are your closest bonds? Big-hearted Leos should schedule a "state of the union" conversation in all your important partnerships between March 23 and June 11, 2023. The reason for this? Transformational Pluto is heading into Aquarius and your seventh house of commitments for the first time since (drumroll) 1798!

And that's not all. This is Pluto's first sign change since January 2008, where it's been slowly rolling through Capricorn and your sixth house of work and wellness for the past 15 years. A dwarf planet it may be, but Pluto's shifts are seismic. This year's transit is a taste of what's ahead. Next year, on November 19, 2024, Pluto officially calls Aquarius home for 19 years—until January 19, 2044—and sets the stage for Leos to have soulful, metamorphic shifts in the relationship realm.

As Pluto weaves back and forth between Capricorn and Aquarius for the next two years, you have a chance to assess your day-to-day habits and look at which ones are winners and which are counterproductive to your happiness and vitality. Since 2008, Leos have put some serious muscle in their hustle. More than most signs, however, you may be feeling on the verge of burnout—or perhaps, ready to make some sort of change to the *way* you do your work. With Pluto in Aquarius powering up your partnership sector, the next 21 years will serve one masterclass after another in the "sharing is caring" model.

Whatever throne you've held since 2008, we're betting you've felt the weight of responsibility. Heavy is the Leo head that wears the crown! Even undeniably privileged Leo Kylie Jenner poured her creative capital into work, transforming from gangly kid sister to the billionaire CEO of Kylie Cosmetics during this Pluto cycle.

The sixth house is the service sector and hard-driving Pluto in Capricorn made sure that every victory you celebrated (privately or publicly) was earned through the school of hard knocks. To wit, Leo Barack Obama was elected President a few weeks prior to Pluto's final move into Capricorn in November 2008 (although Pluto had already visited Capricorn from January 25 to June 14 that year). He spent the first half of this cycle in the Oval Office, through 2016. His victory as the first Black President was in and of itself a Plutonian event, shattering the notion of who could hold the greatest position of power in the United States. Since Capricorn is the sign that rules government and the economy, Obama's first mission was to bail out banks and clean up a mortgage crisis.

Your mission for the remainder of Pluto's time in Capricorn—which is all of 2023 except for March 23 to June 11—is to get your life in an orderly groove. What processes can you automate with smart devices and apps? If you've nailed your system for achieving certain tasks, get that information out of your head and into an orientation manual. Get down with SOPs. (Standard Operating Procedures, in case you're wondering...) Even if you only share your proprietary materials with one trusted soul, that's fine! Your growth during the forthcoming Pluto in Aquarius cycle is directly proportional to your willingness to transfer your knowledge to others.

Need a little more motivation to clean up your act? Running a tight ship is key to attracting the right partnerships—or creating the right conditions for current partnerships to flourish. We're talking budgeting, scheduling, eating clean and working out, not exactly a playful Leo's favorite activities lineup. And while you may need to sacrifice some pricey vacations, hedonistic Fridays and shopping sprees in the name of fiscal—and physical—fitness, you'll gain an appreciation for standing on solid ground before 2023 is through.

And guess what *will* make this punch list a lot more enjoyable? Partnership! And we mean in the most pragmatic, mundane areas of life. Do you struggle to get to the gym? Find a trainer, perhaps one who instructs small groups, and turn those workouts into a social event. Skipping a few (boozy) brunches can open up flow to invest in a support staff of your own. Hire a space organizer if you struggle with clutter; a bookkeeper to do your monthly reconciling. Tight on cash? Use your stellar organizing powers to get a group together for sharing and/or bartering everything from grocery shopping to childcare.

Leos who have been developing a methodology over the past decade-plus may be ready to bring in financial backers. But take your time with this process! There are many roads to funding a business from loans to angel investors to an M&A. The question is, how will you fare when you're not the boss—or others are involved in your final say? That's something to seriously consider as wealth-agent Pluto shifts gears!

Just because Pluto is moving into Aquarius doesn't mean you have to turn *every* soloventure into a joint affair. In fact, the first few years of Pluto in Aquarius could be incredibly bumpy as you road-test prospective partners. This is the planet that rules our unconscious projections, secrets, hidden traumas and the places where we feel "captive" to another's domination. The whole idea of pairing up could feel like a no-go initially—or an epic power struggle. Through this, you may discover that you need something *very* different from a partner in the years ahead.

LEO

Although your urge to merge will intensify over the next two decades, if you aren't with the "right" person, you'll want to bolt in the opposite direction. While Pluto's in Aquarius, you simply can't deny hidden feelings and buried truths. But warning! Pluto is the projector planet, which makes it too easy to point your finger and blame others for your unhappiness. Before you make any regrettable, permanent decisions, we recommend doing some serious soul-searching. If you then decide it's time to part ways, at least you can do so without dragging a ton of hurt, anger and baggage into your next bond.

We're not going to sugarcoat this: Even the most happily married Leos out there may weather a test of spirit while Pluto enters Aquarius. If it doesn't happen between March 23 and June 11, you may at least have a bit of foreshadowing. We recommend shifting your expectations, like *now*. Rather than looking for a conflict-free relationship, let Pluto in Aquarius draw you deeper into the places where you don't see eye to eye. There's rich terrain to explore here, Leo, but it may feel "threatening" to go there at first. Pluto in Aquarius reveals layers of desire that *you* didn't even realize were there. Unnerving? Yes, but also hot!

Pluto rules our long-term wealth and, while in Aquarius, joining assets can become a big deal. If you break up a relationship, the legalities could get super complicated! Bear that in mind if you're *entering* something new. It may feel romantic to, say, buy property together and merge all your possessions, but if there were ever a time when a Leo needed a contract and a pre-nup, these twenty years (2023-2044) would be it.

With great power comes great responsibility. And with crystal clarity comes a rock-solid union. There's so much potential awaiting in Pluto's vault! Yes, there are also trials by fire. Work your way through them and you may soon team up as a dynamic duo, supporting one another's dreams and building a legacy!

VENUS RETROGRADE
In the looking glass

Venus in Leo

June 5 to
October 8, 2023

Venus Retrograde

July 22 to
September 3, 2023

If you can't help but emit a vocal "rawr" every time you catch your reflection or snap a selfie, well, who could blame you? Beauty goddess Venus struts through your sign for four whole *months* in 2023—from June 5 to October 8. Yes, that's four times as long as her usual visit to a sign and 30 percent of the entire year. You're already the charming and vibrant center of attention. But with your first house of identity lit, your powers of attraction will be even *more* powerful during this magnetic cycle. You're on fire, oh royal one!

All that adulation comes with a catch. (Sorry!) On July 22, Venus slips into retrograde and backs up through Leo until September 3. During this six-week timeout, you won't just re-examine your relationship with your adoring fanbase, but also with yourself. Are you living your most authentic life or spewing platitudes to keep the peace? Are the rose-colored lenses of a relationship slowly slipping off? A little self-reflection will help you find clarity about why you're in these situations in the first place. Just be careful not to lean too far in either direction during these six weeks. Going to extremes to ice people out or warm them up with overbearing love isn't going to solve anything.

While Venus spreads loved-up warm fuzzies all over Leo, consider this entire four-month transit a time to extend that same feel-good energy to yourself. Leos can fall into the trap of needing constant validation and praise to feel

ℒ

valued, but here's your 2023 challenge: Can you generate self-love *without* an external source? It's easy to lose your identity (or build a new one) inside a relationship—but that's when things get problematic for your sign. The reflective retrograde may be just the thing you need to figure out who you are outside of the crowd. And yeah, it's like the RuPaul adage goes, "If you can't love yourself, how the hell are you gonna love somebody else?"

66

In 2023, new

relationship energy

can become intoxicating

99

If you're single, don't be afraid to swipe out of Tinder entirely and focus on personal goals between July 22 and September 3. This will lay the groundwork for a more fulfilling relationship when you're ready to open up again—or improve the one that you're already in. Venus may reignite your creative spark for passion projects and cup-filling hobbies like art and music. Just don't get *so* busy working on that large-scale oil painting that you miss the flirtatious clues a certain someone is dropping.

Not only will you be excavating your innermost self during Venus retrograde, you'll also be a curious cat primed to dive below the surface with new love interests and friends alike. But keep clear boundaries in place. New relationship energy can be intoxicating, and if you're already spoken for, it's probably best that you don't stay up all night (every night) talking to a cute coworker who has decided to bare their soul. An emotional affair is still an affair!

Because you're spending all this time in the astrological looking glass, you'll naturally start to ponder a style update. All good while Venus is in direct motion from June 5 to July 22 and again after September 3. But during the retrograde? Press pause on that thought, Fierce One! Venus is the planetary beauty queen, but while in reverse, regrettable decisions are often made. You could wind up with four more inches of hair than expected on the floor of the salon—or a tattoo that you have to cover up later. Put your ideas on a mood board and wait it out! Same goes for any cosmetic treatments that can't be easily reversed.

Here's something special: Every eight years, Venus revisits one of the same five zodiac signs during a retrograde, which, if you connected the dots on the zodiac wheel, would form a perfect star! (Yes, even while retrograde, Venus is still making things pretty.) "Lucky" you, Leo, you are one of the signs that gets to host backspinning Venus once per decade.

The last time Venus reversed through your sign was from July 25 to September 6, 2015, so you might flip back in your timeline to see what was happening for you then. Keep an eye out for recurring themes and feelings this year, like old passions coming back to life or people from your past making a comeback in an unexpected and inspiring new way.

NORTH NODE IN ARIES
Wanderlust strikes

Lunar North Node in Aries

July 17, 2023
to January 11, 2025

Leo a go-go! As one of the zodiac's three intrepid fire signs, faraway lands are always whispering your name. Get your passport up to date. When the lunar North Node points its compass into your ninth house of global expansion this July 17, the call of wanderlust could become too loud to ignore! Across the zodiac wheel, the karmic South Node lands in Libra, heating up action on the local scene. No matter where you find yourself during this 18-month cycle, fun and adventure will follow!

The lunar nodes are not actually planets, but special points in the sky that are associated with eclipses. Every 18-20 years they position themselves in a specific, opposite-sign pairing that directs your fate for a year and a half.

From January 18, 2022 to July 17, 2023, the North Node is in Taurus and your career-driven tenth house while the South Node is activating your home and family zone. Work-life balance? That's the equation you'll be tooling with in the first half of the year.

Expect to feel a whole lot freer as the nodes shift to Aries and Libra on July 17, 2023. If you've felt like a corporate servant and caretaker, that all changes *now*. During this cycle, which lasts until January 11, 2025, anywhere *but* "the usual places" are where you'll find the most enriching opportunities for growth. Begin dreaming early in the year by making a list of all the locales you'd love to visit. (A great way to "multitask" during that protracted, all-hands meeting on Zoom.) Are there historical sites you'd love to see? Special training you'd like to be certified in—at an overseas university or an eco-chic retreat center? Pin away! When you're ready to book, don't fill every second of the journey with a packed itinerary. Wandering off the beaten path could bring the most game-changing moments of all. One minute you're "out on a walk," the next you're slipping into an after-hours tango club or meditating with locals at

> 66
>
> *Horizons will expand,*
>
> *even if you never*
>
> *step foot out of*
>
> *your time zone*
>
> 99

a full moon ceremony on the beach. By the same token, don't leave it *all* up to chance. Research the area before arrival and you'll have a far smoother integration period—especially if you book those coveted show tickets or get an appointment with the area's raved-about healers, readers or bodyworkers.

What we can say with certainty is that from July 17, 2023 until January 11, 2025, your horizons will expand, even if you never set foot out of your time zone. You can widen your viewfinder with online classes and spiritual pursuits. When you can articulate your soul's mission statement, reach out to like-minded folks and see who might be leading a virtual training or mastermind.

Leos in the market for a move might suddenly consider a totally different zip code—or country code—after July 17. Work may require you to travel, perhaps back and forth between two cities. If you're geographically locked down, you may begin to work remotely with people in another part of the world.

Speaking of work, you may become a lot more entrepreneurial in the second half of the year. Keep paying your dues and making those VIP connections while the North Node treks through Taurus until July 17. A leadership role has your name written all over it and you'll want to pounce on that opening should it arise. But the point of this exercise is *not* to saddle yourself with a zillion new tasks. Rather, make it your mission to become the doyenne of delegation. When the North Node shifts gears into free-spirited Aries, the more playtime you have in your calendar the better.

But "playtime" might look like developing your own entrepreneurial venture, even if it begins as a side hustle to your 9-to-5. With the Aries North Node whetting your entrepreneurial appetite (not to mention your independent streak), you could develop a profitable venture that lets you set your own hours and work from anywhere. Maybe you'll parlay your savvy social media prowess into a digital marketing company with a roster of mid-sized business clients. Consulting work could pay you handsomely. If you've been itching to escape the grind, now's your opportunity—perhaps on a multi-city tour as a digital nomad.

Simultaneously, the equally influential South Node is doing a balancing act in Libra and your communication and local activity HQ. Any sort of writing, media-making or teaching is favored under this nodal cycle. Got a vision for a workshop you'd like to create? (Trauma-informed dance therapy or creative visualization 101...) Has a YA novel series been rattling around in your head? This could feel like a legit calling after July 17. Start that manuscript!

Most Leos love to be involved in community affairs, but you could go next-level with it after July 17. (Not you, Leo, organizing an after-school tutoring program, spearheading the block party, running for city council and convincing your favorite pub to host a weekly karaoke night? ...With you as MC, naturally.) To call you a "fixture on the neighborhood scene" might be an understatement in the second half of 2023. With culture-vulture Libra guiding your moves, you could turn your area into a thriving hotspot for the arts!

But hang on there, Leo. You're not one to ride the brake, much less step on it, ever. Yet, the Libra South Node could deliver some harsh lessons about the dangers of spreading yourself too thin. The road to hell is paved with good intentions. If certain initiatives aren't met with community support, the answer is NOT *you* picking up the slack...or taking on all the work. Burning yourself out to produce a talent show at your kid's elementary school, say, could leave you too exhausted to enjoy the holidays with family. (Not worth it!)

The third house rules cooperation and communication. Let any "failing" initiatives be a sign that you need to bring in more support—*not* don your superhero's cape to get this thing to the finish line come hell or high water. In fact, partnerships could be quite profitable with the Libra South Node in this position. Stop suffering as a solo act and turn your missions into a tag team effort. The third house rules peers, like siblings and close friends, as well as neighbors and coworkers. Cast in these categories and you could have a dynamic duo on your hands before you know it. Just make sure you've outlined the criteria in advance. When people know what's expected of them, they can have an easier time rising to the occasion.

Even if a verbal agreement would suffice, don't leave the future up to chance. Pinky promises made between besties turn into televised cases on *Judge Judy*, like, daily. (And those aren't the IMDB credentials any Leo needs.) Awkward as it may be to draft a formal agreement with, say, your sister, if you design this together, it will feel like an insurance policy for your relationship instead of a dominating power play.

ECLIPSES IN 2023
Passion: unbound

Hybrid Solar Eclipse in
Aries (new moon)

April 20 at 12:17AM

Penumbral Lunar Eclipse
in Scorpio (full moon)

May 5 at 1:24PM

Annular Solar Eclipse
in Libra (new moon)

October 14 at 2:00PM

Partial Lunar Eclipse
in Taurus (full moon)

October 28 at 4:15PM

times in eastern time

APRIL 20:
SOLAR ECLIPSE IN ARIES
HYBRID SOLAR ECLIPSE 29°52,
12:17AM ET

Your passion will be uncontainable
during this energizing solar (new
moon) eclipse in Aries—the first to
activate your ninth house of expansion
and wanderlust since 2015! What's
next for you, Leo? Take copious notes!
All kinds of ideas stream in under
this ultra-rare hybrid solar eclipse,
which begins as an annular "ring of
fire" eclipse and transforms into a
total eclipse for part of its path. The
only "rule"? Look in a new direction!
Whether that means exploring
different philosophies or pondering
travel to an unexplored part of the globe, this new, two-year eclipse series
awakens you to a brand new set of possibilities. Self-employed Leos could
hit the jackpot when a passion project or entrepreneurial venture reaches
a milestone moment by March 2025. Stay with it: You're still building
momentum, and embracing the learning curve is what will create the
miraculous outcome.

MAY 5: LUNAR ECLIPSE IN SCORPIO
PENUMBRAL LUNAR ECLIPSE, 14°52, 1:24PM

Feelings, nothing more than feelings? Ha! The May 5 lunar (full moon) eclipse in Scorpio will crank up the volume on your emotions. You're an empath, psychic sponge, and in moments, a little bit of a basket case (sigh). Give yourself lots of room for processing, with one caveat: Don't allow yourself to take out your feelings on other people. Blaming, raging, and guilt-tripping are officially off limits, Leo! This eclipse could bring a family or domestic situation to a pivotal point, too. A relative may require extra support over the coming two weeks. If you're in the market for a new address, the eclipse could reveal an incredible real estate opportunity for you. Book those movers!

OCTOBER 14: SOLAR ECLIPSE IN LIBRA
ANNULAR SOLAR ECLIPSE 21°10, 2:00PM ET

Friends, foes, or frenemies? There will be no denying what category a certain someone belongs in before this day is through. With an earth-shaking annular "ring of fire" solar eclipse in Libra—the first eclipse to land in this sign since 2016—in your house of amigos, some hidden information about one of your allies could come to light. On a positive note, you might discover that this person has been going to bat for you behind the scenes—we certainly hope this is the case, Leo. But don't turn a blind eye to any unsavory clues you've been picking up on. If there's a snake in sister's clothing lurking, she will be outed, soon.

OCTOBER 28: LUNAR ECLIPSE IN TAURUS
PARTIAL LUNAR ECLIPSE 5°03, 4:15PM ET

Take a well-deserved bow, Leo! As the third and final Taurus lunar eclipse in a two-year series activates your career zone, you may have a professional milestone to celebrate. What have you achieved since November 2021? Even if you haven't hit all your benchmarks yet, this is an important day to appreciate your progress—and acknowledge everyone who's helped you rise to the top. For some Leos, this eclipse will bring a long-awaited epiphany about your next professional move. First move: Dress for the part you want to play, even if you're not fully there yet. If funds are available, make an investment in your future, like a specialized training or crucial equipment for the job.

MORE BOOKS
BY THE ASTROTWINS

HOW TO GET ALONG WITH ANYONE (*YES, EVEN THAT PERSON)

Any two zodiac signs CAN be compatible, as long as they understand what makes the other one tick. The AstroTwins simplify the secrets of synastry—the 7 unique energies encoded in the distance between your signs. Take your relationships from difficult to dynamic and start bringing out your best.

SUPERCOUPLE

Unlock the astrology secrets to sizzling attraction and deep connection, and get through the hard stuff fast! Did you know that your relationship has a zodiac sign and chart? The Supercouple system is the ultimate guide to finding true compatibility—by understanding why you came together and what your divine destiny could be!

MOMSTROLOGY

Parenting DOES come with instructions! This ultimate guide to raising your kids AND flourishing as a mom takes you through every season of parenthood, from birth to toddler to school years and leaving the nest. A favorite baby shower gift, featured by *Good Morning America* and a #1 Amazon bestseller.

START READING NOW AT **ASTROSTYLE.COM/BOOKS**

2023

—

VIRGO

WHAT'S IN THE STARS FOR

VIRGO

How close is too close for comfort, Virgo? In 2023, you need ample personal space AND tight, soulmate-level bonds. There are only so many hours in a day, and you want to spend yours on people and pursuits that enrich and transform you. View everything as an investment in 2023. Will you get a good "return" on the time, money or energy you put in? Focus on quality over quantity whether in relationships, work or life experiences. While your introverted side will crave privacy, a sexy plus-one could shimmy behind those velvet Virgoan ropes to join you. Maybe you'll jet off to a far-flung locale together, as travel is a big 2023 theme. Vacation with friends or hit a wellness retreat and start racking up those frequent flier miles. Virgo is the sign of health, and paying attention to the mind-body-soul connection in 2023 will bring you vibrant, balanced wellbeing. That backache might be a sign that you need to stretch after workouts—but it could also be a sign that you need more emotional support. Read between the lines!

VIRGO WILL BE LUCKY WITH:
Money, sex, travel

VIRGO WILL BE CHALLENGED WITH:
Commitments, staying healthy

LOVE

A sex-positive year is on deck for Virgos, which will be more of a "private screening" than a public display. Expand your erotic borders while bawdy Jupiter slinks through Aries and your scintillating eighth house until May 16. Since you need both lust *and* trust, exploration may happen within a relationship—or in flexible agreements with clear-set boundaries. Good thing, candid Jupiter makes it easy to talk about everything from protection to fantasies to consent this year. Simultaneously, serious Saturn moves into Pisces and your partnership zone on March 7. Relationship matters become weightier during this three-year cycle, a trend that continues once the lunar North Node heads into Aries from July 17 to January 11, 2025. Before 2023 is through, you may take on a big responsibility with a partner, like a mortgage, marriage or a lifestyle change that impacts you both.

CAREER & MONEY

Is it a wise investment or a risky bet? Play it safe while Jupiter, the galactic gambler, rolls the dice in your big money zone (the eighth house) until May 16. Yes, "buying low" is a sound strategy in a bear market, but keep a diversified portfolio. If you're going to purchase NFTs or a fixer-upper property, mix it up with mutual funds or other safer assets. With Pluto heading into Aquarius for a brief preview lap from March 23 to June 11, your job interests evolve in a new direction. This powerful cycle lasts for 21 years, so no rush! But start exploring a new field. Or deepen knowledge in your chosen industry. You could slowly move into a management or leadership role. But stay on your grind! When the South Node settles into Libra from July 17 until January 11, 2025, you may have to hustle to pay the bills.

WELLNESS

Take care "down there," Virgo. Reproductive and sexual health are front and center for you in 2023 as Jupiter and the North Node pass through Aries and your eighth house. Schedule that gynecology or urology exam, get a mammogram or colon screening if you're due. Virgos in the babymaking conversation may get some swift support from abundant Jupiter before May 16—which might even signal the birth of multiples or the start of successful IVF treatments. Venus will be in Leo and your twelfth house of elimination and detoxification from June 5 to October 8. For a summer glow-up, you might try a food-based cleanse, colon hydrotherapy or, of course, chugging H2O with electrolytes. If you're ready to kick a bad habit like smoking or sugar addiction, get support from Venus from June 5 to October 8.

FRIENDS & FAMILY

Who are your truest, best-est friends, Virgo? Since the South Node moved into Scorpio on January 18, 2022, your inner circle has grown tighter. Until this cycle rounds out on July 17, let people in slowly and make sure they earn your trust. (Especially near the May 5 lunar eclipse!) You'll be ready to branch out again once Jupiter swings into Taurus on May 16, activating your worldly, exploratory ninth house for a year. Take a vacation with your BFFs—or travel with a group and make some new global connections. Close to home, joining a sports league or book club could be a great way to bond and make friends in your area.

JUPITER IN ARIES
Clear commitments

Jupiter in Aries

December 20, 2022
to May 16, 2023

Let the bonding begin! And for the record, we mean deep, soulful bonding, Virgo. Expansive Jupiter sails through Aries and your intimate eighth house during the first five and a half months of 2023. This circuit, which you experienced last year (from May 10 to October 28), shines a spotlight on the inner workings of your closest commitments.

For much of last year, Jupiter traveled through Pisces and your relationship zone, giving you free rein to branch out. A business partnership may have taken off like a rocket—or it might have fizzled out due to Jupiter's blithe optimism. Enthusiasm doesn't always spell staying power where the red-spotted planet is concerned. With 2022's emphasis on pairing off, some Virgos committed to one special person. Others might have outgrown a connection and moved on. Stale relationships encountered growing pains, compelling you to evolve as an individual. Virgos in long-term relationships may have rediscovered a shared passion and taken on an endeavor together.

As Jupiter bounds back into Aries from December 20, 2022 until May 16, 2023, the focus turns back toward lasting (binding) commitments, like marriage and joint business ventures. The eighth house is the province where "two become one" in an official way. These mergers can be equal parts titillating and terrifying for you! Virgos who like to be in control of every aspect of their lives and this level of involvement will require an adjustment. Once you're beholden to, say, a spouse, a bank loan or a financial backer, you're no longer doing things on your terms alone. You'll need to embrace the conundrum of exploring freely within the confines of a binding commitment. So pace yourself!

Sex falls under the eighth house's jurisdiction. Exploratory Jupiter in this zone can take erotic adventures to a whole new place. You'll be drawn to modalities like Tantra and other techniques that add a spiritual dimension to carnal delights. Instead of hitting the sheets in the heat of passion, how about setting the scene? Delayed gratification can be a spicy pleasure-extender. Jupiter in "anything goes" Aries will inspire YOU to experiment with positions—and while it circuits through your high-intensity eighth house, it can be sexy to explore power dynamics with BDSM or other role-playing.

But be warned that in Aries and the eighth house, Jupiter can amplify any jealous tendencies. You may feel like you can never get quite enough of your boo's undivided attention, but is that really the case? Feels will intensify in the first half of 2023, and it's important that you run them against empirical data.

If you're in a relationship, forging a powerful bond without losing your identity is your #LoveGoal. Perhaps you'll take a major step like buying a place together, putting a ring on it or starting a joint business. While optimistic Jupiter in Aries is cheering, "You've got this!" its tour through your guarded eighth house is bearing down on every one of your trust issues. Be super selective about who you invite in. The word "casual" simply won't be in your vocabulary until May 16.

Even in platonic relationships, you may find yourselves patrolling the borders of your social circles and closing ranks. Rather than maintaining a million acquaintances, you'd rather keep company with a handful of true friends who you trust with your deepest secrets. Business-wise, you could connect with some influential VIPs. Socialize strategically in the first half of 2023. The membership fee of an exclusive industry group could pay dividends, hooking you up with clients, an agent or other way-showers who guide you to revenue sources you couldn't nab so quickly on your own.

If you harness the laser-focused energy of this cycle, you'll end it richer in so many ways. And yes, we mean that literally! The eighth house rules outside financing such as royalties, commissions, tax refunds, inheritance, and other money that doesn't qualify as earned income. Better yet: Abundant Jupiter here wants to shower you with cash.

> 66
>
> *Forging a*
> *powerful bond without*
> *losing your identtiy*
> *is your #LoveGoal*
>
> 99

But be warned! Jupiter is also the planetary gambler. The crypto bros could lure you down a garden path. And even if digital currencies and NFTs *are* the way of the future, high-risk investments should be handled with kid gloves this year.

If you're seeking investment capital, advance with caution. Hire an attorney to negotiate contracts or protect your intellectual property. Improve your insurance coverage if you're a property owner. This is the year to secure specialists. We don't need to tell a Virgo that the details matter!

JUPITER IN TAURUS
Emerging from the cave

Jupiter in Taurus

May 16, 2023 to
May 25, 2024

Jupiter Retrograde

September 4 to
December 30, 2023

Ready to burst out of that confining cocoon and fly free? Circle May 16 on your calendar, Virgo. After Jupiter's intense deep dive in Aries, the bountiful planet sails into Taurus, taking aim at your ninth house of travel, expansion and global adventure until May 25, 2024. You've rested your wings for the first part of 2023. Now, you're like a butterfly coming out of the chrysalis. Ditch the tunnel vision and flip to a wide-angle lens. With Jupiter sailing through your global ninth house for the first time since 2011-2012, you have a whole year to study, travel and take some bold risks, all in the name of personal growth.

When Jupiter segues from Aries into Taurus, it's like emerging from a dark cave into a bright room. Let your eyes adjust, then look around! You'll see intriguing faces from all walks of life; people who are ready to share brand-new perspectives and worldviews. This shift can be overwhelming at first, but resist the urge to scurry back into hiding. The Virgo explorer is back at the wheel until May 25, 2024—and beyond!

Jupiter is the natural ruler of the expansive and optimistic ninth house, bringing a double shot of good fortune while in Taurus. Suddenly, anything and everything feels possible...and it really is! Life may literally imitate the refrigerator-magnet quote, "If you can dream it, you can do it." Corny or not, you might as well make that your mantra. With your lofty visions *this* elevated, the power of positive thinking is truly in effect.

VIRGO

Even more fortuitous? While in Taurus, Jupiter forms a flowing 120° trine to your Sun in Virgo. This energy-boosting transit unleashes a torrential downpour of passion. Virgos can expect to feel more playful and outgoing than you have in ages!

Allies arrive in all packages starting May 16, so get ready to receive them with open arms. You might learn a foreign language or become involved in a diversity, equity and inclusion initiative in your state or your company. Spread your inspiring message far using your Virgo gifts of mediamaking and teaching, which also happen to be two of Jupiter's specialties. A win-win!

Now for the most exhilarating prescription. Go big with your travel plans in the second half of 2023. What would an epic getaway look like for you? Let yourself dream, Virgo: Get your advanced open water certification and go on a dive trip in the Maldives. Hike the Scottish Highlands, or go on a photo safari (and textile sourcing mission!) through the colorful streets of Marrakesh.

Travel can happen in the figurative sense, too. If you're ready to embark on a new chapter in your career, this is an optimal time to apply to grad school or enroll in a class on a subject that has always fascinated you—especially if it's taught in a retreat setting overseas.

Are you an entrepreneur? Jupiter in Taurus brings a big boost in that department. Secure investors for your start-up or get the beta version going by yourself. Did Jupiter in Aries bring a big payout? Invest some of those profits toward your own venture. Since the ninth house rules media, that might mean writing a book or launching a new content platform. All that wisdom you've gathered over the years is ready to go *somewhere* outside of your inner thoughts (and journal pages). Pick your platform, Virgo, and share your visionary ideas with the world!

MARS IN GEMINI
Your network is your net worth

Mars in Gemini

August 20, 2022 to
March 25, 2023

Mars Retrograde

October 30, 2022
to January 12, 2023

Ready to knock those 2023 resolutions straight outta the park? Step up to the plate, Virgo, and aim for the major leagues! Go-getter Mars is on a seven-month tour through Gemini, firing up your tenth house of career ambitions from August 20, 2022 to March 25, 2023. This is truly a lucky break for you since, normally, the red planet only hovers in a single sign for about seven weeks.

The only hiccup? Mars turned retrograde on October 30, 2022, which may have stalled your fast-moving plans. Initiatives you hoped to push through before the EOY may have hit supply chain and shipping snags or maybe a key decision-maker went offline for the holidays without giving you the green light.

Whatever the case, don't let any seasonal slowdowns discourage you, Virgo. On January 12, Mars corrects course and blasts ahead through Gemini, reheating your goal-getting tenth house until March 25.

First mission of 2023: Refresh your loftiest intentions and get back in touch with promising alliances who may have drifted away in late 2022. Then, buckle up, buttercup. Life's about to move at a *much* faster pace.

While you might not want a permanent pass into the world of "hustle culture," Mars only visits Gemini every two years. Stay on your grind for

Q1 and you'll set yourself up for long-term gains. And while that might spin up some anxiety, know this: With the fierce provocateur planet spurring you on, you're ready to field any challenge that comes flying your way.

What *can* trip you up in early 2023? Modesty. Mars brings nonstop swagger, and Gemini is a notorious smack-talker: two things that make a Virgo break out in hives. But if you don't want to get passed over in early 2023, toot your horn a little (or a lot!) louder.

This ain't about ego, Virgo. And we're not suggesting you fake it 'til you make it. (As if!) It's about making it easy for the world to understand your (obviously merit-based) capabilities. Put them in a presentation deck and seed them across social media. Work with a branding expert who can help you polish any rough edges. As creative synergies emerge, *you* can be the one to boldly spin them into profitable business deals.

Thinking of opening a business in 2023 or perhaps expanding the one you own? You're in luck! Mars provides a solid tailwind for Virgo-powered ventures. In partnership-oriented Gemini, you might team up with a collaborator or expand into a second location. This is a bright time for producing mobile products like apps or anything that can be scaled easily, such as a subscription-based offering. Let your inner mogul out to play!

SATURN IN PISCES

Commitment is in the cards

Saturn in Pisces

March 7, 2023 to
February 13, 2026

Saturn Retrograde

June 17 to
November 4, 2023

What does a "mature relationship" look like, really? While the answer can take many forms, get ready for some eye-opening developments in early 2023. On March 7, responsible Saturn drops anchor in Pisces and your seventh house of partnerships for the first time in 29.5 years. As the ringed planet reigns here until February 13, 2026, all of your important ties, from romantic bonds to close friendships, could go through an important evolution. Are they built to last? With Saturn's stress tests, you'll discover which connections are strong enough to endure and which should be relocated to the "memories" folder.

You can start by examining the integrity of your closest connections. Are they based on mutual give-and-take? Maybe you've gotten so caught up in supporting your S.O.'s aspirations that you've lost sight of your own, and your stifled ambition has led to anger and depression. On the other hand, your own ambitions may have dominated the relationship in recent years, leaving your boo feeling like an underappreciated fan. You can't ignore an imbalance when Saturn visits your seventh house. Time to course correct!

Lucky for you, Virgo, with accountable Saturn in your opposite sign of Pisces, you have a clear view across the way of how you "do relationships." Between March 7, 2023 and February 13, 2026, every Virgo will see key relationships put through their paces while the taskmaster planet is parked precisely opposite your Sun. Since the Sun provides vital life-force energy, this opposition will try your patience and also sap your strength until you simply can't suffer fools (a blessing in disguise!). Who has earned an engraved invitation to your inner circle and who needs to be demoted to the D-list? You may have to shuffle the deck soon.

For the same reason, playing the blame game is a no-go on Saturn's watch. This transit forces you to look in the mirror and hold yourself accountable for actions that you might have projected onto others in the past. Consider the role you habitually play because it's familiar and comfortable. If you're the "fixer" who swoops in and solves everyone's problems, what are the chances that they'll miraculously begin acting like team players and pull their own weight? (Hint: not high.) If you want equality, you need to teach people how to treat you from the start—or make it clear that there's a new, non-enabling Virgo in town! Then follow up by establishing firm boundaries (one of Saturn's favorite things).

Saturn is the planet of status, so during this three-year circuit, Virgos could become half of a legit power duo. Does that mean you should spend every waking minute in the couple bubble? Nope. With boundary-hound Saturn putting you through paces, the best relationships are ones that draw a line between "mine" and "ours." Half of you is ready to pair up, and the other half is serious about preserving your autonomy. Separate checks, separate rooms, separate offices. Virgo, the sign of deconstructing and dissecting, can easily grasp this concept, which might be the recipe for longevity in your VIP unions.

Unattached Virgos could take time off from the dating game or an exhausting friendship to evaluate the ROI. Or you might sever ties with a business partner who's not holding up their end of the bargain. You could also decide to make a blossoming relationship official by jumping the broom or entering into a formal professional collaboration.

VIRGO

With border-defining Saturn in your relationship zone, couples might be kept away from each other through physical distance. Even if you're committed, unavoidable duties could separate you geographically. It may be true that absence makes the heart grow fonder, but too much space may cause you to grow apart from a loved one. Lean into Saturn's love of structure and put a schedule in place that supports your relationship. For example, you each fly to the other's home base once a month and FaceTime nightly at a set time.

The clock could wind down during timelord Saturn's tenure if a long-term connection has been running out of gas. But because this is the planet of karma, you need to ask yourself if the two of you have fulfilled your purpose as a pair. Don't give up without one last push, unless you're absolutely sure it's over. Regular sessions with a couple's therapist (at least six months) may help repair the cracks in the foundation. If you split up or get a divorce, do your utmost to keep everything civil and mature.

As Saturn powers through Virgo, work relationships call for the same level of integrity. The key is to start investing in business affiliations that will go the distance. Chasing clients who string you along or partnering with people who don't do their fair share? Not in 2023! Give that draining trend a rest and start working with people who pass Saturn's discerning tests.

While you're evicting the lightweights, begin teaming up with heavy hitters who can take your ideas to the big leagues. Creative Virgos might sign with a pro who negotiates your contracts and helps you gain traction with the public. Experienced Virgos could work with agents and reps who will sell your work for a higher price than you could command by yourself. Maybe you'll get *your* license and represent undiscovered talent. Who knows!

PLUTO IN AQUARIUS
Evolving organically

Pluto in Capricorn
Janury 1, 2023
to March 23, 2023

June 11, 2023 to
January 20, 2024

Pluto in Aquarius
March 23 to
June 11, 2023

Pluto Retrograde
May 1 to
October 10, 2023

Step off the red carpet, Virgo, and onto... lush, green grass? You reclaim your earth sign "field cred" beginning March 23, 2023, as transformational Pluto spins into Aquarius and your sixth house of natural wonders until June 11. Your health-conscious, mindful sign is always looking for ways to live in tune with Mother Gaia. That calling will lead you through a 20-year personal evolution, starting in March. Wellness warrior? Trauma-informed bodyworker? Biodynamic farmer? A new role could soon materialize, even as a tiny seed of possibility.

The sixth house is the "administrative department" of the zodiac wheel. It directs our daily rituals: self-care, wellness and work routines. It's also the "service sector" of the zodiac wheel, the place where you are called to help others and where you will enlist people as support staff when you need a hand. This is a comfortable zone for you! The sixth house shares similar qualities to Virgo, the sixth sign of the zodiac. So when any planet orbits through progressive, humanitarian Aquarius—the ruler of your solar sixth house—you feel very much in your generous, industrious element.

That said, 2023's two-month Pluto-in-Aquarius cycle probably won't be a walk in the park. Pluto guides our "shadow work," the healing that we resist doing because, damn it, it's painful there! Yet, life-altering magic can arise when we bravely follow Pluto through a hero's journey.

VIRGO

In your sixth house, Pluto forces you to confront any self-defeating habits that could be harmful to your health. Has your job become too sedentary? Are you taking proper care of your body with clean, nutritious food and regular exercise (in the right amounts of both instead of too little or too much)? How much stress and anxiety are you attempting to metabolize each day?

Because Pluto only switches signs every 12-21 years, its transits are a major deal. Consider any developments that arise between March 23 and June 11 a preview of what's ahead. On November 19, 2024, Pluto will return to Aquarius for 19 more years (until January 19, 2044), laying out the path of transformation.

In preparation, prescribe yourself large doses of preventative medicine. Don't wait until you have an actual health issue before you clean up your diet and get back on the cardio and yoga bandwagon. What can you do, like *now*, Virgo, to make sure all systems are running smoothly? As the ruler of the hidden realm, Pluto can conceal things that aren't apparent to the eye or even showing up as symptoms. To be on the safe side—and get the relief you deserve—book all those routine checkups and bloodwork in 2023. The earlier you make adjustments to anything that's out of balance, the better your odds are of nipping it in the bud before it turns into a chronic condition.

Digestion is ruled by the sixth house and with subterranean Pluto journeying through this zone, you can't ignore the old "you are what you eat" maxim. Much research has been validated about the role of gut health in everything from strong immunity to curbing depression and anxiety (serotonin is produced in the gut). In 2023, fermented foods like kimchi could become staples for you, along with probiotics and mood-stabilizing supplements such as 5-HTP or L-Tryptophan. Colon hydrotherapy can support your digestion as well—and if you're one of the many Virgos who has a fascination with elimination, well, this might just become a recurring treatment. (Let's talk about poop, baby!) Get your doctor's advice on all such things, of course.

Let's also look at what you're phasing out while Pluto finishes its current journey through Capricorn. Since January 2008, Pluto has been in the sign of the Sea Goat, creating all kinds of fluctuations in your fifth house of fame, romance and artistic expression. That dramatic arc surely informed Virgo Beyoncé's *Lemonade* masterpiece, a visual album ode to what it feels like to have Pluto in your solar fifth house. Relationship breakdowns may have pushed you into your own transformational work over the past 15 years, from breaking up with a toxic ex to dealing with love addiction, codependency or an overreliance on outside validation to shore up your self-esteem.

66
Prescribe yourself large doses
of preventative medicine
99

Virgo Jada Pinkett-Smith's lived experience was certainly an illustration of this. After her private decision to open her marriage became tabloid fodder, she took command of the narrative with a candid *Red Table Talk* episode that included her husband Will Smith. So much for letting other people scandalize your personal choices!

While Pluto's been in Capricorn since 2008, Virgos have enjoyed stirring up energy in the limelight. But you, more than many, also saw the ugly side of the fame game. Virgo Tarana Burke's #MeToo movement went worldwide during Pluto in Capricorn—with support from Virgo celebrities including Rose McGowan, Selma Hayak and Evan Rachel Wood—and exposed Hollywood's most notorious sexual predators and abusers.

Prince Harry, a Virgo, joined wife Meghan Markle for a candid *Oprah* special, lifting the royal curtain on the palace's conspiracy with the paparazzi that fractured his family ties, perhaps irreparably. Themes of loyalty and betrayal are Pluto's domain. Over the past 15 years, you too may have been forced to choose sides in an emotionally treacherous way.

And no, Pluto in Capricorn hasn't been all bad—not by a long shot! You've wined and dined and lived the glamorous life, too, we're betting. But all that may start feeling like an embarrassment of riches now. Sharing is caring for Pluto in Aquarius and the sixth house of service...*not* being the kid who's all alone with the most toys. In other words, Virgo, you're switching from a competitive mindset to a more cooperative one. This forthcoming cycle isn't merely humbling; it is a surefire way to create the kinds of loyal, heartfelt relationships that stand the test of time.

Workwise, you could also feel a new path emerging between March 23 and June 11. Even if you aren't changing jobs per se, you may change the *way* you do your work on a daily basis. Not only can Pluto in Aquarius "smart" up your systems, it can also help you lower your footprint while making a bigger, positive impact. Confidentiality is key where Pluto is concerned, but that doesn't mean you should keep all your notes on paper. Electronic security, encryption, VPNs...if you're not on the ball with current data security standards, educate yourself.

There's a deep calling within every Virgo to be of service to the world. When Pluto heads into humanistic Aquarius, you'll hear it ten times louder. How can you make this place better, not only for citizens of the planet, but for the Earth herself? From affordable healthcare to environmental justice to green energy, don't be surprised if your attention shifts in a socio-ecological direction.

Again, we share this with you as an invitation to start dreaming—not a call to figure everything out by the end of 2023! Pluto will be in Aquarius until January 19, 2044, giving you two full decades to flow through its up and down cycles. The journey is as crucial as the destination so forget about taking shortcuts. But know that you *will* emerge wiser than you ever thought you could be!

VENUS RETROGRADE
Making amends

Venus in Leo

June 5 to
October 8, 2023

Venus Retrograde

July 22 to
September 3, 2023

Ready to patch up some pain points and heal your heart? From June 5 to October 8, you'll get gentle, loving support from Venus herself. The planet will be on a long, slow roll through Leo and your twelfth house of forgiveness and transitions. Normally, Venus hangs out in a sign for four weeks, but she's sliding into her every-18-months-retrograde from July 22 to September 3.

During the retrograde, old pain may dredge itself up from your subconscious. We've all been hurt—and we've all hurt other people—it's part of being human, alas. If it's time to make amends, the doors are wide open during Venus' four-month trek through Leo. That said, we recommend getting the ball rolling on those conversations *before* the July 22 retrograde.

It's healthy to mourn a breakup, a lost friendship or an opportunity that slipped away. And if you don't bolt away from the emotions, you stand a solid chance of finding the closure you crave. Sometimes, your solution-oriented sign wants to rush ahead and find the latest therapeutic modality that brings you back to your happy place. (Which explains why you know so much about tapping, somatic breathwork, Abraham Hicks, sound baths...shall we go on?) This time, let yourself experience the entire Gottman Institute feeling wheel, Virgo. The twelfth house is the final wedge of the zodiac wheel and there are no shortcuts here.

Prep for some big feels and treat yourself with kid gloves. And most of all, get support if it all feels too overwhelming to process on your own. You don't have to barrel into your frenemy's life with a bushel full of olive branches and pumped-up bravado! Truth is, it might take multiple interactions before you both arrive at a place of peace. In some cases, the forgiveness work can (and should) be done alone, particularly if you're dealing with someone who is incapable of handling an intimate conversation, or worse, triggers a trauma response in you.

If your task-rabbit nature needs activities to make this all easier, process memories by writing them down (and safely burning them if you must). You could make a scrapbook or vision board of the person or feeling you miss. Then, pack it away when you feel you've adequately exorcized the demons.

Even Virgos in happy, healthy relationships don't get a hall pass to skip this introspective Venus cycle. Insights abound during the retrograde, including ways *you* might be repeating defensive (or *glug* offensive) habits from your past that push your sweetie's buttons. You don't have to be in crisis to benefit from couple's therapy. A few sessions can provide the fine-tuning you need to *really* unite and flourish.

Another option? Slipping off for a couple's retreat might be the perfect retrograde remedy. Issues are going to arise, no matter what, between July 22 and September 3. You might as well work them out with a master teacher's guidance, while camped in a beachside bungalow in paradise, right?

No matter your GPS coordinates, Venus in the twelfth house serves lesson after lesson in boundary-setting. In this sacrificial zone, caring can bleed into codependence. And as the sign of service, you often lose sight of when it's time to *stop* giving and let others stand on their own two feet. With Leo ruling this sector of your chart, you can flip the script by treating yourself like royalty. Pump up the self-care and spoil yourself with luxury between June 5 and October 8.

But this advice also comes with a Venus retrograde warning label: Make a budget for your indulgences. Although those price tags look promising, a retrograde isn't the time to rehaul your closet or revamp your living room. It is, however, a chance for a well-intentioned redo.

If you said goodbye to a love connection without giving each other a fair chance, they may pop up again, willing to give it another shot. It may take a while to decide whether or not to take the plunge—and that's smart! Make a pros and cons list or review the sitch with trusted friends. Put those planning powers to good use and if you don't see a future with the person in question, let them go and remember the future is full of infinite possibilities.

Single Virgos, watch out for pitfalls in the dating landscape. Beware of old hookups trying to slither back into your good graces, only to ghost you once more. Because it's easy to develop dating amnesia during Venus retrograde, block the people you know will hurt you if they get the chance. Close those chapters so you can move on to better things, which are definitely heading your way once Venus heads into Virgo on October 8!

NORTH NODE IN ARIES
Sensuality unleashed

Lunar North Node in Aries

July 17, 2023
to January 11, 2025

While you'll begin the year feeling like an international superstar, come in for a landing on July 17. After 18 months in Taurus and your worldly, expansive ninth house, the fate-finding lunar North Node shifts gears mid-summer and heads into Aries and your eighth house of intense bonding until January 11, 2025. That's quite a compass shift!

It's been nearly two decades since the North Node sashayed through Aries—and if you're anything like Virgo Beyoncé, you'll definitely enjoy the irresistible mojo this newfound nodal energy brings. While you may be the sign of the virgin, you're hardly the zodiac's prude. And the Aries North Node gets you deeply in tune with your sensual powers. Behold: a new wave of sex magick!

How comfortable are you with your erotic identity? We're talking about the persona that emerges when you're lit up and turned on (think: Beyoncé as Sasha Fierce). Or should we say personas. You're a mutable sign after all and no one's putting you in a box. Not surprisingly, these "characters" are often a direct departure from your everyday self—and that's the beauty of this pleasurable playground you're being beckoned to explore.

While the North Node twerks its way through Aries, your romantic life may feel like a sexy costume party and a dance across the dom-sub continuum. You don't have to install restraints on your bedposts—unless, of course, you want to. But if you want to live a more integrated life, get more acquainted with your raw desire. In other words...own it, Virgo! No matter what you're trying on, the Aries-Libra nodes are sure to nudge you toward greater empowerment.

Simultaneously, a stabilizing influence is happening across the zodiac wheel, as the karmic South Node positions itself in Libra and your sensible (yet sensual!) second house on July 17. Talk about a blessing! The experimentation you're in store for can make even the most confident Virgo feel vulnerable. Fortunately, the balancing Libra South Node helps you find that solid ground to stand on when feelings are shaken and stirred. There's plenty of lust, but what about the trust? Reliability and consistency are essential if you're going to allow anyone into your field. (And they'd better be damn good at aftercare.)

Do you have questions about your potential person? Pace yourself, even if that requires extreme willpower. You can test the waters with a few soulful revelations, but actions speak just as loudly as words now. Do they show up on time? Pull their weight? Respect your needs and honor your desires? Little by little, you could gain the confidence to drop your guard and embrace the kind of intimacy that leads to sultry AND spiritual interactions.

Virgos in relationships could plunge into deeper waters once the nodes hit Aries and Libra. Try to load up on as many dopamine-fueling adventures (traveling, socializing, expanding your roles in the world) *before* July 17, while the nodes linger in Taurus and Scorpio. You may need to lean into those memories mid-summer as the Aries North Node forces you to deal with the emotional landscape of your relationship. The financial one, too! The eighth house rules joint ventures, shared investments and soulful transformations—and with take-no-prisoners Aries ruling this zone of your chart, you may have to initiate some hard conversations in order to realign about the future. Don't avoid them! Taking a fearless inventory of everything involved in "the state of your union" is what will bring back the sizzle and help you two soar.

Has your life together gotten mired in complicated details and draining obligations? You may realize that you need to outsource a few tasks, sell off some property or otherwise simplify your shared mission to bring more peace to your partnership. You love to be there for your people, Virgo, but at what price? Supporting every grown adult in your universe might mean shortchanging your innermost circle of besties and your *amour*.

The challenge? The power of your pull is undeniable during this 18-month cycle, and everyone wants a piece of your time. Be careful what you wish for! Words manifest into reality at an accelerated pace—which would be fine if you could take them back. Aries and Libra are like war and peace. A heated moment of frustration could destroy important relationships— and a feelgood vibe could cause your mouth to write a check that your ass simply doesn't want to cash. As a rule, only make promises if you're willing to follow through to the finish line. Otherwise, you could wind up paying a hefty fee for your liberation. Start practicing these words, Virgo: "Let me get back to you on that!"

Financially, this nodal cycle gets you thinking long-term. With the North Node touring inventive Aries, you'll have no shortage of original ideas that you can take to the bank. And with your eighth house of big money activated, funds could arrive in a lump sum such as royalties or dividends. Inheritances, legal settlements and tax returns could also fill the coffers between July 17, 2023 and January 11, 2025.

If you have a product to bring to market, take time to perfect it. Make sure everything's in compliance, tested and in prime condition so you can nail five-star reviews right off the bat. Line up your marketing plan. You may have the greatest idea in the world but if you're not showing people how it can absolutely make their lives better, you're leaving money on the table!

Got debt to pay off? Luck is on your side for settling it—and you may finally clear up your credit or put an end to ongoing litigation. Rather than waiting for an ominous letter to arrive in your mailbox, set up a payment plan. Integrity sets you up favorably when it comes to negotiation.

VIRGO

The South Node is the comfort zone, and while transiting through Libra and your second house of work, be careful not to get complacent on the job. Having a steady paycheck is great but are you underearning,? Figure out what it will take to get yourself bumped into a higher pay grade—special training, software certification, proving yourself to an office VIP—and do *that*. If you're overly dependent on someone's resources, be hardcore about weaning off their supply chain. You'll never know what you're capable of (which is *so much more*) if you don't take a calculated risk.

Pick off any freeloaders who have been draining *your* precious resources, too. Peace holds a high value in your world, but at what price? Slackers might not appreciate "2023 Virgo," and that is 100% *their* problem. Same for anyone who is abusing power, gaslighting you into believing you deserve less or manipulating your emotions.

The Aries North Node makes you a total baddie when it comes to fighting for yourself. Confronting inequities is never easy, but armor up, Virgo. In the second half of 2023, you may have to report an abuse of authority or fire someone from your squad. We hope circumstances don't pull you down to this extreme, but it's only fair to warn you. Firm limits are recommended after July 17, so set your boundaries and take note of anyone who is repeatedly violating.

You're in a great earning cycle, too, so think "abundance!" If you have extra cash left over after the bills, here's your chance to learn more than you ever thought you could about investing it. No one loves a beauty closet raid more than a Virgo, but those mink lashes and lip kits aren't going to put food on the table. We're not suggesting you turn your back on your Pat McGrath or close the door on Dior! Just remember these two magic words: compounding interest. From NFTs to real estate to the stock market, it takes money to make money, Virgo. Tuck your funds into assets that are likely to grow in value over time and you'll be sitting pretty (in Bali, Copenhagen, Buenos Aires...wherever!) for years to come!

ECLIPSES IN 2023
Sharing is daring

Hybrid Solar Eclipse in
Aries (new moon)

April 20 at 12:17AM

Penumbral Lunar Eclipse
in Scorpio (full moon)

May 5 at 1:24PM

Annular Solar Eclipse
in Libra (new moon)

October 14 at 2:00PM

Partial Lunar Eclipse
in Taurus (full moon)

October 28 at 4:15PM

times in eastern time

APRIL 20:
SOLAR ECLIPSE IN ARIES
HYBRID SOLAR ECLIPSE 29º52,
12:17AM ET

A relationship could reach a turning point—or get an exciting jumpstart—thanks to an ultra-rare hybrid solar eclipse in Aries, the sign of new beginnings. This is the first eclipse to activate your eighth house of seduction, joint ventures and investments since 2015, and because it begins as an annular "ring of fire" eclipse and evolves into a sky-darkening total eclipse, you may see a glimmer of possibility in a formerly hopeless place. But only you can say which side of the fence you'll land on. Is it time to get engaged...or call the whole thing off? This is the first eclipse in a two-year series so you may be uncertain about which direction you'll take. What can you do now? Begin a fearless deep-dive to figure that out, searching your soul while also scouring for real-deal facts and figures. This lunation can also bring sweeping financial change, especially of shared resources. It's a good time to explore opportunities in real estate, raise venture capital (or take out a business loan) or look for a way to earn passive income.

♍

MAY 5: LUNAR ECLIPSE IN SCORPIO
PENUMBRAL LUNAR ECLIPSE, 14°52, 1:24PM ET

Who are the people in your neighborhood? As the May 5 lunar (full moon) eclipse in Scorpio electrifies your third house of local activity, it reveals hidden opportunities that have been sitting right under your nose. Take a moment to read the community blogs and analog bulletin boards at your neighborhood coffee shop. You could spy the very opening you've been waiting for. A platonic partnership that's been percolating since the corresponding solar eclipse in Scorpio on October 25, 2022 could hit a pivotal point today. Time to make that joint venture official and get the creative braintrust in gear!

OCTOBER 14: SOLAR ECLIPSE IN LIBRA
ANNULAR SOLAR ECLIPSE 21°10, 2:00PM ET

Cha-ching! You're ready to make some money moves as today's annular "ring of fire" solar eclipse in Libra activates your second house of income. Some huge opportunities could flood in over the coming two weeks, ones that require you to stretch out of your comfort zone—and possibly pick up a new skill set. But secretly, you've been hoping for a change just like this. Don't fixate on whether or not you'll nail it on the first go. There's always a period for orientation and learning. If you're intrigued by an offer, it's absolutely worth exploring. This eclipse also gives you the nerve you need to raise your rates or ask for a salary increase if the right time has come to charge more.

OCTOBER 28: LUNAR ECLIPSE IN TAURUS
PARTIAL LUNAR ECLIPSE 5°03, 4:15PM ET

It's time to leap, Virgo! And you've got wind in your sails as the lunar (full moon) eclipse in Taurus—the final one in a two-year series—powers up your daring, expansive ninth house. What have you been dreaming about? This is the time to step off the sidelines and out of your safety zone as Lady Luck spurs you to action. An entrepreneurial venture or media project could get off the ground in a huge way. Reach out to friends in far-flung places and start talking about a visit. A cross-cultural connection that's been simmering could heat up over the coming two weeks, so make your move!

2023

—

LIBRA

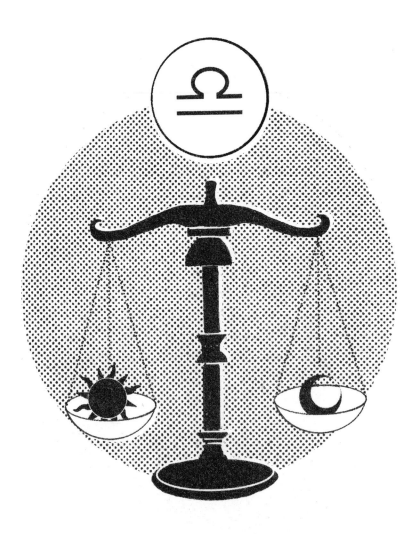

WHAT'S IN THE STARS FOR

LIBRA

Relationships are a central theme of #LibraLife and a huge focus of your 2023. Finding that all-important sweet spot between other people's needs and your own identity will be a balancing act. You'll crave more freedom in all of your connections—nobody's fencing you in this year! The most attractive feature you can cultivate in 2023? Your own identity. And while you're busy getting excited about being YOU, why not pursue financial self-sufficiency as well? A regular fitness routine that targets your core and gut health will complete your total life glow-up. Gaining strength everywhere—from your body to your boundaries to your bank account—makes you feel utterly vibrant. Many Libras have been drawn to energy medicine, sexual healing and spiritual transformation in the past few years. You may add these to your suite of superpowers in 2023, as you learn to work with your own "life force energy." Kundalini: rising!

LIBRA WILL BE LUCKY WITH:
Relationships, money

LIBRA WILL BE CHALLENGED WITH:
Staying organized, setting firm boundaries

LOVE

Partnerships are always a priority for you, Libra, but while free-spirited Jupiter roams through Aries until May 16, no one's clipping your wings. To keep relationships from devolving into a power struggle, fill your shared calendar with active adventures. Novelty releases dopamine, which might be your primary bonding agent this year! Meanwhile, the lunar North Node continues its tantric trek through Taurus until July 17, luring you into new erotic terrain. Get ready: Your turn-ons may evolve before your eyes, especially once Pluto dips into Aquarius and your fifth house of romance from March 23 to June 11—the beginning of a 20-year cycle. The snug vibes that warmed your heart (and other body parts) for the past fifteen years could suddenly feel like a too-tight suit. There's no denying your urges once the karmic South Node lands in Libra from July 17 to January 11, 2025—its first visit here since 2004-06. Developing your personal passions is the quickest way to bringing sexy back...not trying to "fix" your partner or find a new one.

CAREER & MONEY

Let your money work hard for you, Libra! With the fateful lunar North Node in your eighth house of investments until July 17, learn all you can about emerging tech markets, cryptocoins and NFTs—yes, even if the bottom seems to have dropped out on these. There could be a few "buy low" opportunities worth leaping on after lucky Jupiter lands in Taurus for a year on May 16. Libras could make a nice profit on the sale of a property, perhaps near the October 28 lunar eclipse. But stick to your budget and keep your sleeves rolled up. On March 7, industrious Saturn lands in Pisces, giving your sixth house of systems and efficiency a workout. Simplify your processes and you'll see greater profits.

WELLNESS

Shoulder back, core tight! Structured Saturn heads into Pisces this March 7, kicking off three years in your sixth house of healthy routines. The bones, teeth and joints are governed by the ringed taskmaster: all areas that could use extra focus and protection in 2023. In addition to dental and chiropractic checkups, try using a stability ball as a desk chair or investing in a standing desk. Need to do some emotional healing? When the South Node dips into Libra from July 17 to January 11, 2025, you'll be ready to push past ancient blocks, perhaps with guidance from therapists, shamans and bodyworkers.

FRIENDS & FAMILY

Have BFF, will travel! Global Jupiter swings through Aries until May 16, so embark on an epic winter- or spring-break getaway with a BFF or visit a long-distance *amie* in her city. Your ruler, social Venus, rolls through your communal eleventh house from June 5 to October 8, boosting your popularity skyward. Don't forget your ride or dies during Venus retrograde, from July 22 to September 3, which would be the perfect time for a reunion. With Pluto finishing its tour through your family zone, you may need to support a relative who is aging or going through tough times. Playing caregiver? Make sure you have enough support for yourself during the process.

JUPITER IN ARIES
Finding "me" within "we"

Jupiter in Aries
December 20, 2022
to May 16, 2023

Every Libra knows that it takes two to tango. And after a year of hard work and self-discovery, you're yearning for companionship—with someone who sees you, honors you and wants to grow with you. Well, guess what? Before 2023 even begins, your wish is the stars' command. Starting December 20, 2022, expansive Jupiter pivots back into your opposite sign of Aries, broadening horizons in your seventh house of partnerships until May 16. Roll the dice on anything from a legendary love affair to a booming business alliance. With your risk tolerance elevated, this could be the year when you make things official or extricate yourself from a situationship that doesn't work for you anymore.

You got a first taste of this last year, when Jupiter took its first of two circuits through Aries (from May 10 to October 28, 2022). In 2023, the galactic guru continues to expand your relationship skill set. If you're open to a sequel, bonds that formed during that period last year could get a second wind. But should they? Thrillseeking Jupiter loves to gamble as much as it lives to serve up a golden lesson. Allowing "last season" characters to reprise their roles in your life story could also be your undoing, Libra. Don't invite trouble back into your life.

Was it merely bad timing that sent you and a prospective partner drifting to separate ports? In cases like that, luck may be on your side. If you're already joined at the hip, worldly Jupiter lays out a mission of shared adventures that can liven up your connection. Reflect back on a prior Jupiter-in-Aries cycle, from January 2010 to June 2011, for themes that could crop up again.

While you're at it, brace yourself for enlightening role reversals in your current partnerships. For example, if you're usually the chatty raconteur, you may pivot to being the active listener. Libra homebodies may suddenly remember how much you love a glamorous night of painting the town red. If you typically bite your tongue to avoid conflict (a Libra pitfall), forthright Jupiter nudges you to voice your feelings—yep, even the ones that could stir up a fight. Polish your already impressive negotiation skills with Jupiter's encouragement. Anything from couples' retreats to managerial training could put a feather in your cap. But no more self-silencing, please. You deserve to be heard, Libra!

> 66
>
> *In 2023, love gets*
> *"repackaged" for Libra*
>
> 99

What you don't want to lose, however, is your keen diplomacy. Outspoken Jupiter in Aries pulls no punches, but is the timing right? Wait a beat before you attach to any snap judgments—not only because your impulses could be misguided, but to give yourself a chance to see the big picture. How important is it, *really*, for your date to know that the restaurant across the street got better reviews than the place they chose? (Hint: not important, but possibly destructive to bond-building.) Apply Jupiter's optimism to emphasize what you *do* like about your dining experience, like the attentive service, the perfect wine recommendation and the sinfully delicious tiramisu.

If you've got weddings on the brain, Jupiter reads your mind like a cosmic clairvoyant. In 2023, even the most gun-shy Libra could put a ring on it. Thanks to Jupiter's global influence, you might plan a destination wedding or celebrate your roots with an ancestral tradition, like a Scottish handfasting ritual or a "jumping the broom" to honor your bygone Black relatives.

The only catch to all this? While in Aries, Jupiter directly opposes your Libra Sun. With the red-spotted planet furthest away from el Sol in the zodiac, you could leap excitedly straight into a blind spot. Before you go out on a limb for another person, create a checklist of criteria. Your judgment could be askew, or it might take a while for you to locate *your* truth that's being drowned out by a cacophony of opinions.

Single? Boundary-buster Jupiter could open your eyes to someone who was previously way off your radar. In 2023, love gets "repackaged" for Libras. Your soulmate may hail from abroad; maybe they grew up in a religious or cultural setting totally opposite from your family of origin. While this *will* add a dimension of complexity, it hardly needs to be a dealbreaker. Variety is extra spicy for Libras while Jupiter is in Aries.

And don't knock a long-distance relationship, should one appear. Nomadic Jupiter is all in favor of racking up frequent flier miles and could find you relocating for a special someone. Check out prospects in different zip codes (or even country codes) on the dating apps. This could turn out to be the ideal arrangement, leaving room for those contemplative monk moments many Libras cherish. And, let's be real, Libra, you're always down to prolong the honeymoon phase, and there's no better way to do that than keeping your "secret single behaviors" (waxing, plucking, squeezing, etc.) hidden in your own private vault for as long as you can.

Been together for years? Enterprising Jupiter inspires new ideas for co-creation. In 2023, you could join forces to get a profitable independent business off the ground. (Time to open that car detailing shop...or the vegan food truck?) Learning and growing together could lead you to all sorts of spaces, from a tantric retreat to a shamanic medicine ceremony. Even when you're on a "casual date night," elevate your planning. Go see live music, take a salsa lesson, drive to a vineyard.

Has a certain relationship passed its expiration date? Magnanimous Jupiter makes it easier to part on friendly terms—or at least polite ones. And it won't be long until a bevy of fresh prospects appears. You may enjoy a few casual encounters to ease your way back in. But because Jupiter in this committed sector makes you catnip for serious types, you could segue from one commitment straight into another. Although serial monogamy often suits your companionship-loving sign, don't bypass the self-discovery journey that Jupiter wants to take you on. Shacking up together too soon or sprinting to the altar could get messy down the road, even if you're "positive" this person is The One.

The same holds true for any business partnerships. Enthusiastic Jupiter in your house of contracts can spur you to sign on the dotted line. Fortunately, gambling on some promising joint projects could pay off in 2023. It goes without saying that you should *not* overlook red flags in your hurry to seal a deal. Don't get carried away; conduct your due diligence. Hire an attorney for a couple of hours to ensure that your rights are protected. If you get the green light, awesome! You'll have peace of mind when you form an alliance that passes all the integrity tests.

JUPITER IN TAURUS
Intimacy ahoy!

Jupiter in Taurus

May 16, 2023 to
May 25, 2024

Jupiter Retrograde

September 4 to
December 30, 2023

If the urge to merge passes you by in the first half of 2023, there's no dodging it come May 16 when Jupiter plunges into Taurus and the intimate waters of your eighth house. This cycle, which lasts until May 25, 2024, won't make you desperate to be half of a supercouple. Quite the contrary! With your discernment filters sharpened like a ninja's throwing star, only the most qualified candidates will make the cut.

Your indecisive sign has perfected the art of fence sitting, but that perch is off limits come May 16. From emotional bonds to joint financial ventures, there's no "half in and half out" now, Libra. It's all or nothing for you! Expect to feel pressured one minute, exhilarated the next. Because once you make your final choice, you can actually get rolling in a clear direction. And that's when the adventures begin.

And here's the juicy part: Taurus rules your erotic eighth house. With open-minded Jupiter slinking through this sector, a sexual awakening could be in the cards. This could be the year that you expand your "menu," perhaps with a different kind of partner or by trying things that rev up untapped aspects of your sexuality. Since Jupiter governs education, you could open up portals of pleasure by working with a sensuality coach or taking a course in orgasmic massage.

If you haven't already gleaned this, the eighth house is no place for lightweights! If Jupiter in the seventh house (Aries) was the wedding, Jupiter in the eighth house (Taurus) is the marriage itself. With the bouquet dried and pressed in the scrapbook and the slice of cake frozen solid, you are faced with what's ahead. The reality of merging two complex human beings with their own individual lives is...gulp. Intimacy can be as intimidating as it is exhilarating—and it's what Jupiter in Taurus has on tap for you to learn. So if you're in any sort of partnership, face down your trust and control issues. Navigating these seas is not meant to be a solo excursion.

66

This could be one of your most prosperous cycles in a long time when you experience windfalls and master the art of wealth planning.

99

The eighth house rules joint investments. In 2023, coupled Libras could set things in stone by co-signing a mortgage or collecting NFTs—or making a baby, the ultimate "investment." The pendulum might swing the other way, with some Libras breaking up and splitting shared assets. If a courtroom battle ensues, most Libras can expect a favorable outcome with custody, alimony, or asset division. Know your worth and find counsel who can properly represent you.

How's your privacy policy? With Jupiter in this interior zone, life can take a quieter turn. Feelings may be tender during this vulnerable, 12-month cycle, so get ready for some ups and downs. Anger and hurt that you repressed could resurface, sounding the call for transformational healing. Prepare to do some intense and private work to process the swirl of deep emotions. Talk therapy can be highly beneficial during this period, but you might also release calcified pain through energy healing or somatic work that helps you uncover trauma that you're holding onto in your body.

In the business arena, Jupiter in Taurus can help you to score an investor or ink an interesting joint venture. This could be one of your most prosperous cycles in a long time when you experience windfalls and master the art of wealth planning. If you're pondering a move, bountiful Jupiter will be on your side and you might buy or sell real estate.

You'll be drawn to metaphysical mysteries and won't have any problem suspending logic to go places that were previously off-limits. As an added bonus, your esoteric explorations might pay off in the material world, as you become well-rounded and richer in every sense of the word.

There's a good chance that friends will send out an APB during this introspective Jupiter phase. Going against your social-butterfly grain, you're prone to flying under the radar between May 16, 2023 and May 25, 2024. Whether you're obsessed with a passion project that demands total focus or sobbing on your acupuncturist's sofa after a mind-blowing session, your attention is absolutely internal. Stay the course, knowing that you'll burst free from the chrysalis as a beautiful butterfly by mid-2024. For now, shed your skin and transform.

MARS IN GEMINI
Embracing independence

Mars in Gemini

August 20, 2022 to
March 25, 2023

Mars Retrograde

October 30, 2022
to January 12, 2023

The wider world is calling, Libra—and starting January 12, you're ready to answer the WhatsApp message, then book your international flight. Go-getter Mars blasts out of a 10-week retrograde and sails ahead in Gemini and your ninth house of global adventures until March 25.

Normally, Mars spends seven weeks in a single sign, but due to its biennial backspin (which began October 30, 2022), it's touring Gemini for seven *months*—from August 20, 2022 to March 25, 2023. If your independent spirit has yet to ignite, just wait until January 12. No one's fencing a Libra in, no way, no how.

Libras fall in love easily—with people, places, pastimes—so much so that it can be hard to settle on a "favorite" of anything. Good news! In early 2023, there's zero pressure to drop anchor. In fact, you might want to drop *out* of the rat race for a minute and play digital nomad. Soul-quenching spiritual retreats and pilgrimages can rewire you.

With lusty Mars in the picture, single Libras might just meet a lover in every port. Maybe you already have since the red planet first zoomed into Gemini on August 20, 2022. Does one connection have long-distance relationship potential? Make it your mission to find out in early 2023.

The directive for happily coupled Libras? Level up your baecation goals! Why go to a ski lodge when you could book a room in a *chateau*? That all-inclusive resort? Gorgeous, for sure, but no replacement for the far-more authentic experience of renting a cabaña in a secret little surf town. Surprise, Libra! You might not need as many of those creature comforts as you convinced yourself you did; in fact, Mars in the unbridled ninth house can make you jungle-cat wild!

Can't get out of town? Expand your horizons through education, another ninth-house domain. Whether you're applying to grad school or diving right into an online masterclass, your mind will be hungry to learn. Get a certification under your belt if it brings professional legitimacy and, by extension, access to greater profits. Fitness instructor, app developer, tantra coach: What is your soul longing for?

Is there a book rattling around in your head? Since the ninth house rules publishing, it's officially go time! Maybe you began the manuscript last year but lost steam during the retrograde. After January 12, you might create an official proposal to give to an agent or explore the many self-publishing tools on the market. For entrepreneurial Libras, Mars in Gemini puts wind in your sails. Write that business plan, pitch angel investors or test-market a new offering. Just take that calculated risk already while Mars is in this daring position. Planning is great, but you won't know 100% how the market will receive you until you start testing the waters.

The only red flag? Diplomacy, which normally comes naturally to Libras, may feel out of reach between January 12 and March 25. Hotheaded Mars is particularly brash in mouthy Gemini and the outspoken ninth house. You may be quick to anger or clap back at people who you assume are insulting you. (But are they?) Or, you could fall into the "open mouth, insert foot" trap by spewing unsolicited advice.

Unless you're actively seeking to burn a bridge, bite your tongue and plan to take lots of cooldown breaks. If someone has crossed a line, find a kind yet firm way of letting them know their behavior was unacceptable. Just wait until you're back in control of your emotions before confronting them on their misdeeds.

SATURN IN PISCES
Life gets back on track

Saturn in Pisces

March 7, 2023 to
February 13, 2026

Saturn Retrograde

June 17 to
November 4, 2023

Breathe, Libra. After a few years of nonstop curveballs, 2023 offers a lot more predictability. Beginning March 7, orderly, meticulous Saturn lands in Pisces, parking in your sixth house of work, wellness and daily routines until February 13, 2026. For the next three years, integrate fresh systems into your repertoire—and make them stick. Wax on, wax off!

Although this methodical groove isn't everyone's jam, it could be music to a Libra's ears if you're ready to dial down your stress and restore more balance to your life with healthy regimens. Sign you up! With the planetary personal trainer in your corner, improving your life will be a marathon, not a sprint. Rather than trying to change your behavior overnight, shift your mindset and focus on developing sustainable habits. Skip the 30-day challenges and instead, cultivate practices like morning meditation, meatless Mondays and balancing your budget on Sunday evenings. You could even come up with a mantra for your self-improvement campaign and have it tattooed on your wrist. In any case, Saturn in Pisces can help you pull off a whole life tune-up.

If you're used to Googling health information, now you'll need to be sure that guidance comes straight from the pros. Serious about your workouts? You might invest in sessions with a trainer who can correct your posture and demonstrate how to fend off injuries. When it comes to medical care, consult a board-certified doctor (MD or ND) for check-ups and procedures. Work with practitioners who integrate traditional medicine with complementary and alternative treatment like homeopathy and biofeedback. And remember that an ounce of prevention is worth a pound of cure.

Saturn rules the bones, teeth and skeletal system, and these may be sensitive areas in 2023. Pay particular attention to your posture and make sure you're sleeping on a good mattress. Regular visits to the chiropractor, along with therapeutic massage, may be necessary. Dental issues could crop up if you haven't been brushing well enough, especially around your gumline. And don't skip the floss, Libra!

Gut check: The sixth house is associated with the digestive system. The enteric nervous system, often referred to as the "second brain," is located here, and it's connected to the actual brain through a vast network of neurons. Soothing yours can aid anxiety this year. Get serious about creating serenity in your life in 2023. Among its many side effects, stress can wreak havoc on your stomach because when the brain triggers a stress response, the gut gets involved. With heavy-hitting Saturn in this house, it's essential to keep your gastrointestinal tract in optimum working order— and yes, calming down can support this. Undiagnosed food allergies and sensitivities may flare up, triggering a host of symptoms, including fatigue. It would be worth your while to have a panel of tests done to see how your body responds to things like gluten, dairy and other hard-to-process "inflammatories."

Whether you're experiencing problems or not, there are so many benefits to improving gut health. Restoring intestinal flora (AKA "the good bacteria") directly improves your immune system. You might try taking a probiotic supplement, eating fermented foods like kimchi and tempeh, or doing a short-term cleanse, especially if you've been on antibiotics.

Mindfulness practices can be game-changing for Libras this year. Those of you who are processing trauma or living with PTSD may reap the rewards of body-centered, somatic therapy. Deeper healing from issues that have been passed down through ancestral lineage is possible with karmic Saturn here. Generations of conditioning affect us on a cellular level. Who knows? By courageously addressing such issues, you could turn the tide toward healing for your entire family—present *and* future.

The sixth house rules your work—not your career path, but the plug-and-play daily job duties that keep food on the table. In 2023, you could be more process-oriented than results-oriented. Effective Saturn will enable you to upgrade your systems so you're working smarter, not harder. Answer this honestly: What tasks are you tired of? Rather than looking for lifehacks to relieve the misery, consider long-term solutions like delegating or outsourcing. Not an option? Reshuffle your workflow and you might add pleasure to your productivity.

If you're just breaking into a field of work, disciplined Saturn in your service-oriented sixth house rewards humility. Even if you were the biggest fish in the pond you just leapt out of, you might be a mere minnow in a vast new ocean now. Check your ego at the door, pronto. Ask how you can help. Spend extra time learning new skills or brushing up on a company mission. Make yourself indispensable to the top brass. Some people believe you're never too old for an internship. Even a few weeks of working for "free" (in exchange for the pure gold of contacts, learning on the job and getting an insider view) could be the smartest move you make.

Saturn is a big fan of systems, so you could write an operations manual for your company, create guidelines for your department, design training programs or delegate tasks to new hires and show them the ropes. Try out a few project management apps like Basecamp, Asana or Trello, too. Maybe you'll hire a virtual assistant to manage your workload—or add staff on the home front with a house cleaner, dog walker or nanny.

PLUTO IN AQUARIUS
Unpacking your magic

Pluto in Capricorn
Janury 1, 2023
to March 23, 2023

June 11, 2023 to
January 20, 2024

Pluto in Aquarius
March 23 to
June 11, 2023

Pluto Retrograde
May 1 to
October 10, 2023

A creative metamorphosis is coming for Libras, the likes of which you've never seen in your lifetime. (And that's saying something for folks who share a zodiac sign with Ta-Nehisi Coates, Halsey and Doja Cat!) On March 23, enigmatic Pluto changes signs for the first time in 15 years, darting forward from Capricorn and your domestic fourth house into Aquarius and your passionate, flamboyant fifth. Although this first transit only lasts until June 11, make no mistake, Libra: these two months will be life altering. In fact, you can consider them a dress rehearsal. Next year (on November 19, 2024), mystical Pluto dons Aquarius' technicolor dreamcoat for another 19 years, giving you a backchannel to the Muse until January 19, 2044.

Sounds scintillating, doesn't it? Now, let us give you the full picture. Pluto rules the underworld. Death, rebirth, transformation. Sex, drugs, rock and roll. Which means you're probably not going to be painting sunshine and rainbows across the canvas. (Libra Mark Rothko's color fields were of another time.)

Whatever métier you choose is likely to be informed by "shadow work," arising out of the emotional depths that you rarely reveal to the world. Heck, Libra, you might not even admit them to yourself. Or maybe you do, with your trademark balance of sadness and joy, like poet and *Milk and Honey* author, Libra Rupi Kaur. Her verse is fitting for how you may feel while Pluto weaves into Aquarius from March 23 to June 11 this year:

"like the rainbow
after the rain
joy will reveal itself
after sorrow"

In a strange way, this plunge into Pluto's subterranean studio will be *such* a relief! While Libras prefer to look on the bright side of life, there's a point where that level of forced cheer veers close to toxic positivity. Whether you make trauma-informed art or simply give yourself permission to *not* have to wrap up every tough situation with a pretty bow, a fuller spectrum version of yourself is slowly emerging. (Resistance is futile!)

The emotion ocean is not an unfamiliar place to you, however. Since 2008, Pluto has been paddling along at the bottom of your solar chart, in Capricorn and your fourth house of foundations, family and roots. In a desire to "anchor" yourself, you may have moved through some pretty intense spaces—literally, for many Libras! Your home lives have been filled with changes of address, some turbulent, others as a result of wealth-agent Pluto's sage direction.

One public example of a Plutonian journey through the fourth house of home and family is Libra Kim Kardashian. During Pluto's tour through Capricorn, she had a 72-day televised marriage to Kris Humphries, wed and divorced Kanye West and gave birth to her five children with the Gemini rapper-turned-private-school-owner. After dating and splitting with Scorpio Pete Davidson in 2022, Kardashian purchased a $70.3 million Malibu dream home. With direct access to the beach and three acres of land, it was among the highest-priced homes sold in Malibu all year. Meanwhile, the L.A. mansion she designed with Kanye—in a self-described (and oh-so Plutonian!) "minimal monastery" style—is on the market.

Before you start scanning Zillow listings, note that Pluto's final leg through Capricorn—which picks up again from June 11, 2023 to November 19, 2024—doesn't *have* to portend a change of residence. The way you "do" home and family, however, is going through a fundamental transformation. For one thing, you are *so over* mothering everyone at your own expense. If you've been carrying the load for capable adults, look out! Your emotions could read at level Fire Breathing Dragon.

Pluto pulls no punches though! While it's essential to set boundaries with your inner circle, the real growth comes from examining your own role in these lopsided dynamics. Perhaps you unconsciously enabled someone's underearning, underfunctioning or under (fill in the blank) because it gave you a sense of purpose. That "need to be needed" has its place; it certainly keeps you from feeling lonely. The trouble comes in when your identity gets wrapped up in a particular role: nurturer, healer, rescuer, sage. As Pluto wraps up its last two years in Capricorn, you're ready for fluidity. Wouldn't it be nice to have more give and take in your relationships?

Careful not to swing to the opposite extreme though—a real pitfall with Pluto. Just because you've given at the office (and in the bedroom, family room, kitchen and everywhere in between) doesn't give you the right to turn into an entitled diva. Ditch the scorekeeping mindset, Libra, and just aim to reset everything on a level playing field. As Pluto pops into Aquarius and your regal fifth house, avoid "spoiled royal" behavior like the plague. The game of thrones can get ugly if you get locked into power struggles, but it's going to be a little too easy to do.

As you prepare to graduate from a decade and a half of Pluto in Capricorn, your true power emanates from your rootedness! And with Pluto in Aquarius shifting you out of the cocoon and into the colorful garden of the fifth house, you don't want to lose sight of all the key lessons you've learned since 2008. Being calm, centered and in your body (your true home!) is something you worked hard to learn. What's coming next will be a time of great power, but also great responsibility, so you *want* to stay grounded.

While hidden talents emerge during this new Pluto cycle, remain the ever-unhurried Libra. Why not revel in the experience of developing these gifts? Where complex Pluto gets involved, the process itself is a critical part of the final outcome. Since the fifth house rules fame, don't expect to fly under the radar. By the same token, private Pluto beckons you to keep parts of your experience *off* social media—for the sake of your own sensitivities—until you have crafted the narrative in a way that you can stand behind. Whatever you put out there will draw scrutiny. If you can back it up with confidence (and in some cases, data!), you might even position yourself as a go-to expert in the field.

Romantically, Pluto's shift into Aquarius will make it impossible to accept anything less than a soul-deep connection. But that comes with a very large asterisk! When this stormy, obsessive planet first shifts into a new sign it can feel like a hurricane blowing down everything in its path. In 2023, Libras may be especially susceptible to power struggles in their love life. Without realizing it, you could get stuck in polarizing dynamics like "victim and rescuer" again. In extreme cases, you may even confuse a sense of danger with romantic intensity and form a trauma bond. We're not writing this to scare you, but to put you on high alert. Even healthy people can slip into these roles when the heady rush of romance is involved. Awareness is crucial for Libras who are dating and mating in 2023.

This is *not* the year to rush right into a relationship. Behind those intense attractions there may be hidden clauses or secrets you should know about—from unfinished divorce paperwork to outstanding debt. The last thing you need is to be stuck with the wrong person. And even if they are the *right* person, rushing in complicates feelings, leaving you flooded with guilt and obligation.

If you have kids, they will need more focus and attention—and get ready, Libra, because your little ones could really test you. Expect Plutonian control issues to rise up as you figure out how much rule to exert and where to let them learn a few tough lessons sans interference.

66

While hidden talents emerge,

remain the ever-unhurried Libra.

99

Should you find yourself in a tough place, consider taking a short dating hiatus. Or if you're in a relationship, find a way to give yourself more space. Getting yourself to a core foundation of strength may take you through some powerful emotions around loss, rejection and abandonment. Metabolizing them in a therapeutic setting means no longer dragging them into your romantic relationships. Imagine a life where you didn't need your partner to fill that hole in your soul—but could work with your wounds in a way that brought the two of you closer together.

And here's some happy news! Because Pluto rules permanent mergers, the next twenty years hold the promise for all sorts of soulful connections. Proposals and pregnancies could be in the cards—or another co-created project that you team up on with a soulmate.

VENUS RETROGRADE
Experimenting and exploring

Venus in Leo

June 5 to
October 8, 2023

Venus Retrograde

July 22 to
September 3, 2023

Novel romantic opportunities will be right at your fingertips between June 5 and October 8. The question is, Libra, how experimental are *you* willing to be? As your galactic guardian Venus whirls through Leo for a prolonged, four-month passage, she shoots off sparks in your cutting-edge, tech-savvy eleventh house. Pushing the envelope? That's putting it mildly. You may be ready to take on a far bigger, er, package, when it comes to romantic (and erotic!) exploration.

Single and looking? Fire up Tinder, Hinge, Raya, Match and the rest of the go-to apps and get to swiping. While the online dating landscape can feel as thorny as a *Naked and Afraid XL* Amazon jungle challenge, chances are good that *someone* worthy of a superlike is out there. If you're happily paired-off, take that techie buzz right into the bedroom with a new toy or two to spice things up.

While Venus is direct in Leo (June 5 to July 22 and September 3 to October 8), you have lots of room to talk about fantasies—a topic that might be triggering during other times of the year. Maybe you know it's time to explore BDSM, threesomes, group sex, whatever. And if you go there, it will all feel so incredible in the moment! But the smart Libra will pad these experiences with lots of pre-game discussions about boundaries and comfort levels. And when you come down from the high, take time for "aftercare," creating a safe space for everyone to share their full range of feelings—from excitement to fear—about whatever went down at your play parties.

All this electricity will be undeniably exciting! But just like any wired-up appliance, it comes with a warning label. From July 22 to September 3, Venus creates shockwaves of her own with a six-week retrograde. While love won't come to a grinding halt, watch for hazard zones. Instead of rushing into a situationship, test the waters with a few extra coffee dates or happy hours—without going home together after the second drink. Hit up Google (or better yet, LinkedIn) to make sure a potential partner is the real deal and not a catfisher or chronic ghoster.

Even if their credentials *do* check after your detective work, ease into anything new during the retrograde. Because your eleventh house rules future plans, you'll be inclined to think every great date is a sign that you're destined to be together. Pace yourself Libra and embrace that beautiful balance you're known for,

When the love planet dims her light, things *can* get confusing, even if you've been paired up for ages. Riding on assumptions could be a misstep for coupled Libras, so how about scheduling a "state of our union" conversation? Are you on the same page when it comes to careers, kids, living situations, matrimony and everything else that comes with a long-term relationship? You could be surprised at your partner's views on these crucial topics. This could either be a good thing or a sign that it's time to explore a new arrangement. Maybe you're set on moving and your partner wants to be closer to family, or you're still undecided on whether or not you want a child. These big (huge!) discussions *can* bring you closer.

Has an old friend been on your mind? Ring them up! Are you missing an old coworker? Shoot them an email and see what projects they have cooking. Get the squad together for a summer beach rental or plan a winter vacation you can look forward to when the snow falls. Lean into Venus's pleasure-seeking potential and treat yourself to quality time with people you love.

NORTH NODE IN ARIES
Karma calling

> **Lunar North Node in Aries**
>
> July 17, 2023
> to January 11, 2025

Karma is calling, Libra, don't ignore those texts! On July 17, the lunar South Node settles into your sign, spinning you into a deep inquiry around identity, personal passions and self-expression. This cycle hasn't come around for nearly two decades! The last time the South Node toured Libra was from November 30, 2004 to June 19, 2006. Significant themes around individual growth, identity and partnership may recur this year. You might even pick up where you left off or resume a path that you thought you'd finished for good. Surprise, surprise!

Even if you're too young to remember that last time the South Node paddled through your sign (November 30, 2004 and June 19, 2006), this promises to be an interesting moment in your personal development! While the South Node occupies your sign from July 17, 2023 to January 11, 2025, it helps you "true up" with your goddess-given gifts, the ones you've had for as long as you can remember. (And probably before then, too!) Get ready to (re)discover your superpowers, Libra. You may have packed them away, hiding these gifts for fear of being ridiculed or misunderstood. Perhaps you even forgot that these parts of yourself existed!

As the South Node pings your sign beginning July 17, you're like Sleeping Beauty awakening to your own power and magic. Like a calling that can't be ignored, you're invited to unveil the *real* you to the world—in a way that inspires others to live out loud.

Transparency? Authenticity? You're here for it! But don't expect this transit to be a walk in the park. As willing as you are to bare your soul, you hate the idea of *not* looking good when you do. This process could get a little messy, causing people to question you. Take heart, Libra! With a little courage and conviction you can help them understand the message behind your "madness."

So, Libra, who do you think you are? That exploration could take you on a fascinating voyage between July 17, 2023 and January 11, 2025. You may feel a call to "rebrand" yourself—not as the person who has it all together, but rather, as someone relatable who can own their mistakes and is figuring it out along the way. (Libras Will Smith, Kim Kardashian and Gwyneth Paltrow may lead the charge.)

Have faith! While the karmic correction of a South Node transit can be unsettling, there's a reason its tests are pushing you past the edge of reason. Breaking up stagnant energy is the path to this next round of transformation. Even if you've done 20 plant medicine ceremonies, decades of therapy and dismantled your ego structure under a guru's tutelage, the "work" is never done. (Sigh.)

If you've outgrown certain situations, there's no need to start pulling plugs. But gently begin untangling yourself from these bonds. Goodbyes can be excruciating for gentle Libras and you prefer when they're done with love. And you never know! The universe may bring you back together again in the future after you've both evolved.

Plus, there's another half to this equation. The lunar *North* Node will concurrently travel through the opposite pole of the zodiac in Aries and your seventh house of partnerships. Until January 11, 2025, you'll have repeated opportunities to find, develop or improve on a special dynamic duo. You'll already enter the year feeling a strong urge to merge, thanks to the North Node's trek through Taurus and your "all or nothing," erotically-charged eighth house. That cycle began on January 18, 2022, and no doubt made for some intense ups and downs in your closest partnerships last year.

Thankfully, when the North Node shifts into Aries (the nodes move backwards through the zodiac) on July 17, you're entering a more romantic, playful stage of partnership. You'll feel eager to take the plunge or give something untested a serious go. This can be your romantic interest, a writing or performing partner or a professional associate. But whoever it is, there's some weight behind the connection—that feeling that fate brought the two of you together.

For many Libras, the Aries North Node may bring a milestone moment for relationships. If you're ready to tie the knot, there couldn't be a more beautiful moment for it. (Just mind the Venus retrograde cycle from July 22 to September 3, a less-than-ideal astrological time for weddings.) Maybe marriage isn't your thing and you want to openly embrace ethical non-monogamy and

> 66
>
> *There's no greater aphrodisiac than a little bit of space...yes, even when every cell in your body is screaming, "I want more!"*
>
> 99

date several people seriously. However you define "relationship bliss," the Aries North Node gives you a warrior's determination to pursue your love goals.

But forget about living for other people's approval ratings! To manifest great relationships, you need to remain deeply in touch with yourself. Pleasing your partner is one thing—and Libras are skilled lovers and romantics. But if you feel like you're coming out of your own skin to make someone happy (or that you crash when they aren't able to meet your needs for a night), let that be a sign that you need to actually pull back and focus on your own independent goals. Counterintuitive as it sounds, nothing creates a more magnetic field for relationships than self-love and healthy boundaries. Sure, you'll dip into the couple bubble plenty in 2023. But with autonomy-loving Aries guiding this operative, the last thing you want to do is "lose yourself." (Sorry, Libra Eminem!)

Advance warning: When the inner work feels too hard, you might want to go for your favorite fixes—tapping the apps for a steamy date or getting wrapped up in solving other people's problems. But don't! That's just an unconscious avoidance technique. Creating drama in existing relationships is another sneaky distraction tactic you'll want to avoid.

For Libras in relationships, there may be temporary turmoil as everyone adjusts to new roles. But ultimately, there's no greater aphrodisiac than a little bit of space...yes, even when every cell in your body is screaming, "I want more!"

Figuring out what makes you happy is a process. Set up a sanctuary, chill space, meditation room, whatever, so you can slip off for reflective alone time. The sooner you start thinking about these quiet spells as "personal growth and development sessions," the faster you'll evolve toward your true north. Until then, keep bravely looking into the shadows—with as many coaches, healers, therapists, shamans and guides as you need to help you hear the sound of *your* beautiful inner voice.

ECLIPSES IN 2023
Renewing your outlook

Hybrid Solar Eclipse in
Aries (new moon)

April 20 at 12:17AM

Penumbral Lunar Eclipse
in Scorpio (full moon)

May 5 at 1:24PM

Annular Solar Eclipse
in Libra (new moon)

October 14 at 2:00PM

Partial Lunar Eclipse
in Taurus (full moon)

October 28 at 4:15PM

times in eastern time

APRIL 20:
SOLAR ECLIPSE IN ARIES
HYBRID SOLAR ECLIPSE 29º52,
12:17AM ET

When you compare you despair, Libra, and that goes for your closest relationships, too! So stop following other people's scripts, okay? Today's new moon solar eclipse in Aries—the first eclipse in a game-changing, two-year series on the Aries-Libra axis!—can bring illuminating insights about how you'd like to "do" partnerships. Not only is this the first eclipse to hit Aries since 2015, but it's also a super-rare hybrid solar eclipse, beginning as a "ring of fire" (annular) eclipse and transforming into a sky-darkening total eclipse along its path.

Metaphorically, you may have a lightbulb moment about the "rules of engagement" you'd like to play by with a particular person in your life. Will they be aligned? That part requires conversations and, in some cases, contract negotiations. You have two years to ride the waves of this new eclipse cycle so don't be too quick to bail on a situation that still holds a glimmer of promise. (Just make sure there's more than just potential to work with here!)

Don't believe in love at first sight? You might just change your mind. A budding bond could cross into exclusive terrain, thanks to a confessional conversation you have over the coming two weeks.

MAY 5: LUNAR ECLIPSE IN SCORPIO
PENUMBRAL LUNAR ECLIPSE, 14°52, 1:24PM ET

You're a money magnet this May 5, as the brilliant lunar eclipse in Scorpio lights up your second house of income. Since eclipses reveal shadows, hidden sources of revenue could crop up out of the blue. This could span the range from a 9-5 job offer to a steady client who fills your coffers on a regular basis. Cha-ching! Luxe-loving Libra, have you been overdoing it on the high-end purchases? Overspending could catch up with you today, too, forcing you to lock your wallet shut. Some extreme budgeting measures may be required for the next couple weeks to help you bounce back. Rolled up sleeves and a tightened belt is a good look for you.

OCTOBER 14: SOLAR ECLIPSE IN LIBRA
ANNULAR SOLAR ECLIPSE 21°10, 2:00PM ET

Reinvention time begins in 3, 2, 1... Today is a historical moment for Libras! As the first eclipse to land in your sign since 2016 arrives as an annual "ring of fire" solar eclipse, it calls forth the slumbering (and incomparable) parts of your personality. Are you ready to dazzle the world with your starpower? If so, you have planetary permission to put yourself out there in a bold and attention-getting way. One caveat: Eclipses can bring unexpected results, so make sure you're ready to field a mix of reviews—and to use them as a chance to improve whatever you're working on. (You might even invite people to give honest feedback and let them be part of the fun.) If you've been stuck in a rut, this eclipse puts a chain on the proverbial tires and hauls you right out of the ditch. You could blast off on a brand new path—one that feels so true to your soul's urges—while these eclipses wage on for another year and a half.

OCTOBER 28: LUNAR ECLIPSE IN TAURUS
PARTIAL LUNAR ECLIPSE 5°03, 4:15PM ET

Your passion levels are skyrocketing, just in time for cuffing season. Thank (or blame) the lunar eclipse in Taurus—the third and final in a two-year series—that's turning up the heat your erotic eighth house. Your urge to merge may be irresistible, and luckily your seductive powers are finely tuned. But make sure your actions align with your soul. It may be hard to keep things casual under with such a strong pull to bond. Don't settle for a situationship if you want a rock on your finger. Over the coming two weeks, a lucky swipe on the apps could bring a deeper-than-expected connection. Attached? Let this eclipse shine a light on what your next shared step is. Ready, set, go!

2023
—
SCORPIO

WHAT'S IN THE STARS FOR

SCORPIO

Ready to turn your power back on? In 2022, many Scorpios went underground, and even felt invisible. While your mysterious sign likes to keep people guessing, this felt beyond your control—and it was. Good news: In July 2023, you can emerge from this karmic cocoon, hopefully with stronger relationships and vibrant good health. Let's show the world what they've been missing! But before you leap into the spotlight, make sure your game is tight. Polish your presentation and tweak your talents to compete in the modern marketplace. (Training from a pro-level mentor or expert is advised.) Relationships could turn super-serious in 2023. Is it time to make this one official? The second half of the year sets the stage for that. Just don't forget to have fun, Scorpio—a little lightness goes a long way. In the spring, you may start gently snipping the cords with family, or transitioning into a more adult relationship with your clan. You can still maintain close bonds while setting boundaries that allow you (and them) to express your individuality. The ties that bind need not constrict! Your home also becomes a "manifestation station" so clear the clutter and create a space that attracts abundance.

SCORPIO WILL BE LUCKY WITH:
Healthy living, relationships

SCORPIO WILL BE CHALLENGED WITH:
Making time for fun, home and family

LOVE

Serious relationships are a Scorpio's jam but with weighty Saturn plunking down in Pisces on March 7, careful that they don't get *so* heavy that you forget the romantic parts! During this three-year Saturn cycle, you're tasked with making magic, one conscious action at a time. That will be easy starting May 16, when adventurous Jupiter soars into Taurus and your coupled-up seventh house. Not only does this bring some breathing room to your bonds, but it might open your mind to new arrangements: long-distance, cross-cultural, LAT (living apart together). If you're a solo Scorpio, get yourself back into a seductive headspace so that you're in the right "vibration" to attract *amour*. Start by moving your body and planting yourself in social situations where you can make friends who know someone they can fix you up with! If you're on the fence about a union, you could hit the make it or break it point by the October 28 lunar eclipse.

CAREER & MONEY

Werk, Scorpio! Enterprising Jupiter zips through Aries, pouring high-octane fuel into your industrious sixth house. You won't even mind the grind if you're learning new things. With the karmic South Node in Scorpio until July 17, keep hustling quietly to monetize your passions or doing something that feels like "soul work." A breakthrough result could arrive near the May 5 Scorpio lunar eclipse! And once the destiny-fueling North Node heads into Aries on July 17, you'll have 18 months of accelerated professional growth. Network like it was your side gig from June 5 to October 8, while enchanting Venus struts through your elite tenth house. The VIPs could get behind your vision. A past colleague could go to bat for you while Venus is retrograde from July 22 to September 3. Reconnect!

WELLNESS

Vitality-boosting Jupiter revs its engines in Aries and your wellness zone until May 16, providing ample energy for fun, upbeat workouts and winter sports. Gut health will be especially important this year, particularly after July 17 when the lunar nodes shift into Aries and Libra—the rulers of your sixth house of digestion and twelfth house of elimination. Learn more than you thought you wanted to know about microbiomes and join a gym with a sauna for regular, detoxifying sweats. Hit the dance floor with a plus one when active Jupiter bounds into your partnership zone for a year this May 16. Who knows? With your competitive streak activated you might even win a mirrorball trophy!

FRIENDS & FAMILY

Friendships are going through a transition this year, as your ruler, Pluto, makes its first sign change since 2008, moving from Capricorn and your outgoing third house to Aquarius and your intimate fourth. While this transit only lasts from March 23 to June 11, it's the warm-up for a 20-year cycle of Pluto in Aquarius that kicks off again next year. Close relationships have always been your style, but this year, you could form a solid inner circle and build a stronger support network than you've had in a while.

JUPITER IN ARIES
Health is wealth

Jupiter in Aries

December 20, 2022
to May 16, 2023

What's the secret of success, Scorpio? While energizing Jupiter rockets through Aries and your sixth house of wellbeing from December 20, 2022 until May 16, 2023 you'll live by the words "healthy, wealthy and wise." Eat clean and renew your commitment to fitness. And be sure to think holistically! Allow a "self-care first" strategy to permeate every area of your life, from home to work to relationships with family and friends. That's how you'll thrive!

You already got a taste of this vitality-boosting vibe last year, when Jupiter made the first of its two passes through Aries (from May 10 to October 28, 2022). Although that period wasn't the *sexiest* time of your life, it was undeniably productive. With optimistic Jupiter back in this administrative zone for the first half of 2023, make an adventure out of tackling the little things. Finding the magic in the mundane—and allowing gratitude to wash over you for what each one provides—isn't merely a beautiful way to live. The positive energy actually raises your vibration making you a magnet for miracles. (You might even put a gratitude app on your phone to record these moments.)

Try not to sweat the small stuff though. With amplifier Jupiter in your persnickety sixth house, there will be a lot of it to wade through! The 12-Step mantra of taking things "24 hours at a time" can come in handy should you start to spiral.

You can mitigate stress by creating a savvy system for your workflow and productivity. Look around! If you have a thousand Post-It notes and desktop icons, it's no wonder you are struggling to focus. Lean into your analytical side and get your life running like a well-oiled machine. If you struggle with organization, hire a coach who can help you implement a process that jibes with your unique workflow. Once you set up your "storage systems" upkeep will be easy. Could you learn to live with less? Downsizing could be a game-changer for you this year! We see a label gun, drawer organizers and a whole lot of cute baskets and bins in your future.

Jupiter is the god of the feast and in fiery Aries, you should think about food as fuel. Since the sixth house rules the digestive system, it's worth it to figure out which foods agree with yours, Scorpio. Aim to improve your gut health by taking a daily probiotic, eating more fiber or trying colon hydrotherapy. Every aspect of your life could shift from this effort. Not only does a healthy gut boost immunity, it's also where feel-good serotonin is produced.

While eating lower on the food chain—and eating the rainbow of produce—can get you glowing, you may not be able to get your full nutritional RDA from food alone. Should you be taking certain vitamins or minerals to supplement your healthy diet? Have your doctor order a bloodwork panel to find out. And if you're into reading labels, don't forget to peruse the ones on your beauty products. Eliminating specific ingredients can improve your skin.

While you're on this self-improvement quest, give the concept of *wabi sabi* a try; it's a Japanese worldview based on embracing imperfections. Without checks and balances, Scorpio, you may veer into obsessive territory. Bodies are meant to be used, food is meant to be eaten and books are meant to be read. Focus *less* on posing, plating, and color-coding. Appearances can be beautiful and asymmetrical at the same time. While you'll grow from being more disciplined this year, magnanimous Jupiter would never advocate sucking the joy out of everything. Being patient with your process doesn't make you a slacker.

For some Scorpios, Jupiter in Aries may bring a health diagnosis to light, necessitating a lifestyle change. This may very well be a blessing in disguise, particularly if it means early detection. The link between stress and disease is well-established, so even the fittest among you should unwind in every way that you can. If you spend a lot of time sitting, get up and move around every hour or try a standing desk.

Got your hands full? Since the sixth house is the domain of helpers, Jupiter in Aries could introduce you to the service providers of your dreams before May 16. Everyone from a virtual assistant to a nanny can lighten your load significantly, but screen candidates rigorously and start with a trial period. Given Jupiter's blithe optimism, you could rush into an arrangement that leaves you feeling angry, or worse, stuck.

If you've hit a wall with your job, Jupiter may send you searching for a new gig. Don't jump into something permanent if you're still testing the waters. Free-spirited Jupiter in your administrative sixth house suggests that you might take a "bridge job"—something temporary and easy that doesn't sap your vital energy. After you clock out, take training to enhance your skillset and qualify you for higher-paying positions in the future.

Some Scorpios may gravitate to the service sector or a green industry like sustainability consulting or environmental justice. Or you could dip into an up-and-coming segment of wellness work and thrive there. A creative job, perhaps for a world-bettering cause, could be part of 2023's cosmic plan. Regardless of where you land, shift into the mindset of gracious service and you'll naturally ease into greater responsibilities.

JUPITER IN TAURUS
Power couples and power plays

Jupiter in Taurus

May 16, 2023 to
May 25, 2024

Jupiter Retrograde

September 4 to
December 30, 2023

Ready to make it a double, Scorpio? The power of partnership becomes glaringly obvious starting May 16 when ever-expansive Jupiter marches on to Taurus, love bombing your seventh house of partnership for an entire year, until May 25, 2024. Relationships that have been stuck in a holding pattern may take off at a gallop—in any and every direction! Grab the reins, but keep your grip loose. For a change, you'd rather enjoy the ride and see where it takes you, even if that means giving up a solid measure of control.

It's been more than a decade since Jupiter roamed through Taurus and your seventh house of partnership. Flip back to June 4, 2011 to June 11, 2012 if you want to see precisely what was happening in your life that go 'round. Similar themes could permeate your partnership strategies in the second half of 2023. Perhaps you're craving more erotic freedom and experimentation—or you're ready to expand through co-creation of a business venture that could use a certain skillset that's out of your wheelhouse. There's no dodging the trouble spots in your closest connections, but optimistic Jupiter can help you approach them with a positive, proactive mindset.

And it *will* be exciting! This Jupiter circuit, which lasts until May 25, 2024, pours Miracle-Gro on your closest connections. Single and looking? As the zodiac's sexiest sign, you'll have a buffet of potentials to pair off with, thanks to bountiful Jupiter's tempting offerings. With all these compatible people entering your orbit, you might find a long-term romantic partner or an inspiring business collaborator—or both.

Conversely, you may lean into the indie-spirited planet's *joie de vivre* and keep your options wide open. Scorpios prefer to bond deeply, so it may come as an epiphany that every attraction doesn't have to morph into the be-all and end-all for you. There's a paradox to navigate when freedom-loving Jupiter lands in traditional Taurus and your committed seventh house. You'll covet people's company but also treasure your freedom—and that's fine. Be candid about it so you don't lead anyone on. No matter your status, you will need some room to roam this year. Relationships should happen by choice, not obligation now (and maybe not forever).

Have translator app, will travel? Globetrotting Jupiter could spark synergy with someone from another culture or background during the second half of 2023. You could meet someone while journeying abroad or connect through a virtual introduction. Perhaps you'll launch an entrepreneurial venture with an offshore collaborator or actually *not* write off a long-distance love interest because of the miles between you. Galactic gambler Jupiter dares you to cast a wide net!

There's just one hitch: While transiting through Taurus, Jupiter will directly oppose your Scorpio Sun. With the red-spotted planet furthest away from el Sol on the zodiac wheel, you might be eager to take a leap of faith without peering into the abyss first. To protect yourself, come up with a checklist of criteria before you roll the dice. Your judgment may not be 100% on point, or it might take you a bit longer to home in on *your* truth when the chorus of opinions around you is at fever pitch.

If you're already half of a dynamic duo, your relationship could evolve in fascinating directions. As you fine-tune the levels of give-and-take, you'll establish more equality and harmony. Longtime couples may take a bucket-list vacation together, renew their vows (on a black sand beach on the Greek Isles), or evolve into different roles. For example, if your mate has been bringing home the most bacon for a while, you might become the household's bigger breadwinner. If you're the perennial sidekick, get ready to step into the starring role.

With free-spirited Jupiter here, you might move the boundaries, perhaps pursuing more extracurriculars—or in some cases, trying on an open relationship for size. Jupiter is a risktaker, and while in Taurus, you're more willing to dance on the edge. But don't be cavalier about this, Scorpio! You of all people know the possible pitfalls of anything that could spin up your jealousy or obsession. Pick the brains of people who have been down this road themselves so you understand what you're getting into. A solid read of books like *The Ethical Slut* and *More Than Two* can be eye-openers for Scorpios pondering polyamory.

Has a certain someone overstayed their welcome in your heart? If life is pushing you onto different paths, magnanimous Jupiter supports a "conscious uncoupling." (Or at least an amicable split.) Don't bank on flying solo for long, however! Jupiter in Taurus invites in promising contenders who balance you out beautifully.

A word of warning: The exciting people you attract in late 2023 may be busily engaged in their personal pursuits, limiting the time you can spend together. But with adventurous Jupiter at the wheel, you'll embrace the challenge of being with a partner who has a full life of their own! (As long as you still get *some* time to hide out in the couple bubble....) Besides, a little less togetherness means more time to devote to your own pursuits, perhaps with a script writing partner, bandmate or a coder who can bring your digital dreams to life.

MARS IN GEMINI
Mojo rising!

Mars in Gemini

August 20, 2022 to
March 25, 2023

Mars Retrograde

October 30, 2022
to January 12, 2023

♏

The year is off to a sex-positive start for Scorpios—and we're not just talking about the stock-in-trade sultriness your sign emits. After languishing in a lowkey retrograde since October 30, red-hot Mars corrects course on January 12. As the lusty planet forward-thrusts through Gemini until March 25, it reignites a bonfire in your erotic eighth house. Yes, Scorpio, you are officially back in your element: magnetic, alluring and deliciously mysterious.

Not that you weren't already there. Mars has been on this extended sashay through Gemini since August 20, 2022. But when the retrograde began on October 30, 2022, the planetary provocateur went into energy-saver mode, disrupting the vibes. That may have been a saving grace for Scorpios whose relationships got a little too "Martian." (Read: wild, ferocious or obsessive.) Spicy connections that sizzled in late summer may have fizzled by cuffing season; or circumstances may have literally short-circuited a promising bond. On the other hand, if lust has been AWOL, you may have found yourself fantasizing about someone besides your so-called other half.

No judgments! No matter where you are on Cupid's continuum, you'll be reflective about your relationship status for the first couple weeks of 2023. Did you get in too deep too fast only to feel suffocated by the commitment you swore you couldn't live without? Do power dynamics need a serious recalibration? Perhaps you'd like to revamp the day-to-day structure of your life to make space for a partner—or for yourself!

Whatever the case, all the ruminating and reflecting may come to an abrupt end on January 12. Body-based pleasures, on the other hand, regain priority. Scorpios can dwell in their heads like no other sign (except perhaps a Pisces). And with your rich imagination, fantasy can far outpace

> **66**
>
> *If you're not getting*
> *your needs met,*
> *2023 is the year to*
> *turn that all around.*
>
> **99**

reality. Still, there's no replacing legit physical touch, even if your willful sign *can* stay in #MonkMode until you forget what you're even missing. Eternal celibacy does not have to be your fate! If you're not getting your needs met, 2023 is the year to turn that all around.

Let's be honest, Scorpio: To captivate your sensual interest (and keep it!), physical attraction is only the beginning. Partners must drive up a deep sense of longing in you that lingers hours (days!) after you've left their company! Yes, you want security, but you also like to be kept on your toes. If you were nakedly honest, you wouldn't mind a few cat and mouse games—and even some consensual power plays. And guess what? This *can* be learned. If it's been ages since you were in the mood for more than falling asleep watching Netflix, with a tiny bit of effort, that can change in 2023.

Your mission, should you choose to accept it, is to take the risk of exploring your desires! Yes, we did say, "risk." Scorpio Brené Brown talks about "foreboding joy," the fear that arises when we get too excited and suddenly everything feels out of control. You're going to have to get vulnerable (another Brené favorite word) if you want to grasp that orgasmic grail of erotic rapture. And Scorpio, you've got this!

Another way Mars in Gemini could play out? Shared resources, investments and joint ventures could become exciting areas of discovery—or major sore spots—until March 25. You'll need to manage your anxiety and jealousy (and anger and competition). With inflammatory Mars here, basic talks about finances could spiral out of control in a heartbeat. If you're feeling unhappy about the way things are divided up, don't let your temper overtake you. But *do* pay attention to red flags and be unstoppable about getting everything back onto an even keel.

Scorpios with larger loans to pay off may feel an accelerated urge to pay back IOUs. With rash Mars in this position, avoid borrowing money that will be hard to pay back. Instead, get resourceful. From ride shares to cooperative living to passive income earned from, say, Airbnb-ing your basement, creative financing is the name of the game until March 25. And let us say it again, Scorpio: You've got this!

SATURN IN PISCES
Quality over quantity

Saturn in Pisces

March 7, 2023 to
February 13, 2026

Saturn Retrograde

June 17 to
November 4, 2023

Can you feel the pressure lifting, Scorpio? For the last three years, you've shouldered a heavy load as serious Saturn in Aquarius plowed into a tough square (90-degree angle) with your Sun sign. But on March 7, 2023, the cosmic taskmaster eases off, shifting into your fellow water sign Pisces and powering up your creative, romantic and flamboyant fifth house until February 13, 2026. Talk about a gift from the gods! Although Saturn never gives away anything for free, this will be a much lighter cycle, with more opportunities to enjoy life's pleasures—and far fewer existential crises and arduous unpacking of emotional baggage. Truthfully, you could use a break from all that internal processing!

When Saturn spins from Aquarius into Pisces this March 7, it's like emerging from a dark cocoon and finding yourself on...the catwalk! Pisces rules your fashion-forward fifth house, and systematic Saturn is here to help you assemble a tastefully chic wardrobe—or give you an excuse to rock the one you've already curated. But don't stop there. Like Scorpio style icons Bjork, Chloe Sevigny and Willow Smith, your game-changing sensibilities could inspire others to turn their wardrobe into wearable art. Set up the photo shoots and start your feed!

Membership has its privileges while status-conscious Saturn moves through Pisces and your glamorous fifth house. Saturn can restrict your time, so aim for quality over quantity when it comes to human interactions. Are tryouts needed to join the team? Do you have to be referred or voted into a certain club or masterclass? Without turning into a snob, keep it "exclusive and elite" in 2023.

For Scorpios who work in the arts, the three-year Saturn-in-Pisces cycle may ignite some of your best work ever. And if you're ready to go public, Saturn in your fame-fueled fifth house will help you gain recognition slowly but steadily. This isn't Internet-famous, viral TikTok stardom. Rather, it's hard-won acknowledgment for your genuine talents.

On that note, be mindful of what you put out into the public forum. If you've already come out with your first hit, you could easily follow with a "sophomore slump" by rushing a half-baked product to market. Take the time to hone your craft, Scorpio. Only attach your name to work that reflects your stellar taste. For example, maybe you're an actor who wants to be on camera as much as possible when you're not going on auditions and waiting tables. Make sure that appearing in your friends' short films won't stain your budding reputation, even if you never put them on your reel.

Power couple fantasies spring to life with impressive Saturn here, and thanks to the persevering planet, a romantic connection can have staying power during this cycle. Saturn knows you have to take the "bad" with the good. It's all part of adulting, a vital lesson that the planet of maturity and time is here to teach you.

In case you require an excuse to pamper yourself unapologetically, Saturn in Pisces decrees self-care as a necessity more than a luxury. But blowouts and facials only offer a temporary boost, so think beyond the manicure mindset. To really go after your galactic glow-up, work at a deeper level. Relax your furrowed brow with meditative breathwork, get your lifeforce energy flowing with Qi Gong, try facial acupuncture.

Pisces oversees your fifth house of romance, creativity and procreation, and under Saturn's watch, these areas could become subjects of serious conversation. What starts as a lighthearted love affair may steadily evolve into a real-deal relationship. Pregnancy could be an all-consuming topic for some Scorpios. Since Saturn can slow things down, conceiving might prove challenging. Scorpios could explore IVF treatments—or freezing your eggs if you want children someday, but not right now. Clarifying Saturn may bring a calm decision to *not* have kids (or more kids), and instead, to redirect your energy toward birthing a creative "baby." The bigger message is to ensure that your life can withstand the upheaval that often accompanies the joy of a new family addition. Saturn loves a long-range plan!

A short-term plan, too! If you want those weekly date nights and regular romps to actually happen in 2023, commit them to a shared calendar. While that may not sound remotely romantic or sexy, relying on spontaneous impulse will be a recipe for disappointment. Carve out non-negotiable blocks for the quality time you crave. Couples who have done this successfully often take turns surprising each other with the actual date planning. Trade off and have fun researching new venues and activities. There's science behind this, too. Novelty releases dopamine, which in turn, turns up the heat between you!

Unattached Scorpios won't be in any rush to give up the curated life you've created for yourselves. Hey, why rock the boat when you've already settled into a solid groove? You may be a passionate soul, but you harbor few illusions about the "disruption" that an intimate relationship causes. This may be one of the reasons you're hesitant to get involved. Many Scorpios have specific tastes, from an obsession with Art Deco design to a love of arthouse cinema. (And let's not get started on those complex nightly rituals.)

You probably won't take kindly to your mate's comic books messing up the 1930s movie-set vibe of your ebony and chrome coffee table...or their late-night TV habit clashing with your early bedtime. No, Scorpio, there's nothing like a relationship to reveal your hard edges. Maybe you're as strong-willed as everyone suspects. And that's okay! Let yourself go through this process, Scorpio—and don't rush it. It might take you until Saturn leaves Pisces, on February 13, 2026, to arrive at the best decision for YOU. Search the depths of your soul, as only a Scorpio can.

PLUTO IN AQUARIUS
Reimagining home

Pluto in Capricorn
Janury 1, 2023
to March 23, 2023

June 11, 2023 to
January 20, 2024

Pluto in Aquarius
March 23 to
June 11, 2023

Pluto Retrograde
May 1 to
October 10, 2023

m,

Home sweet...somewhere? You might feel like Dorothy waking up in the technicolor land of Oz beginning March 23—disoriented but determined to make it back to Kansas. This sudden compass shift comes courtesy of your ruling planet, transformational Pluto. For the first time since January 2008, the icy dwarf is changing zodiac signs, darting forward into Aquarius, your fourth house of family, security and roots, until June 11.

In case you're wondering, this is a *huge* deal, Scorpio. The last time Pluto visited Aquarius was from 1778 to 1798, which means no one alive has ever experienced this transit. While you'll only get a two-month hit in 2023, don't sleep on whatever Pluto stirs up. On November 19, 2024, your small-but-mighty cosmic guardian paddles back into the sign of the Water Bearer for 19 more years, until January 19, 2044.

In preparation for this tide-turner, you may want to start speculating on what "home" looks, feels and sounds like for you. (Feel free to click the heels of your ruby slippers three times if it helps.) Surprise: What you visualize may be a huge departure from your current living situation. While there's no need to pull up the stakes immediately, take note of these new requirements.

Pluto's been paddling through Capricorn and your curious, frenetic third house since January 2008. During this time, you've been all about "location, location, location." Or should we say, *locations*. If you didn't change your home address, you may have shuttled back and forth between cities for work or another purpose. While you're not inherently a social butterfly, this people-powered Pluto circuit has been an interactive one. Wherever you landed, you wanted to click with the *vibe*, from the cultural activities to the overarching mindset of the community.

As Pluto weaves back and forth between Capricorn and Aquarius from March 23, 2023 to November 19, 2024, shelter needs may fluctuate. Environmental triggers that you once shrugged off—honking taxis, limited parking, a lack of green spaces—may suddenly be a solid "no." You may long for more square footage, privacy, open sky. Maybe it's time to buy a building or land and start that intentional community with your friends...

Since the fourth house rules your kin, a move could be predicated upon the needs of a relative, like an aging parent or a family member who has invited you to come work at their business. Pluto rules death and wealth: You may come into an inheritance that allows you to purchase your apartment or buy a vacation property.

Happily-nested Scorpios may open up your home to a relative, adopt a pet or build an addition. While Pluto's been in Capricorn for the past decade and a half, your friend count has grown, but your interactions may be quantity over quality. Ready to flip that script? Tighten up the radius of your inner circle. If you've been floating on the periphery, pick one group and *really* get involved. While Pluto's in Aquarius for this 20-year lap, friends will be more like chosen family. Rejoice, Scorpio! Superficial exchanges have never been your thing anyway.

But how to attract your kindred spirits? That's where this final leg of Pluto in Capricorn comes in. With your communicative third house catching fire, your job is to sharpen your messaging. What you put out into the world boomerangs back, which is good news because it means you have control over what you're attracting. Whittle down to your core values. Can you express your fundamental philosophy on life in three sentences or less? What do you want to convey to the world? See what happens if you align every aspect of your presentation from your social media to your personal style to the words you speak when you're in conversation with others. (And um, do you even have a photo of yourself on your Instagram profile?)

We're not telling you to be inflexible, of course. No one has this all figured out—plus, we're eternally evolving beings. But there are some fundamental parts of your interior world that feel like *your* truths. This is the year to craft your personal mission statement, mantra or operating guidelines.

Also review the past 15 years! Scorpios have gone through epic identity shifts while Pluto's been in Capricorn. Scorpio Caitlyn Jenner began this cycle as Bruce and transitioned near the halfway point in 2015. While your personal evolution may have taken a different path, take time to reflect on ways you've transformed.

Look too, at where you got stuck. Scorpio Hillary Clinton's run for U.S. President was dogged by Plutonian subterfuge, including an FBI investigation of "those emails" right before the election. For many born under your sign, the hurdles since 2008 came from outside sources: gossip, shady friends or perhaps your own secrecy. If you weathered any betrayals, do what you can to get closure, whether it means talking it out or changing your personal narrative about the situation so that *you* can have peace and move on.

Accepting your own "imperfections" may be enough to bring a Plutonian phoenix moment. Clinton's rise from the ashes of the 2016 election led her in a very third house direction: mediamaking and documenting stories. Her 2022 series, *Gutsy*, debuted on Apple TV+, highlighting courageous women across genres including Amy Schumer and Megan Thee Stallion. The former Secretary of State shares fascinating stories from her own arsenal, including this little-known tidbit: Her pantsuit obsession began early in her career, as a uniform of self-defense, after she accidentally flashed a Brazilian news photographer and drew unwanted attention. If you didn't believe she was a Scorpio before...

Owning your full story is exactly what this final circuit of Pluto in Capricorn is about. Before Pluto officially moves on to Aquarius in November 2024, challenge yourself to lift the curtain and share your authentic, vulnerable self. This can be regenerative, if not redemptive, for you!

How "at home" do you feel in your body right now? (AKA your soul's address here on Earth.) Your relationship to your physical form could shift during scintillating Pluto's passage though Aquarius. That's especially true if you have disconnected from your sensual nature or have, perhaps, turned to food, drink or another vice for a primary source of pleasure.

While Scorpios are known for being the zodiac's sex symbols, your erotic nature is complex. For all the intensely seductive energy that you exude, your own potency can overwhelm or even scare you. Long spells of celibacy are not uncommon for your sign. Sometimes, you're using that "sex magick" for another creative purpose in your life, like a business that fills your every cell with passion. At other times, you simply don't want to deal with all the complex emotions that arise when you open that tantric door: jealousy, anxiety, obsession, self-doubt.

The key to transformation while Pluto is in Aquarius is to build a strong foundation. The fourth house sits at the base of the zodiac wheel, representing our "anchors" like home, trustworthy supporters and financial security. Bodywise, physical movement—as in pleasurable (not punishing) forms of exercise—can make you feel strong, safe and rooted in your own skin. From that centered place, body-on-body action is a whole lot more appealing.

Whatever the case, in 2023, try some lower-chakra healing. Hip circles, reiki or other forms of energy work can get the stuck chi (life force) flowing. Any form of touch can be healing, Scorpio, whether it comes from a massage therapist, a romantic partner or friends in a cuddle puddle. As Pluto casts a long shadow into your fourth house, there's a risk of unconsciously dissociating from your body by doing mental, intellectual work at the expense of your physicality. Watch for that! While your beautiful mind is always worth tuning in to, make movement a non-negotiable priority.

What conversations do you engage in? Words matter mightily while Pluto wraps its time in Capricorn and your language-based third house. Question the topics of your echo chamber. The connection between food and mood is also emphasized. Between March 23 and June 11, you might detox your diet of stimulants or add in foods that boost your energy. Read up on the Ayurvedic doshas. Get your levels checked to see if there are any allergies or digestion issues at play. Pluto rules all things hidden, so it might take a blood draw to get a clear read.

It's a fine time to work on your fiscal fitness, too. While your resourceful sign can thrive during lean and supple years, you always feel better when you have a solid nest egg. Wealth-agent Pluto can make an investment whiz out of you over the coming twenty years. It's never too late, but depending on your age, there *are* better places to tuck your funds than others. Whether tech stocks, mutual funds, real estate—or a combo platter (ideal)—your money moves could pay off in surprising ways.

Bottom line, Scorpio: Be gentle with yourself. Your sign tends to be change-averse—maybe because your cosmic ruler gets cozy in each sign for such a long time, from 12-21 years. Even if nothing shifts in your external realm, your emotional needs will demand more airtime. After 15 "heady" years, your intuition will soon send its strongest signals from your heart. The softer side of Scorpio is peeking through!

VENUS RETROGRADE
Polish your pitch

Venus in Leo

June 5 to
October 8, 2023

Venus Retrograde

July 22 to
September 3, 2023

Grab the brass ring of romance, Scorpio! From June 5 to October 8, ardent Venus rolls out a long, red carpet in regal Leo and pours her love potion into your tenth house of ambition and success. Time to trot out your relationship goals and make them known! Secrecy is your stock in trade, but shrouding yourself in mystery is *not* going to get you what you want during this transit.

Whether it's love, leadership or both that you're after, you are poised to crush it like a heart-centered boss while Venus tours Leo for a whopping 30 percent of 2023. Normally, the planet of romance and beauty lingers in a sign for four weeks. But due to a retrograde (yes, we said it) from July 22 to September 3, Venus extends her journey in Leo for four *months*. Which means you have four times longer than usual to tap into this status-boosting magic, even if the backspin brings a few bumps in the road.

If the thought of confessing your deep-down desires fills you with dread and fear, well it's understandable. Naked authenticity might be a cornerstone of intimacy, but being exposed is nowhere on the list of "Scorpio's Favorite Things." Which means you may have to build up some courage before you stage any big reveals.

SCORPIO

Good news! Venus in confidence-boosting Leo is like a worldwide pride parade. Start by finding a few role models who fiercely own their truth. They might be celebrities (Leos Jennifer Lopez and Madonna come to mind) or your badass neighbor who drives a turquoise pick-up truck like our Scorpio friend Juli. The "who" matters not, as long as you can siphon off some juice from their unapologetic vibes.

Ready to go platinum as a power couple? Scorpios in long-term relationships could find fulfillment by teaming up on a mission between June 5 and October 8...and beyond. Where on your romantic Venn diagram do your dreams overlap? Maybe you both always wanted to own a rustic cabin in Idyllwild or to start a vegan meal delivery service. (Note: Simpler visions like learning to duet on guitar or traveling to Portugal are also more than valid.) When June 5 rolls around, take these plans seriously, Scorpio. They might be the glue that gets you through rocky retrograde moments later in the summer.

Be strategic about every move during Venus' retrograde from July 22 to September 3. This reversal happens every 18 months, causing roadblocks that aren't insurmountable but *can* stop you in your tracks temporarily. The key to pushing past them? Keep your eye on the long-game instead of getting tripped up by details, like your partner's slower timeline for cohabitation or your desire for more partner-induced orgasms during boo's busy season. Venus retrograde is like a yellow caution light, not a glaring red one. From July 22 to September 3, slow and steady wins the race when it comes to future planning. You can quietly start sourcing ethical wedding ring jewelers even if it's not time to discuss a proposal.

Of course none of these milestones matter if you aren't building a strong foundation for your relationship. And that means getting the quality "just us two" time a Scorpio longs for. Anyone who is worthy of you will *not* find this trait "needy," FYI.

Single Scorpios may be caught up in the frayed and faded memories of former loves. And if you're not, get ready! Venus retrograde could stir up some uninvited thoughts, sending you back down another "I wonder if..." trail. Be as honest with yourself as you can, Scorpio: Are you romanticizing the past because you're afraid to open your heart again? Whatever brought this relationship to its unceremonious close had to hurt. (Even if you were the one who ended things.) You may still be nursing wounds, months (or decades!) later. But could you start to open up space for someone else? As much of a one-soulmate lover as your sign may be, what if the universe had a small soul circle waiting for you?

In rare cases, Venus retrograde can bring people back together. If you broke up due to bad timing or life circumstances beyond your control, a second chance might be possible this summer and fall. Advance cautiously and don't set anything in stone until after September 3. And yes, this includes trying to mend fences and start a "friendship" with an ex.

Because Venus in Leo charges up your career-obsessed tenth house, this four-month window is an ideal time to cultivate work connections. Coworkers from the past could be ideal creative collaborators during the six-week retrograde, leading to profitable results for 2023. Do you own a business? Network like it was your side hustle, and not just for prospective clients but for future collaborators, too. Well-connected Scorpios, stop hesitating! Reach out to your circle (and your circle's circle) for leads.

♏

SOUTH NODE IN SCORPIO
Trust your guides

**Lunar South
Node in Scorpio**

January 18, 2022 to
to July 17, 2023

Until July 17, life could feel as surreal as a Banksy NFT. The karmic lunar South Node finishes out its final seven and a half months in Scorpio, putting you through one test of spirit after another. Long-range planning hasn't been easy during this cycle, which began on January 18, 2021. Ever since, you've likely had a frustrating series of starts and stops. Just when you *thought* you nailed the right formula for success, boom! The universe tossed another curveball, sending you back to "seeker" mode. Our advice? Stay fluid.

Detours can be frustrating, we get it. But they *are* taking you somewhere—have faith! When the South Node checks into your sign every 18-19 years (for 18-19 months) it brings answers according to divine timing. Unseen pieces of the puzzle will click into place before this transit ends on July 17. Your job, Scorpio, is to tune in to the subtle cues and clues. Listen to your gut rather than solely relying on intellect. Then put one foot in front of the other and unravel the mystery.

Scorpios who are spinning their wheels may have to move a few barriers out of the way. The first half of 2023 is *the* time to face your fears head-on—and vanquish their hold on you! With the lunar South Node opening your psychic channels, you'll find the strength to do that inner work.

Spiritually and creatively, you'll feel dynamic! And with the lunar North Node in your seventh house of partnership, people will take note! Since you're still "in process" until July 17, don't rush to form any official mergers. Yet if you see a clear path forward with someone who has met all of your requirements—and, of course, passed your loyalty tests—this

> 66
>
> *Unseen pieces of the puzzle will click into place before this transit ends on July 17. Listen to your gut rather than solely relying on intellect.*
>
> 99

could be the year when you officially become half of a dynamic duo. That's music to your ears, whether you find your songwriting partner, a silent investor for your ethical business or the person you want to marry. Soul-deep connections is what Scorpios live for! Want to speed up the laws of attraction? Pop open the hood to your psyche and get to know yourself better.

NORTH NODE IN ARIES
Doing meaningful work

Lunar North
Node in Aries

July 17, 2023
to January 11, 2025

Woosah, Scorpio. When the moon's karmic South Node moves on to Libra on July 17, you'll be ready for a celestial sabbatical. Take it! After 18 months of hosting this lunar point in your sign, you may feel a bit depleted, as if you're emerging from a dark night of the soul. Painful though it's been at times, it's also been a beautiful process of "true-ing up" to your genuine self. This heavy round of internal searching won't come again for nearly two decades. Whew.

Not that you're *completely* out of those deep, reflective woods. On July 17, the lunar nodes reposition themselves across your axis of health and healing—Aries and Libra—and help you integrate your insights into your self-care routines until January 11, 2025. Dialing down stress will be an especially important mission for Scorpios in the second half of the year. If you've been making too many sacrifices, you could hit a burnout moment. The remedy? Simplify your life, then systematize your workflow.

You'll get a lot of support from the lunar *North* Node in Aries, which begins a cleanup mission in your sixth house of efficiency on July 17. Think in terms of getting your house—and your body, mind, spirit and finances—in order. Tempting as it will be to tackle these all with your laser-focused determination, take a more holistic approach. What got you here in the first place? Start by observing how you think on a daily basis. Pay attention to your unconscious habits, limiting beliefs and defensive moves that were birthed in childhood trauma like people-pleasing or rushing in as the "fixer." With the South Node moving through your healing twelfth house (Libra) until January 11, 2025, awareness is the key to alchemy.

Trigger alert: The South Node in your twelfth house can poke at old wounds. You may have a few more tears to shed as you process grief, ancestral trauma, pain over abandonment and breakups. Don't resist the painful feelings! The sooner you unblock emotional dams, the faster you'll get back to your happy place. Watch sad movies, go to a sound bath, do what you can to get things flowing. Bottled up feelings lead to all kinds of unwanted things, from literal weight on your body to chronic disease. This healing nodal cycle helps you shed whatever you've been holding in. Let go and let yourself be liberated!

Reminder from the North Node in Aries and your healthy sixth house: Your body is your soul's address here on Earth. Mid-summer, get pumped to eat clean and get back into a regular fitness groove. If you've been ignoring aches and pains, you'll need to deal. Vitality is the goal, so make sure you're also loading up on preventative medicine. Eating clean, taking supplements and holistic treatments (acupuncture, Chinese medicine) can go a long way to keep you humming.

Since Aries rules the cranium, the North Node's journey through this sign can turn your attention to neuroplasticity. While many neural pathways are formed during childhood, they aren't all hard-wired. Because of the brain's plasticity, new pathways *can* be formed, often through repetitive activities such as breathing exercises or learning a new word every day. Novel activities like traveling, crafting and reading fiction have also proven to boost brain activity. As a sign that loves to treasure hunt and make things by hand, this is right up your alley, Scorpio.

Or hack your body's responses with epigenetics, which studies how environment and behavior affect the expression of genes. Moving to a new area or cultivating a daily habit won't alter your DNA per se. But it *can* change your body's response to stimuli, for example, the way your nervous system reacts to intergenerational trauma.

With the Aries North Node accelerating the pace of your sixth house of daily routines, work could get insanely busy. Unless you're feeling passionate about the job, however, you may find yourself slipping into "quiet quitting" mode. With this destiny-driver pointing you toward professional growth, you're well positioned to find a new job—or perhaps create one for yourself at the company you already work for. Don't rush a resignation. If you're a valued employee with a solid track record, at least *try* to have a conversation about carving out a more suitable, fulfilling position for yourself. You may be pleasantly surprised!

No matter what, before January 11, 2025, make it your mission to add more meaning to your work. Already there? Now's the time to do a health check. Have you slipped into martyr mode, working around the clock or without clear boundaries? Burning out is never a good look, Scorpio, so let the Aries North Node help you reclaim personal limits—and systematize your workflow so you have time to prepare a healthy dinner, hit the gym for an evening cardio class and enjoy weekend trips.

The last time the nodes were in this position was from November 30, 2004 to June 19, 2006. Significant themes around health, spirituality and work could arise again between July 17, 2023 and January 11, 2025. Revisit parts of your life that fed your soul back then. Nostalgia aside, you may discover that they nourish 2023 you!

ECLIPSES IN 2023
Reclaiming your time

Hybrid Solar Eclipse in
Aries (new moon)

April 20 at 12:17AM

Penumbral Lunar Eclipse
in Scorpio (full moon)

May 5 at 1:24PM

Annular Solar Eclipse
in Libra (new moon)

October 14 at 2:00PM

Partial Lunar Eclipse
in Taurus (full moon)

October 28 at 4:15PM

times in eastern time

APRIL 20:
SOLAR ECLIPSE IN ARIES
HYBRID SOLAR ECLIPSE 29°52,
12:17AM ET

Wellness check! The first eclipse of 2023 arrives in Aries and your sixth house of healthy routines. Because it kicks off a new, two-year series across your healing axis, you may get a wakeup call to manage stress and take better care of your body. Or maybe just a giant burst of motivation! This is a super-rare hybrid solar eclipse—beginning as an annular "ring of fire" eclipse and evolving into a sun-blocking total solar eclipse—that shifts your attention to new modalities. For some Scorpios, this may be the first time you try acupuncture or colon hydrotherapy. Others among you may need to mix some modern medicine in with the natural healing, so look for a Functional MD who blends both. During this eclipse cycle, you'll benefit from a more structured routine: nutritious meals and daily meditation will go a long way toward helping you feel more balanced and peaceful. Get ready for big news on the work front. You may be offered an opportunity that really lets you shine. You're poised to make a name for yourself between now and March 2025!

MAY 5: LUNAR ECLIPSE IN SCORPIO
PENUMBRAL LUNAR ECLIPSE, 14°52, 1:24PM ET

Feel this moment, Scorpio. Today marks a stunning lunar eclipse in your sign, a day for letting your full-bodied personality out to play. Your efforts of the past six months (since the corresponding solar eclipse in Scorpio on October 25, 2022) could come to a magnificent milestone, helping you put your name on the map in the days and weeks ahead. Get yourself camera ready because the media could knock! While your secretive sign tends to have mixed feelings about being in the public eye, accept your role as "the reluctant superstar." Life is too short to hide your light under a bushel. And once you start promoting yourself and what you have to offer, you'll quickly see what an incredible difference you make for others.

OCTOBER 14: SOLAR ECLIPSE IN LIBRA
ANNULAR SOLAR ECLIPSE 21°10, 2:00PM ET

Epic fail...or a life-changing epiphany? Today's annular "ring of fire" solar eclipse in your twelfth house of closure helps you see beyond the doors that seem to be shutting in your face. This is an opportunity to turn in a new direction, Scorpio. Miracles can happen simply because you surrender and let life take its natural course. Forcing an outcome only feels like hitting your head against the same brick wall. A mentor figure who is an "earth angel" of sorts could appear to support you with your change. You are so ready for this, don't even doubt it for a minute.

OCTOBER 28: LUNAR ECLIPSE IN TAURUS
PARTIAL LUNAR ECLIPSE 5°03, 4:15PM ET

A key relationship could take a turn in an exciting direction as the potent lunar eclipse in Taurus—the third and final one in a two-year series—activates your seventh house of partnerships. You've grown exponentially since November 2021, and your needs from a mate may have fluctuated in kind. How can you and your "other half" combine your skills for an even more rewarding win-win? If you've been negotiating with a business collaborator, you might finally settle on terms and ink a deal. If you're craving more commitment from the object of your affections, conversations should be productive—and passionate!

2023

—

SAGITTARIUS

WHAT'S IN THE STARS FOR

SAGITTARIUS

You're falling in love again, Sagittarius—and this year, it's with your life! While the 2023 stars will be happy to offer romantic escapades and high-octane fun, the main event is happening on any stage you strut across. Got a gift to share with the world? The first half of the year holds special promise for increased visibility, perhaps with a global audience. A long-distance attraction could also heat up. Taking care of your body is also a huge new hotspot, as the stars reward your efforts to eat green, clean and lean. Transform yourself from the inside out by reducing stress and shifting your mindset—then go break a sweat with an endorphin-pumping workout (epic playlist required!). Your home life turns serious and structured for the next couple years. You could buy or sell property, or care for a relative in need, such as an aging parent or a child who requires more attention. Over the past decade, your fluctuating finances have taught you huge lessons and revealed limiting beliefs. Ready to graduate from "feast or famine" into power and prosperity? A sneak preview of this new chapter arrives in spring and summer 2023.

SAGITTARIUS WILL BE LUCKY WITH:
Romance, healthy living

SAGITTARIUS WILL BE CHALLENGED WITH:
Home and family

LOVE

A romantic renaissance or reckoning? 2023 is sure to bring both. You'll have your hands full of admirers while your ruler, bountiful Jupiter, rolls through Aries and your fifth house of *amour* until May 16. During this heavenly high season, squeeze as many playdates on the calendar as you can. Proposals, weddings or babymaking could be on deck for Archers through mid-May, or perhaps a renewed relationship chapter that feels like a second (or third) honeymoon. Venus goes on an extended tour through Leo and your global ninth house from June 5 to October 8 making summer ideal for a baecation or a long-distance romance. But be warned! While Venus spins retrograde from July 22 to September 3 you could rebel against anything that feels challenging or restrictive. The truth could get slippery then. Don't make promises you can't keep—or change your entire life based on a charmer's sweet nothings!

CAREER & MONEY

Lights, camera, Sagittarius! A long red carpet rolls out for Archers in 2023 starting with Jupiter's strut through Aries and your fifth house of fame until May 16. Don't miss this prime opportunity to increase your reach, whether you're delighting fans with live TikToks or getting your research published in a journal. When Jupiter settles into Taurus on May 16, it's all systems go—provided you have solid processes in place. Simplify and streamline your workflow so it's easy to step out and shine without having to manage the same mundane matters over and over again. The North Node heads into Aries on July 17, sending up another call from the cosmos to stretch out of your comfort zone and into the public eye. Keep a sensible budget in place. With restrictive Pluto weaving in and out of your money zone this year, stability is as important as visibility this year!

WELLNESS

With the lunar nodes on your axis of healing (Taurus-Scorpio) until July 17, you are carrying on 2022's health quest. Detoxifying your diet, improving gut health and reducing stress are all tantamount to your vitality in 2023. Getting yourself into a routine has always been challenging for you, but once your ruler Jupiter arrives in Taurus for a year on May 16, you'll relish the repetition, especially once you start to feel (and see!) results. Bake pleasure into the process! Rather than cutting out "bad foods," get excited about tasty recipes that use fresh, unprocessed ingredients.

FRIENDS & FAMILY

Family duty calls! Not exactly the clarion call your indie-spirited sign loves to hear, but with Saturn dropping anchor in Pisces and your fourth house of roots this March 7, you're heading into a three-year cycle of increased responsibility. A child, parent or beloved friend may need extra support. Conversely, *you* may need to lean on a relative a little more than you'd prefer. Your home situation may change or settle down after a period of uncertainty. Thankfully, friends will be there to hit the town when you need some fun! The Libra solar eclipse on October 14 could usher you into an exciting new group or elite organization!

JUPITER IN ARIES
Step into the spotlight

Jupiter in Aries

December 20, 2022
to May 16, 2023

Wardrobe! Styling! Are you ready to strut back onto the main stage, Archer? Call in hair and makeup and find your best angles. The public began clamoring for your gifts December 20, 2022, when your ruler, larger-than-life Jupiter, zoomed back into Aries, spotlighting your fifth house of fame, romance and self-expression, until May 16, 2023. From your refreshingly quirky personality to your creative gifts, you won't keep much under wraps.

Even luckier still? In Aries, Jupiter forms a flowing 120° trine to your Sagittarius Sun. This energy-boosting transit unleashes the Niagara Falls of passion in the first half of the year. Expect to feel more confident and flamboyant than you have in a while.

You already got a taste of Jupiter in Aries last year when your red-spotted ruler zipped through this headline-grabbing zone from May 10 to October 28, 2022. Once again, you'll draw the spotlight your way in 2023. And this time you have a few important lessons about the "fame game" under your belt. Being a public figure comes naturally to bubbly, live-out-loud Sagittarians. Whether that means a spot on a TV show or the PTA President is entirely up to you. If you're being 100% honest, you thoroughly enjoy doses of admiring praise!

What you don't dig about #IconLife is when people start pigeonholing you. And then there are the obligations that being an in-demand figure puts on your time. You were just trying to share some sparkle with the world! How did you wind up being typecast as a role model...and do you *really* have to create a posting schedule for your Instas and TikToks? Grrrr. Most Archers would rather spontaneously twirl in their living rooms like Sagittarius Britney Spears when the "touch of rose" strikes than queue up a month's worth of posts on Creator Studio.

Don't resist structure! There's freedom to be found from, say, batching out content or picking one day a week to record some videos. Jupiter may rebel against rigidity and predictability, but getting yourself into a steady stride has its benefits in the audience development department. When people know when and where to find you, they'll return—and if they're into your vibe, they'll share your feeds with friends.

> **66**
>
> *Sharing BTS videos and works-in-progress could win you even more approval for your no-joke work ethic.*
>
> **99**

With worldly Jupiter minding the store, cast a wide net to reach a global audience. This could be the year when you're randomly discovered on TikTok, YouTube or another self-starter platform. Don't worry about making everything perfect. Sharing BTS videos and works-in-progress could win you even more approval for your no-joke work ethic.

But do leave space on your jam-packed calendar for romance. Aries is in charge of your passionate fifth house, and while heat-seeking Jupiter visits, a tepid attraction could start to sizzle. With cosmopolitan Jupiter playing matchmaker, cross-cultural romance and vacation flings will be hot, hot, hot! But what will you do with the boatload of admirers who want to drop anchor on your shores? Single Archers may decide to play cruise director and enjoy the attention from a multitude of sexy sources without feeling pressure to settle down.

Even more good news? You won't have to worry about directing every scene. (But you can still produce a few that fulfill your fantasies!) With free-wheeling Jupiter playing Cupid in your decadent fifth house, you can simply focus on pleasure. If that results in a happily-ever-after, great. In the meantime, let your hair down and diversify your dating portfolio. That will be an education in and of itself.

Already off the market? You can still reap the benefits of this romance-boosting circuit. Forthright Jupiter helps you to express your desires, which could spark a new flood of experimentation. That could include anything from, "I want to have a threesome" to "Let's plan a trip to Croatia this spring" to "Let's make a baby." And not for nothing, the fifth house governs fertility. Consider yourself on notice that the stork may have you in his crosshairs until May 16.

Warning: Pursuing an extracurricular attraction may be tempting before May 16, especially if your erotic life has become a bit too predictable. But Jupiter the gambler doesn't offer you the greatest foresight. Opening things up is always complicated. Whatever the case, clear agreements are a must. For example, you might want to loosen up restrictions around flirting with other people. Innocent crushes happen! But how far can you push it without making each other spiral into fear and jealousy? As long as you and your partner establish mutually agreed-upon boundaries—and respect them— you can enjoy Jupiter's last lap through Aries without losing your integrity.

JUPITER IN TAURUS
Muscle for the hustle

Jupiter in Taurus

May 16, 2023 to
May 25, 2024

Jupiter Retrograde

September 4 to
December 30, 2023

Ready to come back down to earth, Sagittarius? On May 16, Jupiter segues out of Aries and your fantasy-filled fifth house and lands like a weighted balloon in Taurus and your sixth house of service, efficiency and wellness. Suddenly, your priorities shift from play to work, and not a moment too soon! Your early 2023 hedonism was about to creep into "touring rockstar" territory. Fun for a while, but not a sustainable groove for anyone, even you!

While Jupiter visits Taurus until May 25, 2024, the wellness wagon becomes your ride of choice. No longer will a Bloody Mary be your sole veggie serving of the day, nor will raising it to your lips count as a bicep curl. This holistic cycle calls for clean living across the board. Get ready for a big shift, Sagittarius. In the second half of 2023, you're more interested in reading nutritional labels than debating what you should label your latest situationship.

If you fell into unhealthy habits in early 2023, you could pull off a major lifestyle pivot mid-year. Chronic aches or doctor's orders to get your BP or cholesterol under control may be the catalyst you need to make this shift. And with Jupiter in just-do-it Aries, you have all the motivation you need to bite the bullet and go for broke. Eliminating alcohol, nicotine, or sugar could save some Archers from bottoming out. But deprivation works for very few people—and certainly *not* a Sagittarius. Turn the focus to discovery instead.

Try eating for your blood type, soothing inflammation with ayurvedic recipes like turmeric golden milk or learning to cook paleo meals in a Moroccan tagine.

66

Jupiter in Taurus may serve bigger projects than you've tackled in the past—ones that could involve travel or interfacing with people all around the world.

99

With sporty Jupiter in earth sign Taurus, make fresh air and sunshine regular "supplements" in your daily regimen. Sagittarians love any excuse to be out, moving around under the open sky. Motivate yourself to exercise with *al fresco* fitness. Sign up for tennis lessons or join a cycling club; learn Stand Up Paddleboarding or rent a kayak. Make a point of walking or biking places you'd normally drive. If you live in a hilly area, an e-bike may be the best investment you make. Adopting a dog is also a Sagittarius-strong incentive to get out and about.

With your industrious sixth house activated, Jupiter could lead you to the wellness field or even the service sector. Many Archers will crave freedom while no-limits Jupiter sails through this 9-5 realm. If you're still searching for your next passion, a "bridge job" with flexible hours and low stress could help you pay the bills in the meantime. Use any extra time and energy to take skill-building classes and earn certifications in your area(s) of interest.

Already thriving in your field? Jupiter in Taurus may serve bigger projects than you've tackled in the past—ones that could involve travel or interfacing with people all around the world. If you're the typical Sag, your enthusiasm often outpaces the systems you have in place. It might be hard for you to slow down and get others up to speed so they can pitch in. But try! If you want to take advantage of Jupiter's growth potential, you'll need to delegate.

Don't expect people to knock it out of the park the first time they step up to bat. Put them through an orientation process and set a trial period. With this systematic sector lit, document processes in a training manual. This could be as useful for *you* as it is for the contenders jockeying for a spot on Team Archer. Getting organized is the secret to your success—and the key to your peace of mind—in the second half of the year.

MARS IN GEMINI
Parallel play and partner dancing

Mars in Gemini

August 20, 2022 to
March 25, 2023

Mars Retrograde

October 30, 2022
to January 12, 2023

Power to your partnerships! Actually, Sagittarius, make that turbo-charged power with twin engines. On January 12, mojo-revving Mars wakes up from a 10-week retrograde in Gemini, and your stalled libido starts turning over again. Until March 25, Mars blasts ahead through Gemini and your seventh house of relationships, accelerating your drive to connect with anyone who holds dynamic duo potential. Whether you're inking a deal as a brand ambassador or co-signing a lease, take the initiative!

No one on your radar? Gemini rules local activity and peer groups, making this the perfect winter to be a joiner. Network with industry players or jump into social activities where you can meet (and maybe fall head over red soles for) people who love to buzz about the same fascinations, from Portuguese cooking to fantasy lit. Career-wise, Mars also fans the flames. Set up chemistry meetings with people you'd like to collaborate with—and hit 'em with a pitch deck that sizzles! With Mars shortening attention spans, first impressions need to be *hot* now, Sagittarius. Start with an attention-getting question. Then, show them why your solution is the best and obvious answer.

The red-hot planet only visits Gemini every other year and this particular circuit is a special one. Normally, Mars hovers in a sign for seven weeks, but when it spins retrograde every two years, its extended stays last for seven *months.* And that's exactly the case in 2022-23! You've had the red planet in your relationship zone (Gemini) since August 20, 2022. No doubt, this got you thinking about the state of your unions—or lack thereof. While you can be perfectly content on your own, Mars in Gemini reminds you that it's also nice to have a "someone" to sip morning coffee with or share the client load during busy months at the office.

Many Archers had a shakeup in their unions since combative Mars arrived in Gemini on August 20, 2022—especially once the retrograde began on October 30. Chaos, upheaval, forward momentum? Disorienting as the backspin has been, did it snap you out of complacency? Drive you to shift stale dynamics...or possibly leave a relationship that you've outgrown? Martian energy is anything *but* gentle. Still, you can't deny the results
it delivers.

Are you the sort of Sagittarius who is open to all sorts of people? Discernment isn't your eternally optimistic sign's top trait, Archer. (FOMO, on the other hand...) Starting January 12, however, fuzzier notions about romantic fulfillment could sharpen dramatically. Questions like, "What are you looking for in a partner?" or "Where do you see our relationship heading in the future?" won't leave you at a loss for words. But you might not tell people what they want to hear! That's fine. Pleasing people is not the goal; in fact, that may have been the problem all along. Until March 25 (and beyond), lean into your sign's penchant for speaking your truth. All you have to do is remember that your word won't be gospel for everyone. Express what *you* want—and put it on the negotiating table. With Mars in logical, cooperative Gemini, remember that it's a two-way street. Get just as eager to discover where all the VIPs in your life stand. Their preferences are not your command, and vice versa. They are simply a jumping-off point.

The real question is, can you carve out a path of workability, one that allows you both to get your needs met? Lofty as this goal may be, it's not an impossible stretch. But if it is? Courageous Mars can help you fly free—and quickly. Go ahead and have the ugly cry, primal scream and body-racking grief if that's what you need. Mars can help you move that energy through your body, metabolizing it all.

Have you had a hard time letting someone go? After January 12, you'll get clarity around why this person has you in their thrall. Mars is the planet of passion and lust, but chances are the attraction is more than that. How do they make you feel when you're together—or even just communicating? Stating the obvious: Sexy and desirable are great feelings, but if you know this person is trouble, you need to weigh the emotional cost against the (ego) benefit. Bottom line: Listen to indie-spirited Mars' message that you don't have to get your validation from anyone else, least of all an insincere player.

Beyond the real-life interactions, this activating energy is essential for clearing out stagnant energy and rebuilding things on rock-solid ground. Mars churns up heavy emotions and passions, but you don't get to cherry-pick them. When anger, jealousy or resentment arise, accept it for what it is but then probe beneath the surface. Where is this really coming from? You may need to work with a therapist to get to the root of this, but it's vital to get there. Otherwise, you'll only be putting Band-Aids on surface cuts and never get to heal the core wounds.

If you're willing to bravely dive in and face relationship stumbling blocks head on, you can expect profound results. While it takes two to tango, there's only one person you *can* control: yourself. With that in mind, Sagittarius, what's your next move?

SATURN IN PISCES
Dropping anchor

Saturn in Pisces

March 7, 2023 to
February 13, 2026

Saturn Retrograde

June 17 to
November 4, 2023

Settle in, Archer! As steady Saturn drops anchor in Pisces on March 7, a three-year security-building cycle gets underway in your foundational fourth house. Until February 13, 2026, your lesser-seen homing instinct kicks into high gear. Yes, even the zodiac's most notorious nomad needs to put down roots every now and again—even if Casa Archer is a base station you can nest in between your worldly jaunts. As the ringed planet points you toward smarter ways to live comfortably within your means, you might feel less inclined to rush off on the next adventure.

On that note, how *is* everything at Chez Sagittarius? With serious Saturn adding heft to your domestic plans, you could plant deeper roots, perhaps buying (or selling) property, renovating your home or moving to a location with a better cost of living. You have a gift for creating a lively hub, no matter how much square footage you have to work with—and how rarely you're home to enjoy it!

That said, your housing needs may change dramatically over the next three years, as you evolve under karmic Saturn's maturing influence. You may reach the bittersweet conclusion that you've outgrown the studio apartment on a buzzy cosmopolitan avenue that you've rented (for cheap!) since your halcyon days. Conversely, some Archers will get inspired to embrace a minimalist lifestyle that conforms with Saturn's austerity plan.

If you rehome yourself, there's no need to rush the process. Take a methodical approach—but not *so* slow that you fail to gain traction or miss a plum opportunity to invest in a great piece of property.

Coupled Archers struggle to give up their bachelor(ette) ways, but surprise, surprise! In 2023, you may decide to take the adult plunge and cohabitate. After March 7, the search for your love nest could become an obsession. But how ready are you for this *really*? If you're amped up with new relationship energy, Saturn warns you that fools rush in. Giddy decisions should be based in practicality, not *just* romance. (Sorry, Sagittarius.)

Discuss every possible scenario, from how you'll divide housing costs to what function each room will serve. That "creative cave" your boo is picturing might be the square footage you hoped to utilize for your home office—something to consider before you settle on a floor plan.

For other Archers, strict Saturn may shift your lifestyle, limiting the time you spend together. Maybe one of you has to relocate temporarily for work or see a family member through an illness. There will be details to work out, so practice patience! Even if there are no extenuating circumstances, do you simply want your own space? Separate addresses might mean amplified romance for some Sagittarians who live by the rule of "absence makes the heart grow fonder."

Since Saturn governs structure, building storage systems or working with a professional organizer could prove beneficial. We're not saying new shelves will change your life...but we're not saying they won't, either!
This won't be the easiest Saturn cycle in the world. While in Pisces, Saturn forms a tense 90-degree angle (called a "square") to your Sun. Squares force us to stop dawdling and take concrete action. If your foundation has been shaky of late, the coming three years will help you strengthen it. Learning to nurture yourself is part of the program. Regimented Saturn wants you to schedule self-care, not just talk about it abstractly. Eat meals at regular intervals, integrate fitness into your daily routine and go to bed at the same

time every night. In other words, act a little more like a Capricorn (the sign Saturn rules) than a Sagittarius. You can do it!

The fourth house rules women and female-identified folks. In 2023, you could link up with a powerful group of ladies or get involved in an organization that moves women's rights forward. A relationship with a female coworker or adviser could turn into a solid business partnership, or maybe you'll profit from an older woman's wisdom. On the flip side, you might assume this role yourself, training a younger upstart or mentoring a colleague. An aging parent or relative may need more help this year, which could lead you to take on a more grown-up role in your family.

Mommy issues ahead: Saturn, the planet of adulting, in your maternal fourth house could trigger a rift with your mother or kids. But this isn't necessarily the worst thing. If you're enmeshed, severe Saturn hands you the psychic scissors and orders you to cut the cord. Personal space and independence can strengthen your bond—even if there's grief in letting go. Cautious Saturn may cause delays with starting or expanding a family—or compel you to seriously change your lifestyle to accommodate this plan.

Sagittarius parents might struggle to deal with a child going through a challenging phase (oh, those tricky tween years) or experience the pangs of empty nest syndrome. During this stoic Saturn cycle, you may not feel the usual warmth and closeness with your kin. It's a time when you need to "do the right thing, not the easy thing." Set loving but firm boundaries.

Truth be told, that's a sound strategy for dealing with *everyone* in your life now. Saturn in your sensitive fourth house teaches you to lead with the right combination of head and heart. You may have learned tough lessons about people who play your soft side like a fiddle or charm you into codependent enabling. In 2023, you have to rework (or even end) draining, one-sided relationships. Let others be accountable for their grown-up choices, and you do the same.

PLUTO IN AQUARIUS
The burden is lifting

Pluto in Capricorn
Janury 1, 2023
to March 23, 2023

June 11, 2023 to
January 20, 2024

Pluto in Aquarius
March 23 to
June 11, 2023

Pluto Retrograde
May 1 to
October 10, 2023

Is money the bane of your existence? The keys to your kingdom? A little bit of both? Since 2008, volcanic Pluto has been simmering underground in Capricorn and your second house of finances. For many Sagittarians, your cashflow's been as unpredictable as lava, coming in hot one minute then drying up the next.

Are you ready to put an end to that feast-to-famine cycle? We'd bet our gold ingots on it. And would you like to enjoy a little (okay a lot) more stability in your financial life? Check! That goal is in closer reach in 2023, as wealth-agent Pluto darts into Aquarius from March 23 to June 11—the first leg of its 20-year cycle through your savvy third house.

Although Pluto will power back into Capricorn for a last hurrah on June 11, it returns to Aquarius from November 19, 2024 to January 19, 2044, its first long trek through the Water Bearer's realm since 1798! Get ready for some major shifts around money and values that could reshape your entire life.

Pluto's journey through Capricorn has put pressure on your bank account since 2008, but it hasn't been a total wash—not by a long shot! This regenerative earning cycle brought exponential growth and some on-the-edge-of-your-seat excitement to your daily work. Money flowed in from different sources, sometimes in large checks. "Hustle" was not a dirty word in your lexicon. (Hell, that's just everyday living for a supersonic Sagittarius.)

While you love to "chase the bag," wouldn't it be nice to keep more of those hard-earned winnings? For every dollar you clocked since 2008, there was another worthy expense demanding your coin. From classes to travel, you invested in your growth! But you felt like a hamster on a wheel who can never stop running and running and running...

Sagittarius Britney Spears is a prime example of the dark side of Pluto in the second house as her family literally wrested control of her millions in a court-mandated conservatorship that left the pop star "a slave" to her father Jamie's whims starting in 2008, the very year Pluto shifted into Capricorn. Fans formed the indefatigable #FreeBritney movement and in 2022, the final full year of Pluto in Capricorn, they helped Britney spring free from her father's iron grip and regain command over her estate, her liberties and her mental health treatment.

If money hasn't been an issue, time may be. While you adore your work, many Archers feel stretched thinner than angel hair pasta. You may have commuted frequently or lived like your digital devices were literal appendages. Work-life balance, uh, what's that? Something's gotta give! Enter alchemical Pluto in Aquarius, the sign of the disruptor, and the ruler of your third house of communication and cooperation. When Pluto shifts into a new sign, it's a major deal. As the outermost (dwarf) planet in our solar system, it hovers in a single zodiac sign for 12-21 years.

As the planet that rules our unconscious behaviors, projections and shadows, Pluto's not exactly a welcome guest when it first casts its spell upon a new area of our lives. But like the path of Joseph Campbell's hero's journey, Pluto lures you into the dark cave. If you heed its lessons, you *will* emerge with a gift.

So what does that mean for you, Sagittarius? Over the next two years, as Pluto winds down its time in Capricorn, you could get a solid handle on this work and money thing. Already found your groove? Get ready to rise into a greater position of power and prestige, perhaps as half of a dynamic duo. After November 19, 2024, Pluto will never return to Capricorn and your second house again in this lifetime. So make sure you track its golden lessons. This evolution has sharpened your values and taught you so much about what is actually priceless to you. By the same token, it's awakened the responsible money manager in you.

How to make life easier from here? As Pluto tests the waters in Aquarius from March 23 to June 11, you don't actually have to scale back or simplify. Instead, do what Archers do best: aim high and expand.

But here's what's different this time, Sagittarius: The "target" you're hitting isn't a pot of gold, but rather a precious partnership that will be a win-win for everyone. Generating wealth, opportunity, excitement? You've traditionally done that as a one-Centaur show. Pluto in your third house throws down a gauntlet: Find people who adore your unorthodox style but can also teach *you* a thing or two!

Feel those control issues rising up? They're going to be a familiar guest at the table as you evolve into this new, two-decade Pluto cycle. There may be a few crash-and-burn test runs in the beginning of this "hands on to hands off" transition, so ease in slowly. Be sure to develop criteria for who you want in your corner rather than whimsically gambling on people who "feel like a good fit." The so-called experts who charm you could be concealing a hidden agenda to dominate entirely. Or maybe they simply don't have the resources they promised, which could stall your fast-moving project when you get into bed with them.

You're going to need a very excellent (and probably expensive) lawyer to support you with contracts over the coming 21 years. Dealmaking is the terrain of Pluto in the third house and a proper, signed agreement is the rock-solid insurance in which you need to invest. What you *don't* want to do is give away too much of your intellectual property. (Remember all the lessons Pluto in Capricorn taught you about valuing yourself?!) Starting off on a clear, unambiguous note might feel awkward, but you're setting yourself up for a win-win.

The third house rules communication and intellect, and with piercing Pluto in Aquarius here, nothing gets past you. But does that mean you should blurt out your observations in a ranting tweet or with one of your off the cuff "jokes"? Neither strategy worked well for Sagittarians like Chrissy Tiegen and Steve Bannon while Pluto was in Capricorn—and that warning goes triple when Pluto enters Aquarius. Don't get yourself #canceled in the heat of the moment!

Sagittarius media makers, get ready to create some of the most profound material of your life. Pluto in Aquarius is prime time to pour your spiritual beliefs, experiences and philosophies out into the world. Record that podcast, write a book, create an online course. Just make sure you're super clear on the point you're trying to make. If it's salient enough, it could create a cultural movement!

Say goodbye to any superficial friendships. With your social third house getting tagged by Pluto, you need people who will embrace you on a sunny day *and* have your back when you're doing your shadow work. Loyalty is everything to your truth-dealing sign. But if you want your relationships to fulfill their potential, you have to open up more of yourself, too.

Letting yourself be seen by people won't be easy when Pluto in Aquarius drops its cloak of invisibility over your soul. So lift it up, willingly. Pluto in Aquarius will serve lessons in "being with" your hard emotions rather than running away, changing the subject or turning them into a sketch comedy. The realest, fullest you is emerging from the shadows, slowly but surely.

VENUS RETROGRADE
Take a chance on romance

Venus in Leo

June 5 to
October 8, 2023

Venus Retrograde

July 22 to
September 3, 2023

Your wide-angle view on love could broaden ten times further in its scope this summer! (Think: fisheye lens.) From June 5 to October 8, ardent Venus sails through Leo and your ninth house of global connections. Summer lovin' won't just "happen so fast," it could also go down on at least three different continents. Or maybe you'll finally take the baecation that has been on your bucket list since, ohhhh, your first crush.

No matter your GPS coordinates, you'll perk up for a *patois*; get enchanted by an accent. From there, it's anyone's guess what might spontaneously combust, especially with pleasure-seeking Venus in the sign of the fierce jungle cat. But don't rush to be caught in any one hunter's net. The ninth house is the one associated with your independent sign. With Venus in this freedom-loving zone, you're like Sagittarius Nelly Furtado's bird that will "only fly away" if someone tries to cage your spirit or restrict your trajectory in any way.

So what's a solo Archer to do? Pack your bags, obviously. No one ever has to ask you twice to fly the friendly skies or hop in your car for a cross-country drive. (Though you might want to coordinate schedules with your coworkers first.) Exploring a new region provides the ultimate dopamine rush for a Sagittarius, making you feel like your sexiest self. Who knows? The person sitting next to you at the twee roadside diner could be your next great love—or a hot summer fling.

During Venus' nostalgic retrograde, you might even take a road trip to visit an FWB who you vacation-flinged with earlier in the year. Oops, that's right, we said the R-word. From July 22 to September 3, Venus shifts into reverse, a disruptive cycle that comes around every 18 months. Much like a Mercury retrograde, Venus' periodic retreats can scramble signals. The difference is, as the love planet, Venus takes specific aim at your close, interpersonal relationships.

Warning: Since Leo rules your outspoken, honest-to-a-fault ninth house, you're likely to wind up with a stiletto in your mouth at least once or twice this summer. But you can head that risk off at the pass with early intervention. What are the triggering hotspots in your relationships, Sagittarius? Not just with lovers but family and friends? Try to address these while Venus is flowing in forward motion from June 5 to July 22. While tripling down on tact is recommended, don't be afraid to drop the façade and speak your truth. Pretending that everything's okay when it's clearly dysfunctional is not actually "keeping the peace." As a matter of fact, Sagittarius, pointing out the neon pink elephant in the room is kind of your job in the zodiac. Once the air is clear, you'll see smoother sailing for all parties involved.

For coupled Sagittarians, absence will make the heart grow fonder from June 5 to October 8. But don't confuse "absence" with "abandonment"! Even while apart, you need to fill your relationship's emotional bank account with deposits of quality attention. Leaving that up to chance is inadvisable. Book regular slots to FaceTime—and don't even think about rescheduling unless it's truly an emergency.

If you need to end a dry spell, head back to a place that makes you feel like the enchanting siren you are, especially between July 22 and September 3. It could be a beloved beach, a favorite dive bar or your childhood home. Trips like these can reinvigorate your pure power and potential. And there's nothing more attractive than a Sagittarius in love...with yourself!

NORTH NODE IN ARIES
Playing the fame game

**Lunar North
Node in Aries**

July 17, 2023
to January 11, 2025

Wardrobe! Styling! Although the year begins on an industrious note, it probably won't end that way. On July 17, your official uniform could change from athleisure to athluxury—or full-tilt glam! For this, you can thank the destiny-driving North Node, which is returning to Aries and your fifth house of fame, romance and creative expression for the first time since 2004-2006. And frankly, you'll be more than ready for the playful, frisky vibes this cycle brings.

But first...work, work, work, work, werk. Until July 17, the North Node will wrap up the final third of its tour de Toro that began on January 18, 2022 when it landed with a thud in Taurus and your industrious sixth house. In this service sector, you've had your sleeves rolled up so often that you're ready to go strapless. You probably already gave someone the shirt off your back anyway.

As the North Node pivots into Aries, you might not even be ready for the rewards it brings. Like Cinderella easing her foot into that glass slipper, you could suddenly go from broom duty (sweeping up other people's messes) to belle of the mother****ing ball!

Sashaying down the street looking runway-fierce is one thing, but the North Node is the cosmic *destiny point*. Which means that you need to play a much more "high-exposure" game between July 17, 2023 and January 11, 2025. TikTok supernova, star of your own TV series, keynote speaker: Where do you *know* your talents can shine? Get all your ducks in a row and your workflow solid in the first half of the year. That way, you'll have the perfect springboard to soar into the spotlight. Now's the time to let your hair down—and boost the volume with a blowout, curl cream or a mammoth wig. During this showstopping cycle, even the most chill Archers will get a thrill out of turning heads.

66

If you're not 100% comfortable in front of the lens, do what your sign does best: study until you ace it.

99

The camera will love you during this North Node cycle. If you're not 100% comfortable in front of the lens, do what your sign does best: study until you ace it. Livestreaming is a no-brainer when it comes to raising awareness of one of your endeavors. But why stop there? If you've mastered a skill, get into the expert industry. Develop motivational talks and courses, write a book. Media has always been your playground as the sign that rules publishing. All that's missing? Your beautiful face on the screen!

And maybe on the dating apps? The North Node in Aries spells "peak romance" for you! No matter your status, this 18-month cycle calls for dress up dates, baecations, and quality time with your boo. After a certain point, relationships don't "just happen." If you want yours to thrive, feed it a steady diet of time and energy. There's something to be said for the comfort of "parallel play," where you and your S.O. are both engaged side by side in your respective projects. But make sure you have enough interactivity in your relationship, too. This may require you both to break a few bad habits, like checking messages in bed or watching TV during dinner, effectively blocking out moments where intimate communication could arise.

Single Archers won't be in a hurry to settle down. Enjoy the tasting menu but don't be surprised if someone special sweeps you off your feet—and possibly down the aisle! This destiny-dusted cycle could bring you straight to your soulmate—or into a more solid arrangement with someone you've been dating for a while. Your fifth house also rules fertility. Those with bambinos on the brain might get some pregnancy news by January 11, 2025.

Across the zodiac wheel, the lunar *South* Node finds a brand-new balance point in Libra—the opposite sign of Aries—activating your eleventh house of teamwork and technology for this full 18-month time span. The South Node is what we call the "karmic comfort zone," stirring slumbering gifts within you.

Indie-spirited Archers attract great people, but you aren't always the best at organizing a collaborative approach. It's not for lack of desire! You'd happily let go if only you knew how. When the Libra South Node kicks in this July 17, you'll get a master class in project management and team systems. Seek that out for yourself! Life doesn't have to be such a struggle.

It's possible that you've been giving the wrong people a chance over and over, as dating prospects, friends, service providers, employees. Don't lose faith in the human race! Use the harmonizing gifts of the Libra South Node to find your inner serenity. Forgive yourself for making "mistakes," and distill the lessons. Then, experiment! You won't get a different result until you try a different tactic. And in the second half of 2023, that may involve playing in a much bigger league than you have in the past!

ECLIPSES IN 2023
Healing your heart

Hybrid Solar Eclipse in
Aries (new moon)

April 20 at 12:17AM

Penumbral Lunar Eclipse
in Scorpio (full moon)

May 5 at 1:24PM

Annular Solar Eclipse
in Libra (new moon)

October 14 at 2:00PM

Partial Lunar Eclipse
in Taurus (full moon)

October 28 at 4:15PM

times in eastern time

APRIL 20:
SOLAR ECLIPSE IN ARIES
HYBRID SOLAR ECLIPSE 29°52,
12:17AM ET

Make way for another archer—Cupid, that is! The first Aries eclipse since 2015 shoots a quiver full of arrows into your fifth house of romance, fame and creative expression, waking up your slumbering passion. Eclipses bring swift and sudden opportunities and this one could reveal a heaven-sent romantic click. Since it's a super-rare hybrid solar eclipse—starting off as an annular "ring of fire" eclipse and transforming into a sun-blotting total eclipse midway—you can't ignore fluctuating feelings. Wondering where a love interest stands? You're going to need answers soon—and so will they! Which means if you've been wavering about your own affections, lovers may hold your hands to the fire. Choose or lose, Sagittarius. The fifth house also rules fertility, which might even herald a pregnancy. And make sure you're "camera ready" as a glamorous and starpowered opportunity could come out of the blue.

SAGITTARIUS

MAY 5: LUNAR ECLIPSE IN SCORPIO
PENUMBRAL LUNAR ECLIPSE, 14°52, 1:24PM ET

Forget about going gently into any goodnights. The game-changing lunar eclipse in Scorpio and your twelfth house of completions wants you to celebrate an important passage in your life. Be proud of the threshold you've crossed; celebrate with friends. Helpful guides may come out of the woodwork, opening doors and helping you circumvent any barriers to success. Although you could feel a little overwhelmed by it all, surrender to the growth opportunities that crop up over the coming two weeks. You'll figure out how to handle it all, Sagittarius, just like you always do.

OCTOBER 14: SOLAR ECLIPSE IN LIBRA
ANNULAR SOLAR ECLIPSE 21°10, 2:00PM ET

Your taste in friends is always evolving, Sagittarius, probably because you are the type who never stops growing and learning. The annular "ring of fire" solar eclipse in Libra—the first eclipse to land in this sign since 2016—could bring a shift in your social life. You may suddenly realize that you've outgrown a certain group. Simultaneously, you may encounter the very crowd you've been dying to meet. And given the ephemeral nature of eclipses, these introductions could come quite out of the blue. Eclipses reveal hidden opportunities. As this one illuminates your tech sector, lighting the way to some prosperous digital ventures or someone with soulmate potential waiting to be swiped on. Get the intros rolling, but take your time, since some information may be concealed that could inform your future consideration.

OCTOBER 28: LUNAR ECLIPSE IN TAURUS
PARTIAL LUNAR ECLIPSE 5°03, 4:15PM ET

Three, two, one, expand! The final lunar (full moon) eclipse of a two-year series in Taurus illuminates your sixth house of work. And as it does, it could spotlight a massive opportunity for ascending the ladder of success. Along with the added prestige also comes an incredible surge of responsibilities. Already maxed out with your current workload? If you're willing to relinquish a bit of your independence in the name of leading a team effort, it's definitely doable. After all, Sagittarius, you are just one person.

2023

—

CAPRICORN

CAPRICORN

Your long reinvention tour is nearly complete. Since 2008, your sign has been going through a slow but intense inside-out transformation. This spring and summer you'll get a sneak peek of what life will feel like on the other side, as you emerge with new levels of power and influence. You may start putting your money where your morals are, and long to make a greater impact with your work. On a personal note, your home is a hub of activity all of 2023, and possibly the site of your next genius innovation! Family ties, especially with female relatives, can reach healthy new levels of honesty. You might hunt for a home or upgrade your current abode. In the second half of the year, love takes top billing as a romantic renaissance sweeps in. This is also a prime period for fame, so get yourself camera-ready. The company you keep is crucial now. Preserve those cherished lifelong bonds, but start moving in some new, established circles where you can meet industry colleagues who will open doors. For the next couple years, it really is about "who you know." Bring YOUR generosity to the party, and foster a genuine network that helps each other thrive.

CAPRICORN WILL BE LUCKY WITH:
Home and family, romance

CAPRICORN WILL BE CHALLENGED WITH:
Communication, financial management

LOVE

Keep on stretching, Capricorn! The destiny-driven North Node lingers in Taurus and your romance house until July 17, bringing nonstop insights about dating and relating. Once lucky Jupiter arrives in Taurus on May 16, you'll be Cupid's darling—and ready to cash in on all your self-discovery work. Single Sea Goats might mesh with someone from another culture or spark up a long-distance love affair. No matter what, bring on the decadence, pleasure and playtime. A sexy summer is in store as Venus simmers in Leo and your intensely seductive eighth house from June 5 to October 8. Schedule any "state of our union" conversations *before* Venus turns retrograde from July 22 to September 3—a time that could spin up jealousy and lovers' quarrels. If you're ready for that next big step, this Venus-in-Leo cycle gives you the courage to leap.

CAREER & MONEY

Switch it up! Powerhouse Pluto, which has been touring Capricorn and your self-authorized first house since 2008, darts into Aquarius from March 23 to June 11, beginning a 20-year cycle that could evolve your approach to work and money. Capricorns who have been paying your dues could soon cash in on a venture. Do you need more consistency with your income or time to yourself? You may give up some "excitement" for the ease of a steady paycheck. When the karmic South Node slips into Libra on July 17, it begins an 18-month trek through your leadership zone. Duty calls, but that crown will get heavy if you don't delegate. You'll connect to all kinds of power players while convivial Venus launches a charm offensive in your eighth house from June 5 to October 8. If you want to secure funding or a loan, you're in luck—but vet people carefully and negotiate favorable terms, especially while Venus is retrograde from July 22 to September 5.

WELLNESS

Your year is off to an energetic start as of January 12 when action planet Mars powers forward through your wellness zone until March 25. You might even join a health club that has a social component or take your winter vacation at bikini bootcamp or a yoga retreat. Preparing healthy meals could become your favorite way to socialize, as feast-god Jupiter hangs out in your nourishing fourth house until May 16. Forget the wine club—how about a vegan supper club? Structured Saturn heads into Pisces on March 7, putting focus on your hands, wrists and arms. If you do computer work, prevent carpal tunnel with stretching, posture and an ergonomic mouse.

FRIENDS & FAMILY

Family time is always important to your devoted sign, whether with blood relatives or your esteemed "chosen family." And with both Jupiter and the destiny-driven North Node visiting Aries and your house of kin this year, you may go out of your way to connect to your inner circle. (Time to take that trip to your ancestral homeland!) Get involved in activism while the South Node's in Scorpio and your community zone until July 17. With serious Saturn in your BFF sector starting March 7, you may outgrow certain people, but never fear! A new friend circle will form quickly, especially if you get involved in local activities.

JUPITER IN ARIES
Home sweet anywhere

Jupiter in Aries

December 20, 2022
to May 16, 2023

When was the last time you stopped to feel your feelings, Capricorn? And have you been treating them like honored guests at the table? Your first New Year's resolution of 2023 might be to revel in the richness of your inner landscape—and even make friends with the demons that are hiding in the shadows.

It's not like you could avoid your emotions if you tried. (And oh, how a business-first Capricorn *will* try...) On December 20, 2022, maximizer Jupiter barreled back into Aries for its second (and final) lap through your "big feeling" fourth house, moving your personal life to the front burner until May 16. Whatever you've been sweeping under the carpet could come flying forth for examination.

Our recommendation? Be proactive and set up support networks of friends, mentors and therapists who can help you process and metabolize whatever arises. You've been the rock for so many people, Capricorn, and now it's your turn to have a lean. The biggest barrier to feeling held, however, may be your own fear of being judged. Thankfully, Jupiter in confident Aries will supply large doses of truth serum, making it easier for you to open up about whatever's in your heart.

Could you use a little "mama energy," Capricorn? With Jupiter anchored in this nurturing part of your chart, you'll gravitate toward the types of people who can shower you with TLC. This may be a departure from the buttoned-up business bros and stylish influencers your sign tends to gravitate toward. (Whether you care to admit it or not.) Your relationship with your mother or an important elder in your life may grow closer before May 16. Is it time to evolve into new roles instead of relating to each other via outworn dynamics? You're in a great place to get some transformation rolling here.

If you have children, they could occupy both your time and your thoughts. However, independent Jupiter in this zone suggests that you may be letting go a little—and in the process, giving them a "fly zone" to test their wings without your instruction or interference. We're not saying this will be easy! Since Jupiter rules education, you could be busy trying to find the right schooling for your kids.

Curious about your heritage? This nostalgic five-and-a-half-month period could be the perfect time to reconnect with your roots, traveling to your ancestral homeland or visiting relatives who perhaps you've never met IRL before. A 23andMe test could bring fascinating results about your genetic makeup and introduce you to new branches of your family tree!

The fourth house sits at the base of the chart, and it represents your foundations—emotional, historical and familial. Meanwhile, Jupiter is the planet of travel and exploration. Does this mashup sound like a contradiction? It doesn't have to be. With the nomadic planet parked in this zone for the first half of 2023, you could reimagine your concept of home life completely. Have you fantasized about moving to another region or trying the digital nomad lifestyle for a few months? The first half of 2023 could be an ideal time to arrange a house swap or put your stuff in storage and head out to explore. If you're curious about van life, rent a rig and see what it's like to take Casa Cap on the road. With bold Jupiter in the fourth house, this is your chance to take a wild leap! "Home" could soon be wherever you hang your beanie and stash the lotions and potions you manage to squeeze into travel-sized bottles.

CAPRICORN

Staying put? Life at base could turn into Grand Central Station with energetic Jupiter buzzing through this realm. You may play host to a revolving door of houseguests or build an ADU on the back of your property to rent on Airbnb for extra cash. If mortgages in your area are unaffordable, you could roll the dice on a vacation property elsewhere.

A word to the wise: You may struggle to set boundaries before May 16, especially with family members and cherished friends. Although your caretaking side is switched on, honor your need for personal space. You'll need to take occasional breaks from couch-crashers, especially during busy work seasons—or when you just need a break from setting up the spare room for the fifth week in a row.

If you're looking for a permanent pad, 2023 is the year you could become a homeowner. While you love working out in the world to achieve your goals, your ambitious sign also thrives in a secure nest that nourishes your body and soul at the end of the day. With bigger-is-better Jupiter in this zone, you could move into a scaled-up place, build an addition or redecorate. Even if you're in a tiny studio apartment, you'll find ways to maximize the square footage.

Under Jupiter's enterprising influence, 2023 is an ideal year to launch or grow a home-based business. Did your company return to the office when pandemic restrictions eased? If not, maybe you won't have to...ever. That side hustle you've been quietly developing may soon need its own dedicated workspace. Create a corner—or take over a spare room—and get ready for your creativity to flourish.

Some Capricorns might take a job where you provide emotional support to others. If you've thought of becoming a healer, coach or therapist, you could be headed back to school, courtesy of erudite Jupiter. You'd do well to lighten your schedule a bit while Jupiter is at its farthest point away from your tenth house of career. Not that you'll ever completely power down, Goat. But you'll make a *lot* more headway from the comfort of your couch (or your neighborhood coffeehouse) than you will in a fluorescent-lit cubicle. If higher-ups want you in the office, make a compelling case for WFH productivity, and they might just agree!

Some Capricorns could get a long-distance job offer—and next thing you know, you're packing up and moving across the country—or the world. Fate and fortune will be on your side in these negotiations. Maybe you got a whiff of this in 2022 when Jupiter visited Aries from May 10 to October 28—or in the circuit before then, from January 17, 2010, to June 4, 2011. Scroll back for clues of what could surface again, particularly around family relationships and your living situation.

There is one hitch: While in Aries, Jupiter forms a difficult, 90-degree square to your Capricorn Sun. So, in the course of all this rapid growth, you could experience growing pains and face a few tough hurdles. It will be worth it to push through such challenges, as long as you learn the lessons and apply them ably to whatever you're working on. Bonus: You'll get stronger in the process!

JUPITER IN TAURUS

Prioritizing pleasure and playtime

Jupiter in Taurus

May 16, 2023 to
May 25, 2024

Jupiter Retrograde

September 4 to
December 30, 2023

You're cordially invited to let your hair down, Capricorn—and also get it blown out, highlighted or dyed cobalt blue! On May 16, Jupiter exits your lowkey fourth house and blasts into your fellow earth sign, Taurus, heating up your fifth house of passion, romance and playful expression until May 25, 2024. After a lowkey entry to 2023, your *joie de vivre* returns with a vengeance. Woosh! It can be disorienting going overnight from behind-the-scenes producer to the center of attention. But don't scurry back behind the velvet curtains, because you'll get your bearings in a short time.

If you want to develop a following, widen your lens. As global Jupiter raises your profile, you're poised to attract an international fanbase. This could be the summer that your band goes on a European tour or maybe you'll fly to Asia to attend a conference. Draw influences from every corner of the world during this 12-month cycle, whether you board a plane or study an ancient modality. As the zodiac's most ambitious sign, you could turn some of the lessons you've learned into your own "edu-tainment"-style course offering. Or you could wind up recording live streams, being followed by a reality TV camera crew or killing your lines like Capricorns Jared Leto and Florence Pugh.

The fifth house is the realm of *amour* and your love life could go through an accelerated growth spurt after May 16. Fresh romance—or rekindled passion with your S.O.—can add sizzle to this 12-month Jupiter-in-Taurus cycle. Even better? In Taurus, Jupiter forms a flowing 120° trine to your Sun in Capricorn, which triggers an avalanche of passion and gives you the most radiant glow-up you've had in years. (Photo shoot!)

Romantic options? You'll have plenty of them. But don't measure everyone by the soulmate standard. The fifth house is the realm of romantic love. (Long-term commitment is the business of the seventh and eighth houses.) It's not that you won't find quality prospects this year. But *you* may want to extend the exhilarating courtship phase (with more than one contender, possibly) before locking yourself into anything longterm.

And note to the sentimental softies who captured your heart in the first part of 2023: Get your swag up to snuff or step aside! As your taste in lovers goes from mild to wild, you need more fire to light up your erogenous zones. But warning: Although your libido may do a U-turn, don't throw the baby out with the bathwater. You're looking for thrills while Jupiter slinks through sensual Taurus, but you'll live to regret it if you throw a good catch back in the water prematurely. After May 16, the fun may lie in being exploratory *together*.

Speaking of which, attached Goats could see the second half of 2023 as the perfect time to blast out of their comfort zone: traveling, learning and exploring new hobbies together. Surf lessons in Costa Rica, a Portuguese culinary tour in Lisbon, or maybe...water birthing classes? The fifth house is the fertility zone and if you're in babymaking mode, abundant Jupiter could bless you with a mini-me (in a twin set, even). If that's not in the cards, a co-created project can give you and your boo an inspired excuse to bond. What *could* you create together...? Start dreaming, then get into action!

MARS IN GEMINI
Cleaning house, making moves

Mars in Gemini

August 20, 2022 to
March 25, 2023

Mars Retrograde

October 30, 2022 to
January 12, 2023

Here's some news that will make your systematic soul sing! Starting January 12, you can restore order to the Capricorn court in an epic way. Momentum-building Mars, which has been retrograde in Gemini since October 30, 2022, corrects course and zooms ahead in your sixth house of efficiency, productivity and well-being until March 25, 2023! Talk about a productive Q1! With this gale-force tailwind at your back, you won't just get organized, you'll create structures that boost productivity and profitability. Boom!

Don't let this cleanup mission impinge on any wild and crazy birthday celebrations, of course. But once you've had your cake (champagne and spotlight dances on every table and surface), you'll be good to go. Life at Goat Central is about to get streamlined, decluttered and polished—as you get yourself into fighting shape in every way.

This *will* take discipline, of course. Luckily, that d-word is one of Capricorn's favorites. As the sign of the steadily ascending Goat, you know that achieving success is a marathon, not a sprint. Set your goals—benching 50 lbs by March, getting to inbox zero—then design the daily habits needed to get you there. Get organized with a game plan and timeline, then pick your progress-tracking app. Not only is it easier to course correct when you're watching the process like a hawk, but celebrating little wins along the way is what keeps you excited! The hardest part might be simply getting off the couch or out the door. Once you're in motion, the momentum will build.

Since the sixth house rules wellness, pay attention to stress levels. Hard-driving Mars can cause you to bite off more than you can reasonably chew—and in overthinking Gemini, it can provoke anxiety from spinning thoughts. Breathwork exercises, like box breathing—4 counts inhale and hold for 4 counts; 4 counts exhale and hold for 4 counts—can ground you in basically any moment.

> ## 66
> *With this gale-force tailwind at your back, you won't just get organized, you'll create structures that boost productivity and profitability.*
> ## 99

Check out what's in your line of vision, too. Clear clutter and move any reminders of daily work *out* of your resting and sleeping areas. Your first "new year, new you" mission may be creating an aesthetically appealing storage system for all your stuff. Group like objects together and keep them in specific areas of your home. (Power cords and beauty supplies do not belong in the same box...)

When it comes to your well-being, you can get ahead of the game with preventative medicine. With athletic Mars in your vitality zone, build in regular workouts, especially ones that have a challenge component. (You love being #1!) Develop a stronger yoga practice, even hire a trainer or tap a fitness buddy to help you stay motivated. Pick up a practice that you began when Mars first moved into Gemini last August 20—one that might have slipped when the retrograde began on October 30, 2022.

And what have you been developing behind the scenes, Capricorn? After the retrograde wraps on January 12, show stealing Mars invites you to trot your work into the public. If the final product is still "in process," how about beta-testing it with a small focus group? Their feedback can save you costly mistakes in Q1. Or video yourself in production. Your "making of" videos might turn into future tutorials that you can market. Plus, your work ethic makes you a fan favorite!

If you're considering any professional plays in early 2023, tap into Mars in Gemini's networking prowess. While you *could* pry open the door by yourself, that may be extra. Could a well-connected friend help you sail in without all that effort? Ask your people with clout if they'll put in a good word on your behalf. Ask clients to write testimonials and gather case studies so you have "social proof" of your abilities. Of course, you have to deliver the promised goods, but there's no shame in using the blessings you have.

Still getting started on your path? Get humble, Capricorn, and pay those proverbial dues. Solid experience is worth its weight in platinum, even if you have to "settle" to get your foot in the door. Don't get caught up in the "quiet quitting" hype. To arrive at a place where you can command top dollar, you need genuine expertise. Starting at the bottom gives you a chance to observe the action—and it won't be long before your ambitious self is on an express elevator ride to the top!

SATURN IN PISCES

The weight of your words

Saturn in Pisces

March 7, 2023 to
February 13, 2026

Saturn Retrograde

June 17 to
November 4, 2023

Say what, Capricorn? Heavyweight Saturn, your galactic guardian and the planet of authority, is broadcasting from Pisces and your communicative, cognitive third house starting March 7. Your words carry more weight than ever during this cosmic cycle, which lasts until February 13, 2026.

If you're going to open your mouth, click "send" on a screed or press "publish" on a post, step into your power first. Saturn, the planetary disciplinarian, challenges you to be impeccable with your messaging. Know your hashtags and keep your finger on the pulse of cultural conversations. Whether you're creating a platform or already standing on one, hefty Saturn lends you influence.

The trick with no-nonsense Saturn is to get to the point and keep it brief. When there's business to take care of, bypass the wordy preamble and philosophical tangents. Brevity is the soul of wit when timelord Saturn is in this position. And frankly...what a relief! Mastering this less-is-more approach to communication is a discipline that could open up space on your calendar.

What will you do with all those extra minutes? And moreover, with whom will you spend them? With status-conscious Saturn here, you could feel judged by the company you keep, or worse, get bogged down in policy debates. Yet 2023 may present prime opportunities to play Community

Ambassador or superconnector. There's a time and place for everything, according to Saturn. Where work is concerned, make sure everyone on your team can be vouched for and verified. You'll never accomplish the mission if you're stuck brokering peace deals.

> **Where work is concerned, make sure everyone on your team can be vouched for and verified.**

How you say things matters, too—including your modulation. If you've adopted the Millennial-era habit of ending every sentence with a question mark, consider that this "upspeaking" might signal a lack of self-assurance and clout. Yikes! You could go as far as working with a vocal coach, but for starters, recognize that your views are valuable. No more apologizing for your opinions, Capricorn. That being said, doublecheck your facts and get your data from credible sources. You could get #Canceled for speaking off the cuff or spreading false rumors.

Refining your message could pay off in other ways. You may gain recognition as a podcaster, writer, blogger or media-maker in 2023. If you've mastered your medium, you might generate revenue as a teacher or motivational speaker. Saturn likes things polished and perfected, so don't improvise. Work from a script or an outline. Make sure you really have something to say—and stay focused. Keep it short and sweet.

If you own a business, update your branding so everything (fonts, logos, colors) is consistent. While Saturn is retrograde (traveling backward) from June 17 to November 4, it's an ideal time to refresh your presentation style, marketing materials and social media profiles. A curated image will take you far! Writers, artists and inventors should protect intellectual property with copyrights, trademarks and even patent applications.

Saturn likes to do everything by the book. If, for example, you fell into a job as a life coach but never got certified, diligent Saturn could prompt you to get some formal training under your belt. An added bonus: You'll feel free to charge more after you acquire additional credentials. Luckily, Saturn in Pisces forms a relatively easy sextile (60-degree angle) to your Sun, so you'll welcome this chance to flex your intellect.

The third house rules siblings, neighbors, cohorts and kindred spirits. With "wise elder" Saturn here, you might have growing pains with one or more of these folks. Or, you could formalize a collaboration with someone whose talents complement yours. Take those synergistic developments slow and steady. Test the waters with a joint project and see how that goes before diving into an official partnership. You could also take on a leadership role in your community, becoming a vocal advocate for a cause you believe in. Whatever it is you have to say, Capricorn, people are listening!

VP

PLUTO IN AQUARIUS
Cashing in on hard work

Pluto in Capricorn
Janury 1, 2023
to March 23, 2023

June 11, 2023 to
January 20, 2024

Pluto in Aquarius
March 23 to
June 11, 2023

Pluto Retrograde
May 1 to
October 10, 2023

A seismic shift is in the stars for Capricorns starting March 23. For the first time since 2008, metamorphic Pluto leaves your sign and moves on to Aquarius, loosening its iron grip on your life. Although Pluto circuits back into Capricorn for one final hurrah on June 11, your world feels noticeably lighter in early 2023. And after November 19, 2024, Pluto will exit your sign for good, moving on to Aquarius and your second house of work and money until January 19, 2044. (More on that in a minute...)

Pluto stays in each sign for 12-21 years. Because of its 248-year orbit, many people will never host the formidable planet in their zodiac sign. But you, Capricorn, were one of Pluto's lucky darlings, chosen to go through a 16-year hero's journey from 2008 to 2024. You've plunged into the depths of the underworld and crawled back into the light. Surviving Pluto in Capricorn has been a huge achievement, so take a moment to congratulate yourself. The cycle is nearly complete!

As a Capricorn, you're quite comfortable with power and authority. Domineering Pluto's transit through your first house of self-expression wasn't the worst thing ever; in fact, it brought plenty of high points that boosted your prestige. To wit, weeks after Pluto entered Capricorn in late 2008, signmate Michelle Obama moved into the White House, breaking ground as the matriarch of first Black First Family. Capricorn Gayle King rose to prominence as a newscaster, shedding her reputation as Oprah's sidekick. The iconic Dolly Parton became a pandemic hero, financing and promoting vaccines. Bradley Cooper, LeBron James, Lin-Manuel Miranda, John Legend—all proved the staying power of your indefatigable sign since 2008.

On the dark side of Pluto, scandals unraveled for Capricorn villains like Ghislaine Maxwell, R. Kelly, Marilyn Manson and Ezra Miller, all accused of various forms of Plutonian kidnapping, manipulation and/or sexual abuse. Scary!

We know that the average Capricorn is *not* dealing with such extreme highs and lows. (A blessing!) But many of you have experienced your fair share of intense developments since 2008. After weathering so much change and turbulence, you probably wouldn't mind relaxing into a more predictable groove.

And so you shall...soon. You'll pass the Plutonian baton back and forth with Aquarius a couple times in 2023 and 2024. We wish we could say this would be an easy process, but this is the underworld planet we're dealing with here. Progressive Aquarius rules your second house of finances, self-worth and values. Over the next couple years, there may be some shifts in your material status. Larger bills may come due but you could also cash in on your hard work!

Many Capricorns identify personally with your job. Who *would* you be without your title and privileges? We're not saying you have to answer that! But it's a question that could send a Sea Goat soul-searching this year, especially if you aren't feeling spiritually connected to your work.

Maybe the money isn't worth the stress or you feel underutilized (or worse, undervalued). Quiet quitting? As furtive Pluto passes through Aquarius this

March 23 to June 11, you may be tempted to slip away slowly. We suggest a more graceful exit, one that leaves your hard-earned contact database intact.

Money is a motivating factor in your decisions, but it's not going to be the only one once Pluto goes full force in Aquarius from November 19, 2024 to January 19, 2044. What does "soul work" look like for you, Capricorn? Don't rush to answer this. Just start contemplating.

Perhaps you've already discovered that meaningful path for yourself and if so, strategic Pluto's pass through your sign can help you figure out how to leave your legacy. Could you systematize what you've built up (AKA "The Capricorn Method")? That would allow you to pass on your work, train others to carry it on and economically empower everyone in the process. Sounds like a huge win-win to us!

As you peer into Pluto's dark crystal ball, you may see an epic lifestyle change, one that will seep in gradually over the next 21 years. While you'll never give up your luxuries 100%, the desire to live simply and naturally will hold greater appeal. Those status symbols you accumulated over the years may not spark the same joy. (Well, with the exception of some genuine favorites.)

Values change as Pluto makes its glacial drift into Aquarius and your second house. Starting this year, don't be surprised if you find yourself longing for more of life's basic pleasures: quality time with loved ones, meaningful interactions, time in nature.

And more body-based activity, please! With transformational Pluto in your corporeal second house, you'll crave relationships with regular TLC—and you may be drawn to somatic therapy, massage and other hands-on healing. And while Pluto can be icy, in Aquarius, it could melt some of your reserve and bring out a warmth you haven't experienced for years.

VENUS RETROGRADE
Getting intimate

Venus in Leo

June 5 to
October 8, 2023

Venus Retrograde

July 22 to
September 3, 2023

Midyear check in for Capricorns: Are your love tanks running on empty? Venus to the rescue! On June 5, the planet of love and beauty sashays into passionate Leo, charging up your eighth house of seduction and intensity for four *months*, until October 8. This sultry summer awakening could jolt your libido out of hiding, turning you from Sea Goat to horny goat in seconds flat.

Or maybe a frisky feline? In luxurious Leo, Venus wants you to purr like a big cat in your own delicious skin. If you planned to lounge around all summer, switch up your strategy. Moving your body gets the sexy endorphins and neurochemicals flowing. Plus, you feel more empowered in your physical form, making it easier to invite any consensual "guests" into your field.

You'll relish your alone time, too! With the cosmic creatrix in this nocturnal zone (the eighth house), you could stay up half the night composing songs for an EP, working on a large-scale painting or video installation. Date nights with the Muse should be booked on the calendar!

Generally, Venus hangs out in a single sign for four weeks, but not mid-2023. Yet the reason for her extended voyage through Leo comes with a caution label. From July 22 to September 3, Venus spins retrograde, an unavoidable cycle that comes around every 18 months and leaves lovers shaken and stirred. During these six frenetic weeks, you could confront everything from buried desires to a few deadly sins.

CAPRICORN

Even if you'd never admit it aloud, you get jealous and possessive, just like the rest of us. This retrograde will be particularly provocative to the green-eyed monster. But there *is* a silver lining! You also have a golden opportunity to create soul-deep intimacy as you peel off the mask and keep it retrograde-real. Yes, Capricorn, you *do* care (a lot!). While there are risks to revealing this intel, you stand to lose a lot more (like, say, the one you love) by pretending to be nonchalant.

Conversely, you may suspect that a partner is hiding something. While you'll be tempted to play Sherlock Holmes, avoid crossing any lines, such as reading their private texts and emails. If you feel compelled to go *there*, deeper issues are brewing. Venus in Leo helps you confront the trust problem in relationships that keep filling you with suspicion.

Since retrogrades rule the past, don't be surprised if a contact you maybe should have blocked reappears on your phone screen in July or August. But Venus retrograde is equally famous for reuniting long-lost lovers, and with this one hitting your alchemical eighth house, you'll see exactly why people say that soul connections are eternal. Question is, can you make it work on the material plane now that time has gone by? Wait until Venus corrects course on September 3 to resolve that question.

Long-term investments fall under the realm of the eighth house domain. Venus in luxe Leo could bring a wealthy windfall through the sale of property or a savvy stock you bought years ago. Joint finances also come into play—and prior to July 22, you might ink a killer deal that pays dividends for years.

Any sort of transaction can get tricky from July 22 to September 3, however, causing major relationship meltdowns. Make sure anyone you're combining funds with is on the up and up. If you're doing business together, avoid ambiguity. It's up to you to project your intellectual property from sharks in sheep's clothing that might be circling around your fortune this summer.

NORTH NODE IN ARIES

Home sweet sanctuary

> **Lunar North Node in Aries**
>
> July 17, 2023
> to January 11, 2025

Ambitious Capricorns are forever climbing higher, but how are things going down at base camp? Starting July 17, the destiny-driving lunar North Node anchors in Aries and your fourth house of home, family and roots. While we're not suggesting you hit the brakes on your dreams, come on down to ground zero and fortify your foundation. This cycle hasn't happened in 19 years, Capricorn, so consider it your once-every-two-decade integrity check. (Inconvenient though it may be to slow your roll.)

Plus, this is pretty exciting! Between July 17, 2023 and January 11, 2025, Sea Goats have the rare opportunity to (re)invent "domestic bliss" according to *your* specs. And with your killer tastes, this could turn into an art project—maybe one that gets you featured on a stylish blog. But no need to turn your space into a public spectacle (unless you want to). What matters most now is that it makes you happy every time you walk up to the front door.

Don't wait too long to make changes, because the unspoken visual cues affect your subconscious in more ways than you realize. If you haven't redecorated post-quarantine, start with switching to less-expensive items, like duvet covers, framed art and paint colors. Reconfigure rooms, tapping into the principles of Feng Shui to harmonize your design plan and hues to best suit the elements: wood, fire, earth, metal or water.

♑

CAPRICORN

In the market for a move? Plans may accelerate after July 17, thanks to the speedy Aries North Node. Whether you're moving into a modern loft apartment with floor-to-ceiling glass or shopping for a historical fixer-upper with great bones, this could be exciting! Just be careful not to bite off more than even you can chew. If you can't get through a remodeling mission on a reasonable timeline (ideally by early 2025), phase it out. A good home is never done!

Whatever your dream scenario—a different (or no) roommate, to live with your love, to move or buy a place of your own—start envisioning it as if it's already taking place. Get really clear about what this new situation looks, feels, even smells, like. (Can you already imagine the custom-blended scent piping in?) The more time you spend "in" that reality, the closer you get to manifesting it.

Warning! Who you spend your downtime with is going to be a lot more important during this 18-month cycle. Your sensitivities will be heightened after July 17, which can make you prickly if people invade your private space. Scientists are studying "emotional contagion," proving that moods are actually transferable. Living (even working) with energy vampires affects your mental health. Some people will never stop disrupting your serenity, leaving you no choice but to distance yourself. Don't waste your breath explaining, because they'll probably try stealing that, too! Quietly craft your exit plan, then bounce.

Even in the happiest households, family roles will need to be negotiated after July 17. In the case of needy friends and relatives, avoid performing the Capricorn trick of turning into an unmovable slab of stone. While their actions may merit this impenetrable stance, that just makes you have to work harder to ignore them. Maybe you simply need to spell your wishes out in a way that they understand. And write them down so they know where your "no" lies. Desired outcome? To make your space work for everyone living under the same roof. But first, get clear about what you need so you can communicate without misunderstandings.

"

Some Capricorns may completely revamp your eating habits in the second half of the year.

"

Don't forget the home you always carry with you: your physical form. The fourth house rules the way you nurture yourself—mind, body and soul. Food and mood are indelibly entwined with the North Node here. Dietary changes can vastly improve health in any year, of course. But you'll have added motivation now to tackle things like your addiction to sweets and adult beverages or excessive coffee consumption. Some Capricorns may completely revamp your eating habits in the second half of the year.

And lest you worry that you'll lose your professional edge... Across the zodiac wheel, the lunar *South* Node is shifting into Libra and your career corner for the same time span, from July 17, 2023 to January 11, 2025. Slumbering gifts wake up when the South Node activates this ambitious part of your life. Charged up by charming, social Libra, your work could involve a lot more networking in the second half of the year.

While few work as hard or fast (or efficiently!) as a Capricorn, there *are* some people on the planet who can roll with your gold-star work ethic. Since Libra is the sign of partnership, make it your mission to seek them out. Teaming up could spell three times the money in the bank! No need to look for a clone. Someone with a complementary skill set could fill in all the blanks, deepening the quality of your offerings—and elevating your profit margin to the sky!

If you're ready for a career pivot, the South Node in Libra may bring a period of soul-searching that's essential to the process. Be patient, Capricorn, because you may need to try out a few possibilities before you find the one that really sticks. Even if you're "just exploring," you could stumble upon an awesome new possibility for a side hustle. If you're ready to shake things up, consider a job in sales or do something very "Libra" like investing in NFTs or working as a sommelier.

Creating harmony is another one of the Libra South Node's superpowers. Have you always had a knack for helping people improve an aspect of their lives? Consider getting certified as a coach, consultant or holistic healer. As that classic Confucius quote reminds, "Find a job you love, and you'll never have to work a day in your life."

ECLIPSES IN 2023
Shifting loyalties

Hybrid Solar Eclipse in Aries (new moon)

April 20 at 12:17AM

Penumbral Lunar Eclipse in Scorpio (full moon)

May 5 at 1:24PM

Annular Solar Eclipse in Libra (new moon)

October 14 at 2:00PM

Partial Lunar Eclipse in Taurus (full moon)

October 28 at 4:15PM

times in eastern time

APRIL 20:
SOLAR ECLIPSE IN ARIES
HYBRID SOLAR ECLIPSE 29°52, 12:17AM ET

All is not quiet on the Capricorn homefront as the first Aries eclipse since 2015 lands in your fourth house of kinfolk and roots. Because it's also a super-rare hybrid solar eclipse, beginning as a "ring of fire" (annular) eclipse and transforming into a sky-darkening total eclipse along its path, you may only see a glimmer of possibility about what's ahead. That can be frustrating for a sign that loves to plan the way you do, but here's a message: Embrace the process! For Sea Goats who are ready to make some changes, this will be refreshing news! Whether it's a roommate swap, kitchen remodel or a full-on relocation plan, eclipses speed along developments. There could be news about a family member that prompts you into action. For some Caps this may simply be a realization that you'd like to spend a lot more time with your loved ones and a little less time with your nose buried in work. Plug those playful moments into your calendar right away.

MAY 5: LUNAR ECLIPSE IN SCORPIO
PENUMBRAL LUNAR ECLIPSE, 14°52, 1:24PM ET

Where do you belong, Capricorn? The year's only lunar eclipse in Scorpio charges up your eleventh house of collaborations, bringing all sorts of insights about who deserves inner circle status—and who does not. It's possible that you've been casually interacting with a group since the corresponding solar eclipse on October 25, 2022. Starting today, your role within the collective may become crystal clear. Perhaps you'll take on a leadership role—or at the very least, become a card-carrying member, devoting yourself wholeheartedly to the mission. Still haven't found your kindred spirits? The eclipse could bring a meant-to-be meeting of the minds over the coming two weeks. Stay open.

OCTOBER 14: SOLAR ECLIPSE IN LIBRA
ANNULAR SOLAR ECLIPSE 21°10, 2:00PM ET

Your power blazer is never far from the front of your closet, Capricorn, and October 14 is the perfect day to suit up like a boss! With an annular "ring of fire" solar eclipse in Libra—the first one to land in this sign since 2016—activating your tenth house of success, you could be launched even further up the ladder. This could happen quite suddenly, so keep your game face on and be prepared to play ball at any moment. What starts out as a casual stroll for pumpkin-spice lattes could turn into an impromptu business chat. Seize any opportunities to prove your loyalty, dedication and skills. Your efforts will not go unnoticed, or unappreciated!

OCTOBER 28: LUNAR ECLIPSE IN TAURUS
PARTIAL LUNAR ECLIPSE 5°03, 4:15PM ET

Here come your accolades! As the zodiac's overachiever, you appreciate the acknowledgement that comes with success—just as long as it's not too over the top. Get ready! Today's lunar eclipse in your fifth house of fame will alert the paparazzi, putting you in the (slightly uncomfortable) position of center stage. Set aside your humility, and graciously accept the attention you've worked hard to earn. Since the fifth house also rules romance, this eclipse could herald some out-of-left-field surprises in your love life. Anything from a positive reading on a pregnancy test to news that your boo is getting transferred to an office out of state could be on the horizon. Whatever comes your way, you've got this, Capricorn. Stay nimble and in a creative mindset.

2023

—

AQUARIUS

WHAT'S IN THE STARS FOR

AQUARIUS

Let freedom ring! If life has moved at the speed of molasses for the past couple years, get ready for a 180-degree pirouette. Also, be a tiny bit careful what you wish for, Aquarius! Starting in March 2023, transformational experiences will be coming by the hour. New friendships, invitations and even job offers could come in. Whether you accept them or not, take it as an affirmative sign that you've done some tough personal growth work. This year, you're ready to reap the hard-earned rewards! Your trailblazing ideas could make you a popular leader in these times, so turn up the volume on your unique personality and quirky concepts. You could gain a fast following! Nonetheless, be careful who you share the reins of power with this spring and summer. You may still be getting your self-confidence "sea legs," and a flattering or manipulative person could slip into the inner sanctum unnoticed. Home and family, particularly female relatives, are big focal points in the second half of 2023.

AQUARIUS WILL BE LUCKY WITH:
Friendships, home and family

AQUARIUS WILL BE CHALLENGED WITH:
Money management, trusting the wrong people

LOVE

Passion is already percolating as the ball drops on 2023, and when white-hot Mars ends its retrograde on January 12, you'll be Aquarius Untamed! Enjoy this thermostat-raising mojo while Mars zips through your fifth house of showstopping *amour* until March 25. Dating could be your favorite winter sport; then get ready for a summer of love! Venus takes a long, sultry sashay through Leo and your relationship house from June 5 to October 8. If you're serious about someone—or need to renegotiate the terms of engagement—the diplomatic, enchanting love planet has your back. Longing for the one that got away? Venus retrograde from July 22 to September 3 could bring a much-awaited reunion or the closure you need to *finally* move on. Pro tip for the happily hitched: Save up for a luxury baecation to take before the year is through.

CAREER & MONEY

Make it rain, Aquarius! On March 7, your co-ruler, industrious Saturn, heads into Pisces, beginning a three-year tour through your income zone. This is double cause for celebration since it means that you're also kissing the ringed taskmaster goodbye. Saturn's been in Aquarius since March 21, 2020, putting you through your paces since the pandemic began. As you graduate from cosmic boot camp (not to host Saturn again for 29.5 years!) you are ready to establish your expertise and increase your earnings. But just as you're settling into a groove, transformational Pluto darts into Aquarius from March 23 to June 11—the warm-up lap of its 21-year circuit through your sign. Don't get so comfortable that you wind up stuck in a rut! Pluto draws out your competitive nature and makes you a shrewd investor. Go beyond 9-5 thinking: money could flow in from property, inventions and even inheritances over the next two decades. The Scorpio lunar eclipse on May 5 may bring a plum offer from on high!

WELLNESS

Detox time! With Pluto in its second-to-last year in your twelfth house of release, there's no more excuses for unhealthy behaviors that have crept in over the years. Whether it's that five-coffee-a day habit, sedentary job or another addictive vice, this is the year to break the habit once and for all. Working with a support group and even a hypnotherapist can do wonders for your process. With Saturn moving into Pisces and your second house, focus on thyroid health. You might try cutting back on fatty animal products and eating more iodine-rich superfoods like seaweed, fish and fresh eggs. Buddy workouts keep you motivated all year with Jupiter and the North Node doing time in Aries and your cooperative, social third house. Join a walking group or cycling club for summer fitness.

FRIENDS & FAMILY

Your social circle swells to exciting proportions in 2023—and what a colorful crew you'll assemble! Thought leaders, artists, and garden variety unicorns will populate the Aquarius entourage as live-out-loud Jupiter and the North Node move through your outgoing third house. When global Jupiter enters Taurus on May 16, it spends a year in your house of roots. Reconnect to long-distance relatives and plan an epic family vacation in the second half of the year. The October 28 lunar eclipse could bring some heart-opening moments, but may also demand that you set boundaries with people in your inner circle who are draining you with their dependence.

JUPITER IN ARIES
Cooperate and communicate

Jupiter in Aries
December 20, 2022 to May 16, 2023

What do you have to say for yourself, Aquarius? Turns out, a lot! On December 20, 2022, outspoken Jupiter soared back into Aries, taking its second (and final) lap through your third house of communication, until May 16. With your mind *and* your mouth activated, you're bringing nonstop mic drops. Start recording those killer one-liners, Water Bearer. Your wit deserves more than dead air. In fact, this could be the year that you finally launch a podcast, write a book or become a regular guest on a friend's popular feed.

With outspoken Jupiter handing you a megaphone, you could take the world by storm via multiple channels—social media, community action, teaching, broadcasting—to spread your message far and wide. Publishing projects could find an enthusiastic audience while media-maven Jupiter rolls through your third house of writing. Try different mediums and platforms until you discover the perfect outlet. Do you want to blog about fashion? Shoot weekly videos where you weigh in on current events? Experiment until you find your forté.

You already got a burst of this loquacious energy when the red-spotted raconteur rolled through Aries from May 10 to October 28, 2022. Your first order of business in 2023 may be to pull out the half-finished screenplay or revive a collaboration you put on hold before the holidays. As an air sign, you know just how to breathe new life into things after they've been collecting dust for a while.

AQUARIUS

If you're not already in full social-butterfly mode, Jupiter's tour through Aries and your locally zoned third house serves plenty of entertainment options close to your front door. Go in search of the "ultimate" everything, from cafés with the best matcha lattes and vegan scones to organic salons with the most innovative nail artists. Instead of guarding your finds, lean into generous Jupiter and alert the whole neighborhood. Help keep the area's businesses thriving, especially the independently owned venues and mom-and-pop shops.

Besides, "superconnector" is a title that suits you well! The first half of 2023 is *the* perfect time to finally introduce all the fabulous people you know to each other. Your skillful matchmaking could do a *mitzvah*, like getting your long-unemployed pal hooked up with her dream job or introducing single pals who were destined to become soulmates.

Be on the lookout for fresh faces, too. Your friends list is sure to swell during this buzzy Jupiter cycle. And with a little luck, a few of these kindred spirits may morph into more defined roles like: guitar teacher, co-leader of a workshop or travel buddy. Even introverted Aquarians will feel the desire for stimulating company and conversation. Nudge yourself out there on a regular basis while beneficial Jupiter traipses through this gregarious zone.

But don't rush to commit to any social structures because now's the time to experiment with different types of bonds. Is a promising collaboration in the air? With indie-spirited Jupiter in this social sector, test the waters with a trial run to see how your styles mesh. To be safe, do this *before* you sign on the dotted line of a binding or exclusive contract. If this alliance isn't a good fit, you can graciously move on after you bring this mission to completion. Or maybe it's kismet! Even then, nothing wrong with starting small and letting the synergy evolve organically.

While scholarly Jupiter occupies these curious quarters, learning is an adventure. Enhance your know-how with mini courses and get a certification if it will give you an edge. But don't embark on any multi-year degree programs unless you're absolutely sure about the path you want to pursue. Have you always wanted to learn how to paint with oils or bake French pastries? When the student is ready (and Jupiter's in the third house), the teacher will appear—and you might even create a curriculum of your own. Share your knowledge in a webinar and hang your shingle, Aquarius!

Playing with the idea of relocating? You'll want to "try before you buy" during this fickle Jupiter phase. Some Aquarians will bop between multiple cities or give bicoastal life a try. Take as many short trips as you can squeeze in, spending a few days in an appealing neighborhood that you *might* want to call home. Go through your daily routine as if you already lived there: Find the running path, the juice bar, the dog park.

After May 16, you may feel ready to begin house-hunting or relocate. Do the research in early 2023. Even if you end up right where you started, it'll reboot your mindset. Like Dorothy waking up in Kansas, your trip to Oz may give you a greater appreciation for that "boring state" or "loud, dirty city" you wanted to escape from. Maybe you just needed a break. Or perhaps you'll move to a different neighborhood that has more of the amenities you care about.

You couldn't find a better excuse to invest in a weekender bag or car that's built to last. Switch up your commute. Ride a bicycle to work to align with Jupiter's love of freedom and sport. If it's within the realm of possibility, you might rent an RV as your remote office for a few weeks here and there.

JUPITER IN TAURUS
Home on the road

Jupiter in Taurus

May 16, 2023 to
May 25, 2024

Jupiter Retrograde

September 4 to
December 30, 2023

There's no place like home? Nesting instincts take flight this May 16, as peripatetic Jupiter heads into rootbound Taurus and your fourth house of home, family and foundations until May 25, 2024. Do you hear the contradiction there? After a breezy start to 2023, you need a moment to hunker down. But where? And for how long? Jupiter is the global adventurer while your Taurus-ruled fourth house wants to drop anchor. Finding ways to satisfy both urges will be quite the exploration.

Modernist loft, tiny house, tricked out Sprinter van? No matter what shape your four walls take, home will occupy a good deal of your thoughts in the second half of 2023. As the red-spotted planet trots through this zone, you'll ponder limitless possibilities for living arrangements, from shared housing to solo dwelling. Jupiter only visits each sign every 12 years and was last in Taurus from June 4, 2011 to June 11, 2012. Look back to that time: Were there changes in your family structure or living situation? Themes from over a decade ago could repeat.

The fourth house sits at the bottom of the zodiac wheel and governs your roots and foundations—from your nest to your *nest egg*. With risk-forward Jupiter here, you could take a bold step like buying or selling property or relocating for work. If you're in the market for a move, cast a wide net. That dream listing could be in a totally different state—or country. If you love your current address, expansive Jupiter may get the ball rolling on a renovation project like opening up the floor plan or putting on an addition. While you don't want to gamble (a Jupiter pitfall), things like adding a second bathroom or finishing the basement can raise your property value. Explore!

Jovial Jupiter is the legendary god of the feast, so if your home is set up for guests, you may entertain regularly after May 16. You'll prefer cozy huddles, like family movie nights and intimate dinner parties, but don't rule out at least *one* epic celebration at Casa Aqua, like a party for a friend's milestone birthday or a New Year's Eve masquerade ball.

Jupiter is the planet of entrepreneurship and while in Taurus from May 16, 2023 to May 25, 2024, your home could be tied to your income stream. A kitchen table side hustle could scale quickly, making it necessary to convert a spare bedroom into an office—or to upgrade from a studio to a two-bedroom apartment so you can work, or host clients, from home. Got more space than you know what to do with? Consider renting out to a tenant, or even building an ADU on your property and turning it into an Airbnb.

There *is* a caveat: While in Taurus, Jupiter forms a challenging, 90-degree square to your Aquarius Sun. Along with all this rapid development, you could experience growing pains and encounter some difficult obstacles. This phase may call for serious hustle, and you'll need to check your ego at the door. Look at setbacks as potential learning experiences, not failures. With the right attitude, you'll pass this test with flying colors.

The fourth house is classically associated with motherhood, though in modern astrology, it represents nurturing parenthood. Jupiter's expansive powers could bring a child into the picture for some Aquarians or get talks rolling in that direction. Are you already a parent? Candid Jupiter could open up powerful conversations with your kids—perhaps about subjects you weren't planning to discuss quite yet, but need to.

Your relationship with your own parents could go through an enlightening transformation, paving the way for you to relate to each other in a more adult fashion. Aquarians with elderly parents could become caretakers in the second half of the year or find themselves on an accelerated timeline to find in-home providers for their folks. If family dynamics need to shift, the time is right, but the process won't be all smooth sailing. Expect some discomfort as the balance between you is recalibrated.

How well do you nourish yourself? There's an undeniable link between food and mood, which may flare up this year. As the zodiac's progressive explorers, many Aquarians are the earliest adopters of vitality-boosting trends, from adaptogenic mushrooms to CBD-infused balms. Animal-loving Water Bearers may go plant-based on principle. Are you getting the right nutrients for your age and stage of life? This is the year to set up a blood panel to test for food allergies and make sure you're not low on things like Vitamin D, which affects your energy level and thyroid function. If you get sleepy after meals, a Chinese medicine practitioner might blend you some bitters, enzymes or other herbs to help with digestion.

Bottom line: Double down on self-care and nurturing during this sensitive cycle. Your moods are bound to ebb and flow, as you sift through big feelings. Solitude can offer you the peace you crave. Spending time in nature, especially near water, will soothe your spirit. You're such a social creature that becoming a bit reclusive for 12 months could give you a whole new perspective on life. But don't hole up by yourself to the point of becoming truly isolated. Just carve out unapologetic sacred space when you need it. You can knit, read, take aromatherapy baths and pamper yourself without anyone clamoring for your on-demand attention. Heaven!

MARS IN GEMINI

Know your audience

Mars in Gemini

August 20, 2022 to
March 25, 2023

Mars Retrograde

October 30, 2022 to
January 12, 2023

Curtains up, Aquarius! The cosmic klieg light beams directly on you beginning January 12 as showstopping Mars wraps up a 10-week retrograde and blazes ahead through Gemini and your fifth house of fame and flamboyance, until March 25. Performers, artists and all creative types will regain direct access to the muse. In Q1, you could be invited to showcase your talents on the stage, podium, in a local gallery or podcasting studio. Say yes!

You already got a wave of this celebrity magic last summer, when Mars first trotted into Gemini on August 20. But when the red planet slipped into retrograde on October 30, 2022, promising leads may have dried up or simply got put on hold. Grab the reins again on January 12! With Mars galloping forward like a sexy steed, the initiative you take can get the whole parade rolling again. People who gazed right past you in late 2022 could sit up and take notice. Do your level best to make sure of that, even if you have to resort to a pinch of shock value. Mars in Gemini doesn't mind when tongues wag if it means you're the subject on everyone's lips.

If you can't quite access the dimmer switch on your spotlight, enlist the pros for help. Designers and stylists can polish the "Aquarius brand" to a platinum gleam. Hire a coach or private teacher who can work with you to amplify your stage presence. Visual materials should pop and your personal style should be a reflection of your rich imagination. Yes, Aquarius, "Martial law" permits you to unleash your rainbow-bright extraness like signmates Alicia Keys and Harry

Styles. Of course, you want to be as authentically self-possessed and assured as humanly possible. And if that requires a photo shoot with five outfit changes, no judgments here!

Since the fifth house rules love, Cupid's arrows could hit the mark a month before Valentine's Day. If you've been harboring a secret crush, good luck keeping it under wraps come January 12. Now that electrifying Mars is powering forward through your house of passionate romance, you're a fired-up Water Bearer on the loose! Your magnetism is reading off the charts, so if you're truly ready to let love in, a few sincere efforts in that direction should yield some worthy prospects. But give 'em a chance before you send anyone on their way. Mars can be flashy, but you might be happier for the long haul with a diamond in the rough than some flashy, splashy bling.

Recovering from a breakup? Down a cup of Martian courage and get back on the apps mid-January. With the red planet in mobile-friendly Gemini, you may have more eligible swipes than expected. Coupled Aquarians could feel an accelerated urge to take a very big, very public step together like shopping for rings, moving in together or spearheading a babymaking project.

This is all cause for excitement, but don't lose sight of self-care! Brash Mars in this hedonistic placement can make even the most modest Aquarius prone to excess. No one's telling you to deprive yourself, but you *do* need to keep your energy high by getting ample rest and eating foods with actual nutrients in them. With so much public attention coming your way, people view you as a role model. Does that feel like pressure for your rebellious sign? Probably. But you won't have this surge of leadership energy again for another two years—and even then, Mars will only tour Gemini for seven *weeks*, not seven months. So you might as well see how it feels to wear the crown. Who knows? You might stir up enough palace intrigue to make any leadership roles feel fresh and exciting!

SATURN IN PISCES

Exhale!

> **Saturn in Pisces**
>
> March 7, 2023 to
> February 13, 2026
>
> **Saturn Retrograde**
>
> June 17 to
> November 4, 2023

Pop the Veuve and spray it all around! Cosmic boot camp is officially over, Aquarius, and you can now catch your breath! After three arduous years of hosting benevolent dictator Saturn in your sign, the ringed taskmaster *finally* exits Aquarius on March 7. With your identity freed from Saturn's tight grip, you have room to explore the vast nuances of your personality—especially the wilder ones that were relegated to lockdown for the past three years. (Welcome back, unbridled joy and explosive laughter!) Better still? You won't have to weather another Saturn-in-Aquarius cycle for 29.5 years. Cheers to that news!

If you're really honest with yourself, however, you've grown tremendously since the challenging planet first orbited into your sign on March 21, 2020. Saturn's strength-training regimen catalyzed a major identity evolution for Aquarians over the past few years. Do you feel bulletproof right now? We're betting so. Water Bearer 2.0 FTW!

That Saturnian hustle might have unlocked career breakthroughs since mid-2020. But as you put your shoulder to the wheel, you became aware of old structures and habits that were due to be dismantled. Gains were offset with losses while Saturn toured Aquarius—not the 1:1 ratio you might have preferred. But learning to navigate the bumps was the point of Saturn's exercise. After all, Aquarius, you are a human *being*...not a human *doing*. Even if you tallied epic wins over the last few years, you also discovered that happiness is an inside job, not something that can be measured purely by external circumstances.

Wherever you're standing on March 7, 2023, the ground beneath your feet should feel a bit more solid. Go ahead and breathe a deep sigh of relief. Let it out! Just don't loosen your belt too many notches. While Saturn tours Pisces until February 13, 2026, it takes up a new role as Chief Budgetary Officer in your second house of financial security. Your lesson for 2023: How *not* to burn as much as you earn. If you've already mastered the art of saving and investing, it's time to compound your profits. Make that hard-earned cash work just as hard for you.

Are you a habitual over-spender? With idealistic Pisces ruling this zone, tap into the sharing economy instead of reaching into your own pocket time and time again. Maybe it's possible to keep enjoying those luxe (and practical) goods without breaking the bank. Pool funds for everything from produce boxes to yard-care tools. As long as your pod is made up of honest, ethical people, this model can work out beautifully. And hey, you might even split the cost of insurance to cover future repairs on big-ticket items. Bear in mind, however, that Pisces is the sign of sacrifice. Guard against over-giving and lean into Saturn's unambiguous penchant for setting up rules for every group.

Slow and steady progress is a hallmark of Saturn in the second house, which could frustrate you at times. Results may take longer to show up this year, testing your patience. Don't despair! When there's a break in the action, concentrate on strengthening your fundamentals. What can you do to fortify your base? Do you need better tools? Are you collaborating with people who have the right expertise? Monitor your everyday routines: What duties are slowing you down? Delegate, outsource or utilize technology to accelerate your processes.

If you want to lighten your workload, start by streamlining and simplifying. That way, you can focus on tasks that are squarely in your wheelhouse. Next, consider ways to redistribute assignments. Does it make sense to hire an employee, get an intern, bring in a business partner, pay a contractor? If you're working your way up the ladder, stay humble. You busted your butt to break into this industry during Saturn's stay in Aquarius, and now that basic training is over, it's time to hone your practice. The next three years could very well be a "chop wood, carry water" tour of duty as you gain mastery by repeating actions over and over until they become second nature to you.

Now that you're out of the pressure cooker, you might feel younger than you have in years. Saturn is the planet of aging, and while it toured Aquarius, it's possible that the stress of this period dimmed your radiance somewhat, especially if you lost sleep while fretting over all the changes in your life. With Saturn in Pisces, you can savor the galactic glow-up that comes from luxuriating in beauty rituals. Wake up a little earlier in the morning to bathe and primp, and start winding down sooner in the evening to prepare for bed. How can you make your nighttime hours more restful? Upgrade to a higher quality mattress and pillows. Relax by listening to binaural beats, pink noise or ASMR on YouTube or a sleep app.

When it comes to your personal life, master the fine art of lovemaking. Revel in the spiritual vibes of Pisces and take a tantric workshop or work your way through the Kama Sutra. (We promise it won't feel like work!) Creating rituals will keep Aquarians connected to your loved ones. Savor quality time, preparing delicious meals and going for long walks together.

If you're dealing with anxiety, depression, trauma or grief, know that you're not alone. Sadly, most people have had to process something heavy since 2020 because of the pandemic. In addition to any aftershocks of the last few years, you may feel ready to tackle longstanding blocks that manifest as physical sensations. With Saturn in your tactile second house, somatic therapy could be especially effective for healing old wounds. This healing modality combines talk therapy and mind-body exercises to resolve issues on multiple levels. Stress may be causing your mind to race, which prevents you from focusing on the things that are important to you. Perfect excuse to carve out time for a calming morning meditation practice.

PLUTO IN AQUARIUS
Stepping into your power

Pluto in Capricorn
Janury 1, 2023
to March 23, 2023

June 11, 2023 to
January 20, 2024

Pluto in Aquarius
March 23 to
June 11, 2023

Pluto Retrograde
May 1 to
October 10, 2023

Metamorphosis! A long period of soul-searching is drawing to a close, Aquarius, while a new chapter of spiritual discovery begins. On March 23, alchemical Pluto voyages into your sign, its first visit to Aquarius since 1778-1798. Although Pluto only hangs out in your sign, initially, until June 11, it's a prelude of what's to come. On November 19, 2024, the dwarf planet settles into your sign for 20 more years, until January 19, 2044!

Come on out of your cocoon and let the games begin! To call this transit profound would be an understatement. It's been two centuries since Pluto toured Aquarius, so we've never experienced this energy in our times. Because of its 248-year orbit, many people will never host formidable Pluto in their zodiac sign. But um, lucky you? As the brand-new host of the planet of unconscious shadows, buried secrets, sex, rebirth, death, mysteries and scandals, life's about to get mighty interesting.

But first...an identity crisis. Since 2008, Pluto has been touring Capricorn, plunged into your esoteric twelfth house. This brought a period of enlightening internal reflection, which, as one of the zodiac's seekers, you were completely enraptured with. But Pluto in Aquarius and your front-facing first house?! Time in your meditation cave is about to be seriously restricted. This new journey is about stepping *out* of the shadows and experiencing your power and allure through other people's eyes.

You're sexy and you know it. (Or do you?) As a sign that traffics in disrupting the status quo—like Aquarians Harry Styles and Megan Thee Stallion—*not* being the rebel can be quite disconcerting. Funny enough, you don't mind judgments and critiques; that's part of your radical style. It's the thought of being *superliked* that can shake up security. But with Pluto in your sign, you will feel potent and magnetic. With great power comes great responsibility, after all. Get ready for both!

Your personal transformation may be televised—or otherwise witnessed by people in a public forum. Unconscious thoughts, which swirled in the background for years (and perhaps came out subversively through your art and mission-oriented career path), suddenly take direct shape. You might even blurt out something utterly unenlightened. *Wait...who said that?* Yes, it was you, Aquarius.

Give yourself lots of grace! Your new, Pluto-inspired brand of "weird" may not be embraced with open arms...at least not immediately in this cycle. Pluto tests your resolve and these tests often begin with a breakdown. Shit could get messy for a minute, Aquarius, but it's part of the transformational process that will envelop you for the coming 21 years.

It can help to think of Pluto's pendulum swings between Capricorn and Aquarius like a two-year detox. As you fill yourself up with nourishing input, you're pushing out all the unwelcome stuff you've unconsciously absorbed. While Pluto worked its way through Capricorn and your twelfth house, you soaked up *so* much in your psyche and energetic and physical bodies. And when it lands in Aquarius, you suddenly realize how heavy and burdensome it all feels!

When Pluto moves from the fog of the twelfth house to the sharp light of the first house, it can be highly disconcerting, as if someone yanked back the blackout curtains and directed the sun right into your eyes. Sadly, this transit is often associated with betrayals—or the realization that a disloyal person has been sitting in your court all along. Or maybe you're just ready to stop carrying capable people on your back. A rallying cry of Pluto in Aquarius? Codependent no more!

What you *don't* want to do? Rage on people who are a legit source of support. While you may be rightfully upset about power imbalances, there are also cases where there were unspoken "contracts" that need to be renegotiated—and can. Were people actually trying to hold you down or take advantage of your kindness? Or were *you* okay with playing a submissive role that you've now outgrown? It's easy to point the finger when Pluto first enters your sign. But unless you were literally in an abusive relationship, start by trying to map out new roles. Your companions may be just as eager as you are to reshuffle the decks.

On the other hand, if you've been forced into the shadows or feeling dominated by a powerful "captor," that all ends now. Some Aquarians will indeed break free from an abusive relationship. While we hope you don't find yourself in such dire circumstances, if so, Pluto helps you rise like a phoenix from those ashes, leaving that prison behind.

What lies ahead for you is largely unscripted, but you'll get some clear foreshadowing while Pluto hits Aquarius from March 23 to June 11, 2023. Your role is to bring Aquarian values out of the shadows and use them to transform the world: Community, a shared economy, a global "one love" mindset, embracing differences? Yes, please!

Technology and space travel, other Aquarius domains, will also get a burst of momentum. Pluto also rules the unconscious so we may see the shadow side of this come forward. Groupthink and echo chambers, data abuse and a loss of privacy: How can we preserve our individuality while still being part of the collective whole? No one knows better than an Aquarius how to navigate that seeming paradox. Now teach the rest of us, would you? We have until 2044 to figure this out!

VENUS RETROGRADE

Romantic revolutions

Venus in Leo

June 5 to
October 8, 2023

Venus Retrograde

July 22 to
September 3, 2023

Slip into that "sexy archaeologist" outfit, Aquarius Jones. Thanks to Venus turning retrograde in Leo and your relationship house from July 22 to September 3, you could find yourself on a "dig" with people from your past. This deep dive into (semi) ancient history could mend broken friendships—and also, broken hearts. Get ready for familiar faces and long-lost places to come blazing back into your life. And try to keep an open mind throughout this journey. You may be sifting through some dirt before you find the valuable artifacts of your connection. This probably won't be an overnight success. But if you genuinely care about each other, it's worth a shot!

Thankfully, you'll have some buffer time before and after the retrograde. In total, Venus spends four months in Leo, from June 5 to October 8—which is 30 percent of the entire year. That's a long time to be so laser-focused on relationships, especially for your indie-spirited sign. But like it or not, they will be a big theme of your 2023. Maybe you're balancing the dynamics in an existing bond or pulling back to figure out how you feel about partnership in general. And during this four-month Venus in Leo cycle, that could be anything from "I'm ready to find my soulmate" to "I'd really love to be single right now."

Truth is, even platonic partnerships take effort to maintain. Are you burning yourself out trying to keep various ships afloat? Uh-oh, Water Bearer. The retrograde blows a Coast Guard whistle on *that* habit. Whether it's a lover, a best friend or a creative partner, you may realize that the "work" you want to put in is trusting that people will still love you if you do less. When you stop overfunctioning, you'll be amazed by what generally transpires. That "unappreciative slacker" may suddenly perk up and start pulling their weight.

Certain wobbly connections may stabilize with a little more structure. Set a weekly date night or monthly brunch and stick to it. Can't get together IRL but totally miss your busy-bee BFF? Set a standing 20-minute Zoom every Friday and enjoy a virtual coffee break.

Dressing up is always a must when beauty queen Venus sashays down fashionable Leo's catwalk. Don't wait for invitations to pour in! Give yourself plenty of excuses to wear all the fierce 'fits that have been gathering dust in your closet since pre-pandemic. Host dinner parties, organize karaoke nights and don't forget the dance marathons!

And let's not ignore date nights. Whether you're dipping your toe back in the Tinder pool or trying to generate a fresh round of sparks with your S.O., stay far away from the usual places. Novelty releases dopamine, a feel-good chemical that blesses your bonds with even more sexiness and staying power. That's good reason to sharpen up your date-planning game by staying abreast of the local cultural activities calendar. You simply can't expect relationships to "just happen" forever. After a certain point in time, Aquarius, you have to generate the chemistry. That might even require you to regulate how much time you spend together. Absence has been known to make the heart grow fonder.

Of course a nostalgic journey *can* be hot while Venus spins back through Leo from July 22 to September 3. Revisiting the quaint little beach town where you first kissed might serve a fresh round of magic moments. Just remember, you're going there during high season—which could actually bring some lows if you have to push through exhausting crowds of tourists.

As mentioned, Venus retrograde could dredge up some "antiques" from your past, which may include exes and FWBs who still hold a flicker of potential. Is the fire worth reigniting? Proceed with care. An old flame could easily strike the match, starting a blaze in your heart (and elsewhere). But when Venus is in reverse, lasting potential is nearly impossible to determine. This could be a fluke or it could be the start of your forever together. What you *don't* want to do, however, is pretend you can start from zero. The past you shared will always be part of the story. Can you live with that? Put unresolved issues and resentments to bed, ideally before heading to bed for a reunion romp. When Venus corrects course on September 3, pieces will fall into place.

Aquarius is the sign of the future and you're born to build! But misaligned assumptions could be a huge source of stress for coupled Water Bearers this summer. Check that bucket list (and goal sheet) you love to carry around. Are you and bae on the same page or are you riding on shaky assumptions? Your hopes and dreams may not be 100% flush, but that doesn't mean you're at the end of the road. You might, however, need to map out a new set of blueprints. How can you flourish individually while also creating enough bonding experiences to bring you together? That's a worthy challenge to take on this summer!

NORTH NODE IN ARIES
Use your words

**Lunar North
Node in Aries**

July 17, 2023
to January 11, 2025

Whatever you're selling, we'll take three! Your silver-tongued charm is back in rare form beginning July 17, when for the first time in nearly 20 years, the fate-fueling lunar North Node returns to Aries. Until January 11, 2025, it sprinkles cosmic fairy dust into your loquacious third house and boosts your popularity to the sky.

With your cooperation zone alight, collaborations could take off like Flamin' Hot Cheetos. (Or, uh, something like that.) Surprise! A so-called competitor could be the missing link in your success strategy. Thankfully, your high-minded sign isn't one to hold a grudge. The third house rules peers such as siblings, friends, coworkers and neighbors. After July 17, these people could be the talent pool from which you draw. But to protect the longevity of these bonds, make sure you spell everything out in writing! Ambiguity breeds contempt.

Got a message to broadcast to the world? You wouldn't be an Aquarius if you didn't have thoughts on the state of our society that were the makings of a podcast, documentary or charitable campaign. (Even signmate Paris Hilton is doing impact work to take on abuse in the "Troubled Teen Industry" of residential treatment centers.) With the lunar North Node in loud, proud Aries, you'll have plenty of opportunities to showcase your skills and take them to the next level, either on an existing platform or your own.

During this 18-month nodal cycle, you may be tapped to play spokesperson or even offered cash to represent a brand as an influencer. Of course, as a principled Aquarius, you're so *not* here to hawk Frappuccinos to Starbucks baristas. Anything that you throw your weight behind had better tick all the boxes: consciously sourced, ethically produced, useful and meaningful...oh, and if it's profitable, too, boom!

The other side of the "coin" to the North Node is the South Node, which will simultaneously circuit through Libra and your global ninth house. Have you cast a wide enough net? While the Aries North Node will definitely shower you with opportunities from your locally grown third house, don't sleep on other zip codes. Did a 23andMe test connect you to long-lost cousins living abroad? Maybe you're itching to explore your ancestral homeland. Trips like these can be profound and life-changing after July 17. Make sure your passport is up to date.

Multi-city living could become the new reality for many Water Bearers after July 17 as you commute back and forth between locations. Traveling may figure into the work you do in 2023, or you may arrange your position to be permanently remote, allowing for global exploration without missing a paycheck. Even if being a digital nomad isn't your ultimate goal, spending a few weeks as a "touring resident" in new cities could be an unforgettable adventure for you in the second half of 2023.

Can't get away—or don't actually want to? The Libra South Node could bring out the seeker and student in you. Have you pondered a grad school program? The ivory tower may beckon after July 17, and before you know it, you're applying for a 2024 PhD program. Spiritual studies could call your name; perhaps you'll return to a path that you stepped away from a while ago. (You might even sign up for the facilitator training!) With the reflective South Node in the zone of publishing, you may be ready to write your memoirs or turn your journey into a healing workshop that you share with the world!

ECLIPSES IN 2023
Circles of influence

Hybrid Solar Eclipse in Aries (new moon)

April 20 at 12:17AM

Penumbral Lunar Eclipse in Scorpio (full moon)

May 5 at 1:24PM

Annular Solar Eclipse in Libra (new moon)

October 14 at 2:00PM

Partial Lunar Eclipse in Taurus (full moon)

October 28 at 4:15PM

times in eastern time

APRIL 20:
SOLAR ECLIPSE IN ARIES
HYBRID SOLAR ECLIPSE 29°52, 12:17AM ET

The friend zone is teeming with possibilities as this solar (new moon) eclipse activates your third house of peer-based partnerships. You haven't had an eclipse here since 2015—and since it's an ultra-rare hybrid solar eclipse (beginning as a "ring of fire" annular eclipse and transitioning into a sun-blotting total eclipse) you may get a once-in-a-lifetime opportunity to buddy up on a project that puts your name on the map. Should such an opportunity appear, leap on it! But if not, no sweat. This eclipse series lasts for two full years. During this cycle, your pioneering ideas draw major attention. So pull out your half-finished projects and get 'em done. If you've been searching for a collaborator for a project, the perfect candidate could be revealed. This may even be someone you've known for months, but under the spell of this eclipse, their fullest potential is revealed. Bursting at the seams to express yourself? This eclipse falls in your third house of communication giving you a way with words. Time to write the book, start that podcast or become a more vocal member of every team you play on.

MAY 5: LUNAR ECLIPSE IN SCORPIO
PENUMBRAL LUNAR ECLIPSE, 14°52, 1:24PM ET

Your career is spotlighted by the year's only lunar (full moon) eclipse in Scorpio, which could bring unexpected openings for growth. A grand goal that you've been pursuing since the corresponding solar eclipse on October 25, 2002 could hit a milestone mark. Two words: strategic promotion. You don't need to be everywhere, Aquarius, just in front of the right people. Since eclipses tend to reveal hidden information, this lunar lift may mark a turning point. Some Aquarians could have the realization that it's time to shift in a totally different direction. Follow the path the universe is lighting for you instead of stubbornly pressing forward on a course that is not yielding the results you hoped it would.

OCTOBER 14: SOLAR ECLIPSE IN LIBRA
ANNULAR SOLAR ECLIPSE 21°10, 2:00PM ET

The siren's song of distant lands grows too audible to ignore, thanks to the annular "ring of fire" solar eclipse in Libra—the first eclipse to land in this sign since 2016—charging up your ninth house of global adventures. One minute, you're perusing a travel feed on Insta, then next you're hitting "Reserve Now" on a dreamy accommodation. Close to home, a cross-cultural connection could rock your world, perhaps becoming an official merger in the days ahead. Enterprising Aquarians could have a brilliant flash about a new business. This is a stellar day to launch a new venture, too, but as eclipses reveal shadows, you might have your hands full with more customers than you're capable of serving. File this under "Good Problems to Have."

OCTOBER 28: LUNAR ECLIPSE IN TAURUS
PARTIAL LUNAR ECLIPSE 5°03, 4:15PM ET

You've got a knack for bonding with people you barely know, Water Bearer. That said, your popularity sometimes gets under the skin of your nearest and dearest who end up taking a back seat to the new kids on your block. Today's partial lunar (full moon) eclipse in your fourth house of family prompts you to redirect your energy back to your loved ones. Give them priority in your life by organizing one-on-one visits they've sorely been missing. Remember, relationships work both ways! If you're ready to pull up the stakes, put down roots or make some hygge season renovations to your space, it's officially go time. Get ready because things could take off at an accelerated pace!

2023

—

PISCES

WHAT'S IN THE STARS FOR

PISCES

Talk about coming into your own! The past two years have kicked off massive personal growth for you, Pisces, as you've explored new pathways and desires. In 2023, it's time to put these discoveries into concrete form. An indie business, a new home, a fresh start? You'll break ground in March 2023, and over the next two years, rise into new levels of leadership and self-reliance. Meantime, there's money to be made, and you can earn a great living doing what you love this year. Pursue your passions while patiently cultivating your sense of self-worth. A secure partner in business or love (maybe both) could stand out from the crowd. New friendships and kindred spirit connections can pop up in the second half of 2023. Branch out!

PISCES WILL BE LUCKY WITH:
Money, making new friends

PISCES WILL BE CHALLENGED WITH:
Building self-confidence, releasing limiting beliefs

LOVE

"Love without limits" might be the Pisces preference, but as boundary-hound Saturn settles into your sign on March 7, you'll be singing a different tune. The ringed taskmaster hasn't visited you since 1994-96, so this is a new groove! During this three-year cycle, everything must be weighed, measured and meted out wisely, including your affections. Keep your heart open, but embrace Saturn's lessons of discernment and energy conservation. The biggest hurdle? Facing down people-pleasing (and codependency) and learning to say "no" to the ones you love. Venus brings another boost in the healthy relationships department from June 5 to October 8, taking an extended tour through Leo and your mindful, revitalizing sixth house. Prep yourself! Venus *will* be retrograde from July 22 to September 3, a time when clear relationship rules are a must. When the karmic South Node swings into Libra from July 17 to January 11, 2025, you'll be ready to deepen a special bond—while also sorting through a few demons like negative thinking, fear and jealousy. It's gonna be intense—but also damn sexy!

CAREER & MONEY

Boot camp starts March 7! The call of duty will be impossible to ignore as heavy-hitting Saturn plants its flag in Pisces for three years. When the lean, mean taskmaster planet visits your sign every 29.5 years, it tests your endurance and forces you to pay dues. But there *is* a reward ahead. Saturn is the planet of excellence and mastery and your hustle builds muscle. Put your focus on a clear goal and humbly forge ahead. Earnings could increase while abundant Jupiter tours your money zone (Aries) until May 16. And after July 17, the Libra South Node helps you stabilize with investments, from real estate to digital assets. Cooperative ventures could spark up mid-year—and while these deals may be short-term, they're bound to be profitable.

WELLNESS

Let the strength-training begin! With endurance-boosting Saturn in Pisces starting March 7, you could get into the best shape of your life. But this will take consistency and effort—two of Saturn's favorite words. This planet rules structure, so take extra care to prevent injury: warm up, learn proper posture and build stamina slowly. Saturn governs bones, knees and teeth—all areas to take special care of during this three-year cycle. From June 5 to October 8, enchanting Venus embarks on an extended tour through Leo and your sixth house of wellness. Skip the punishing workouts and find joy in moving your body, preparing vegan food and working with natural healers. Preventative medicine is the best "cure" of all!

FRIENDS & FAMILY

Branch out socially and discover new aspects of yourself! While the lunar North Node buzzes through Taurus and your outgoing third house until July 17, you may prefer to be a "floating fish" who mingles freely without getting caught in anyone's net. And once free-spirited Jupiter jumps into Taurus for a year on May 16, you won't abide by any restrictive affiliations. But don't miss the opportunity to develop a few enriching connections, especially with people in the local area. If there were ever a year to get a social club membership, this is it, Pisces. That way you can "bump into" familiar folks without getting roped into rigid plans.

JUPITER IN ARIES
Knowing your worth

Jupiter in Aries

December 20, 2022
to May 16, 2023

Ready to add another zero behind that dollar figure? Your financial worth *and* your self-worth are trending up, thanks to abundant Jupiter. On December 20, 2022, the planet of plenty shifted back into Aries, taking its second (and final) lap through your house of income, daily work and self-esteem, until May 16, 2023. Tap Jupiter's wellspring of security—and take it to the bank! When the planet of growth and opportunity visits this part of your chart every 12-13 years, it signals an exciting financial upswing.

You had a lot of exciting ideas while Jupiter visited Pisces in both 2021 and 2022. But getting your plans into motion was another story. In 2023, you can pick the crème de la crème and milk them for all they're worth. This is the year to build from the ground up and steadily save for your future. You got a small taste of this lesson in 2022, when Jupiter visited Aries from May 10 to October 28. Did you shelve a project due to time or cost? Dust it off and see if there's still something worth expanding on.

The second house oversees all things tangible, so you might come up with a product or a business endeavor that has legit legs. A lucrative income stream may flow from the fountain of your goddess-given gifts. Tap into the sophisticated sensibility of the second house and invest in attractive branding that you can use on social media and for your business materials. Visuals are a language unto themselves, as your aesthetically oriented sign understands.

One caveat: This lucrative cycle might not deliver results overnight. Galactic gambler Jupiter is a bit constrained in the fiscally conservative second house. Pursue opportunities that feel like well-calculated risks. What not to do? Get involved in "overnight millionaire" schemes that require you to make a high-risk investment. Delay gratification until you've researched everything thoroughly.

Whether you watch every penny or you never check your bank balance, this cycle will change your approach to spending and saving. Do you tend to swing between feast and famine? Money is not the enemy, but your mindset about it may be. Jupiter in Aries can help you learn moderation. (Note, we did *not* say deprivation.) Jupiter, the ruler of education, encourages you to raise your financial IQ during this transit. Brush up on the basics and master money management. Learn all there is to know about cryptocurrency or compounding interest.

Tuck enough funds away and you'll have something left over for the escapist splurges that Fish love. Spa resort in Austin? Scuba diving in Thailand? Acting workshop in London? Can you imagine how it would feel if the money was in your account the next time inspiration strikes? Before May 16, you may become the kind of person who actually has cash on hand for moments like these.

Gainfully employed Pisces are well-positioned for growth in 2023. Jupiter widens your scopes and sends projects your way that can elevate your profile. Present yourself as a brilliant problem-solver and make yourself irreplaceable. Or take on an "intrapreneurial" project where you spearhead an initiative that raises the company's profile significantly.

Of course, increasing your income won't bring more security if you burn funds as fast as you earn them. Tightening your belt will *not* be easy when

PISCES

Jupiter's large appetite radars in on your luxury-loving second house. It doesn't help matters much that Pisces are famously subject to bouts of extreme retail therapy. Challenge for 2023: Budget for your splurges instead of treating yourself on a whim. You'll enjoy that Italian leather sofa a helluva lot more when you aren't stressing about how to pay your mortgage!

Across the board, look for ways to simplify during this less-is-more phase, whether you utilize savvy lifehacks or just scale back overall. Anything you feel lukewarm about—from social obligations to volunteer activities, needs to be shelved until at least May 16 (and maybe forever). You're better off leaving some white space in your calendar than filling it to the gills with commitments your heart wasn't in when you said yes. Fill those slots with self-care (napping, working out, reading) or something else that's truly meaningful to you.

The pillars of regular waking and bedtime, meals and movement will give you a solid foundation, so make a firm commitment to them in early 2023. Do you have a favorite app that makes all of this easier? Use it! This process *can* (and should) be streamlined. For example, you keep your exercise clothes in your bedroom and hop on your Peloton first thing every morning. You set up the coffeemaker before going to sleep. A little same-old-same-old repetition is preferable to constantly reshuffling your calendar and your priorities, only to miss appointments and get overwhelmed.

JUPITER IN TAURUS
Expanding your reach

Jupiter in Taurus

May 16, 2023 to
May 25, 2024

Jupiter Retrograde

September 4 to
December 30, 2023

Attention Mayor Pisces? Your chill sign can be more of an observer than a joiner, but that all changes on May 16. Magnanimous Jupiter zooms into Taurus, pouring its can't-stop-won't-stop energy into your communicative, cooperative third house until May 25, 2024. Suddenly, you'll hear the call to play social director, rallying friends into cultural activities and organizing community initiatives.

Before this year is through, you could become the most popular fixture in your neighborhood. Is that you, Pisces, dropping off flyers in area coffeeshops and crushing open mics at dive bars? Get more involved in your hometown happenings, attending block association events and city council meetings. During this locally zoned, yearlong cycle, you want to have a say in how things are going in your neighborhood.

Whatever your passion, you'll have lots of local support for your mission! If you spent the first part of 2023 gestating a project, now's the time to show your baby off on social media. Wander around town and you could stumble upon a venue that's been hidden in plain sight. Maybe it's a local theater that will debut your one-Pisces show or a maker's market where you sell handcrafted wares or offer 15-minute tarot readings on the weekends.

But the *real* key to success lies in connecting with people whose skills are a perfect complement to your own. Reach out to well-connected friends who can help you get the word out. Hook up with brand ambassadors, influencers, and word-of-mouth mavens—then put them to work!

For example, maybe you're a mixed-media artist whose large-scale pieces are stacked against the wall of your loft, collecting dust. You've had a couple gallery shows but you're not sure how to get your work out to a wider audience post-pandemic (and maybe get spotted for Art Basel...a Fish can dream!). Team up with a savvy marketing whiz who can help with your social media strategy or an agent who can represent your work for sale. Let go of the idea that you have to promote yourself. As a sign that veers toward self-deprecation you have a strong tendency to underestimate yourself!

Socially, the second half of 2023 is the time to dabble and experiment. Vibrant new friendships crop up and you could find a few qualified project partners amongst the ranks. What *not* to do, however, is rush into binding or exclusive contracts. With the galactic gambler igniting this dynamic-duo zone, it's easy to overestimate potential. To avoid getting hung up in any contractual nightmares, test your chemistry on a trial project and see how your styles mesh.

Since the third house rules peers, a sibling, coworker or neighbor might become a sort of teacher. If your bond has suffered from rivalry or other pettiness, this high-minded Jupiter circuit can help you make headway with your relationship. Genuine dialogue is a prerequisite, and that includes active listening. While outspoken Jupiter is in Taurus, it's easy to sound off, especially if, say, your triggering brother pushes a button that they installed in childhood. It might be worth the money to have a third party mediate, not to mention the surest path to peace. Family therapy works for platonic relationships, too!

With info-hungry Jupiter occupying these curious quarters, learning is an adventure! Have you always wanted to learn how to play drums or custom-blend flower essences? Start with mini courses that build your skills or earn you a certification. With your communication zone lit, this is a great year to take a writing workshop, memoir class or a webinar. Or, maybe you'll be the one putting together a curriculum. Funnel your wisdom into a webinar or workshop and share your wisdom.

Vibrant new friendships crop up and you could find a few qualified project partners amongst the ranks.

If you're thinking of relocating, this is a great year to "try before you buy." With the globetrotting planet in your local action zone, you might hop between multiple cities or become officially bicoastal. Jet off on as many short trips as you can, staying for a few days (or weeks) in an appealing city or district that you're considering calling home. See what it feels like to go through your daily routine as if you lived there. Can you find "your" coffeeshop, hair salon and live music venue? If so, you may be looking at a place to call home in 2024—or a new home away from home to visit regularly.

MARS IN GEMINI
Making your house a home

Mars in Gemini

August 20, 2022 to
March 25, 2023

Mars Retrograde

October 30, 2022 to
January 12, 2023

Home sweet sanctuary? That's the dream for just about any serenity-loving Pisces. But ever since Mars turned retrograde in Gemini and your domestic fourth house onOctober 30, 2022, that little patch peace has been harder to come by. If you weren't in the throes of repair work or moving, you may have been dealing with uncertainty about whether or not you're *really* living in the right place for yourself. Is the thrum of city life that you once adored now making you feel like a rat in a maze? Or maybe you've slipped a little too far off the grid and wound up isolated. Whatever the case, something needs to be adjusted.

For other Fish, family matters could be shifting the tide of your life in an unexpected direction. You're no stranger to sacrifice, but what about *your* precious life? Questions about how to balance your needs and those of parents, kids, spouses, etc. could be keeping you up at night.

Woosahhhhhhh. On January 12, Mars corrects course and gets back on track once again. Better still? Since the red planet remains in Gemini until March 25, 2023, you'll have plenty of can-do momentum for (re)creating the kind of security you need to relax into a space that doesn't just *feel* like home but actually *is* your home.

In a normal cycle, Mars spends seven weeks in each sign during its two-year trip around the Sun. But because of the 10-week retrograde from October

30, 2022 to January 12, 2023, you have seven whole months to work with the agitating-but-exhilarating planet in Gemini and your fourth house of kith and kin.

Thankfully, the 2023 leg of this journey is all about finding the perfect mix of stability and stimulation. Emotions ran hot toward the end of 2022—and here's hoping no bridges were set ablaze during the holidays. There may be amends to make in Q1 of 2023. Thankfully, Mars in Gemini, when direct, has a way with words. But it's not just about delivering a heartfelt apology. Gemini is all about give and take, so lean into active listening. Make sure people know that you've *really* heard them—and that you care about the underlying emotion. You might feel like a parrot at times, but sentences that sound like, "What I hear you saying is X and that you're feeling Y, did I get that right?" could be balm for everyone's soul.

With Mars giving you a home court advantage after January 12, you have a bright green light to redecorate, renovate—or relocate. Some Pisces could be ready to sell or purchase property. Maybe you'll build a tiny home out back that can be rented out on Airbnb.

The fourth house rules your nest egg and Mars here may drive up a desire to plump up your bottom line. With your home zone lit, you could (re)launch a cottage industry from the dining room table. Get ready, Fish! This could take off at a galloping pace, even if the momentum stalled during Mars' retrograde. Mars in multifaceted Gemini can spark all kinds of ideas as well as motivation. Sell vintage collectibles (glasses, frames, pottery), teach an online course. There's nothing limiting your earning potential after January 12!

At the other end of the spectrum, some Pisces will be aching for freedom. A "semester abroad" as a digital nomad gets the Martian thumbs up. Since Gemini rules our vehicles, a cool rig like a tricked-out van or RV might even be part of the journey. With access to some creature comforts, home on the road is home all the same!

SATURN IN PISCES
Doing the work

Saturn in Pisces

March 7, 2023 to
February 13, 2026

Saturn Retrograde

June 17 to
November 4, 2023

Okay, Pisces, brace yourself for incoming weirdness. On March 7, Saturn, the ruler of time, structure and integrity, voyages into your sign for the first time since April 1996. As the zodiac's boundary-dissolving free spirit, this seismic shift is going to change up your flow. In fact, you might feel like a fish swimming upstream for a minute until you can adjust to Saturn's precise and meticulous current.

Everyone gets an audit from Saturn eventually—every 29.5 years, in fact. And from March 7, 2023 to February 13, 2026, your number's up. Resistance is futile so do what a Pisces does best… surrender. Once you do, you'll see that Saturn is only "cruel" to be kind. The boundary-enforcing planet is teaching you, the sign that struggles with any sort of limit, how to create healthy systems that bring you profound satisfaction.

It might help to think of the next three years as astrological boot camp. To level up to the next phase of the game, you've gotta muscle through basic training. That means sacrificing some "unhealthy pleasures" that could be slowing you down and making you feel old before your time. If you're carrying baggage for other people, Saturn hands them back their claim checks and lighten your load. Of course you'll have to deal with your own "need to be needed" in the process. Three years from now, codependent relationships that felt like true love will make you break out in hives.

THE ASTROTWINS

Fortunately, you'll reap rewards galore for paying your dues. Daily drills will build strength, cement healthier habits and create neural pathways that can facilitate a total mindset shift. Getting to Saturn's finish line is a triathlon, not a sprint. To stay motivated, celebrate mini milestones and daily wins. Embrace the process as much as the goal and you could crush this three-year cosmic cycle.

Since Saturn rules experts and elders, this could be the excuse you've been waiting for to train with a cutting-edge leader in an industry you've always wanted to break into. Climate change activist? Permaculture farmer? VR game designer? Pivoting in any direction is sanctioned by Saturn's residence in your first house of self. As long as you're willing to put in the work, this could be the reinvention tour you didn't even know you needed.

Immaculate levels of virtue and responsibility are prerequisites for this journey. That shouldn't be a problem for most Pisces, since you can easily elevate to high-vibe ideals. But Saturn's demand for structure? That's another story. Expect to encounter some obstacles, especially when navigating office politics or red tape. Clock-puncher Saturn can be a buzzkill for your meandering workflow, holding you accountable to other people's deadlines and schedules to an extent you've never known before. Ugh. While Pisces Albert Einstein may have operated in Chiros time, you'll be forced back into Chronos, feeling each minute tick some days.

As Saturn tours your first house of identity until February 13, 2026, give the Pisces "brand" a review. Objectively critique all front-facing assets: websites, social media accounts, profile photos, merch. While we'd never suggest you give up your creative identity, seek a middle ground between "elegant" and "ethereal." Saturn is the planet of maturity, inspiring a sleeker, more grown-up representation. It's fine to be the intuitive empath, artistic soul or the laid-back escapist (or all of the above). Just make sure you show your full range and depth, Pisces. People are ready to see your serious side, too.

Before you begin blueprinting and building anything, however, survey your landscape. Saturn is the astrological architect. Old structures may require a teardown or a renovation that will bring them up to code. Inspect scrupulously! Saturn wants you to construct a historic landmark, not a pop-up shop. With that in mind, create realistic timelines so you don't have to rush development. This is *not* the year to cut corners or pass things off as "good enough." In fact, faking it 'til you make it could backfire. The good news? You *can* boost your status and credibility in 2023. But expect to put in long hours and sweat equity in the process of laying a solid foundation.

Old structures may require a teardown or a renovation that will bring them up to code.

Feeling tired? Saturn's stay in your first house may temporarily deplete your energy, especially if you've been slacking on self-care. If you're used to going out at night and shortchanging your sleep, you may require a more sedate evening routine over the coming three years. Tucking in early with a thick novel and a cup of herbal tea could sound perfectly divine some nights—a shocking departure if you think of yourself as a nocturnal creature. Quiet time can be restorative, but as this Saturn circuit wages on, make a concerted effort to increase your vitality. Clean up your diet, hydrate with water (instead of coffee or your favorite adult beverage) and have a blood panel done to check your levels. You may discover that you're low on Vitamin D or iron deficient. Regimented Saturn enables you to acquire strength through daily practices. Start slowly if you must. A "Couch to 5K" program could be a game-changer if you need to turn potential energy into kinetic force.

Saturn rules aging, and the first house governs appearances. Even the forever young among you may want to put some clock-slowing practices in place. Unwind daily by meditating, spending time in nature and doing breathing techniques. If you're considering anti-aging treatments, conduct rigorous research before you inject anything—and only book with recommended pros (even if you found an amazing deal on Groupon). Note: Saturn will be retrograde from June 17 to November 4, which is *not* an optimal time for cosmetic procedures.

Saturn rules the skin, teeth, bone structure and knees. In 2023, you'd be smart to find a good dentist, esthetician and chiropractor. Remove your makeup every night and apply sunscreen religiously in the morning. Go easy on exercise that strains your joints—and don't forget to floss!

Yes, this is a lot more strategizing than your go-with-the-flow sign is used to, but there's a bright side to this transit. Planning is Saturn's specialty, as long as you're dedicated to whatever scheme you're cooking up. Choose activities that challenge and excite you. Prune the half-hearted engagements from your calendar. Saturn's streamlining effect will condense your list of commitments and casual friends, but that's more than okay. Time is precious, Pisces. Devote yours to whatever (and whoever) means the most!

PLUTO IN AQUARIUS
Tapping your mystical gifts

Pluto in Capricorn
Janury 1, 2023
to March 23, 2023

June 11, 2023 to
January 20, 2024

Pluto in Aquarius
March 23 to
June 11, 2023

Pluto Retrograde
May 1 to
October 10, 2023

Welcome to the Woo Universe! Or should we say, welcome back. Not that a Pisces ever leaves this realm! But you may need to reorient yourself a little to its mysterious depths. The reason for this? On March 23, alchemical Pluto changes signs, dipping into Aquarius and your dreamy, esoteric twelfth house until June 11. While this first cycle is brief, take notes! Pluto returns to Aquarius for 20 more years on November 19, 2024, laying out a new pathway for your soul's evolution until January 19, 2044.

And yes, this is a *very* big deal! Pluto has not passed through Aquarius in over two centuries! (The last circuit was from 1778 to 1798.) That means we living humans have literally never experienced this energy before in our time! And because Pluto hovers in a single zodiac sign for 12-21 years, its shifts can be seismic.

Since January 2008, Pluto has been on a slow roll through Capricorn and your eleventh house of teamwork and technology. During this time, the Pisces Posse has probably gone through some intense highs and lows. The cast of characters in your everyday life may have come and gone, at times without warning. Since Pluto rules harsher subject matter like abuse and death, you may have lost (or let go of) a few key figures over the past 15 years.

With profound Pluto stirring the pot, there was no escaping the influence of the company you've kept. Friends (and frenemies alike) held you, repelled you, dragged you down and lifted you up. Groups you joined were key to your spiritual evolution, but in some cases, you may have discovered nefarious dealings happening behind the scenes. Pisces Ja Rule found himself under legal scrutiny for involvement in the infamous Fyre Festival, a fraudulent "luxury music festival" that left thousands stranded without proper food and shelter (or music!) in the Bahamas. Although the rapper was cleared of the $100M charges, his affiliation with con-man Billy McFarland left a permanent mark on his reputation.

Alas, Pluto's "phoenix" lessons don't come without burning something down in the process. Thankfully, you have lots of experience navigating Pluto in Capricorn. During this final leg of its journey in 2023 and 2024, take stock of what you've learned. You're probably a whole lot more discerning about the people you get involved with! And certainly clearer about which environments are toxic (for you) and which ones support you to flourish and grow. Pisces Drew Barrymore is making the ultimate Pluto in the eleventh house moves by inviting her wide swath of friends on air for her popular talk show.

In this final frontier of Pluto in Capricorn, take a look: Are you making too many sacrifices for the ones you love? Hope springs eternal for the dreamy Fish. You don't believe in lost causes—but there are some people who may be a danger to you, simply because their energy drags you down and steals your life force. These are the ones to keep at a *very* far distance in 2023. In some cases, your only choice may be to end the relationship due to its draining, toxic nature.

When Pluto moves into Aquarius, you'll confront codependency and all the sneaky ways it shows up in your life. Our friend, author Terri Cole, has a name for it: "high-functioning codependency." While it may not interrupt your ability to produce, it steals your joy and destroys relationships. It's an insidious force that you can slowly heal from between now and March 8, 2043.

Boundary-setting has always been...a journey...for your sacrificial, generous sign. Now, Pluto in Aquarius delivers a master class in this form of emotional protection. Yet, don't expect yourself to ace this overnight. You have 21 years, in fact, to complete Pluto's "curriculum." In the early days, you may find yourself swinging wildly between extremes, pulling people close then pushing them away. Controlling, detaching. Freaking out, then feeling illuminated and free. Take responsibility for your emotional fluctuations! Otherwise, you could lose a genuinely supportive person in your life.

Although Pluto is dark and stormy—and generally an unwelcome guest at the party—the twelfth house is your comfort zone. You're the twelfth sign of the zodiac, so you feel "in your element" when a planet travels through this segment of your solar chart. (Yes, even Pluto, the part-time villain.) Plunging into the shadows? Exploring matters of life, death, regeneration and the afterlife? If anyone's here for it, you are, Pisces! Good thing, because Pluto's going to pull you right down the rabbit hole for the coming 21 years. And if you emerge feeling like a modern-day Yoda, we would *not* be surprised!

Forgiveness work is another huge theme that Pisces will face with Pluto in Aquarius. Are you estranged from a relative or dear friend? The rigid wall between you may start to soften between March 23 and June 11 as you come together to work through issues. Go slowly here, of course, because you want to make sure that *both* parties are going to do the inner excavation that's essential to your mutual growth. If revenge fantasies are involved, check yourself. Those will only blow up in your face.

Have you been blaming yourself for a situation that was beyond your control? Perhaps the person you most need to forgive is *you*, Pisces. While Pluto tours Aquarius, your internal landscape will become the most fascinating canvas to explore and interpret. This may even herald an artistic renaissance! Set up a studio to paint, write music, make art for art's sake. Pour your sorrow and revelations into your work.

One caveat: In the twelfth house, depth-plumbing Pluto doesn't have an oceanic floor, and you could get pulled into bottomless obsessing or rumination some days. But that's also where you'll find inspiration for your art and spiritual beliefs. (Hey, you don't share a zodiac sign with Kurt Cobain and Nina Simone for nothing.) And yet, you don't want to get lost in those woods for too long either.

With your subconscious twelfth house awakened by Pluto, the planet of the unconscious, your deepest discoveries can also come through meditation, journeys, and hypnotherapy. Crucial note! Only work with responsible people who are credentialed or experienced in ways that you can take to the bank. Your explorations may tap into trauma that requires a professional navigator to walk you through. This is not the time to go on some rando's "healing retreat."

Our advice? Keep grounded, cheery folks on call! For one thing, you may feel like you're walking around with VR goggles permanently over your eyes. What is reality, anyway? The line could get blurry enough to leave you feeling dissociated and confused some days between March 23 and June 11. Reach out to friends who know how to talk you out of a mood, make you laugh and snap you back to your sensible side. With one toe planted on Earth, you won't get pulled down into Pluto's abyss, but you *will* experience spiritual transformation on a level that is new and unscripted!

VENUS RETROGRADE
Simple pleasures

Venus in Leo

June 5 to
October 8, 2023

Venus Retrograde

July 22 to
September 3, 2023

You've heard what they say about the word "assume," right, Pisces? And if not, well, here goes, "It makes an ass out of u and me." Ba-da-damp. But seriously, Fish, you may want to jot down that little ditty in a reminder notification and have it pop up regularly this summer. From July 22 to September 3, love planet Venus will be retrograde, backing up through Leo and your persnickety sixth house. During this up-and-down period of turgid waters, you may feel like you're swimming upstream. Luckily, you're no stranger to changing currents—and you're not afraid of an emotional challenge. Life vests: on!

Fortunately, you'll have plenty of time to strengthen your lungs and catch your breath—both before and after the retrograde. Venus is taking an extra-long lap through Leo, strutting through the realm of the drama-forward Lion from June 5 to October 8. Normally, Venus hangs out in a single zodiac sign for four weeks. But thanks to her retrograde (which happens every 18 months), she'll court Leo for four whole *months*!

Since relationship friction intensifies during the six-week retrograde (July 22 to September 3), try to deactivate any emotional landmines that may be lying dormant *before* then. And we're talking specifically about the ones planted inside *you*. Your picky side could make an unceremonious appearance, polarizing a once-magnetic attraction into a repellant, fault-finding repulsion. For the record, this happens to almost everyone when their fears of engulfment arise. But if you're worried you might push away a good one, figure out what *you* need to give yourself. Is it more space and solitude? Less touch when you're trying to fall asleep? No interruptions while you're in your creative zone or work mode? Spell out those boundaries, Pisces, and you'll soon see who respects them and who is legitimately what our friend Terri Cole calls a "boundary buster."

Since Leo rules your sixth house of work, wellness and efficiency, the path to peace may lie in putting smart systems in place. What *are* your "work hours," Pisces? When *do* you like to cuddle and have sex? The journey to intimacy begins within, by giving yourself permission to have a full spectrum of wants and needs. You offer that grace to others so generously. Now, how about turning some of that back on yourself?

Since the sixth house is the "admin" zone, Venus here loves the rule of KISS: Keep It Simple Sweetheart. How about syncing calendars and summer schedules with bae, for example? This would be the perfect year to embark on a wellness challenge together. Eat more plant-based fare, train for a 5K, crew a sailboat. The endorphins will only add to your attraction.

Take care of your relationship's health by giving each other quality, undivided attention. Leave the phones off when you're sharing a meal (or in bed). When you're together, make a point of creating a safe space for conversation. If you aren't up for discussing a subject, say so instead of pushing yourself to "go there" then blowing up in frustration. A couple's coach or therapist can be a helpful translator while Venus is retrograde from July 22 to September 3.

Single swimmers, consider what a healthy relationship means to you. Venus retrograde may hold some important answers about unproductive behaviors. Generous Pisces, your sign rules sacrifice, but you can take that to extremes by overlooking your own needs and playing martyr to your boo.

You might wave off help and reflexively say, "I've got this," thinking that you don't want to bother anyone. But guess what? You're also missing a key opportunity to build partnership by solving problems *together*. The journey is actually a lot more enlightening when there are extra hands to help.

With Venus sashaying through your sixth house of *self*-care, give your own body a tune-up, fussing over yourself the same way you would a lover. Book all those checkups, get a monthly massage on the calendar, see your acupuncturist. Gut health is especially salient in the sixth house, and with Venus here, you might visit a colon hydrotherapist or do a food-based cleanse (or both) to kick off your summer.

Do try to get any procedures handled before the July 22 retrograde—especially Venus-ruled beauty treatments, from injections to microblading to cosmetic surgeries. And if you can't change the dates, make sure you're an expert on the matter before you slip into that hospital gown.

Workwise, Venus in Leo puts the emphasis on stress reduction. Any form of exercise helps, as does getting quality sleep so you can triumph the next day. Are you taking on too much and overloading yourself from day-to-day? Perhaps a coworker can step in and lighten the load. Are you constantly redoing or editing a team member's work? Before July 22, have the uncomfortable conversation to set **expectations**. It may feel awkward, but it'll spare you from picking **up their slack in the future**.

NORTH NODE IN ARIES
Security check

> **Lunar North Node in Aries**
>
> July 17, 2023
> to January 11, 2025

Money matters are top of mind for Pisces starting July 17, as the lunar Nodes begin a journey across your financial axis that lasts until January 11, 2025. "Going with the flow" might be your preferred state and we can't say we blame you. But as the destiny-driven North Node parks in Aries and your fiscally responsible second house mid-July, that ephemeral ethos will be, er, bankrupt. Steady, solid work becomes essential, and you may need to downsize in the "luxury" category.

Fortunately, you won't have to look hard to find people who want to hire you. If the prior nodal cycle in Taurus and Scorpio (January 18, 2022 to July 17, 2023) did its job, you developed a powerful network to help boost your net worth. While you're generally more comfortable in the role of the benefactor, it's time to cash in on all those favors you bestowed. Since most people don't share your mind-reading skills, you'll have to speak up and ask for what you need. The squeaking wheel gets the oil!

Regardless of where your earnings come from, personal economics become a key decision driver for Fish after July 17. We're not just talking about putting food on the table and keeping a roof over your head though. How can you make your money work harder for you? Across the zodiac wheel, the karmic South Node brings a new sense of balance from your eighth house of joint finances and long-term wealth. Sharing resources (with the right people) can bring everyone greater security. This may be the year that Pisces shop for VC funding, apply for a mortgage or small business loan.

With the South Node in Libra, sharpen your investment know-how. There's a certain amount of intuition involved (lucky you!) in playing the market. But you don't want to gamble! Close that learning curve and educate yourself on fiscal systems. You could make a mint from a diversified portfolio of mutual funds, real estate, crypto and more.

If you've been working at the same job for a while, leverage your experience, Pisces, and move up the ladder within the company. Or use this feather in your cap to apply for a position elsewhere. Self-employed Fish can raise your rates after July 17—or offer packages or subscriptions to retain clientele and keep recurring revenue flowing in.

Check your mindset! Money is not the root of all evil nor is it a holy grail to pursue. But it *is* a necessary resource to operate in today's world. With the lunar South Node in luxe-loving Libra and the North Node in entitled Aries, tune in to your desires. What's a worthy goal to save up for in the second half of the year—something that would make your daily existence feel deliciously decadent? Rather than buying it on credit, create a special fund for it and start tucking bits away. If you're living beyond your means, what can you scale back on without feeling deprived? How can you earn more to cover not just your lifestyle costs but also tuck funds away for future security?

Surprise, Pisces! Financial security can be sexy! Ask any expert on the planet: Relaxing is fundamental foreplay. Yes, life could be a whole lot more sensual if you gave up adrenaline as your primary fuel source. Whether you're merging bank accounts, tucking more into your retirement account, or adjusting your income-to-expense ratio, *not* constantly worrying about cash means more headspace for fantasizing about seductive pleasures...many of which won't cost a thing!

ECLIPSES IN 2023
Money moves and power plays

Hybrid Solar Eclipse in
Aries (new moon)

April 20 at 12:17AM

Penumbral Lunar Eclipse
in Scorpio (full moon)

May 5 at 1:24PM

Annular Solar Eclipse
in Libra (new moon)

October 14 at 2:00PM

Partial Lunar Eclipse
in Taurus (full moon)

October 28 at 4:15PM

times in eastern time

APRIL 20:
SOLAR ECLIPSE IN ARIES
HYBRID SOLAR ECLIPSE 29°52,
12:17AM ET

Hello abundance! Today marks the first eclipse in a two-year series across your financial axis (Aries-Libra) and could bring a whole new approach to earning and investing between now and March 2025. It's also an ultra-rare hybrid solar eclipse (beginning as a "ring of fire" annular eclipse and transitioning into a sun-blotting total eclipse) so don't scour for opportunity in the same old places. Are you ready to make a dramatic pivot? Now's the time to hit the gas on that. You could be offered a new position or have that long-awaited inspiration for a profitable business idea. If you need training or updated skills to make that bank, invest in your development now. And while you're at it, speak up for yourself. Your hard work could be recognized (at last!) by the movers-and-shakers at your job and any self-promotion can expedite that. Consider this the start of an upward trend in your financial life. It's not just how you earn it, it's how you burn it as well. Budget, please!

MAY 5: LUNAR ECLIPSE IN SCORPIO
PENUMBRAL LUNAR ECLIPSE, 14°52, 1:24PM ET

Should you stay or should you go? The lunar (full moon) eclipse in Scorpio could bring a travel opportunity completely out of the blue, one worth scrambling to pack and, if necessary, get your 24-hour passport handled. A long-distance connection that's been percolating since the corresponding solar eclipse on October 25, 2022, reaches a pivotal moment today, too. Something's gotta give here, Pisces...and that might just mean giving up hope if you can't figure out the logistics of seeing each other face to face more often. On the other hand, a powerful partnership may emerge with someone in another part of the world. Thank goodness for that little thing called the Internet.

OCTOBER 14: SOLAR ECLIPSE IN LIBRA
ANNULAR SOLAR ECLIPSE 21°10, 2:00PM ET

Ready for an extreme makeover, Pisces? Today's annular "ring of fire" solar eclipse in Libra—the first eclipse to land in this sign since 2016—lights up your eighth house of transformation. You've known for a while that an aspect of your life needed to change, but today, you're finally ready to take the bull by the horns. Boil it down to a black or white decision. There's no room for fifty shades of grey now...the bedroom being the exception. The seductive allure of the eighth house could bring a simmering attraction to full boil. Draw the drapes; lock the doors. This is a Do Not Disturb situation.

OCTOBER 28: LUNAR ECLIPSE IN TAURUS
PARTIAL LUNAR ECLIPSE 5°03, 4:15PM ET

True friends fit you like a glove, courtesy of today's lunar (full moon) eclipse in your social third house. There's no need to linger on the periphery of a scene, looking in. As eclipses reveal shadows, you could discover that others were actually afraid to approach you, either out of intimidation or perceived disinterest on your part. Don't wait for an invitation, Pisces, just get in there and participate. Your warm presence and genuine way of connecting with others makes it easy for them to adore you. Add your two cents, and bring on the bonding. Are you in the market for a new set of wheels? With your transportation sector lit, the perfect ride could appear. Just make sure it comes with a warranty!

2023

HOTSPOTS

JANUARY *Moon Phases*

SUN	MON	TUE	WED	THU	FRI	SAT
1 ☽ ♉	**2** ♉ ♊ 9:44PM	**3** ♊	**4** ♊	**5** ♊ ♋ 9:15AM	**6** ♋ Full Moon 6:07PM	**7** ♋ ♌ 9:40PM
8 ♌	**9** ♌	**10** ♌ ♍ 10:15AM	**11** ♍	**12** ♍ ♎ 9:56PM	**13** ♎	**14** ♎ 3rd Quarter
15 ♎ ♏ 7:08AM	**16** ♏	**17** ♏ ♐ 12:33PM	**18** ♐	**19** ♐ ♑ 2:11PM	**20** ♑	**21** ♑ ♒ 1:29PM ♒ NM 3:53PM
22 ♒	**23** ♒ ♓ 12:36PM	**24** ♓	**25** ♓ ♈ 1:48PM	**26** ♈	**27** ♈ ♉ 6:42PM	**28** ♉ 1st Quarter
29 ♉	**30** ♉ ♊ 3:35AM	**31** ♊				

Times listed are Eastern US Time Zone

KEY: ♈ ARIES ♊ GEMINI ♌ LEO ♎ LIBRA ♐ SAGITTARIUS ♒ AQUARIUS
♉ TAURUS ♋ CANCER ♍ VIRGO ♏ SCORPIO ♑ CAPRICORN ♓ PISCES

FM FULL MOON   **NM** NEW MOON   **LE** LUNAR ECLIPSE   **SE** SOLAR ECLIPSE

1

NEW YEAR'S DAY

Welcome to 2023! The New Year begins on a sultry and sensual note as Venus sidles up to Pluto in Capricorn. If you're not snuggled up in bed all day, you might be downloading creative hits and taking notes for a year-ahead project. As you look ahead for 2023, this empowering alignment challenges you to raise the bar to a height that inspires you to elevate yourself. But don't set it so high that you feel like you're grasping, especially since Mercury remains retrograde in goal-getting Capricorn until January 18. Because of this, we recommend waiting to formally make your resolutions until January 21, when the first new moon of 2023 (in Aquarius) aligns your wishes with limitless possibilities. In the meantime, start with a vision board or a first draft of your intentions for the year ahead.

**2 JAN -
26 JAN**

VENUS IN AQUARIUS

Traditional romance takes a backseat to chill bonding as flirtatious Venus sashays into progressive Aquarius, From unconventional arrangements to FWB situations, this freedom-loving cycle could inspire you to mix things up. Single? Aquarius rules technology, bringing a high "clickthrough rate" on the apps. Experiment with blind dates and let friends and coworkers set you up. Attached? Socialize as a couple and strengthen the foundation of friendship in your relationship. Don't feel compelled to play by the rules if you're yearning for something a bit outside the lines. From bringing in a "guest star" to planning for a family, the stage is set for exploration and negotiation. You don't have to actually do any of the things you discuss. Talking about them might be spicy enough during this sapiosexual cycle!

SUN-URANUS TRINE

5
JAN

Expand your horizons and think beyond the box! As the confidence-boosting Capricorn Sun teams up with inventive and original Uranus in Taurus, the spark of possibility ignites! First step? Stop focusing on what you would do instead of actually doing it. Shift your mindset from "Maybe if …" to "Let's try …" during this visionary moment. Bring in tools, technology and cutting edge procedures to manifest your goal.

FULL MOON IN CANCER 6:07PM EST

6
JAN

The first full moon of 2023 glows in warm, caring Cancer. Under these nurturing beams, you'll be closely connected to your emotions—good reason to keep the tissue box handy to dab any tears. Should a dear friend cross your mind, don't let it be a passing thought. With Mercury opposing this full moon, that pull to reach out could be a near-psychic one. A cathartic coffee date could get you both back to center after the buzz (and stress) of the holidays. Under Cancer's domestic influence, home life is equally top of mind. First project of the New Year? Rearranging your living room, updating your bedroom furniture—or changing your address entirely! In love, this lunar light softens hearts and draws out everyone's sentimental side. Cozy up under the cashmere throw with your favorite plus-one (or just by yourself). Binge a new series, cook something simple and nourishing, and talk about your feelings. Yes, really!

1

SUN-MERCURY MEETUP

Open mouth, insert Prada loafer? As the ego-driven Sun greets Mercury retrograde for a tense summit in Capricorn, one thoughtless comment could get you canceled. While you're eager to dive back into the grind, goals may be mired in red tape. Here's the silver lining though: This frustrating mashup could lead you to research new production processes. As a result, you could stumble upon a more economic or efficient way of doing things. Since retrogrades rule the past, the Sun could beam on a former colleague who turns out to be the missing link. Don't hesitate to reach out. If nothing else, they'll have the very advice you need to hear!

MERCURY-URANUS TRINE

Summon your inner genius today as clever Mercury gets in a hive-mind huddle with innovator Uranus. In stabilizing earth signs, you could come up with a wildly profitable idea out of left field. Dig through old files for inspiration since you may already have the seeds of your plan sitting on an half-finished spreadsheet. A lightning-bolt epiphany could also come from an unexpected source, such as a casual conversation with a coworker or, since both planets rule technology, via your apps. Check those DMs today! Mercury is retrograde, so a person from your past could be the catalyst for events. Or, you may have a fabulous idea but no clue how to pull it off. Jot your notes down anyhow, as these two planets will reconvene again at the end of the month when Mercury is back in forward motion and ready to kick things off for real!

VENUS-MARS TRINE

<table>
<tr><td>9
JAN</td></tr>
</table>

Intellectual chemistry could ignite a serious case of the butterflies as cosmic-copilots Venus and Mars soar into a one-day air trine. Venus is in experimental Aquarius and Mars in articulate Gemini, a recipe for radical experimentation...if you're ready to go there. Interactions don't have to get physical to send waves of energy rippling through your body. A flirty text may flicker across your screen or a friend of a friend could be fetching enough to trade contact information. The dating apps could actually turn up a promising prospect, but so could a local hangout. If you're in a relationship, send a playful DM and suggest meeting somewhere for a surprise date. Skip the same-old activities and experiment with something new!

MARS RETROGRADE ENDS

<table>
<tr><td>12
JAN</td></tr>
</table>

Two is the magic number again as passionate Mars blazes forward in persuasive Gemini, ending a dicey retrograde that began on October 30. After weeks of resistance, the tension clears. It won't take much convincing to get people on board with your grandiose schemes. But here's the catch: If you want to maintain their trust, make sure you can deliver the goods! The red planet is spending a rare seven months in the sign of the Twins—as opposed to its usual seven or eight weeks—so there's no wriggling out of any promises, at least not without a penalty. Mars has been in Gemini since August 20, 2022, and will remain here until March 25, 2023. Between now and the start of spring, carefully-vetted dynamic duos could take flight. Caution: This transit can also bring out the fast-talking charlatans and devil's advocates who want to argue for argument's sake, or worse.

1

<table>
<tr><td>

**14
JAN**

</td><td>

WANING QUARTER MOON IN LIBRA

Addressing a conflict may be awkward but avoiding it for another day could quickly create a much bigger mess. Fortunately, the waning quarter moon in Libra steps in like a diplomat helping you broach the topic gracefully. Keep a level head as you wade into potentially turbulent waters—and stay on the high road, even if you're feeling wounded or attacked. If you have the facts on your side, you have nothing to worry about. But how sure are you that you haven't overlooked any details? A little digging may reveal that you're the one who needs to extend an apology. (Yikes!) If you discover that you were in error, own it. With gracious Libra guiding the amends-making, the key to dissolving tension might involve a large bouquet of flowers and a lavish dinner, your treat.

</td></tr>
<tr><td>

**14
JAN**

</td><td>

VENUS-URANUS SQUARE

Stormy emotions and short fuses make it hard to relax today, as peaceful Venus in Aquarius spins into a stressful square with volatile Uranus in Taurus. Brace yourself. People will clamor for your attention and make demands on your time. Meanwhile, all you want is a little bit of space! It's tempting to react when you feel cornered, but take a breather before clapping back or firing off an incendiary email. Even the sweetest souls could snap with little provocation. Feeling bored or claustrophobic in a relationship? You could be tempted to bolt or blur the line between "spontaneous" and "recklessly impulsive". Better just to take a time-out than to make any rash and hard-to-reverse moves.

</td></tr>
</table>

<table>
<tr><td>18
JAN</td></tr>
</table>

MERCURY RETROGRADE ENDS

At last! Communication and technology planet Mercury corrects course after an irksome and disruptive retrograde that began on December 29, 2022. In goal-oriented Capricorn, backspinning Mercury made it tough to commit to clear resolutions. From today forward, that changes, so get those 2023 resolutions in your crosshairs. Figure out what needs to get back on track ASAP, then pick up the pieces and get your plan in place. Career convos are productive and promising while Mercury powers forward through ambitious Capricorn until February 11. Set up time to confer with your boss about Q1 goals, announce your increased 2023 rates or say yes to that exploratory coffee meeting with a potential freelance client.

<table>
<tr><td>18
JAN</td></tr>
</table>

SUN-PLUTO MEETUP

Even the best-kept secrets could be revealed today as the Sun brightens Pluto's shadows, activating your private ambitions. The idea of having your hopes and dreams exposed to the world might seem intimidating, especially if you don't feel "ready." But stepping into your power requires courage during this once-per-year summit. If you've been humble about your hard work, show off the fruits of your labor. Make sure your boss or an industry figure you admire are keenly aware of your capabilities. But be strategic! This planetary board meeting can arouse ego clashes and temper tantrums. Go into every meeting informed about who's in the room and what position they occupy on the pyramid. Handle fragile types with care.

1

SUN IN AQUARIUS

20 JAN - 18 FEB

Start assembling your crew of collaborators and get ready to make magic together! For the next four weeks, let community-driven Aquarius guide you through changing roles and seek out a team that aligns with your values and appreciates your strengths. It may be time to lean into technology to streamline your search, so fire up LinkedIn and get to networking to help you find your people faster. The perfect left brain to your right brain (or vice versa) could be a click or two away! Aquarius is fueled with idealism, so be wary of unrealistic expectations, but don't let fear of failure or being "too ambitious" stop you from reaching toward your goals. Focus on community and inclusivity and make it your responsibility to bring out the best in others. After all, doesn't success feel better when it's shared?

21 JAN

NEW MOON IN AQUARIUS 3:53PM EST

All together now! 2023's first new moon arrives in the sign of the wishful, collaborative Water Bearer, opening the perfect window for setting resolutions and intentions. (A wise idea, since Mercury retrograde was muddling everyone's visionary powers back on January 1.) Team-spirited Aquarius rallies people around a common cause. From social justice initiatives to collaborative projects, make space for different opinions and viewpoints. (Aquarius loves community, not conformity.) This evening also ushers in the Chinese New Year, as we say farewell to the sultry, savvy Water Tiger and welcome the spiritual, abundant Water Rabbit. After a year of strategic stakeouts, we can, er, "hop to it" with the Rabbit's creative flair. But keep your boundaries more firm than fluffy. Without the Tiger's protective prowess, we're more vulnerable to predators under the gentle Rabbit's rule.

22 JAN

URANUS RETROGRADE ENDS

The line between stability and chaos has been shaky since last August 24, when disruptor Uranus pivoted retrograde in Taurus, the sign of daily routines, money and security. Today, the planet of revolution powers forward in this sensible-but-sensual sign. In the days ahead, explore novel approaches to earning money and creating security while also giving credence to proven strategies. Warning: When Uranus "stations" back to direct motion, people's behavior can be erratic and unpredictable. Give the energy a few days to settle before making any major decisions. While you may be headed for an exciting change, it's not something to embark on impulsively. To stay balanced, see what happens if you reduce screen time and increase connection with the natural world.

1

VENUS-SATURN MEETUP

22 JAN

Love is serious business today, as Venus gets swept under Saturn's stern spell. You don't have to give up your fantasies, but for the moment, shift focus to brass tacks. Are you on the same page about your relationship's direction? Even if you're casually dating, clarify basic boundaries around things like scheduling dates and bedroom safety. Couples may need to drop anchor and get real about bigger subjects such as family and finances. Head's up: These no-nonsense discussions may reveal some genuine disparities. Since Saturn rules experts, it may be time to bring in the big guns. A coach or couple's therapist may help you get past a sticking point. Have you been caught up in a never-ending situationship or pining for a lost soul? This planetary pairing forces you to take an unblinking look at reality. Time is precious, and you don't want to waste your life waiting for someone who "isn't ready" and may never be!

WAXING QUARTER MOON IN TAURUS

28 JAN

Time for a tune-up! If you're feeling exhausted or overtaxed, consider it a "dashboard warning light" telling you to stop and treat yourself like a luxury vehicle instead of a cog in the machine. Today's waxing quarter moon in tasteful Taurus is the perfect time to pull out the magnifying glass and see what's under the proverbial hood. Taking the time to keep things humming along happily could save you a breakdown later, so don't wave off the inspection for the sake of speed. Let go of anything that isn't working and plan for what could be looming just beyond your plane of vision. But don't streamline too much! Sensual Taurus enjoys the finer things in life. Upgrade any parts of your life suffering from wear and tear and add some simple elegance.

SUN-MARS TRINE

Welcome to the ideation station! Today's free-flowing trine between the innovative Aquarius Sun and mentally agile Mercury is best used for brainstorming, mind mapping and any sort of "wouldn't it be crazy if..." conversations. Set up a recording app like Otter or have someone take copious notes! With these bold and fired-up planets in cahoots, novel visions come in fast and furious—and you might lose them if you rely on memory. With both heavenly bodies in communicative air signs, don't be surprised if your clever concepts gain a following—and attract a few eager people who want to help make them a reality. But vet everyone before welcoming them aboard. Savvy and smarts are great, but do they have the loyal attitude to back it up? If they pass the litmus test, the more the merrier!

MERCURY-URANUS TRINE

They're baaa-aack! For the second time this month, the two innovative planets fist-bump in stabilizing earth signs, Capricorn (Mercury) and Taurus (Uranus). This time, however, Mercury is out of its disruptive retrograde phase and powering forward in achievement- and status-oriented Capricorn. An "a-ha" moment that struck back on January 8 could now gain real traction. Give it another round of consideration. If it still passes muster, put out the word to any well-connected people in your world. If you're ready to start developing your concept, move from ideation mode to the production phase!

FEBRUARY *Moon Phases*

2

SUN	MON	TUE	WED	THU	FRI	SAT
			1 ♊ ♋ 3:11PM	**2** ♋	**3** ♋	**4** ♋ ♌ 3:48AM
5 ♌ Full Moon 1:29PM	**6** ♌ ♍ 4:14PM	**7** ♍	**8** ♍	**9** ♍ ♎ 3:47AM	**10** ♎	**11** ♎ ♏ 1:34PM
12 ♏	**13** ♏ 3rd Quarter ♐ 8:31PM	**14** ♐	**15** ♐	**16** ♑ 12:00AM	**17** ♑	**18** ♑ ♒ 12:35AM
19 ♒ ♓ 11:56PM	**20** ♓ New Moon 2:06AM	**21** ♓	**22** ♓ ♈ 12:14AM	**23** ♈	**24** ♈ ♉ 3:29AM	**25** ♉
26 ♉ ♊ 10:48AM	**27** ♊ 1st Quarter	**28** ♊ ♋ 9:40PM				

Times listed are Eastern US Time Zone

KEY: ♈ ARIES ♊ GEMINI ♌ LEO ♎ LIBRA ♐ SAGITTARIUS ♒ AQUARIUS
♉ TAURUS ♋ CANCER ♍ VIRGO ♏ SCORPIO ♑ CAPRICORN ♓ PISCES

FM FULL MOON **NM** NEW MOON **LE** LUNAR ECLIPSE **SE** SOLAR ECLIPSE

2

3
FEB

SUN-URANUS SQUARE

Tempers are flaring—and threatening to boil over—as the ego-driven Sun (in Aquarius) goes head-to-head with Uranus in Taurus. With everyone insisting their way is the right way, jockeying to be "right" is probably futile. As you move through the day, weigh out your actions and avoid going rogue. People might get a rise out of pushing your buttons, but don't take the bait! Stooping to their aggression will only inflame the battle further. And you never know...the "loser" you cuss out at the traffic light could turn out to be your new HR director or your best friend's new flame. #Regrets

4
FEB

VENUS-MARS SQUARE

If you're waffling over a love interest, today's clash of romantic duo Venus and Mars may shed light on the situation. You could discover you're just not as compatible as you thought, or maybe there's an issue that's become a serious sticking point. With Venus in soft-hearted Pisces, you may be tempted to go into denial and sweep this matter under the rug. But courageous Mars in talkative Gemini encourages you to address this. Be diplomatic but direct.

2

<table>
<tr><td>5
FEB</td></tr>
</table>

FULL MOON IN LEO 1:29PM EST

Should you post those "tastefully risqué" selfies? Submit your work to a juried competition? Bare your soul to your secret crush? Today's full moon in Leo says, "hell to the yes!" You don't have to be polished or perfect before you put yourself out there. Nope! This lion-hearted lunar lift rewards courage. Although there's a performative energy to the day, try to genuinely connect with people instead of just wowing them with your pizazz. What not to do? Court controversy with wild antics or spark a public feud just to rile people up. Since this full moon locks into a tangled angle with rabble-rouser Uranus, the rebuttal (and consequences!) could be harsher than you anticipate. And with "wounded healer" comet Chiron trining this full moon, spark peace talks instead of using your roar to start a war.

<table>
<tr><td>10
FEB</td></tr>
</table>

MERCURY-PLUTO MEETUP

Intellectual Mercury teams up with investigative Pluto in Capricorn, serving penetrating insights that help you connect the dots on an unsolved mystery. But don't go trumpeting your findings to the world. Under these secretive skies, delicate topics demand careful delivery...or complete confidentiality. Is a hidden agenda brewing? Even the most innocent statements could feel loaded with subtext, provoking your suspicion. If you sense that people are being less-than forthcoming, observe instead of accusing. Working on an important project? Do some behind-the-scenes research and be cautious about who gets the scoop. It's okay to cultivate an aura of mystery under today's intriguing spell! Once you've established a firm foundation of trust, you'll be able to speak freely.

2

MERCURY IN AQUARIUS

11 FEB - 2 MAR

Social butterfly Mercury zips into collaborative Aquarius, kicking team efforts into high gear. Get your online profiles in grade-A shape! People may soon be typing your name into their search bars. Of course, making all-important connections should not be left up to chance. Over the next few weeks, circulate among industry peers and ask well-connected friends to put in a solid word on your behalf. Fresh viewpoints can do wonders to elevate any big projects. Set up a think tank with experienced colleagues or invite friends to test pilot your latest venture-in-progress. (Wine and margherita pizza on you!) Since this transit lasts all month, V-Day plans might be best enjoyed with a crew of couples or singles. Who says Cupid's arrows can't be platonic and professional ones? Play superconnector between friends you've been dying to introduce.

WANING QUARTER MOON IN SCORPIO

13 FEB

Feelings are not facts, though today's waning quarter moon in Scorpio could tempt you to believe otherwise. Watch out for a subtle undercurrent of jealousy. Are your trust alarms going off? It's important to listen to your intuition, but your judgment could also be clouded by insecurity. The darkening moon can cast shadows on the truth and make your true feelings hard to decipher. Dive a little deeper into what's causing these tangled emotions—and get curious instead of closed off! By asking the right questions (a Scorpionic superpower), you may turn a foe into an intimate friend. Never underestimate the power of a "Can you tell me more?" at exactly the right time. A little elaboration and examination could lead to tighter bonds in the boardroom or the bedroom. Don that detective's chapeau and start digging!

2

VENUS-NEPTUNE MEETUP

15 FEB

Enjoy a sultry sequel to Valentine's Day as ardent Venus pairs up with enchanting Neptune—in poetic Pisces, no less! Yes, that's exactly why you're so weak in the knees. This annual cosmic connection brushes relationships with a rose-tinted glow. The only trouble? That blithe optimism can screen out everything but people's brightest potential. Tap the brakes on your pumpkin carriage before you get swept along in a fantasy. (Or forgive someone's egregious misdeeds before they've even apologized.) Boundaries might be the last thing on your mind right now, but unless you're sure that it's safe to surrender, work extra hard to keep sensible ones in place.

SUN-SATURN MEETUP

16 FEB

If today's union of the optimistic Sun and pessimistic Saturn is good for anything, it's to help you weigh the pros and cons. With both planets in Aquarius, logical solutions emerge that can decomplexify ongoing problems. But as the ringed taskmaster casts a shadow over El Sol, your buoyant hopes and optimistic plans could get a harsh reality check. Watch for heavy moods under this annual "downer day." Instead of getting discouraged, go back to the drawing board and put a solid plan in place. If you lose perspective, remember that this weighty energy will pass by tomorrow. Have you been diligently paying your dues? Your efforts could reach their tipping point at last, attracting the hard-earned respect of an industry leader. Give credit where it's due, then accept kudos with grace.

SUN IN PISCES

18 FEB - 20 MAR

The Sun floats into Pisces's idyllic orbit, serving enchantment and empathy. Imagination reigns supreme for the next four weeks—a refreshing change after geeky-freaky Aquarius season. Ditch the algorithms and social theory and reach for your tarot cards and book on attachment styles. With everyone's sixth sense dialed up during this ethereal time of year, your hunches could be as solid a GPS as your Waze app. Nurture your spiritual side and explore an artistic avenue such as music, painting or dance. This unbound creative surge could yield divine downloads from the muse.

Compassion is on trend during this boundary-dissolving solar cycle, but warning—so is codependence and sacrifice. While it's great to focus on people's potential, you could fall in love with a fantasy version of them. Hoisting anyone too high on a pedestal can cause you to miss red flags. Keep your feet on the ground even if your head is in the clouds.

2

20 FEB

NEW MOON IN PISCES 2:06AM EST

The fantasy floodgates open today as the year's only new moon in Pisces awakens your wildest imaginings. Since the spiritual veil is thin under these moonbeams, this is one of the best days of the year to download divine inspiration. Get yourself into a quiet space where you can receive the guidance of your inner voice. Start an artistic venture or sign up for training in a spiritual modality. Anything from life drawing workshops to Human Design astrology could make the winter months fly by. But heed this planetary PSA: Compassion does not equal codependence. This sacrificial lunation may find you playing the role of caretaker instead of companion. It's great to lend a hand when people need extra support. But if you're feeling drained, set boundaries around your availability. A healthy "no" or "not right now" saves you from resentment in the future and lays the groundwork for a healthier relationship where everyone pulls their weight. Got a secret wish or desire? Dare to bare it!

20 FEB - 16 MAR

VENUS IN ARIES

It's getting steamy in here! Vivacious vixen Venus sprints into fierce, fiery Aries, raising temperatures right after Valentine's Day. Don't melt the ice too quickly, though. In impulsive Aries, Venus is in "detriment," a challenged position for the typically slow-burning seduction planet. Romance can sizzle then fizzle under this fast-moving sign. One day you'll be glued together and the next, ghosted. (But don't worry, they'll be back...then gone, then back again.) Coupled? Scorching chemistry with someone outside your relationship can take you by surprise. No need to act on it; just bring that surge of feisty energy back home to your partner. If you've hit a dating plateau, Venus in courageous Aries can inspire you to get back out there and circulate.

21 FEB

MERCURY-URANUS SQUARE

As tempting as it may be to flout the rules, rebellious moves could backfire as Uranus pushes mischievous Mercury's buttons and sets everyone on edge. Mercury is stirring the pot in renegade Aquarius bringing a double warning to not go ranting and raving across social media—or in any social setting for that matter. Meanwhile, Uranus in Taurus could cause you to stubbornly cling to a highly questionable idea. The threat of cancellation looms large under these skies. If you're sharing a new idea or presenting a clever defense, do the work to organize your sources and stats before you circulate your findings. Otherwise, you could come off like a loose cannon or worse, uninformed.

22 FEB

MERCURY-MARS TRINE

Mic drop! As raconteur Mercury trines high-key Mars, a colorful story could leave everyone spellbound. And with both planets in savvy air signs, pepper in clever quips and well-researched data for a standing ovation. This galactic glow-up bodes well for pitches and presentations, so if you're ready for the attention to swing your way, it's showtime! Take that professional leap and make sure you've covered all your bases. Along with your polished bio, potential employers or collaborators may be scanning your social media.

2

**27
FEB**

WAXING QUARTER MOON IN GEMINI

Pairing is caring under today's waxing quarter moon in Gemini. A budding connection or meeting of the minds could set the stage for a longer-term collab down the line. Since this lunar lift lands in the sign of the twins, you might be tempted to partner with someone who thinks and acts just like you. Reconsider! While some common ground is necessary, you may fare better by joining forces with the person who leads with their left brain versus your right, for example. Since this is a gentle quarter moon, no need to rush into anything. Start off small with a short-term project and test the waters. You may unlock talents you didn't know you had or find avenues you didn't realize you were seeking.

MARCH *Moon Phases*

SUN	MON	TUE	WED	THU	FRI	SAT
			1 ♋	**2** ♋	**3** ♋ ♌ 10:16AM	**4** ♌
5 ♌ ♍ 10:38PM	**6** ♍	**7** ♍ Full Moon 7:40AM	**8** ♍ ♎ 9:44AM	**9** ♎	**10** ♎ ♏ 7:06PM	**11** ♏
12 ♏	**13** ♏ ♐ 3:21AM	**14** ♐ 3rd Quarter	**15** ♐ ♑ 8:06AM	**16** ♑	**17** ♑ ♒ 10:25AM	**18** ♒
19 ♒ ♓ 11:12AM	**20** ♓	**21** ♓ ♈ 12:01PM ♈ NM 1:23PM	**22** ♈	**23** ♈ ♉ 2:42PM	**24** ♉	**25** ♉ ♊ 8:42PM
26 ♊	**27** ♊	**28** ♊ ♋ 6:22AM 1st Quarter	**29** ♋	**30** ♋ ♌ 6:31PM	**31** ♌	

Times listed are Eastern US Time Zone

KEY: ♈ ARIES ♊ GEMINI ♌ LEO ♎ LIBRA ♐ SAGITTARIUS ♒ AQUARIUS
♉ TAURUS ♋ CANCER ♍ VIRGO ♏ SCORPIO ♑ CAPRICORN ♓ PISCES

FM FULL MOON **NM** NEW MOON **LE** LUNAR ECLIPSE **SE** SOLAR ECLIPSE

3

<table>
<tr><td>2
MAR</td></tr>
</table>

VENUS-JUPITER MEETUP

Nevermind the depth of your love—how big are those feelings? And what will it take to expand them even further? Venus and Jupiter are known as the "great benefics" for their positive and helpful influence. In the rare moments when they come together, that generosity multiplies. Today, as romantic Venus and limitless Jupiter connect in passionate fire-sign Aries, you've got permission to turn up the dial on your love and let people know how enchanted you really feel!

<table>
<tr><td>2
MAR</td></tr>
</table>

MERCURY-SATURN MEETUP

Today's cranky meetup of mental Mercury and curmudgeon Saturn could make Debbie Downers out of all of us. But don't quit right on the verge of a breakthrough! Apply patience instead of pessimism and you could stumble on an ingenious solution. Saturn rules experts, and if a problem is too big to tackle with your current team, call in the pros. The wisdom of their experience could provide you with a "teachable moment" and some important personal growth. Saturn is in its final days of a three-year tour through Aquarius, the sign of teamwork and technology. Look to those realms for long-term solutions. Casting the right collaborators—or harnessing a new app—could be the key to your ongoing success.

2 MAR - 19 MAR

MERCURY IN PISCES

Listen to your inner voice, not the self-appointed newscasters or handwringers in your group chat. As communicator Mercury charges into boundary-blurring Pisces, it will take extra effort to cut through mixed messages and discern what's really going on. Pay attention to non-verbal cues and body language. What people aren't saying could communicate more than their words! Mercury in this "right-brained" sign awakens your inner artist. Steep yourself in music, painting and dance. Pull out your journal. Your subconscious will be active, especially at night. If you can remember your dreams, write them down! They could contain important messages.

7 MAR

FULL MOON IN VIRGO 7:40AM EST

Spring is officially around the corner, and the annual full moon in Virgo calls in the cosmic cleaning crew. From your fitness to your diet to your space, you'll get a glimpse of where things have gotten messy or disorderly over the winter. Take a page from the zodiac's practical planner and write down absolutely everything on your to-do list. Then, sort through that brain dump and develop a plan of action. Note: That doesn't mean you have to face it alone. Before you get too focused on checking off boxes, think about how to optimize your time and work smarter instead of harder. If hiring a housecleaner twice a month will reduce your inner and outer chaos, add it to the budget. Look into project management or productivity apps to lighten the load. This applies to your health and wellness, too; consider changing up your treadmill workout for a swim session. With the moon forming a helpful trine to disruptor Uranus, a radical departure from business as usual could be in order. But don't rush: La luna is also embroiled in a tense square to hasty Mars and impatience could lead to a careless error.

SATURN ENTERS PISCES

7 MAR
2023
-
13 FEB
2026

3

Get ready to go (and grow) with a new kind of flow. Structured Saturn departs heady Aquarius, where it's been since March 21, 2020, and shifts uncomfortably into unstructured Pisces. For the next three years, Saturn will put clear boundaries around our compassionate hearts, reminding us to empower rather than enable. Both Saturn and Pisces are associated with karma in different ways. The world will have to reckon with some of its own messes and clean up any breaches of integrity. Pisces rules the oceans and it's no secret they need our help. Restrictive Saturn in this imaginative and spiritual sign could be challenging for artists, creatives and healers. On the plus side, it will separate the real-deal practitioners from the untrained charlatans, forcing everyone to step up their spiritual game. *Read our extended predictions for this transit in the Saturn section of this book.*

WANING QUARTER MOON IN SAGITTARIUS

14 MAR

Is it possible to be "too honest"? The waning quarter moon in candid Sagittarius sounds the call for authenticity with a heaping helping of tact. An issue you've been processing since last week's full moon may be weighing on your mind. But "workshopping" every thought out loud is not advised, especially when you're in the company of people who tend to be critical or rejecting of your ideas. That's not to say you should remain mum. Just choose your audience wisely. With the right "philosopher friends," you can put matters into perspective and maybe even glean a silver lining. Warning: This moon could find you talking in circles or embroiled in a never-ending debate. (Insert the GIF of Oprah saying, "So what is the truth?") Instead of getting stuck on who's right and who's wrong, open up the discussion to a variety of perspectives and try to see things from all angles.

MARS-NEPTUNE SQUARE

14 MAR

Passive, meet aggressive. Today marks the third and final dust-up between submissive Neptune in Pisces and combative Mars in Gemini. Their dizzying squares have been skewing perceptions since they clashed last October 12, then duked it out again on November 19. Since then, you may have jumped the gun in a conflict, taking sides before you had the whole story. Or perhaps you rushed into a situation that was too good to be true. While you're the wiser for it, stay on your toes today. This final grudge match between quickfire Mars and illusory Neptune could obscure facts so deeply that you get taken for that same damn ride. Someone could give you the old razzle-dazzle, talking a big game with no follow-through. If you're the song and dance person in question, don't make promises you can't keep. Save those jazz hands for when you're better equipped to get things done. And think twice before volunteering support! With sacrificial Neptune in Pisces, you could get pulled underwater trying to fix someone else's problems.

SUN-NEPTUNE MEETUP

15 MAR

Silence can be truly golden today as the Sun and Neptune unite in transcendent Pisces, inviting you to daydream along with them. Take a breather from constant chatter and declare this a day for introspection. You'll be amazed by what you notice when you aren't distracting yourself with small talk, social media or the 24-hour news cycle. Meditate, get out in nature or queue up some instrumental music. Don't feel guilty for keeping to yourself today. Reschedule any stressful appointments if possible. (Or stick to a tight agenda!) When it comes to supportive interactions, you can relax rigid rules in favor of a more "go with the flow" approach. This cosmic summit only happens once a year. It's a great time to take leadership on a spiritual or artistic project.

16 MAR

MERCURY-NEPTUNE MEETUP

Communication could get murky today as Neptune meets up with cerebral Mercury in Pisces, blurring the lines between fantasy and reality. Conversations could be clouded in confusion, and it will be hard to focus. Don't force a definitive outcome. Instead, let your imagination and intuition guide you. Have you been tough on people—or yourself? These empathic skies call for a heartfelt approach. Don't be surprised if you have a few teary-eyed moments today. If you've been struggling with a painful pattern, you could have a healing insight.

16 MAR

SUN-MARS SQUARE

As the passive Pisces Sun clashes with headstrong Mars in verbal Gemini, it won't take much to set off tempers or provoke someone to storm out of the room. A snarky retort could accidentally come across as a confrontation or insult. Big egos are at play, but beware the temptation to match someone's bloviating with your own simulated swagger. You might not be able to kill them with kindness today, but at least you can keep your dignity intact!

16 MAR

VENUS-PLUTO SQUARE

Watch out for emotional landmines and look before you leap! Control freak Pluto in Capricorn bumps up against vibrant Venus in Aries (right before it heads into Taurus), raising red flags all over town. If jealousy and anger well up, step back and sort out where they're coming from inside of yourself, rather than projecting them onto a love interest. Someone's secretiveness could be causing problems, but that doesn't mean your suspicions are confirmed. Deal in the realm of facts, not fears. Couples should avoid poking at sore spots today in order to keep the peace at home, as one false step could cause a blowout.

16 MAR - 11 APR

VENUS IN TAURUS

Sweet, sensual Venus glides into its home sign of Taurus today, bringing a stabilizing energy to the game of love. Would you rather be soul food than eye candy? That's a great place to start. But don't forget the basics, like sharing common values. Those are the glue for couples during this annual cycle. From money to spirituality to lifestyle, you'll be happiest in the presence of people who view things close to the same way. But try to leave room for open discourse instead of digging in your heels like that stubborn Bull at the first sign of disagreement. Venus in Taurus can make us all a touch old-fashioned, placing a high premium on comfortable, consistent companionship. Wherever you are on the romantic continuum, relationships grow ever-more serious under the traditional spell of Taurus. Pamper yourself liberally and spoil the ones you love. "Too much of a good thing" feels like the perfect dose of pleasure now.

17 MAR

MERCURY-MARS SQUARE

Stop! Don't send that inflammatory text! With mouthy Mercury in Pisces squaring confrontational Mars in Gemini, the slightest provocation can read as fighting words. Inner turmoil could be just as turbulent, especially if you're worrying about something that doesn't have an easy solution in sight. Avoid rushing into a quick fix. Nip paranoia in the bud as soon as you notice it's starting to spin up. Talk to people who calm you down and avoid fearmongers who agitate your anxiety.

3

17 MAR

SUN-MERCURY MEETUP

Dream a little dream—then make it a reality! With the forthright Sun and expressive Mercury aligning in imaginative Pisces, your creative ideas will meet a warm reception! But watch out for any deals that seem too good to be true. Under this rose-colored cosmic glow, it's too easy to get snowballed by a hustler's pitch. If you've hit a wall, go absorb some inspiration. Wander through a museum, listen to a newly released album maybe while waiting in the eternally long line to try that brick-oven pizza people can't stop talking about. In other words, take in the energy of people who love their craft, then watch as your own channels open right up!

19 MAR - 3 APR

MERCURY IN ARIES

Feeling the need for speed? The world has a collective case of the "zoomies" for the next three weeks, as communicator Mercury blazes into firecracker Aries. Losing focus for even a few minutes could cause you to miss out on important information or get swept away by a fast-talking flirt. For the next few weeks, stay alert and simplify, simplify, simplify! Instead of talking in circles, get to the (bullet) points and don't underestimate the power of a well-timed one-liner.

SUN IN ARIES
(SPRING EQUINOX)

20 MAR - 20 APR

Now entering the realm of the Ram! The spring equinox catapults us into Aries season and hits refresh on the astrological calendar. Hopefully your seatbelt is firmly fastened, because it could be a wild four-week ride that breaks the speed limit. This energetic, physical fire sign snaps us out of hibernation and prompts us to get moving. Head outside and get your hands dirty (spring bulb planting, anyone?) or throw on a scarf and sip your chai latte on a park bench. With the Sun in novelty-seeking Aries, you can turn up the volume on life and love. But easy on the dials: Aries season can bring out a competitive and even selfish side in all of us. Set your eyes firmly on the prize and share in the glory once you get there!

21 MAR

NEW MOON IN ARIES #1 1:23PM EDT

The new moon in trailblazing Aries delivers a burst of momentum to your personal projects and passions. Forget being wishy-washy; allow yourself to fire on all cylinders! A month from now (on April 20), a rare second Aries new moon (which will be a potent solar eclipse) promises high yields for ventures you start today. Make a vision board, set up a meeting with an expert in your field or take the leap into a new opportunity. Don't keep those plans to yourself either! Later today, the moon will meet up with communicator Mercury, urging you to share your big idea with someone who will champion it.

3

PLUTO IN AQUARIUS

23 MAR -
11 JUN

Get ready for a whole new era! A huge and historical day arrives as seismic Pluto enters Aquarius for the first time since the American Revolution was winding down from 1778-1798. The icy dwarf makes lengthy stays in each zodiac sign, and these periods indelibly shape history. Pluto does a brief initial lap through Aquarius until June 11, then returns to Capricorn until January 20, 2024. This sneak preview will give us a flash of what Pluto has in store for the rest of its 21-year visit, which will last until January 19, 2044. *See our chapter on Pluto for a deep dive on this historic transit!*

MARS IN CANCER

25 MAR -
20 MAY

Home is where the HEAT is for the next couple months, which could be equal parts sexy and stressful. After seven long months in Gemini, hot-blooded Mars blazes into domestic Cancer, energizing your abode and amplifying emotions. While the change of pace is welcome (farewell cacophony of Mars-in-Gemini opinionated insanity!), be extra patient with relatives and roommates. Mars in Cancer will increase the cosmic chaos under your roof. Dive into decluttering, decorating and deep cleaning for spring. When cabin fever spikes tension with your housemates, get out in the fresh air for regular walks or bike rides. Aspirational Mars could spark the idea for a cottage industry. Don't be surprised if your home becomes a hub for entrepreneurial inspiration! Considering a move or trying to get pregnant? Family matters accelerate under the red planet's influence, so make sure you're ready before you start trying. Results could come faster than expected.

28 MAR

MERCURY-JUPITER MEETUP

Grand visions and big ideas are awesome, but without a hype-person to spread the word, those dreams may never reach a critical mass. Today, mouthy Mercury and jubilant Jupiter get all fired up in passionate Aries. Shout your message from the rooftops—and enlist as many people as you can to join the effort! Under this bold and fearless conjunction, the world will respond to your confidence. Similarly, you could get inspired by a person who speaks with great conviction. Just make sure you're not getting caught in a slick sales pitch.

28 MAR

WAXING QUARTER MOON IN CANCER

Revive your hive! Today's waxing quarter moon in Cancer might not be the day for a total remodel, but that's more than okay. Sometimes a new living room layout or a colorful duvet set is all that you need to fall back in love with your place, not to mention the people who inhabit it. How about warming up the vibe with a home-cooked meal? If you have "recipe fatigue" from those same-old soups and roasted root vegetables, treat yourself to an inspiring cookbook. Looking for a new place to hang your hat this spring? This lunar lift inspires good real estate karma for any searches. Or maybe it's time to exchange keys with a special plus-one?

MARS-SATURN TRINE

30 MAR

Timing is everything—and if you slow down and observe people's subtle signals, you'll know just when to make your move. Hasty Mars in Cancer gets speed-checked by circumspect Saturn in Pisces, but since they're flowing together in a cooperative water trine, they help you discover the perfect pace for all your interactions. Under this tuned-in transit, you're able to ask for what you need directly without mincing words. If you've been hesitant to voice your needs and feelings, this graceful trine sets the stage for a constructive heart to heart.

VENUS-URANUS MEETUP

30 MAR

Love goddess Venus and provocateur Uranus shake things up when they get together, but that instability is actually their "gift." As the planets collide in sensual-yet-sensible Taurus, they could spark an unexpected love connection. Prepare for declarations of desire to catch you off guard (in a good way!) or for things to take a surprising left turn. This unstable union could push a rocky relationship to a breaking point. Avoid impulsive moves though, because you may feel differently tomorrow. But if you're sure it's time for a jailbreak, this could be your moment. Single? Start swiping to unlock a cosmic connection. Coupled? Get experimental. Try something new both in and out of the bedroom.

APRIL *Moon Phases*

SUN	MON	TUE	WED	THU	FRI	SAT
						1 ♌
2 ♌ ♍ 6:57AM	**3** ♍	**4** ♍ ♎ 5:51PM	**5** ♎	**6** ♎ Full Moon 12:34AM	**7** ♏ 2:29AM	**8** ♏
9 ♏ ♐ 8:57AM	**10** ♐	**11** ♐ ♑ 1:33PM	**12** ♑	**13** ♑ 3rd Quarter ♒ 4:42PM	**14** ♒	**15** ♒ ♓ 6:57PM
16 ♓	**17** ♓ ♈ 9:09PM	**18** ♈	**19** ♈	**20** ♈ Solar Eclipse NM 12:13AM ♉ 12:30AM	**21** ♉	**22** ♉ ♊ 6:11AM
23 ♊	**24** ♊ ♋ 2:58PM	**25** ♋	**26** ♋	**27** ♋ ♌ 2:30AM ♌ 3rd Quarter	**28** ♌	**29** ♌ ♍ 2:59PM
30 ♍						

Times listed are Eastern US Time Zone

KEY:

♈ ARIES	♊ GEMINI	♌ LEO	♎ LIBRA	♐ SAGITTARIUS	♒ AQUARIUS
♉ TAURUS	♋ CANCER	♍ VIRGO	♏ SCORPIO	♑ CAPRICORN	♓ PISCES

FM FULL MOON   **NM** NEW MOON   **LE** LUNAR ECLIPSE   **SE** SOLAR ECLIPSE

MERCURY IN TAURUS

Want to turn a wish into a reality? Cunning Mercury heads into workhorse Taurus for ten weeks, helping you map out—and begin—the necessary legwork. First step: Figure out what you need to support your mission, like a streamlined invoicing system or a special tool. Could your workstation use a makeover? Let tastemaker Taurus lead the way to a new standing desk, an air-cleansing plant or a colorful keyboard. If it makes productivity pleasurable, it's a worthy (and Taurus-approved!) splurge. Caveat! Mercury spins retrograde in Taurus from April 21 to May 14, which is why the bean-counting planet stays in the Bull's pen for so long. Try to get the "project management" piece in place before then and stick to your budget so you don't burn through cash faster than you earn it.

MERCURY-PLUTO SQUARE

Copycats and spotlight-stealers are everywhere today as Mercury in headstrong Taurus collides with secretive Pluto in Aquarius. If you've been cultivating a big idea, don't be too quick to share it with the world. Not only could you encounter what feels like a lukewarm reception for your hard work, but too-eager eyes could be peeping your project to steal those brilliant ideas for their own. There IS a bright side to these mixed messages, though. If you hear a resounding "no" from a key stakeholder, you'll be able to see exactly where you need to home in and tighten for a stronger deliverable. If you're on the receiving end of a promising offer, conduct your due diligence before signing on the dotted line.

FULL MOON IN LIBRA 12:34AM EDT

Peace, love and harmony! The year's only full moon in Libra unlocks happy, healthy and balanced relationships. Ready to leap into a larger commitment? This could be one of the most exhilarating days of 2023 for couples who want to talk commitment, cohabitation, or anything involving a ceremony. But heads up: Because this full moon opposes both healing Chiron and candid Jupiter, opening those floodgates could unleash more than planned. Be prepared for partnership pivots of all kinds as you navigate any "discoveries." If you feel like your plus-one isn't pulling their weight, call a summit. Maybe you need to divide up household duties differently or align around love languages. Have a few thoughtful questions in your back pocket to keep conversation flowing, like, "Can you tell me more?" or, "Am I hearing you right?" When your energies are balanced, there's more time for pleasure and less for picking fights over who last unloaded the dishwasher.

VENUS IN GEMINI

Friends become lovers, lovers become friends. As romantic Venus eases into variety-loving Gemini, you may need a new labeling system for the people in your life. Before you break any barriers, consider what's at stake. Blurry lines will inevitably complicate things, especially if one person is thinking "FWB" while the other is internally screaming, "At last!" But if you can get on the same page about status, welcome to your spring awakening. Longtime couples can spice things up by adding an element of surprise to your playtime. Scavenger hunt date nights and weekend getaways keep things fresh. Venus in Gemini makes people endlessly curious, eager to ask and answer questions. Another way to light the fire in this loquacious planetary pairing: A good old-fashioned game of Truth or Dare.

SUN-JUPITER MEETUP

11
APR

Fortune favors the bold! The magnanimous Sun teams up with boundless Jupiter for their once-per-year alignment, an annual event so brimming with optimism that astrologers have nicknamed it "The Day of Miracles." In 2023, they connect in trailblazing, novelty-loving Aries, supporting the boldest and most daring actions. Whatever is in your path, this dynamic duo tints with a rosy, can-do glow. But read the safety precautions and make sure you proceed with some sort of plan. It's easy to overshoot the mark when everything feels so... limitless.

VENUS-PLUTO TRINE

11
APR

Power is an intoxicating aphrodisiac today, as romantic Venus in Gemini pair bonds with impresario Pluto in Aquarius. Even if you're just watching out of the corner of your eye, seeing someone command social spaces will be a major turn-on. Do what you can to align with well-connected people during this potent air trine. Maybe you RSVP "Yes" to a private party or show up at a ticketed event where you can hobnob with the who's who. What begins as a casual conversation could evolve into a long-range (and highly profitable!) collaboration, for business, love or maybe both!

<table>
<tr><td>

13 APR

</td><td>

WANING QUARTER MOON IN CAPRICORN

Are you tracking towards your goals? Today's waning quarter moon in Capricorn is a great time to stop and check on progress. You may find a team member isn't pulling their weight or you're close to blowing a deadline. It's not too late to salvage this, but you may have to burn a little midnight oil to keep your mission afloat. This lunar checkpoint helps you realign with your project partners. Is everyone clear on deadlines and deliverables? Do you all feel supported? Address any potential molehills before they turn into mountains. What could you achieve together before the month is through? One small victory brings the confidence boost for the next one after that.

</td></tr>
</table>

4

<table>
<tr><td>

14 APR

</td><td>

VENUS-SATURN SQUARE

Speed check! Romantic Venus is in breezy Gemini, bringing a fun and chatty vibe to the dating scene. But if you've been cruising along on assumptions, Saturn pulls the emergency brake. Because the restraining ringed planet is bearing down in Pisces, it puts the kibosh on any unrealistic relationship plans. Pull yourself back to the present instead of fixating on those "someday" dreams. How doable are these...really? One (or both) people may be stewing in resentment or feeling frustrated that certain relationship milestones haven't come to fruition. Diplomatic Venus helps you deal with any unvoiced issues and come up with a more manageable timeline. But first, you'll need to forgive each other for not being mind readers.

</td></tr>
</table>

SUN IN TAURUS

| 20 APR - 21 MAY |

Welcome to Taurus season! After four weeks of Aries' feisty ambition and vigor, it's time to buckle down with the Bull. The Ram lit your creative fire and shot you out of its realm through a solar eclipse cannon. Now you can polish a few of your rough-cut visions into sparkling diamonds with the help of practical Taurus. Let the assembly lines and production roll! Just don't forget to incorporate the Bull's love of luxury into your plans. Beauty is an essential ingredient during Taurus time, not an optional one—and enjoying it doesn't have to cost a million bucks as far as this pragmatic sign is concerned. Since Taurus is both sensible AND sensual, the next four weeks are as much about ritualizing a process as they are about yielding results. Carefully consider every detail. The little things matter now!

NEW MOON IN ARIES #2 & SOLAR ECLIPSE 12:12AM EDT

20 APR

Bonus round! A rare second new moon in pioneering Aries arrives today, a month after the prior one on March 21. This, folks, is how Aries season goes out with a bang! There's even bigger news: This new moon is a changemaking solar eclipse, the first one to land in the Ram's realm since 2015! Think of it like a turbo-charged fresh start, one that might require you to leave a piece of your old life behind. And it kicks off a new eclipse series on the Aries-Libra axis that will power up some of our new and full moons between today and March 29, 2025.

4

SUN-PLUTO SQUARE

20 APR

Right as Taurus season begins, overbearing Pluto and the egomaniacal Sun lock into a tense tug of war—a "game" they play twice per year. A cool head and calm demeanor will build bridges, but good luck remembering that today. Steer clear of triggering situations that you know will provoke intense emotional reactions. (In you or the other person involved!) Because both planets are in stubborn fixed signs (the Sun in Taurus and Pluto in Aquarius), you'll want to push and shove to get your way. Take a breather and wait until you stop seeing red before attempting to reach a resolution.

4

<table>
<tr><td>

21 APR - 14 MAY

</td><td>

MERCURY RETROGRADE IN TAURUS

Mercury, the planet of communication, technology and travel, makes a retrograde U-turn in Taurus, plunging the world into a global state of stubbornness. Plans that were plodding along could sputter to a stop for the next three weeks as schedules clash and people dig in their heels. Don't go charging through barriers like a temperamental toro. Instead, use this slowdown to streamline your systems and catch up on "boring" busy work. You may not see the hidden blessing of this time-out just yet, but you will. Go easy on the spending, especially with luxury goods.

</td></tr>
</table>

<table>
<tr><td>

27 APR

</td><td>

WAXING QUARTER MOON IN LEO

Please take your seats—the show is about to begin! As the waxing quarter moon debuts its theatrical talents in Leo, don't go full Phantom of the Opera on your audience! The moderate quarter moon encourages, well, moderation. It's okay to tease them and save the best for later. Feeling romantic under the leonine skies? Instead of pouring out your heart in an epic soliloquy, do something that you know will delight your sweetie (not provoke a lover's quarrel).

</td></tr>
</table>

MAY *Moon Phases*

SUN	MON	TUE	WED	THU	FRI	SAT
	1 ♍︎	2 ♍︎ ♎︎2:09AM	3 ♎︎	4 ♎︎ ♏︎10:32AM	5 ♏︎ Lunar Eclipse FM 1:34PM	6 ♏︎ ♐︎4:04PM
7 ♐︎	8 ♐︎ ♑︎7:33PM	9 ♑︎	10 ♑︎ ♒︎10:05PM	11 ♒︎	12 ♒︎ 3rd Quarter	13 ♒︎ ♓︎12:39AM
14 ♓︎	15 ♓︎ ♈︎3:56AM	16 ♈︎	17 ♈︎ ♉︎8:28AM	18 ♉︎	19 ♉︎ NM11:53AM ♊︎2:48PM	20 ♊︎
21 ♊︎ ♋︎11:28PM	22 ♋︎	23 ♋︎	24 ♋︎ ♌︎10:35AM	25 ♌︎	26 ♌︎ ♍︎11:05PM	27 ♍︎ 1st Quarter
28 ♍︎	29 ♍︎ ♎︎10:51AM	30 ♎︎	31 ♎︎ ♏︎7:45PM			

Times listed are Eastern US Time Zone

KEY:

♈︎ ARIES	♊︎ GEMINI	♌︎ LEO	♎︎ LIBRA	♐︎ SAGITTARIUS	♒︎ AQUARIUS
♉︎ TAURUS	♋︎ CANCER	♍︎ VIRGO	♏︎ SCORPIO	♑︎ CAPRICORN	♓︎ PISCES

FM FULL MOON   **NM** NEW MOON   **LE** LUNAR ECLIPSE   **SE** SOLAR ECLIPSE

PLUTO RETROGRADE

1 MAY - OCT 10

Starting today, group dynamics could shift into covert power plays as Pluto slows its calculating roll and backs into its annual five-month retrograde, first through collaborative Aquarius (until June 11), then hierarchy-loving Capricorn. If you can't gain traction with your team or goals, take a break instead of trying to force a "all for one and one for all" sense of unity. Use this introspective phase for soul-searching but keep your wits about you. A person with a shady scheme or hidden agenda could slip past your radar if you relax your rules of engagement too much.

SUN-MERCURY MEETUP

1 MAY

No second-guessing yourself! As the bold Sun unites with articulate Mercury in straight-shooting Taurus, just call it like you see it. The best solution may be the simplest one, at least if you're doing "triage" today. Start there before you complexify a problem that may be an easier fix than anticipated. With both planets in the sign of ethics and values, conversations could veer into the ever-so-tricky terrain of politics, religion or general beliefs. If you're going to follow that thread, watch for a dogmatic or dictatorial cadence. Be confident in your message, but give others the freedom to disagree instead of insisting you're right.

VENUS-NEPTUNE SQUARE

4 MAY

Beware the misinformation maelstrom, as two-headed Venus in Gemini and disorienting Neptune in Pisces throw shade on your parade. That fog could make it hard to discern what's real and what's in your head, especially if others are too eager to tell you what they really think of your current romantic status. Here's an idea: Keep some details to yourself. There's no law that says you have to share your private life intel with anyone. If your emotions overwhelm you, which they could today, confide in a trusted source only, and do some self-soothing to get to a grounded place. Gentle reminder: Feelings aren't facts!

<table>
<tr><td>5
MAY</td></tr>
</table>

SCORPIO FULL MOON &
PENUMBRAL LUNAR ECLIPSE 1:34pm EDT

Control is an illusion, so allow yourself to be swept into the universe's greater plan. 2023's only full moon in mysterious, alchemical Scorpio is also a game-changing lunar eclipse. And because it's opposing shock-jock Uranus, this one could bring some bonus surprises that leave jaws on the ground. From power mergers to scandals to sudden transitions, all sorts of secrets will be exposed. For best results, be an open channel for creative and spiritual downloads. These could send you racing to your "studio" to make music, art or love! (Scorpio is the zodiac's sultriest sign, after all) Investment opportunities may appear unexpectedly, or someone may offer to fund your work.

Caveat: Since eclipses always bring an X factor, harness Scorpio's investigative powers and thoroughly research anyone you're getting into bed with, literally or figuratively. Existing partnerships might reach a pivotal, "make it or break it" point within a month of the eclipse. If you plan to proceed, a rock-solid commitment is advised. Over the coming weeks, leave no stone unturned when mapping out the "deal points" of your exclusive arrangement. Time to go your separate ways? This lunar leveler landmark could hasten your departure—and in furtive Scorpio, slipping off discreetly may be your best exit strategy.

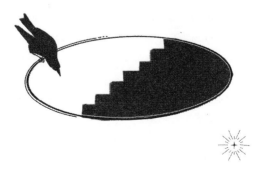

7 MAY
- JUN 5

VENUS IN CANCER

Unleash the emojis! Spring flings get a whole lot sweeter as Venus nestles into sentimental Cancer. Hold hands, write love notes (on actual paper), hug people for at least 20 oxytocin-releasing seconds. With Venus' copilot, lusty Mars, riding shotgun in Cancer until May 20, home is where the heart AND the heat can be found. If you needed incentive to serve breakfast in bed, here it is. (Whether you serve lemon ricotta pancakes or chocolate-dipped strawberries and champagne is your call.) Romantic gestures could lead to trading keys, apartment shopping or even adding a new member to the family. (Pets count!) Single? You might feel especially shy or sensitive when meeting new people. A workaround? Let your inner circle make introductions. This doesn't have to be obvious! Just start showing up at all the picnics and barbecues they invite you to. The intimate vibes could help you make a genuine, heartfelt connection.

9
MAY

SUN-URANUS MEETUP

Could a burst of change do you good? Don't wait for it to befall you, get proactive today as the can-do Sun and spontaneous Uranus team up for their annual conjunction. This year, they're linking arms in tactile, terrestrial Taurus, encouraging you to take charge of plans that have grown stale and predictable. You can still stay on top of the details AND be your most nimble, adaptable self for any quick-turn moments. But be warned that it will take some extra effort to stay grounded today. Channel your innovative powers into crafting a sustainable solution for a common problem. Who knows, you might even be able to monetize this.

5

<table>
<tr><td>12
MAY</td></tr>
</table>

WANING QUARTER MOON
IN AQUARIUS

Who's creeping on your data? Today's quarter moon in digitally native Aquarius wants you to download a password manager and check your sharing settings, stat! With every app you add or online purchase you make, your precious data is being used and, sometimes, abused. Check your tracking to make sure Instagram isn't following you around all day or call on a savvy friend to make sure you're protected from the dark web. It's also a good idea to verify that the "news" you saw on TikTok or Twitter is legit and not a bot blurring the lines between online and off-line.

5

<table>
<tr><td>13
MAY</td></tr>
</table>

VENUS-SATURN TRINE

Time to make things more official, or at least, establish that you're both feeling an emotional connection? As romantic Venus forms a lovely trine with solidifying Saturn in sensitive water signs, talking about your feelings is not only a good idea, it will help you decide on your next steps. Saturn loves a future-focused plan, so couples might discuss a next big step. If the other person's not feeling the love like you are, take it like a grownup: thank them for the experience and keep things moving. Be grateful that you didn't waste any more time with the wrong match! And if you're the one who doesn't see a long-term megahit here, do the mature thing and set 'em free instead of stringing them along.

14 MAY

MERCURY DIRECT IN TAURUS

Bye Mercury retrograde! (You won't be missed.) Technology, communication and day-to-day life resumes its normal flow as the messenger planet ends a signal-scrambling three-week backspin and powers forward in Taurus. If you held off on a commitment or put a project on hold, break out your calendar and start scheduling. It's officially "get back in the game" time. But proceed with caution when re-examining any pricey splurges and mile-high promises. It's all about integrity in Taurus-land, so read the fine print and do your homework before signing on the dotted line. The Bull is the most stubborn sign in the zodiac, so if a certain situation just won't resolve with the usual tactics, see how you can make things move in a positive and productive direction.

15 MAY

MARS-NEPTUNE TRINE

Sensitivity alert! This is not the time to play fast and loose with your opinions. Aggravating Mars in tender-hearted Cancer brings a tinderbox of fragile feelings to compassionate Neptune in Pisces, setting the scene for big emotions and even bigger reactions. This is a day to exercise restraint if you can; instead of blowing up, take a deep breath and dig deep to find your Zen. Take extra care to be respectful of people's triggers today—you never know when you might accidentally set one off. If you've been bottling things up, however, today's planetary connection could pop the cork and let it all spill out.

JUPITER IN TAURUS

16 MAY - 25 MAY '24

Starting today, advancing one step at a time will get you to your destination faster (and safer!) than attempting a giant leap. Supersizer Jupiter beams into sensual, stabilizing Taurus for twelve months, helping us all make practical magic. The red-spotted planet here could bring financial growth and can turn one of your ideas into an entrepreneurial success. No need to come up with any wild escapades under down-to-earth Taurus' reign. Your most brilliant concept could be hiding in plain sight. The simpler, the better! Jupiter's last visit here was from June 2011 to June 2012, so look back to that time for clues of what could resurface after May 16.

5

JUPITER-PLUTO SQUARE

17 MAY

Massive power struggle: incoming! As pioneering Jupiter in Taurus locks into a challenging square with powermonger Pluto in Aquarius, intense forces pull us in dueling directions. On the one hand, there's a current sweeping us toward major change, demanding that we try a radically new way of doing things. An equally strong force will resist these new attempts: If it ain't broke, why fix it? With traditional Taurus and progress-driven Aquarius in the mix, the schism only intensifies. With these two dominant planets at the negotiating table, compromise won't be comfortable—or easy to find. Do your part by at least hearing the other party's desires, even if they sound more like demands (and unreasonable ones at that).

**19
MAY**

NEW MOON IN TAURUS 11:53AM EDT

Come back to your senses—all five of them—as the year's only new moon in Taurus focuses our attention on the physical and material world. Here's an invitation to get back into your body. Slow down and savor the pleasures that you might normally rush right through: the first sip of morning coffee, the feel of your softest sweater against your skin, a tree-lined view on your commute to work. This megadose of Taurean stability couldn't come at a better time, since the first half of May has been filled with so much radical change. Take a clear-eyed look at the practical pieces of your life, such as budget and schedule. Could you cut back on expenses or contribute more to your retirement fund? Arrange your appointments so they don't disrupt your most productive work hours? Since new habits are supported by this lunar liftoff, try adding a practice like morning meditations or cardio workouts that you do the same four days every week. In the coming six months you'll see real-life results if you create a simple, sustainable plan. Less is more!

MARS IN LEO

20 MAY
- 10 JUL

Let your inner big cat roar as fierce Mars charges into Leo for the first time in two years. And throw in a little performance art if you must! With everyone vying for the spotlight, standing out will require a little extra effort. Good thing there's no such thing as "too much" during this two-and-a-half-month transit! Wardrobe, hair and makeup: Why not? As long as you remember that a warm personality and contagious enthusiasm will outshine any OOTD. Leo's rule: Lead with your heart and accessorize from there. For lovers, this fierce connection can cause friction, but instead of fighting it out via text or over dinner, take that feisty energy to the bedroom. Mars in Leo can awaken lust-out-loud, sheet-tangling passion. (Did someone say make-up sex?) Just beware: This cycle begins with a Mars-Pluto opposition on May 20, which could drive up dormant desires but also a boatload of suppressed resentment that may need to be cleared first. To the most courageous will go the spoils!

5

MARS-PLUTO OPPOSITION

20 MAY

Tempers, egos and mind games, oh my! As hotheaded Mars in proud Leo opposes power-tripping Pluto in Aquarius, the tension could reach a breaking point. Without knowing it, you may step into a minefield of psychological warfare, easily taking the bait and losing your cool. Composure will be your greatest asset—and biggest challenge—today. Be mindful of what you post on social or download on your devices. If there were ever a day to protect your tech and everything stored on it, this potentially data-breaching transit is it. Update your passwords and move private files to a more secure place.

SUN IN GEMINI

21 MAY - 21 JUN

Whether you're hanging poolside or hopping from picnic to barbecue, it's officially social season as the Sun beams into Gemini until June 21. Mingling isn't just an art form now, it could be your new cardio for the coming four weeks as this mobile sign keeps you on the move. Invest in comfy-chic sneakers (or maybe an e-bike) and take the scenic route whenever you can. Not only does Gemini season ignite the spirit of discovery but this locally zoned zodiac sign rules hometown happenings. Wandering between appointments could bring the added benefit of "discovering" indie hotspots that were hiding in plain sight, from food trucks to music venues to community gardens that become your favorite reading spot.

Gemini season is prime time for communicating and connecting, so look for ways to amplify your message. Time to start that podcast or put together a TedX talk? Whatever sparks dialogue is worth exploring. Writers, educators and broadcasters could produce some epic work during these four weeks!

<table>
<tr><td>

**21
MAY**

</td><td>

SUN-PLUTO TRINE

Don't hide your light—but don't blast it directly into anyone's eyes, either! As the attention-seeking Sun and secretive Pluto merge their superpowers, a microdose of captivating charisma will be just enough. Work the art of the tease to leave people curious and wanting more. Play up your mystique by moving through every room with quiet confidence. And if you dress the part in something sleek and stylish all the better. On social media, play with posting a BTS selfie with a message like, "I can't wait to tell you all about this in a few weeks." Stop short of being manipulative, however. With the Sun in Gemini and Pluto (retrograde) in Aquarius, you'll need to answer a few questions directly.

</td></tr>
</table>

5

<table>
<tr><td>

**22
MAY**

</td><td>

MARS-JUPITER SQUARE

Is it really that big of a deal? Hard to tell today, as feelings and egos can be inflated under a tense standoff between fierce Mars in egocentric Leo and supersizer Jupiter in stubborn Taurus. Everything will seem disproportionately urgent, and it will be hard to temper reactions or find a moderate stance. Narcissistic behavior could be on full display, and in general people are acting obnoxious and extra. Do your best not to add to the cacophony. Summon your patience, don't interrupt and slow down before bulldozing down every barrier. Feeling restless? This square could shake up a stagnant part of your life and embolden you to take a much-needed risk. Under this disruptive aspect, you may not have any other choice but to adapt to sudden momentum.

</td></tr>
</table>

<table>
<tr><td>

**27
MAY**

</td></tr>
</table>

WAXING QUARTER MOON IN VIRGO

If there were ever a day to sweat the small stuff, here it is. The waning quarter moon in flaw-finding Virgo raises a magnifying glass to expose the tiniest mistakes. Though you may feel pressured to hand off a project, don't rush through! You could overlook an important detail that winds up costing you time and money. Ask for help or clarification when you need it instead of trying to patch the dam. Give your work a healthy once-over before sending it off. (You may win points for its perfection!) While you're at it, assess your wellness with an equally keen eye. Summer's right around the corner and the clean, green influence of Virgo is here to help energize you for it!

<table>
<tr><td>

**28
MAY**

</td></tr>
</table>

SUN-SATURN SQUARE

Were your plans too ambitious? Recalibrate today. A cosmic standoff between inspector Saturn and the overconfident Sun serves up a semiannual reality check. Don't stop dreaming up new ideas. But before you tip too far into any "imagineering," measure this against some of your material-world needs: time, money and resources. Doing so might actually be heartening! With a tangible plan in place, something you thought was just a pipe dream could turn out to be far more doable than you realized. Take time to crunch the numbers and research the facts.

JUNE *Moon Phases*

SUN	MON	TUE	WED	THU	FRI	SAT
				1 ♏	**2** ♏ ♐ 10:03PM	**3** ♏ ♐ 1:03AM FM ♐ 11:42PM
4 ♐	**5** ♐ ♑ 3:31AM	**6** ♑	**7** ♑ ♒ 4:42AM	**8** ♒	**9** ♒ ♓ 6:14AM	**10** ♓ 3rd Quarter
11 ♓ ♈ 9:20AM	**12** ♈	**13** ♈ ♉ 2:31PM	**14** ♉	**15** ♉ ♊ 9:46PM	**16** ♊	**17** ♊
18 ♊ NM 12:37AM ♋ 6:58AM	**19** ♋	**20** ♋ ♌ 6:04PM	**21** ♌	**22** ♌	**23** ♌ ♍ 6:35AM	**24** ♍
25 ♍ ♎ 6:57PM	**26** ♎ 1st Quarter	**27** ♎	**28** ♎ ♏ 4:55AM	**29** ♏	**30** ♏ ♐ 10:59AM	

Times listed are Eastern US Time Zone

KEY: ♈ ARIES ♊ GEMINI ♌ LEO ♎ LIBRA ♐ SAGITTARIUS ♒ AQUARIUS
♉ TAURUS ♋ CANCER ♍ VIRGO ♏ SCORPIO ♑ CAPRICORN ♓ PISCES

FM FULL MOON **NM** NEW MOON **LE** LUNAR ECLIPSE **SE** SOLAR ECLIPSE

VENUS-NEPTUNE TRINE

2 JUN

It's almost too easy to get swept away by romance as touchy-feely Venus in Cancer and impressionable Neptune in Pisces link up in emotive water signs. If your heart is a wide-open space, you might want to install a security device at its entrance. At least for today, your desire for compassion and comfort could weaken your screening process, leaving you susceptible to someone who tugs your heartstrings, or worse, takes advantage of your kindness. If you've been overly guarded, however, the Venus-Neptune alliance helps lower your defenses and give the hopeful contenders a fighting chance.

6

FULL MOON IN SAGITTARIUS 11:41PM EDT

3 JUN

Adventure calls! And with the Sagittarius full moon illuminating your path, it's anyone's guess what corner of the globe will lure you over the coming two weeks. Keep your suitcase at the ready for work travel and weekend jaunts alike. With this full moon forming a fast-moving trine to passionate Mars, there could be romance or a daring activity wrapped up in those getaway plans! The Archer loves learning and personal growth. Sign up for a weekend workshop or pick up some metaphysical reading material. If you'd rather teach, perhaps you can create a course of your own and earn some cash in the meantime. The next two weeks are the ideal window to kickstart any big projects you've been dreaming about. But curb the gambling tendencies of Sagittarius, as this full moon will form a limiting square to cautious Saturn in Pisces.

MERCURY-URANUS MEETUP

4 JUN

Lively Mercury and lawless Uranus throw a wrench in the works of any play-it-safe plans as they unite for one day in material-minded Taurus. You'll have the urge to disrupt anything too steady and to rebel against anyone who tries to fence you in. Do you keep returning to the "same old, same old" instead of trying something new? Take on a "growth mindset" instead of a fixed one and make it your mission to learn about cutting edge technology and innovative ways to make your day-to-day duties more efficient—and interesting!

VENUS IN LEO

5 JUN - 8 OCT

Take your love life from mild to wild! Venus struts into glamorous Leo, draping summer's cosmic catwalk in eye-popping colors and sexy, sequined sizzle. Colossal courtships are on Cupid's menu—and not just for a night or two. The love planet lounges in Leo for an extra-long, four month showcase instead of the usual four weeks. The reason for this extended visit, however, might not be your favorite announcement. But here goes: From July 22 to September 3, Venus will be retrograde, a disruptive cycle that comes around every 18 months. Brace yourself: During the backspin, Leo's "lights, camera, action" energy could spin your personal fairy tale into a straight-up soap opera. Get ahead of the curve by working through any brewing lovers quarrels now. Does your branding need a refresh? Competition could get fierce during the retrograde, so make sure your visuals are on-point and sending out the right message to the world. Summon design star Venus and pick your fonts, themes, palettes and overall "lewk."

6

5 JUN

VENUS-PLUTO OPPOSITION

Trust issues flare as hotheaded Venus in Leo locks horns with furtive Pluto in Aquarius. It's wise to be self-protective today, but stop short of secrecy. Share any helpful data that others need for their own productivity or decision-making. And don't air personal information that could circle back in a damaging way (to you or others). If people's motives are not transparent, you may be tempted to fire off an interrogation. Trouble is, this could set off their defense mechanisms. It may be wiser to "innocently" observe anyone who trips your emotional alarm system. Surface activity won't tell the whole story, however, so dig deeper with your investigations. Do you feel like someone's gaslighting you? Don't take the bait!

6

10 JUN

WANING QUARTER MOON IN PISCES

Desperately seeking stimulation! As the waning quarter moon lands in imaginative Pisces, you can break out of a rut by feasting your eyes on other people's creativity. Street style fashion and murals can be just as inspirational as a meander through a highbrow shopping and arts district. Is a situation you once lived for now failing to excite? You may not see much hope for moving forward...but under the forgiving light of this quarter moon, it may be worth it to explore what can be salvaged. (At least if there's still SOME sort of "there" there.) If there were no barriers here (time, money, annoying people), how would you want things to develop? Allow the waning quarter moon in Pisces to help you weave that dream. Then tap into the Law of Attraction, focusing on your idealized picture—and maybe turning it into a vision board for further psychic stimulation. Ask your angels, guides and earthly mentors for an assist with making this so. Today, support could show up in "hidden" places.

VENUS-JUPITER SQUARE

11 JUN

Does the grass look greener everywhere but under your feet? The two "benefic" planets (named that for their positive, helpful influence) are at odds today, making people selfish and impossible to satisfy. With Venus in demanding Leo and Jupiter in particular Taurus, it may feel like nothing you do is good enough for other people—and vice-versa. Hold off on making any major decisions, whether that's on the status of your relationship or whether to book that summer vacation Airbnb that has a couple of questionable reviews.

6

PLUTO RETROGRADE RE-ENTERS CAPRICORN

11 JUN - 10 OCT

Power monger Pluto slips out of Aquarius and takes one of its two final laps through Capricorn before leaving the Sea Goat's sanctum for good on November 19, 2024. While this retrograde wages on until October 10, it demands a deep inspection of our finances, structures and relationship to power. Pluto only comes to each sign every 248 years, leaving an indelible imprint when it does. Since 2008, Pluto's been rocking government, business and the economy, leaving them all forever changed. In the United States, the tiny avenger entered and exited Capricorn in pivotal election and economic years. Instead of throwing your hands up, heed the call to step into your own leadership and "be the change."

MERCURY IN GEMINI

11-26 JUN

Conversations are the ultimate catnip starting today, as chatterbox Mercury hosts a three-week kiki in loquacious Gemini, one of its two home depots. No subject is off-limits! A single conversation could swerve from dissecting swimsuit trends to an intellectual discourse on trans kids' rights in the educational system. Got a message to broadcast? Grab the mic during this media-savvy transit. You never know... guesting on a podcast or livestreaming on social could make you Internet famous! In "twinning" Gemini, you could meet someone with BFF credentials. But watch for fickleness. Mobile Mercury could send you across the fence to see if the grass is really greener on the other side. Don't ditch your loyal crew because you've met some shiny, new people.

MERCURY-PLUTO TRINE

11 JUN

As clever Mercury in Gemini fistbumps charismatic Pluto in Aquarius, you'll get lots of mileage out of a well-timed quip or thoughtful opinion. But use your powers of persuasion strategically. Be concise about your request (people are busy) while also creating a sense of urgency with your "limited time offer." You don't have to go overboard with a hard sell; in fact, be clear about how your plan benefits others before you pitch it. If you're not sure yet, use today for research and development. Do a competitive analysis to see what others in the "space" are doing. In all conversations, read people's body language and non-verbal cues. With subterranean Pluto in the mix, what they're NOT expressing is every bit as crucial to the communication!

MERCURY-SATURN SQUARE

15 JUN

Practice the power of the pause as repressive Saturn in Pisces issues a gag order to motormouth Mercury in Gemini. It's too easy to flood people with TMI, so take a breath between statements and give people a chance to answer any questions that you're firing off. Mercury in Gemini makes people prone to gossip, but playing fast and loose with the tea could find YOU steeped in hot water. Err heavily on the side of being polite and "appropriate," even if it feels awkward or formal. Not sure what someone meant? Request further explanation before you jump to conclusions.

6

SATURN RETROGRADE IN PISCES

17 JUN - 4 NOV

Inspect to protect! Cosmic auditor Saturn begins its annual four-and-a-half month retrograde today, and for the first time since the mid-90s, it's backing up through Pisces, the sign of soulful and subconscious healing. If you've gotten a little too swept away in your fantasies, this retrograde could put the kibosh on your escapism and force you to deal with reality. (Annoying, but it's for your own good.) This entire, three-year Saturn cycle is optimal for cultivating your spiritual or artistic talents. During the retrograde, take time to master the basics or polish your core skills before hanging your shingle.

18 JUN

NEW MOON IN GEMINI 12:37AM EDT

Planetary PSA from today's collaborative new moon in Gemini: Twinning is winning! Whether you're looking for a workout buddy or a writing partner (or whatevs!), set yourself to "discovery mode." Your ideal other half could be hiding in plain sight (oh, hello!) or hanging in the outskirts of your social group. That's more incentive to get out and mingle. Since Gemini rules local activities, RSVP yes to your neighbor's solstice BBQ or rally friends for al fresco drinks on that hotel roof deck. The point is to get out and circulate because this lunar lift is sure to connect you to kindred spirits. Footnote: With boundary-blurring Neptune squaring this new moon, reserve judgment before declaring a new acquaintance your insta-BFF. You could be easily distracted today, too—all the more reason to team up with a clever colleague or have a wingperson to go out with in case you need someone to call you an Uber.

6

19 JUN

JUPITER-SATURN SEXTILE

It's always a good day when the planet of expansion (Jupiter) and the planet of structure (Saturn) play nicely with each other. Their last sync up was nearly six years ago, so we're overdue for this medley! Jupiter in Taurus brings the excitement and sensuality while Saturn in Pisces brings a dose of sobering sensibility. We won't just figure out what needs to be done, but we'll also see how to do it. Discuss your dream scenario, then put a solid plan in place for achieving the next steps.

21 JUN - 22 JUL

SUN IN CANCER

Step into summer! Cancer season begins today, announced (as it is every year) by the solstice. The longest day of light in the northern hemisphere illuminates our most treasured bonds, from beloved relatives to friends who have earned "chosen family" status. Set up the backyard loungers, prep the grill and sangria pitcher. Homey and heartfelt Cancer season is ideal for nesting and guesting. But don't fill up every inch of whitespace on your calendar with visits. Tender emotions could surface, which you might prefer to process in solitude—then, turn into cathartic works of art. Creativity reaches peak levels during Cancer season and this deep-feeling water sign helps you pull inspiration from intimate experiences.

25 JUN

MERCURY-NEPTUNE SQUARE

You know what they say about assumptions, right? Take nothing at face value during today's muddling Mercury-Neptune square. (Unless you want to "make an ass out of u and me," that is.) As foggy Neptune in Pisces obscures any data that intellectual Mercury in Gemini brings to the surface, no one's speaking clearly. If you're bogged down by details or confused about what someone is actually saying, be forthright and ask for clarification. And don't be afraid to repeat yourself if you're the one confusing things. Avoid taking sides, unless you're certain about where you stand on a matter.

WAXING QUARTER MOON IN LIBRA

26 JUN

Where do you draw the line between "good judgment" and simply being judgmental? That question hangs in the balance of today's waxing quarter moon in Libra. Bring awareness to your decision-making process: Do you write people off after seeing one photo or reading a few sentences of their bio? While your instincts may be spot-on in many cases, it's equally possible that your selection criteria has become a wee bit TOO discerning. Do an experiment and allow yourself to be pleasantly surprised by people's hidden talents. On the other hand, if you keep getting burned by people who take advantage of your kindness, put a stricter screening process in place. Those loyalty points should be earned, not handed out freely!

6

MARS-URANUS SQUARE

26 JUN

Avoid making impulsive relationship moves today as hotheaded Mars in Leo spins into a combative square with volatile Uranus in Taurus. An irresistible attraction might feel too strong to ignore, but that doesn't mean you should leap into bed and minimize the consequences. (Even if you're fired up for a round of revenge dating!) The line between love and hate is so thin today that you really could be attracted to an "enemy" in the heat of the moment. Since you probably don't want to deal with the fallout from that choice, steer clear of that hot-but-triggering person in the office. Even if you're ready to sit down for peacemaking talks, stall for a few days. This is a climate given to stubborn standoffs and explosive emotions, not diplomatically hearing each other out.

MERCURY IN CANCER

26 JUN - 11 JUL

Update your privacy policy and your confidentiality clause, too. Chatty Mercury flies under the radar in Cancer for the next few weeks, encouraging heart-to-heart connections with your innermost circle. Since all sorts of emotions are bound to well up, these aren't the kinds of discussions you'd want recorded for public consumption. Make sure the people you're opening up to have genuinely earned your trust. Socially, this is a perfect time for small, intimate gatherings. Arrange your space to maximize conversation and bonding. Make sure you've got provisions to throw on the barbecue or a charcuterie board. You could find yourself hosting an impromptu game night or heading to a potluck picnic with little notice!

6

SUN-SATURN TRINE

28 JUN

Take command of a stressful situation today as the courageous Cancer Sun trines authoritative Saturn in Pisces. But use a gentle touch while getting your hands back on the wheel. Emotional and social intelligence will get you farther with the "troops" today than barking out orders like a military general. Read between the lines. People may be gripping tightly to the past because they can't see a promising outcome. Try asking open-ended questions (and validating people's answers!) to get to the bottom of their concerns. Or guide the discussion by offering a couple of creative solutions that shift people from a fear mindset to a growth mindset.

NEPTUNE RETROGRADE IN PISCES

**30 JUN -
6 DEC**

Cue your Calm app and blow the dust off your dream journal. Prophetic Neptune begins its annual retrograde today, pushing you deeper into the waters of your subconscious. The oceanic planet, which is sailing through its home sign of Pisces until 2026, will demand extra contemplation and reflection until it corrects course in early December. But this backspin can actually roll back the fog of denial, distraction and delusion and help you process a stuck situation for once and for all. With the muse hovering in the background, use this time to revisit unfinished creative projects or heal another layer of emotional trauma. While your open mind and receptive energy are great for self-discovery, they can also make you more susceptible to picking up toxic energy or attracting untrustworthy people. Be sure to shield your field from energy vampires with an extra layer of protection like healthy boundaries, crystals, salt baths and therapy.

MERCURY-SATURN TRINE

**30
JUN**

Accountability is the cornerstone of trust, so make sure you're backing up your words with actions. As communicative Mercury in Cancer teams up with responsible Saturn in Pisces, feelings could be damaged if you carelessly ignore a promise or backpedal on a commitment. Even simple assurances like, "I'll call you tonight" or "I'll have that on your desk by 3" need to be respected. If you can't uphold your end of an agreement, send a text and let people know what you are able to do. And if you *do* come through with the full package, you could win yourself a coveted gig—or at the very least, the respect of an important person.

JULY *Moon Phases*

SUN	MON	TUE	WED	THU	FRI	SAT
						1 ♐
2 ♐ 1:20PM	**3** ♑ Full Moon 7:39AM	**4** ♑ ♒ 1:30PM	**5** ♒	**6** ♒ ♓ 1:33PM	**7** ♓	**8** ♓ ♈ 3:19PM
9 ♈ 3rd Quarter	**10** ♈ ♉ 7:55PM	**11** ♉	**12** ♉	**13** ♉ ♊ 3:26AM	**14** ♊	**15** ♊ ♋ 1:13PM
16 ♋	**17** ♋ New Moon 2:32PM	**18** ♋ ♌ 12:39AM	**19** ♌	**20** ♌ ♍ 1:13PM	**21** ♍	**22** ♍
23 ♍ ♎ 1:54AM	**24** ♎	**25** ♎ First Quarter ♏ 12:55PM	**26** ♏	**27** ♏ ♐ 8:24PM	**28** ♐	**29** ♐ ♑ 11:44PM
30 ♑	**31** ♑ ♒ 11:58PM					

Times listed are Eastern US Time Zone

KEY: ♈ ARIES ♊ GEMINI ♌ LEO ♎ LIBRA ♐ SAGITTARIUS ♒ AQUARIUS ♉ TAURUS ♋ CANCER ♍ VIRGO ♏ SCORPIO ♑ CAPRICORN ♓ PISCES

FM FULL MOON **NM** NEW MOON **LE** LUNAR ECLIPSE **SE** SOLAR ECLIPSE

SUN-MERCURY MEETUP

1 JUL

Inspire the troops! As the confident Sun and clever Mercury embrace in emphatic Cancer, today is the ultimate merger of head and heart. Presenting an idea? Tell a moving or funny story to illustrate your point or share a testimonial from someone who's benefitted from whatever you're pitching. The more you can make people feel something, the better! In personal interactions, try to read the room before you unleash. The extra minute you take to tune in to people's emotional cues could mean the difference between a heartwarming connection and a triggering clash.

VENUS-URANUS SQUARE

2 JUL

Suddenly single? You might feel like making a break for freedom today, as liberated Uranus T-bones romantic Venus. Your autonomy should not be the price of entry for partnership, so talk through a solution. If someone's smothering you, just take a day or two for yourself, rather than doing anything extreme. Radical moves are likely to be regrettable ones. If you've been biting your tongue a bit too much, vow to speak and act more authentically, starting...now!

<table>
<tr><td>

**3
JUL**

</td><td>

FULL MOON IN CAPRICORN 7:38AM EDT

</td></tr>
</table>

Check in on those New Year's resolutions! (Remember those?) The full moon in goal-getter Capricorn sets the stage for a "midterm" review. What's the 2023 progress report? Pinpoint what's working well and X off anything that's proving to be an impossible task. This midyear review is the perfect time to revamp your strategy and set different milestones if you need to pivot. Industrious Capricorn is an ambitious high-achiever, but don't forget to celebrate any and all accomplishments you've made thus far in 2023. No one gets a shiny gold star for being a martyr. Acknowledge your progress and thank people who've been part of your growth. Are you ready to go bigger? Maximalist Jupiter is fistbumping the full moon, which can help you expand your vision. But capture any big ideas in writing! With the moon opposite mental Mercury, relying on your memory won't cut it.

7

<table>
<tr><td>

**9
JUL**

</td><td>

MERCURY-NEPTUNE TRINE

</td></tr>
</table>

Under a creative and compassionate mashup of communicator Mercury and psychic sponge Neptune, your empathy is so strong you're practically psychic. While it won't be easy to set firm boundaries today, you CAN finally listen to someone or feel fully heard. This could be the path to resolving an issue that's dogged your relationship for far too long. Creative and spiritual pursuits are especially favored today. Open your channels to the divine by free-writing, meditating or asking your guides to send a signal pointing you in the right direction.

<table>
<tr><td>

9 JUL

</td><td>

WANING QUARTER MOON IN ARIES

</td></tr>
</table>

The squeaking wheel gets the oil, but the proactive wheel gets the premium-grade, solar-powered fuel. Under today's waning quarter moon in Aries, just speaking up won't cut it. (And neither will playing the dude or damsel in distress.) If you want support, spark interest without tipping people into aggravation and stress. Even if there's a problem brewing, modulate your pitch and speak with a compelling and confident tone. Most of all, come to the conversation with a can-do attitude. People want to be part of the winning team, especially when competitive, assertive Aries is on the court!

7

10 JUL

MERCURY-PLUTO OPPOSITION

Scandal, intrigue, hidden agendas? As cunning Pluto and expressive Mercury draw their swords, it's best to keep your opinions to yourself. While your powers of observation are strong, there may be more to the story than initially meets the eye. Ask clarifying questions and do more research. Conversations can feel laced with subtext and innuendoes. If you sense a power struggle brewing, gracefully bow out before you get triggered.

<table>
<tr><td>10 JUL -
27 AUG</td></tr>
</table>

MARS IN VIRGO

Class is in session! Action planet Mars blazes into diligent Virgo, pumping you up to put plans, budgets and schedules behind your lofty ideas. This fix-it-fast, health-conscious transit encourages you to improve every part of your life, from cleaning out cupboards and closets to finally hopping on the spin bike. You'll have a lot of productive energy during this period, but you may come across more aggressively than you intend, especially if you're dishing out advice. When wordsmith Virgo collides with warrior Mars, people can get judgmental or critical. Simple conversations can combust into heated debates that get nasty. Remember this: You'll catch more flies with honey than you will with your "helpful hints."

7

MERCURY IN LEO

11-28 JUL

Crank up the creativity! As idea-machine Mercury prowls through playful, passionate Leo, grandiose visions are ready to be "imagineered" into something that you can touch, taste or feel. If you're making a pitch or presentation, use storytelling techniques and bold visuals to underscore your message. With heartfelt Leo on the mic, express yourself with warmth, excitement and even a little gushing. Laying it on thick might actually work, as long as you're genuine in your sentiment.

NEW MOON IN CANCER 2:31PM EDT

17 JUL

7

Serve it up family style! Warm-fuzzy vibing is on the menu as the new moon in Cancer beams its nurturing energy into the ether. Who are the stars of your innermost circle? It's easy to take those unwavering supporters for granted, but today, treat them like VIPs. Feeling drained from too much giving? Maybe you've forgotten where other people's "shells" end and yours begins. Turn up the volume on self-care and begin a practice of saying "no" to requests that are certain to exhaust you. Besides, there are pool parties and beach weekends to enjoy, as this watery lunation reminds. This domestic new moon could reveal a dream listing or inspire a remodel or decorating spree. Time to clear some negativity from your space? La luna's opposition to shadowy Pluto and a harmonious trine to spiritual Neptune sets the stage for Feng Shui, a deep decluttering or a house-blessing ritual.

17 JUL - 11 JAN, 2025

NORTH NODE IN ARIES & SOUTH NODE IN LIBRA

Do your relationships support your personal growth or are other people's dreams crowding out your goals? The balance between "mine" and "ours" hits a critical tipping point today as the lunar nodes shift into Aries (North Node) and Libra (South Node) until January 2025. Take inventory of your inner circle and cut ties with the energy vampires. But note that the real evolution comes from owning the role you've been playing in any lopsided dynamics. The Aries North Node inspires new levels of confidence and leadership. Simultaneously, the Libra South Node delivers a scathing review of any unproductive relationship habits, such as people-pleasing, stonewalling or trauma bonding. As you stretch into Aries' self-authorized terrain, how can you assert yourself with Libra's love, grace and dignity? Get ready to learn! This important cycle hasn't come around for nearly two decades, helping us all unlock the fine art of diplomatic negotiation.

7

20 JUL

SUN-NEPTUNE TRINE

The universe has its eyes and ears open, so get in front of it and speak your desires into existence. The Sun and spiritual Neptune connect today, opening a window to manifest your "impossible" dreams and innermost wishes. And stay open to miracles! Someone close to you, whether it's a friend or a collaborative coworker, could have the perfect serendipitous solution. Pro tip: Be as detailed as you can about what you're looking for and request that these blessings arrive with grace and ease.

MARS-SATURN OPPOSITION

We'd never suggest you give up a dream, even when obstacles are showing up left, right and center. But when vigilant Mars in Virgo faces off with censuring Saturn in Pisces, you may be forced to pull the emergency brake to avoid veering off course. Plant your feet as you hatch your lofty plans. Use the slower pace to ground your vision with market tests, solid research or a rebalanced budget. Call up a trusted mentor and seek advice from seasoned pros. Once you circle back on the details, success will be yours for the launching!

7

SUN-PLUTO OPPOSITION

Pluto's signature power grabs and veiled intimidation tactics are in high gear today, stirring up power struggles with the ego-driven Sun. You may feel extra defensive and apt to take things as a personal affront. Check in with yourself before reacting aggressively when you think you've been slighted or overlooked. Chances are, you're projecting your own insecurities onto the situation. That said, if you sense any brewing tension or feel unsafe, trust your gut and exit the scene swiftly. Better to be safe than sorry.

SUN IN LEO

22 JUL - 23 AUG

All the world's a catwalk as the Sun struts into glamorous Leo for its yearly four-week show. This annual solar cycle is high season for all things glamorous, romantic and creative. Like Leo Madonna (who sang the anthem!), it's time to express yourself. It doesn't matter if you're wearing a cone bra or a Victorian corset dress...or leggings and a T-shirt. The point of Leo season is to let your mane down, no matter what the neighbors think. Does your name belong in lights? Or maybe a history book or the hall of fame? Visualize it, then start positioning your personal "brand" for that ascent. Need some inspiration? Do some competitive research analysis. What are the ballers in your industry doing? How would YOU put your own unique spin on this? If you have a finished product to promote, put a final coat of high-gloss polish on it, then, schedule your big reveal!

VENUS RETROGRADE IN LEO

**22 JUL -
3 SEP**

Cupid hits a six-week speedbump as Venus turns retrograde in Leo until September 3. During this cycle, the planet of love, beauty and romance shifts from being an "evening star" (appearing at dusk) to a "morning star" (glimmering in the sky just before dawn). Metaphorically, this is a key time to assess your love life and think about what issues you'd like to put to bed. Maybe it's time to say "ni-night" to a habit of dating financially-draining users or coddling your messy spouse instead of insisting they help clean up. Since retrogrades bring back the past, don't be surprised if an ex resurfaces out of the blue. A problem you thought was resolved in a relationship could flare up again. Obsessing over you-know-who? During this befuddling backspin, you could waste hours trying to strategize your next best move. Instead of fanning the flames, reach out to get the right help and support. Thankfully, Venus only turns retrograde every 18 months—and it doesn't have to dump rain on your summer lovin' parade! Nostalgia is the magic elixir. Do things that revive a bygone era, like revisiting a place you haven't been to since the honeymoon phase.

MERCURY-URANUS SQUARE

**23
JUL**

Talking a big game but not following through? Today's Mercury-Uranus square could deliver a tough lesson that forces you to recalibrate. Sure, it's sometimes necessary to fake it 'til you make it. But in this case, your genius ideas will never see the light of day if you overpromise and underdeliver. Simplify your master plan and scale back to phases. Better to celebrate a small milestone than to do a massive premature victory lap. Those little wins are the very thing that add up to a genuine triumph.

CHIRON RETROGRADE IN ARIES

23 JUL - 6 DEC

Wounded healer Chiron slips into its annual retrograde today, backing up through self-aware Aries until December 6. During its journey through the Ram's realm (2018-2027) the "wounded healer" comet is teaching us all lessons in self-empowerment and the constructive use of anger. (Arguably, the world's got a long way to go with that!) If you're feeling silenced, shut down or resentful, this backspin provides an important window for introspection. Are you using the power of your voice to silence or dominate others? If you've been playing a game of "the person who speaks the loudest wins," switch your strategy to active listening, where the goal is to understand rather than respond. For those who feel perpetually talked over, this retrograde gets you closer to the core of any confidence issues that may be standing in the way of your self-expression.

7

WAXING QUARTER MOON IN SCORPIO

25 JUL

Today's balancing Scorpio quarter moon helps you discern what's appropriate to share and what should be kept under wraps. If you're maddeningly mysterious, people may get frustrated, especially if they can't figure out what's really going on. But if you unload too much information at once, they could feel flooded and overwhelmed. This is the midpoint between last week's emotional Cancer new moon and next week's friendly Aquarius full moon. Your best bet? Be approachable AND appropriate. Let people earn your trust—but don't demand that they pay an excessive entry fee for it! By asking questions that get THEM to open up, too, you'll establish a more equal footing. Then, next week's full moon will reveal who your true allies are.

MERCURY-VENUS MEETUP

27 JUL

Overthinking alert! Mental Mercury bumps into Venus—who is currently retrograde in Leo, escalating a "do they love me or love me not?" drama. It's one thing to be intuitive and read the tea leaves. But if gauging someone's interest level feels like a guessing game, consider that you might be projecting qualities onto them that may not be there. One way to test the connection? Spend more time together, but without any pressure to move the relationship in a particular direction. Extend an invitation today and see what gives. If you've been guarded, open up more so people can determine if you're a good match. The more authentic information you provide, the better.

7

MERCURY IN VIRGO

28 JUL - 4 OCT

Mental Mercury kicks off an extended visit to its home sign of efficient, analytical Virgo. Bring order to any chaos by organizing, tracking and budgeting. With the communication planet in this healthy sign, you can successfully start (and sustain) new habits by writing things down and planning ahead. While this is a great time for editing, perfecting and inspecting a pet project, there's a downside: Mercury's protracted stay in one sign is because the planet will be retrograde for part of the time—all the more reason to be extra vigilant now and avoid a costly mistake that takes time and resources to fix. Get your plans in order before the summer ends!

AUGUST *Moon Phases*

SUN	MON	TUE	WED	THU	FRI	SAT
		1 ♒ Full Moon 2:32PM	**2** ♒ ♓ 11:05PM	**3** ♓	**4** ♓ ♈ 11:19PM	**5** ♈
6 ♈	**7** ♈ ♉ 2:25AM	**8** ♉ 3rdQuarter	**9** ♉ ♊ 9:05AM	**10** ♊	**11** ♊ ♋ 6:52PM	**12** ♋
13 ♋	**14** ♋ ♌ 6:36AM	**15** ♌	**16** ♌ NM ♌ 5:38AM ♍ 7:14PM	**17** ♍	**18** ♍	**19** ♍ ♎ 7:53AM
20 ♎	**21** ♎ ♏ 7:22PM	**22** ♏	**23** ♏	**24** ♏ ♐ 4:07AM ♐ 1st Quarter	**25** ♐	**26** ♐ ♑ 9:05AM
27 ♑	**28** ♑ ♒ 10:32AM	**29** ♒	**30** ♒ ♓ 9:56AM ♓FM 9:36PM	**31** ♓		

Times listed are Eastern US Time Zone

KEY: ♈ ARIES ♊ GEMINI ♌ LEO ♎ LIBRA ♐ SAGITTARIUS ♒ AQUARIUS
♉ TAURUS ♋ CANCER ♍ VIRGO ♏ SCORPIO ♑ CAPRICORN ♓ PISCES

FM FULL MOON   **NM** NEW MOON   **LE** LUNAR ECLIPSE   **SE** SOLAR ECLIPSE

8

1 AUG

FULL MOON IN AQUARIUS 2:31 PM EDT

Team up for the win! The year's only full moon in Aquarius helps your collaborations take flight. An activist or community project could make a powerful impact. Seek out kindred spirits and people who think outside the box, then put your heads together for a common cause. Is a certain acquaintance worthy of being promoted to "true friend" or squad member status? These clarifying moonbeams will help you discern whether to open that door or keep them at arm's length. Already part of an elite squad? Over the coming two weeks, you could be celebrating a major victory together. Make a point of publicizing shared missions. Supporters could come out of the woodwork, or you may be invited to showcase your collective talents. Casting for collaborators? Take extra efforts to keep your crew inclusive. With the full moon squaring global ambassador Jupiter, you want a dynamic chorus of unique voices, not an echo chamber.

8

1 AUG

MERCURY-SATURN OPPOSITION

Stubbornness alert! You could spiral into analysis paralysis today, as fussy Mercury in Virgo faces off against perfectionistic Saturn in Pisces. If you've colored too far outside the lines, this transit sounds the call to rein yourself in and make sure you've covered the bases. Learn the rules before you break them. You might realize that some tenets are worth keeping intact while only a handful require an official amendment. See how much work you just saved yourself? Whew.

SUN-JUPITER SQUARE

6 AUG

Egos could run amok today as the "pick-me!" Sun and blowhard Jupiter inflate people's sense of their own importance. Everyone knows best and nobody's listening to anyone else. This might not be the day to get a decision-maker's signoff, unless of course, you appeal to their need to feel special. (One tactic: Make them think it was THEIR idea!) If you don't mind putting your own ego aside for that, you might be able to slip past the velvet ropes and get what you really want.

WANING QUARTER MOON IN TAURUS

8 AUG

Focus time! The quarter moon in Taurus brings you back to your priorities and principles, reminding you that certain things are not worth your energy. Bottom-line the basics, clean up unnecessary clutter and cut any superfluous expenses. If your no-frills approach starts to feel too austere, you can re-introduce luxuries one at a time, or on a more affordable scale. Taurus is a pleasure-loving sign—but a practical one! This resource-conscious moon can inspire you to organize a clothing swap, shop in your own closet or upcycle goods that simply need a modern tweak.

8

VENUS-URANUS SQUARE

9
AUG

Feeling smothered is not sexy, and when you can't get one minute to yourself, the single life starts to feel very compelling. Freedom-loving Uranus squares off against lovestruck Venus today, blurring the boundaries between personal space and close-knit relationships. Even if you're obsessed with your partner, overzealous love and affection can be stifling. Before doing anything drastic, book a night off to spend solo. You may return refreshed and ready to snuggle up again. Single? Take a break from the apps if you're feeling discouraged. An opportunity for a no-strings summer fling could present itself today.

8

MERCURY-JUPITER TRINE #1

9
AUG

All fired up with...somewhere to go? As two of the most experimental and impulsive planets form their first of three earth trines in 2023, you get the urge to take action on a unique idea. Veer away from the status quo and approach an old problem from a fresh angle. Write with your non-dominant hand; take a new route to your usual destinations. Swing far out of your comfort zone in relationships and conversations. The novelty will give your brain a burst of mojo!

SUN-URANUS SQUARE

15 AUG

Egos, tempers and tantrums...help! Narcissistic tendencies are on breathtaking display, thanks to a volatile square between the domineering Leo Sun and disruptor Uranus in Taurus. People may be quick to snap or send nasty emails, so do your best to fly under the radar and stay away from tantrum-throwing tinderboxes. If you find yourself walking on eggshells, diffuse the situation by calling a timeout instead of further provoking the "opposition." There's zero use in engaging with hotheads today. Break off and do your own thing!

NEW MOON IN LEO 5:38AM EDT

16 AUG

A fresh start to your creative and romantic endeavors arrives with today's Leo lunar lift. Where have you stopped voicing your feelings or sharing your ideas as openly as you could? Let these moonbeams loosen your tongue. Make a vow to speak up when you have something to contribute to the conversation—or simply when you want to know more. Do one thing to put your talents on display or draw attention to your gifts. Has your work-to-play ratio been heavy on the responsibility side of things? Generate more fun for yourself, even if you're busy. Productivity is bound to speed up when you're taking breaks to relax your mind and enjoy downtime with friends. Poolside happy hour? Let's go!

8

16 AUG

MARS-URANUS TRINE

See ya later, comfort zone! Today's hookup of strong-willed Mars and impulsive Uranus strikes a match and lights things up fast. With Mars in perceptive Virgo, this is a day of quick decisions followed up with action. If a relationship isn't working, examine it from another angle or let it go and move on. In need of more satisfaction? Tap inventive Uranus in Taurus to add an element of surprise to your playtime. That spark of novelty may be just the thing you need to get the passion back.

22 AUG

VENUS-JUPITER SQUARE

Once again, the two "benefics" are at odds, and this time, Venus is retrograde in Leo. A case of grass-is-greener syndrome could return, making it tough to feel like anything or anyone is enough for you. With Jupiter in straight-shooting Taurus, don't mince words. If you're not happy with the amount of romance, affection or attention you're getting, have a talk about it. Who knows? If you dare to state your desires without apology, a consenting companion could happily make them come true. But don't act on the FOMO in ways you'll regret.

22 AUG

MARS-NEPTUNE OPPOSITION

Know thy limits! As relentless Mars opposes boundary-blurring Neptune, it will be hard to find the "stop" button. But you'll be risking burnout if you push things too far. Take breaks in between your go-go-go activities today to replenish your tanks. This transit can drive up the desire to be generous, especially with Mars parked in Virgo's service center and Neptune in sacrificial Pisces. Mind your energy levels and take breaks instead of soldiering through.

8

23 AUG - 22 SEP

SUN IN VIRGO

The Sun settles into Virgo today, turning life into a four-week efficiency mission. After the glitz and glam of Leo season, Virgo's "keep it simple" ethos is a breath of fresh air. Squeeze some al fresco exercise into these last weeks of summer: bike rides to the beach, yoga in the park, lap swims in the saltwater pool. Then, bring some order to your court. From your storage systems to your project management software, give everything a proper review.

This service-oriented sign gets us back in tune with our ethical natures. Skip the fast-fashion specials (yeah, even if they're dirt cheap) and support brands with conscious practices and production models. Go green! With earthy Virgo ruling the skies, it's time to enjoy the summer harvest of fresh produce—all the better if it's locally grown by independent farmers and rich with life-enhancing enzymes.

8

MERCURY RETROGRADE IN VIRGO

23 AUG - 15 SEP

Mercury hits its third retrograde of 2023, backing up through its home sign of Virgo. While the finicky planet is retrograde until September 15, review everything on the finest setting possible. Enlist a third and fourth pair of eyes to edit documents before you hit "send." Need to do more research? You're in luck! This is one of the best times of the year to tumble down the search engine rabbit hole. Be an unapologetic purist when you go on your "sourcing missions." Can you find a greener solution that not only saves you cash but is also environmentally responsible? Watch the judginess! Constructive feedback could come out sideways, so buffer it in a "praise sandwich," starting and ending with the positives.

MARS-PLUTO TRINE

24 AUG

Don't stop 'til you reach the top! As driven Mars and powerhouse Pluto commune, your competitive side comes out full force. Want something? Be proactive and strategic in your pursuit of it. Woo the decision-makers with heart and honesty, and follow your instincts. Mars gives you the courage to make a big ask, while shrewd Pluto reveals different points of entry. Whether you get there through the front door, side door or the service elevator doesn't matter. The end justifies the means.

24 AUG

WAXING QUARTER MOON IN SAGITTARIUS

Too much "elevating" can tip things over the edge and make them feel extra. Shift your benchmarks under the moderating light of the waxing quarter moon in Sagittarius. How can you grow in a way that feels healthy and fulfilling—not stressful and overwhelming? Free yourself from the rat race of competition today and focus on what makes you happy. High-minded Sagittarius shines a light on a different set of considerations. Are you being inclusive to a wide pool of people? How will any expansions impact your environment, your family and people in the area? Review your strategy with a magnifying glass. If something needs to be adjusted, get on that before the full moon, one week from now!

27 AUG

SUN-SATURN OPPOSITION

Hurry up...no—slow down! Mixed messages abound as the pushy and passionate Sun in Virgo plays tug o' war with strict Saturn in boundary-challenged Pisces. There's nothing wrong with wanting to maximize a promising situation, but if things start moving too quickly, one or both of you could get overwhelmed. When in doubt, choose a safe word—whether for challenging conversations or boudoir experimentation. Offset any harsh feedback with an extra dose of compassion and gratitude. Even if you're at odds today, don't lose sight of the fact that you're on the same team.

8

MARS IN LIBRA

Cuffing season is on the horizon, and as lusty Mars blazes into Libra, the zodiac's partnership sign, the urge to merge will be crazy strong. But don't let the impatient red planet get you locked into a serious situation before you're truly ready. It's almost too easy to romanticize when Mars blasts into this "love and marriage" zone every other year. If it's longevity you're after, aim for a balanced view. Can you accept people "for better" and "for worse"? For couples, Mars in Libra adds a dash of spice, but it can also stir up passive-aggressive bickering, especially if one of you is pulling an unequal share of the load. Mars is in "detriment" in Libra, meaning it's an uncomfortable place. And it makes sense: Mars is the god of war, while Libra is all about peace, love and harmony. It will take extra effort to keep your emotional equilibrium now.

URANUS RETROGRADE IN TAURUS

**28 AUG
-
27 JAN,
2024**

Unpredictable Uranus does its annual about-face, backing up through material-minded Taurus for five months. Your grip on finances, good habits and, well, reality, could get slippery. Plan with the best intentions but expect the unexpected between now and January 27, 2024. Progress may be slower than usual during this five-month retrograde, but this forced timeout could provide a hidden window of opportunity to develop an indie venture or side hustle. On a broader level, it's time to take a look: How well are you cooperating with the people in your life? When the side-spinning planet shifts into reverse every year for nearly five months, it's time to recalibrate the ranks and make sure everyone's feeling included and free to voice their opinions.

8

**30
AUG**

FULL MOON IN PISCES 9:35PM EDT

Let your imagination take the reins under August's blue moon—the second full moon of the month. This one lands in dreamy Pisces, illuminating subconscious thoughts and casting a rosy glow over all your interactions. Divine downloads could stream in throughout the day. Whenever possible, get yourself into a meditative space so you can capture the messages from your higher mind—and possibly a few ancestors and guides. Since Saturn's co-piloting this mission, take actual notes. Some of these "fantastical notions" could be the seeds of a future start-up. Because esoteric Pisces is the master of illusion, you might also feel lost in a labyrinth. Stop, breathe, and listen to your intuition, then wait until you feel centered before taking your next step. Do you need to make amends? This compassionate full moon paves the way for deep, soulful healing. Unexpectedly, you may see an "enemy" in a very human light. While you don't have to accept their wrongdoings, you may find a spot of forgiveness in your heart. With no-nonsense Saturn hovering close to the full moon, you may realize that it's time to put up boundaries with a bully. Enough's enough!

8

SEPTEMBER *Moon Phases*

SUN	MON	TUE	WED	THU	FRI	SAT
					1 ♓ ♈ 9:25AM	**2** ♈
3 ♈ ♉ 11:00AM	**4** ♉	**5** ♉ ♊ 4:07PM	**6** ♊ 3rd Quarter	**7** ♊	**8** ♊ ♋ 1:00AM	**9** ♋
10 ♋ ♌ 12:36PM	**11** ♌	**12** ♌	**13** ♌ ♍ 1:18AM	**14** ♍ New Moon 9:40PM	**15** ♍ ♎ 1:44PM	**16** ♎
17 ♎	**18** ♎ ♏ 12:58AM	**19** ♏	**20** ♏ ♐ 10:06AM	**21** ♐	**22** ♐ 1st Quarter ♑ 4:20PM	**23** ♑
24 ♑ ♒ 7:29PM	**25** ♒	**26** ♒ ♓ 8:18PM	**27** ♓	**28** ♓ ♈ 8:17PM	**29** ♈ Full Moon 5:58AM	**30** ♈ ♉ 9:18PM

Times listed are Eastern US Time Zone

KEY: ♈ ARIES ♊ GEMINI ♌ LEO ♎ LIBRA ♐ SAGITTARIUS ♒ AQUARIUS

♉ TAURUS ♋ CANCER ♍ VIRGO ♏ SCORPIO ♑ CAPRICORN ♓ PISCES

FM FULL MOON   **NM** NEW MOON   **LE** LUNAR ECLIPSE   **SE** SOLAR ECLIPSE

9

<table>
<tr><td>3
SEP</td></tr>
</table>

VENUS DIRECT IN LEO

Passion or high drama? It's been hard to tell since Venus turned retrograde in Leo on July 22. But today, the planet of love and harmony resumes forward motion, lifting the curtain on a new scene. With the "pleasure principle" planet motoring forward, you are free to once again engage in the pursuit of happiness. If you've felt out of sync with your partner, this U-turn will restore harmony. You won't have to second-guess someone else's confusing behavior or stoop to manipulative tactics to draw people out. Unions that felt like they were in free-fall may settle down, and you'll gain clarity about where things are going—or at least where you want them to go. Don't try to squish a square peg into a round hole. It's better to cut bait than waste any more precious time on the wrong fit. Single? If your love life went through a recent dry patch, the forecast calls for a deluge! Venus moving forward in Leo gives you the tools for a bonafide charm offensive: A little seduction will go a long way. Give it a week and see if you don't have too many options. No need to rush into anything—including a haircut, tattoo or any other beauty treatment that you've had on hold since late July.

9

MERCURY-JUPITER TRINE #2

Hit that mute button! Not only is Mercury in a signal-jamming retrograde, but today loose-lipped Jupiter is egging on the messenger planet. As they meet for their second of three free-flowing trines, we're all at the risk of rushing to conclusions and, worse, spitting out observations that could come across as offensive. Don't give anyone a chance to screenshot your hasty post (and use it against you). Take a day off from social media to research the date, then, formulate your opinion.

<table>
<tr><td>4
SEP</td></tr>
</table>

JUPITER RETROGRADE IN TAURUS

Keep your eyes on the prize *and* the process. As optimistic Jupiter slips into its annual retrograde, you could easily fall in love with people's potential or let important details slip through the cracks. With the red-spotted titan backing up through methodical Taurus until just before NYE, tighten up any slack in the reins. Get clear on the criteria you need for your elite squad: integrity, reliability, a commitment to excellence. There's always a level of "messy" that comes along with growth. But instead of just "figuring it out along the way," utilize Q4 to set up savvy systems, lifehacks and smarter org charts. Create project plans and budgets—and make sure timelines allow a healthy work-life balance.

SUN-MERCURY MEETUP

As the Sun and friendly Mercury sync up in service-oriented Virgo, look for ways to contribute, no matter how small. Show up with an extra coffee in hand, help a friend assemble bookshelves or offer a ride to the airport. And if you find yourself at your desk (which is likely), don't just dive into "Go!" mode. Instead, make "working smarter not harder" your operating principle. Use apps and trackers to keep organized, and if the load gets too heavy, ask for support. Got some advice to offer? Don't mince words, but follow persnickety Virgo's directive to be clear and make every syllable count.

6
SEP

WANING QUARTER MOON IN GEMINI

Where's the gray area? Focus your attention there because nothing is "black or white" under today's detail-driven quarter moon in Gemini. Keener observations could turn up a missing clue. You might realize that what (or who!) you were looking for was standing right under your nose. Did you rush to make a decision recently? Use this prismatic moon to consider a broader set of perspectives, including the most essential one—your own! If you need to walk back your prior stance, swallow your pride and own up to your choice. It's Gemini's prerogative to change its mind!

8
SEP

SUN-JUPITER TRINE

The glowing Sun forms an expansive trine to bountiful Jupiter, making us all crave...MORE. Since both planets are in material-minded earth signs, the focus falls on financial security. Nothing wrong with wanting to pad your pockets or build a legacy for generations to come. But with Jupiter retrograde, take a look at any counterproductive habits. Where are you leaking money? How efficiently are you using the resources you already own? A thin wallet doesn't mean you're out of options. Work the barter system or see if you can volunteer hours in exchange for access.

9

**14
SEP**

NEW MOON IN VIRGO 9:39PM EDT

If it's time for a life edit, you're in luck. The make-better vibes come flooding in with today's new moon in Virgo, the only one of 2023. Apply a "clean and green" ethos broadly. Set up a new shelving system and fill your house with plants. Get your budget in order and make sure you're supporting companies with ethics you can stand behind. Feed your body food that has ingredients it can actually use for fuel. If you're surrounded by chaos, don't just contain it—tackle it head-on. Make a thrift store drop, meal plan, do all that laundry, and scrub the baseboards. With innovators Jupiter and Uranus chiming in, make your maintenance plan a "smart" one. Put a system in place and let your devices remind you to keep them up.

**15
SEP**

9

MERCURY DIRECT IN VIRGO

Chronic miscommunication gives way to clarity as messenger Mercury wakes up from its retrograde that began in Virgo on August 23. After a choppy three weeks, we'll start seeing eye-to-eye once again. If you've been waiting for a clear signal to sign a contract or upgrade your devices, the smoke is clearing now. With Mercury powering forward through this sensible, savvy earth sign until October 4, you have a few good weeks to bring some order back to your court without retrograde glitches running interference. Cue the sigh of relief!

SUN-URANUS TRINE

15 SEP

The confident Sun and spontaneous Uranus unite in a harmonious trine, emboldening you to leap into new terrain. If your gut is telling you to take a chance, this is the day to follow it. But do look both ways before you swan-dive into something that you haven't researched. The combo of these two impulsive planets can tempt you to abandon common sense. Stuck at a plateau? Mix things up and keep trying different approaches. Under this innovative mashup, your bold and trailblazing attempts could bring a "Eureka!" moment.

VENUS-JUPITER SQUARE

17 SEP

Not again! Love planet Venus and generous Jupiter, normally cosmic BFFs, go for one last round on the mat now that Venus is direct (forward), stirring up FOMO and a few wandering eyes. That said, you don't have to settle for less than you want or deserve. And now that we've just wrapped a six-week inventory of Venus retrograde, many of us have clarified what that is. Put it into practice, whether with your current amour or a new prospect.

9

SUN-NEPTUNE OPPOSITION

19 SEP

Stuck in the muck? Blame nebulous Neptune opposing the decisive Sun, which can derail the best-laid plans. You may think you're focusing and moving forward, yet, too easily you'll get distracted or blown off course. Someone with an ulterior motive may not be showing their hand. Plots and plans may be thrown off course today, but take this momentary chaos in stride and try your best to make progress. Even a few small steps count!

SUN-PLUTO TRINE

21 SEP

Your power is palpable today, so wield it responsibly! It won't take much to make an impact or even to come across as intimidating. Be conscious of how intense you're being, especially in the company of new people. Want to increase your leverage? Hold back a little instead of being an open book. Mystery will work in your favor today as long as you're not so enigmatic that people wind up confused.

WAXING QUARTER MOON IN CAPRICORN

22 SEP

Does "work-life" balance sound more like a riddle than an attainable goal? Make some adjustments—fast—under the equalizing beams of today's waxing quarter moon in Capricorn. Achieving feels great, but think through your path to the finish line. Are you spreading yourself too thin instead of delegating tasks? Trying to "do it all" could logjam an important mission. If career goals are elevating your stress levels, make some adjustments. Rather than pushing to do "one more thing!" see what happens if you start logging out and, say, going to yoga to recharge. Has it been slow-going for your career? These brightening moonbeams could illuminate a work opportunity that (re)builds your skillset. Picking up an extra shift or taking a webinar can get you back in the black!

9

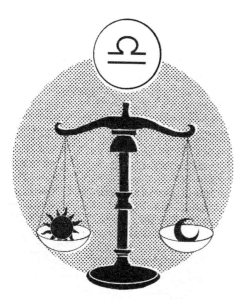

23 SEP - 23 OCT

SUN IN LIBRA

Drop the lone-wolf routine and gear up for a solar-powered month of joint ventures. The Sun kicks off its annual tour of romantic, fair-minded Libra. In business AND pleasure, the name of the game is dynamic duos. You'll increase your chances for happiness and success by keeping an open mind to different types of people—not just those who match the items on your checklist. Should you belly up to a bargaining table, this diplomatic four-week cycle can help you negotiate an equitable deal. Relationships that you're already a part of could grow more serious. Add an exclusivity clause, put a ring on it, or figure out what the next level of the game is for you!

9

MERCURY-JUPITER TRINE #3

25 SEP

Can you repeat that please? For the third and final time, messenger Mercury teams up with outspoken Jupiter in a friendly earth trine, but it's not quite as copacetic as you'd think. While Mercury has corrected course, now Jupiter is retrograde. And since it's backing up through Taurus, a basic request could turn into a battle of wills. Stand by your convictions but avoid a dogmatic or domineering approach. If someone turns down an offer you extend, don't take it personally—but don't waste time pleading or persisting with them.

VENUS-URANUS SQUARE

29 SEP

Love can't flourish if you keep anyone on a short leash today. Freedom fighter Uranus faces off with tenderhearted Venus, creating a rumble in any relationship that feels possessive or smothering. If your partner thinks "me time" should be "us time," remind them that absence makes the heart grow fonder. Try implementing regular breaks from each other where you do your own thing for the day or the evening, then get together to compare notes. Single? Unavailable types are like catnip today, but trying to reform a player is a fool's errand.

29 SEP

FULL MOON IN ARIES 5:57AM EDT

Werk! Twirl! Steal the spotlight. And don't even think about apologizing for being "too much." A wave of flamboyance washes over the world with the annual full moon in Aries. Let tongues wag! Audience appreciation is not the point here, but self-expression is. Dare to put yourself out there, unvarnished, fully authentic and 100 percent amazing—as YOU define it. Aries loves to be #1, which could raise the stakes for all the competitive types out there. But rather than fighting for headliner status, how about shining a light on other talented souls? That's the kind of leadership this trailblazing sign can get behind! Warning: This lunation could unleash a wave of pent-up frustration and rage. Hit the boxing bag, vent to your work wife, scream into a karaoke mic...just don't escalate the drama!

30 SEP

MERCURY-URANUS TRINE

Eureka! The two most clever planets sync in sweet harmony today. As they merge their innovative superpowers in steady earth signs, put a thoughtful plan behind one of your big ideas. Then, get busy crafting it into tangible form! Making a pitch? There's only so much you can anticipate ahead of time. Stay present (and don't get "salesy") and you'll win them over with your personable style.

9

OCTOBER *Moon Phases*

SUN	MON	TUE	WED	THU	FRI	SAT
1 ♉	**2** ♉	**3** ♊ 1:03AM	**4** ♊	**5** ♋ 8:32AM	**6** Third Quarter ♋	**7** ♌ 7:24PM
8 ♌	**9** ♌	**10** ♍ 8:02AM ♌	**11** ♍	**12** ♎ 8:22PM ♍	**13** ♎	**14** ♎ Solar Eclipse NM 1:55PM
15 ♏ 7:04AM ♎	**16** ♏	**17** ♐ 3:36PM ♏	**18** ♐	**19** ♑ 9:55PM ♐	**20** ♑	**21** ♑ First Quarter
22 ♒ 2:06AM ♑	**23** ♒	**24** ♓ 4:33AM ♒	**25** ♓	**26** ♈ 6:02AM ♓	**27** ♈	**28** ♈ ♉ 7:44AM ☌LE FM 4:24PM
29 ♉	**30** ♊ 11:08AM ♉	**31** ♊				

Times listed are Eastern US Time Zone

KEY: ♈ ARIES   ♊ GEMINI   ♌ LEO   ♎ LIBRA   ♐ SAGITTARIUS   ♒ AQUARIUS
♉ TAURUS   ♋ CANCER   ♍ VIRGO   ♏ SCORPIO   ♑ CAPRICORN   ♓ PISCES

FM FULL MOON   **NM** NEW MOON   **LE** LUNAR ECLIPSE   **SE** SOLAR ECLIPSE

10

THE ASTROTWINS

2 OCT

MERCURY-NEPTUNE OPPOSITION

Keeping track of everything is challenging today as mental Mercury faces off with foggy Neptune. Rather than rely on your memory, write things down or use your voice recorder app for tracking. Do you have a million to-do lists on little scraps of paper? Corral them all into a central location to feel less scattered. If you've been TOO linear or rigid in your thought process, this is a great day for creative visualization or artistic techniques to open your channels.

4-22 OCT

MERCURY IN LIBRA

Have you been too quick to judge? Reconsider a hardline perspective and adopt a moderate one instead. Mental Mercury visits balanced Libra, reminding us all to really hear the other person's viewpoint before leaping to conclusions or talking over them. Even if you "agree to disagree," keep it respectful. Diplomatic talks can restore harmony to your relationships. You may be in a rush, but it's well worth your time to slow down and patiently negotiate. In objective Libra, Mercury wants us to be thorough— that's what allows us to make fair judgments based on facts, not feelings.

10

WANING QUARTER MOON IN CANCER

6 OCT

Wrap that flannel throw a little tighter and pull on the thick wool socks. With the balancing quarter moon in cozy Cancer, the hygge vibes of autumn call us to get domestic. Pause between your social and professional duties to tend to your nest. A solid dose of self-care will bring the Libra season balance you need. Even if you're a powerhouse who runs on fumes and foamy cappuccinos, you can't make your personal life an empty tank. Bring inviting elements of warmth and comfort into your space, from new extra-large mugs made by a local artist to piles of textured throw pillows. If your home will be the go-to for fall hangs and movie marathons, stock up on snacks and sips—then start sending out invites for a small gathering. Maybe even an impromptu one tonight?

VENUS IN VIRGO

8 OCT - 8 NOV

After an extended, four-month strut down the red carpet, Venus leaves hedonistic Leo for healthy Virgo, and suddenly, self-care is sexy. Give your love life a makeover and reboot the routines that restore your glow. If you're still smoothing over a conflict from the July 22 to September 3 Venus retrograde, this sensible shift can help you come to a new understanding with your partner. Before the holiday revelry begins, it's an ideal time to adopt a regimen you look forward to, from dance class to kickboxing, and revel in the endorphins post-workout. Pro tip: Acts of service is Virgo's love language. Lavish your partner with extra TLC and support their dreams with a listening ear or by pulling a little extra weight when they have to pull extra hours. Single? With Venus in verbal Virgo, connect over conversation—this deep and discerning sign encourages you to flaunt your intelligence!

10

<table>
<tr><td>

**8
OCT**

</td><td>

MARS-PLUTO SQUARE

All's NOT fair in love and war—especially today, as firestarter Mars and brooding Pluto challenge each other. Resentment, jealousy, possessiveness...pick your "deadly sin" and these two are ready to light a match under it. It will take all your willpower not to let someone push your buttons. If you're feeling stressed about a relationship, demanding that they have "the talk" will NOT go over well today. Take a time-out and try to release some of those pent-up frustrations through exercise. A good workout will turn anger into endorphins and put you in a much more balanced state of mind.

</td></tr>
</table>

<table>
<tr><td>

**10
OCT**

</td><td>

PLUTO DIRECT IN CAPRICORN

Complexities and conundrums will either clear up or bubble up as secretive Pluto wraps its annual five-month retrograde. Since May 1, intense Pluto's reversal has called for deeper introspection, especially around generational patterns and the people we surround ourselves with. Pluto's direct (forward) turn can help if you've felt blocked around processing anything buried in your unconscious, from grief to resentment to addictive or compulsive tendencies. You may have unearthed some root causes during the retrograde. Now, you can take action to heal and deal. Has a so-called friend or family member revealed themselves to be a toxic force in your life? Admitting that is never easy, but Pluto can help you cut ties or recalibrate to more equal power dynamics. Keep an eye on your newsfeeds: Pluto rules power, sex and money, so we may see a buried scandal (or three) make headlines.

</td></tr>
</table>

10

VENUS-SATURN OPPOSITION

Have you been too lenient in your relationships, ignoring your own better judgment? You know you need firm boundaries; yet in the heat of a certain connection, you could have lost your steely determination. Today's stars help you take a step back and realign. On the fence about a certain someone? Avoid rushing into any decisions under this pessimistic planetary alignment. While you should absolutely pay attention to red flags, your ability to distinguish between a problem and an emergency isn't at its sharpest.

MARS IN SCORPIO

Intensity and intrigue build over the next few weeks, as potent Mars burrows into scintillating and secretive Scorpio. Watch for competitive or jealous flare ups. Power differentials can get more pronounced, but you also have a chance to ascend in a hierarchy. Make sure you don't come across as ruthless or only concerned with your own agenda. Bonds deepen under this transit, and you'll gain a strong sense of who you can trust. In love, you can bring on the holiday season heat! As randy Mars slides into sexy Scorpio, a budding connection could burst into flames of full-on consummation. The red planet is all too happy to set your desire on fire. Warning: Jealousy and possessiveness could run rampant now. If someone's legitimately betrayed you, then use this courageous transit to walk away. But know that your raw emotions could also be provoking paranoia. Investigate before you accuse (and no, that doesn't mean snooping or invading privacy).

13 OCT

MARS-SATURN TRINE

Hit your cruising altitude and let the tailwind guide you! Speedy Mars and cautious Saturn play nice today, helping you know when to push a little and when to pull back. Be excited but not desperate, direct but diplomatic. As long as you're fully prepared to back it up with action and evidence, you can even make a slightly over-the-top claim about why YOU rise above the competition. Radar in on people's emotions, pain points and deepest desires. With Mars and Pluto both in sensitive water signs, you'll need to make people FEEL something if you want to spur them to action.

14 OCT

NEW MOON IN LIBRA &
ANNUALAR SOLAR ECLIPSE 1:55PM EDT

Partner power! Today's new moon in Libra is also a potent solar eclipse—the first one to land in this sign since 2016! And it supercharges a six-month window that will refresh and rewire relationships. Could some part of your work benefit from a collaborator who complements your skill set? With the moon and mindful Mercury making contact, it can help to write down the qualities and capabilities of the person you'd like to attract. Whether that's for a serious relationship or a business alliance, being clear will sharpen your judgment. The moon will also oppose Chiron, so pay attention to the type of people you draw in at this eclipse. Are they mirroring a wound that you haven't resolved? If you sense "more of the same" or an old pattern resurfacing, don't blame the messenger—but maybe don't invite them into your inner sanctum too quickly, either.

10

MERCURY-PLUTO SQUARE

20 OCT

Keep it in the vault! With Mercury fighting secretive Pluto, don't give away any state secrets today. Do your research and check all facts before going public or buying into someone's pitch. People could represent themselves as bigger than they really are. Listen and ask questions, but hold your cards close to your vest. The tendency to project blame is strong today. Before you accuse someone of a transgression they didn't commit, take a moment to contemplate the crime. Could you be the root of the problem in some way? Take responsibility for your part in any breakdowns or misunderstandings.

SUN-PLUTO SQUARE

21 OCT

Watch for power struggles today. If you're picking up cues that someone is being evasive or throwing subtle shade, you might be correct. But don't leap to conclusions! Make a point of observing before you jump into the fray. If you don't know how to react, it's better to keep your opinions to yourself than lash out. Better to quietly catalog evidence than accuse someone prematurely. If you think you're clear to address a simmering issue, step aside for a private chat. Ironclad confidentiality is a must under these skies. Respect the circle of trust! Shield your field against negative energy. Just because a person around you is in a foul mood or seeing the glass as half-empty doesn't mean you need to adopt their pessimistic POV. If you're the one feeling low, be mindful not to dump that on others.

10

21 OCT

WAXING QUARTER MOON IN AQUARIUS

How secure is your data, really? Today's quarter moon in tech-savvy Aquarius prompts a closer look. From turning off location settings to strengthening privacy filters and disallowing cookies, you CAN take some of the power back from the droves of data-tracking apps and sites you use every day. Offline, take inventory of the people you surround yourself with. Is there trust and confidentiality on your team? Wean yourself off the gossipy chat threads, especially if you bond with coworkers over a common enemy. Maybe it's time to suggest a morale-boosting brainstorm or offsite day, where people can get reinvigorated and start bringing their best to the table again. Haven't seen your core crew in a while? It's the perfect moment to suggest a fall group outing, like apple picking or a costume party for Halloween—which is just around the corner!

22 OCT

VENUS-JUPITER TRINE

Sometimes there's a fine line between a stable commitment and a stranglehold. As the "great benefics," romantic Venus and adventurous Jupiter, team up in stable earth signs, you're in search of that sweet spot. Today, you can put your relationship to the test to see if your level of attachment makes you feel free yet grounded—or leaves you desperate for space. A calm and loving discussion could help you restore the balance. Single? Set off traveling or enroll in a class: You don't need to start off with a partner to end up with one!

10

MERCURY IN SCORPIO

22 OCT - 10 NOV

Keep it under wraps? Messenger Mercury slides into secretive Scorpio, urging you to strengthen your filters. Adopt an air of mystery and maintain a measure of control. You'll build intrigue by keeping them guessing a little. Not ready for a big announcement? Hold off on the big pitches and press releases. The next couple weeks are ideal for researching, editing and crafting your magnum opus behind the scenes. Keep confidential information safely stashed away and strengthen those passwords while you're at it. Prepare for a loyalty test or two as people will be more suspicious under this transit. Are your trust alarms going off? Catch yourself if you start questioning someone with a little too much fervor. No need for an FBI-level interrogation—just slow down and let trust build (or rebuild) naturally, one step at a time.

MERCURY-SATURN TRINE

22 OCT

Take the time to think every detail through today, as analytical Mercury and mature Saturn form an alliance. Whether you're making a big decision or finishing a project, wise Saturn rewards you for meticulous work. In emotional water signs, these planets prompt you to reach out to your close inner circle for support. A well-connected or experienced person could help you get to the next level. Be prepared to follow through if you ask them to make an introduction. Remember: Your work will reflect on the person who vouched for you.

10

SUN IN SCORPIO

Power is the name of the game for the next four weeks, as the Sun slinks into intimate, seductive and magnetic Scorpio. During this resourceful time, there's strength in numbers, so consider teaming up on a joint venture, passive income opportunity or co-op venture. Where could you consolidate what's "yours" and what's "theirs" for a mutually beneficial win-win? That could be as potent as a group investment or as personal as sharing a babysitter or carpooling to work. Resourceful Scorpio helps increase your bottom line by exposing where you're spending inefficiently. Reduce waste, trim needless costs and watch the profit margins multiply. Scorpio rules transformation, so be mindful of what you focus on. Energy flows where your attention goes, and during Scorpio season, your manifesting powers are dialed up. Don't be surprised to get a text from a person you were "just thinking about." If that happens to be a steamy message during sexy Scorpio season, don't say we didn't warn you!

10

SUN-SATURN TRINE

Step into your power and leadership today. As the confident Sun and disciplined Saturn unite in compassionate water signs, a calm but comforting approach will win the day. Know the difference between reacting and responding. Instead of flying into action at every provocation, step back and assess the best course of action. Smart solutions are best when backed by wisdom.

FULL MOON IN TAURUS &

PARTIAL LUNAR ECLIPSE 4:24PM EDT

Over and out! Today is the third and final lunar eclipse in fiscally fit Taurus, the sign of money, material security and hard work. This eclipse series, which began rippling across the Taurus/Scorpio axis on November 19, 2021, has been radically revamping the economy and our personal financial habits for the past two years. No need for austerity, though. Sensible but sensual Taurus loves luxury (this sign is ruled by pleasure goddess Venus). The key is making sure you've got enough resources to cover the basics while enjoying those earthly delights. Over the next few days, an exciting money-making opportunity could show up. You could have second thoughts about your job satisfaction or an epiphany about better work/life balance. As Taurus rules our daily routines, this lunar eclipse gives a big push to finally break a bad habit and put a life-affirming practice into place. Instead of focusing on some impossible goal ("I'm cutting out sugar, carbs and dairy!"), set a sustainable shift that fits with your lifestyle—enough of a change to make an impact, but not so gargantuan that you give up before it gains traction.

10

MARS-JUPITER OPPOSITION

28 OCT

Face-off! This combustible day comes with an active trigger warning. As hotheaded Mars locks horns with know-it-all Jupiter, no one's backing down from their righteous stance. Since Mars is in secretive Scorpio, you might not even see an offensive coming. Stay on guard for passive-aggressive behavior, a warning that something bigger may be brewing. Normally Jupiter in Taurus would favor a candid conversation to clear the air, but approaching the "enemy" directly right now could inflame the situation. Be watchful and strategic and keep classified information in the vault.

MERCURY-JUPITER OPPOSITION

28 OCT

Know-it-all alert! Today could feel like everyone is carrying on their own conversations and nobody's hearing anyone else. Don't add to the cacophony. Put on your headphones, turn on the white noise station or your favorite music for productivity and drown out the drama. Is someone trying to pitch you a big idea? If it sounds too good to be true, this starmap practically ensures that it is.

10

MERCURY-MARS MEETUP

29 OCT

Retract your claws! Fights could get ugly and people could play dirty today. Don't fan the flames by tossing out cruel barbs. Discussions and negotiations could get intense, so make sure you know exactly what you are and aren't willing to settle for before you open talks.

VENUS-URANUS TRINE

31 OCT

In the dating doldrums? Break out of the box with the help of romantic Venus and change-making Uranus. You might even let your alter ego take the wheel on this one. It *is* Halloween after all! In stabilizing earth signs, this experimental trine will demand a fine balance. Too short a leash will constrict you, but breaking too free from convention will leave you spinning out. This mashup could spark up chemistry out of the blue, perhaps with someone who's not your usual type. (Like that hot vampire ordering a pumpkin lager?) If you're single, make the most of it! But if you're part of a couple, watch where you dabble. Either be upfront about your desires or find another way to satisfy your urge for novelty. Play a game of "What if we...?" and come up with something fresh that neither of you has done before—inside or out of the boudoir.

10

NOVEMBER *Moon Phases*

SUN	MON	TUE	WED	THU	FRI	SAT
			1 ♊ ♋ 5:30PM	**2** ♋	**3** ♋	**4** ♋ ♌ 3:21AM
5 ♌ 3rd Quarter	**6** ♌ ♍ 2:39PM	**7** ♍	**8** ♍	**9** ♍ ♎ 3:08AM	**10** ♎	**11** ♎ ♏ 1:39PM
12 ♏	**13** ♏ NM 4:27AM ♐ 9:23PM	**14** ♐	**15** ♐	**16** ♐ ♑ 2:41AM	**17** ♑	**18** ♑ ♒ 6:28AM
19 ♒	**20** ♒ First Quarter ♓9:29AM	**21** ♓	**22** ♓ ♈ 12:19PM	**23** ♈	**24** ♈ ♉ 3:29PM	**25** ♉
26 ♉ ♊ 7:40PM	**27** ♊ Full Moon 4:16AM	**28** ♊	**29** ♊ ♋ 1:54AM	**30** ♋		

Times listed are Eastern US Time Zone

KEY:

♈ ARIES	♊ GEMINI	♌ LEO	♎ LIBRA	♐ SAGITTARIUS	♒ AQUARIUS
♉ TAURUS	♋ CANCER	♍ VIRGO	♏ SCORPIO	♑ CAPRICORN	♓ PISCES

FM FULL MOON   **NM** NEW MOON   **LE** LUNAR ECLIPSE   **SE** SOLAR ECLIPSE

SUN-JUPITER OPPOSITION

3 NOV

Don't believe the hype—at least, not before you dig for the real storyline! As the ego-driven Sun locks horns with spin-doctor Jupiter, someone might talk a big game with little capability to back it up. Enjoy the colorful stories but know the difference between the truth and a tall tale before you sign on. Under this conflating cosmic confab, be careful not to exaggerate or over-promise anything yourself.

VENUS-NEPTUNE OPPOSITION

3 NOV

Mixed signals much? As charming Venus faces off against hypnotic Neptune, it will be hard to tell if someone's interested in you or just casting an irresistible spell. Don't assume anything under these obfuscating romantic skies. People could be extra sensitive today. Tread lightly to avoid pushing a thin-skinned person's buttons. Are you looking at someone through rose-colored glasses? Don't diminish the downside of their less-than-angelic traits. Better to see people realistically, flaws and all.

11

SATURN DIRECT IN PISCES

4 NOV

Taskmaster Saturn straightens out after a long retrograde period in healing, watery Pisces. Since June 17, Saturn's backspin brought plenty of soul-searching, inner growth and harsh but necessary lessons. You may have learned a lot about trust, vulnerability, surrender and forgiveness. No one would call a transit like this fun, but the growth and maturity that it can bring is priceless. Got an artistic or spiritual gift to contribute to the world? Practice the skills that lead to mastery. Saturn rules mentorship. With mature Saturn correcting course, you may be able to contribute to someone else's inner growth by sharing the wisdom of your own experience.

MERCURY-URANUS OPPOSITION

4 NOV

Don't expect your mouth to be able to keep pace with your thoughts today! The cosmic collision of irreverent Mercury and erratic Uranus sends your mind into overdrive. But hold your tongue before rebellious Uranus seizes the mic. In this case, the first thought probably isn't the best thought. Polarizing discussions can flame up fast today, and rabble-rouser Uranus won't want to back down from a debate. Consider whether you're sowing chaos and contention rather than actually promoting progress. You don't have to force everyone to agree (that's not happening today) but at least reach a place of common decency and respect. With Mercury in sharp-tongued Scorpio, your zingers come with stingers. Just because you've thought of the prizewinning comeback, doesn't mean you should say it out loud.

11

<table>
<tr><td>5
NOV</td></tr>
</table>

WANING QUARTER MOON IN LEO

A little bit "extra" could be just the right amount today, as the modulating quarter moon in Leo polishes the chrome in the dull areas of life. If you've lapsed into a rut or settled for basic-ness, it's time to bring a little glamour. Life was meant to be lived! But no need to go overboard, because a pinch will do the trick. Leo fashion icon Coco Chanel used to advise removing one accessory before leaving the house. Stay out of flashy terrain and think dress-up event, not costume party. Have you been carrying a lot of other people's stress? Leo rules the heart and spine. A cardio dance workout or a chiropractic adjustment could get you back in balance.

<table>
<tr><td>6
NOV</td></tr>
</table>

VENUS-PLUTO TRINE

Smoldering! As magnetic Venus and potent Pluto unite in tactile earth signs, the definition of "sexy" could be a mashup of intense passion and a grounded, reliable connection. Can you possibly find that all in one person? If there was ever a day to, this is it! But careful not to fall for the outward trappings of status and displays of wealth or power—what's under the hood might not be "as advertised." Couples could deepen their bond or revel in a mind-body-soul connection. Get a little more vulnerable and let your partner in a layer deeper. With Venus and Pluto in resourceful earth signs, it's a good day for a "state of the union" on your shared finances.

11

| 6 NOV |

MERCURY-NEPTUNE TRINE

Ask and you shall receive! Not everything requires laborious effort to pull off. Instead of swimming upstream, float *with* the current. Today, as mental Mercury tunes in to mystical Neptune's frequency, use the Law of Attraction to your advantage and visualize what you want! Under this flowing mashup, your intuition may be borderline psychic. Read the reports and check the data, but then follow your gut.

| 8 NOV - 4 DEC |

VENUS IN LIBRA

Amorous Venus makes a luxurious landfall in Libra, the love planet's stylish home base. Give your closet a pre-holiday update and add new pieces for the social season ahead. Take the time for thoughtful touches and decorative flourishes—those little gestures get a lot of mileage now. Does it feel like everyone's flirting with you? That's how cosmic coquette Venus operates in this lovely and gracious sign. Practice your witty one-liners and disarm with your charm. Relationships can turn official while the love planet's in this companionable realm, at the height of Cuffing Season no less. But Venus in Libra responds to gentle wooing, not guilt trips and love bombing. Dial down the pressure and turn up the thoughtful gestures.

11

MERCURY IN SAGITTARIUS

Dream it, do it! As the messenger planet jets through Sagittarius for the next three weeks, you'll be able to articulate some of your grandest dreams. Corral your crew for some blue-sky brainstorming and big-picture visioning. Have you made your 2023 plans yet? Start now, because Mercury will turn retrograde in a little over a month (from December 13 to January 1), making New Year's Eve a little less lucid than usual. The Mercury in Sagittarius period is perfect for identifying the exciting goals you want to pursue in January, even if they get off with a slight delay. Caution: This can be a big talk, little action transit. Some people will be blowing hot air, but excitement could fizzle as quickly as it sizzled. Luckily, there will be no shortage of adventurous opportunities to explore. Don't hold back! With chatty Mercury in honest Sagittarius, a few truth bombs could be dropped. If things get uncomfortably candid, don't underestimate the power of a well-timed joke or witty comeback. Mercury in Sagittarius knows a thing or two about the healing power of laughter.

**10
NOV**

MERCURY-SATURN SQUARE

Rigid much? Watch for a tendency to be stubborn or argumentative today. When you find yourself resisting something "on principle," take a look at what that might really be about. Are you afraid of losing control or being exposed as not having all the answers? Keep the imposter syndrome in check but do make sure you've done all your homework.

11

11 NOV	

MARS-URANUS OPPOSITION

Pure genius—or a recipe for chaos? Under today's combustible mashup of energetic Mars and volatile Uranus, you could have a major epiphany that leads to a breakthrough. But play it cool. People will have hair-trigger tempers and could explode for no apparent reason. Dodge the dramatic divas and skeptics who just want to insist that something won't work. Spend your time around folks who are open to trying things a new way!

13 NOV	

NEW MOON IN SCORPIO 4:27AM EST

Dive into the depths! The year's only Scorpio new moon opens a new chapter for all of your investments: emotional, spiritual and financial. A bond that begins today could develop into a deep soul connection over the next six months. Can this connection go the distance? If it's got permanent potential, explore! In resourceful Scorpio, this new moon turns your attention to shared finances, passive income and property matters. Keep your ears perked, too, as a helpful connection to motivator Mars could bring an investment opportunity. The tricky part? Erratic Uranus and illusory Neptune could make you susceptible to a flash-in-the-pan scheme—or worse, a scam. Better to hang on to what you've got than risk it on something untested that you haven't had time to research. With pushy Mars involved, your first warning is someone pressuring you to sign on the dotted line.

11

<table>
<tr><td>

**13
NOV**

</td><td>

SUN-URANUS OPPOSITION

</td></tr>
</table>

Volatility alert! As the boldfaced Sun faces down radical changemaker Uranus, egos could get testy. Avoid thin-skinned people and rabble rousers who just want to push your buttons. This isn't the day to demand a firm answer or make a binding decision. Plans could change without notice. If you must pivot quickly, adopt a flexible attitude instead of digging in your heels. A completely original approach could actually lead to a breakthrough. Free yourself from any "box" of what's been done before and innovate!

MARS-NEPTUNE TRINE

**17
NOV**

Trust your hunches! Insistent Mars in psychic Scorpio is harmoniously connected with tuned-in Neptune, which is parked in intuitive Pisces. Serendipities, coincidences and "signs" are practically announcing themselves in bold neon lights today. Don't dismiss these directives from the universe! Couples could find the perfect balance of lust and trust, as compassionate Neptune softens the red planet's raw intensity. Single? A sultry person with a strong spiritual side will be more appealing than the sparkly unicorn with sheer animal magnetism.

11

WAXING QUARTER MOON IN AQUARIUS

People-pleaser alert! If you've sacrificed your individuality to make others happy, today's waxing quarter moon in Aquarius offers a chance at a correction. Being a team player is great, but if you're "going along to get along" at the expense of your values, this collaboration will eventually run its course. Before things crash and burn, test the waters. How would people respond if you voiced a (genuinely) dissenting opinion or let your inner unicorn out to play? Under these broad-minded moonbeams, you may be pleasantly surprised by the results of your experiment.

SUN IN SAGITTARIUS

NOV 22 - DEC 21

The Sun blazes into worldly, inclusive Sagittarius for a month, encouraging you to move beyond your core crew and connect with others outside of your familiar zone. Be welcoming and open to diverse perspectives and backgrounds. Play superconnector for your friends or dip into a new talent pool for potential collaborators. Sagittarius also encourages transparency and honesty, so if you need to have an air-clearing talk with someone in your life, do it now before you get swept away in holiday festivities. "Anywhere but home" always seems like the ideal destination for Sagittarius season, but we recommend getting your travel in early this year. Mercury will be turning retrograde at the tail end of this solar cycle, starting December 13 (and ending on January 1). That's a good excuse for a gift shopping road trip...or a long weekend jaunt, perhaps one that requires a passport!

11

SUN-SATURN SQUARE

23 NOV

Too much too soon? This twice-a-year conflict between the confident Sun and speed-checking Saturn can make you feel pessimistic about the future. It's also an important reality check. You might not be able to realistically deliver what you're promising within the budget and timeline—so better to speak up now. Instead of getting discouraged, go back to the drawing board or tighten up your plans. Consider this (brief) pause a blessing in disguise. You could spot an error or a flaw in your plans just in the nick of time.

MARS IN SAGITTARIUS

**24 NOV -
4 JAN,
2024**

You don't need to wait until the new year for your ambitious plans to take flight. Start thinking of your most inspired 2024 dreams as passionate Mars blazes into entrepreneurial, wisdom-seeking Sagittarius. The surge of optimism and can-do energy has a ripple effect across your life. From bucket-list travel plans to an idea for an independent business venture, you'll suddenly have gas in your tank to go for it. Load up on inspiration. Dive into an online workshop or a metaphysical book instead of binging on another round of Elf or eating yourself into a holiday leftovers food coma. When it comes to love, you can forge into bold new romantic or sensual terrain for the rest of the year. That could mean giving someone wildly different than your usual "type" a chance or planning a dream trip with your partner. If you're traveling for the holidays, invite your favorite plus-one along—or skip some of the extra family festivities and slip off somewhere for just the two of you. Ringing in the new year on a gorgeous beach or looking at the lights in a far-flung city? That change of scene could do wonders for your connection.

11

<table>
<tr><td>

**25
NOV**

</td><td>

MARS-SATURN SQUARE

Slow down or speed up? As hasty Mars and cautious Saturn square off, it's like having one foot on the gas and the other on the brake. Don't overlook red flags or wave them away as inconsequential. Though it's tempting to minimize trouble signs and focus on fun and fantasy, rushing in without due diligence is not advised now. On the flip side, if you've got TOO many walls up, you may find a relationship is stalling or hitting a plateau. Push yourself to show a little more emotion or transparency. Real relationships require some risk or they never progress.

</td></tr>
</table>

<table>
<tr><td>

**27
NOV**

</td><td>

FULL MOON IN GEMINI 4:16AM EST

People can't read your mind, so if you want something, speak up! The full moon in garrulous Gemini urges you to articulate your wishes and dreams. Post about your passions and share your original views. With the full moon in this kindred spirit sign, you never know who might be moved by your message and respond. An opportunity to collaborate could also appear under these dynamic duo moonbeams. Ready to transition your career? Reach out to former collaborators or colleagues you admire. If you've been waiting for news or an answer, you could finally hear it today. Look back six months to the Gemini NEW moon for clues of what could come together now.

</td></tr>
</table>

11

<table>
<tr><td>

**27
NOV**

</td></tr>
</table>

MERCURY-NEPTUNE SQUARE

Follow your feelings or think it through? You're torn under today's battle between left-brained Mercury and right-brained Neptune, which tugs you between head and heart. With both planets in mutable signs, making a decision is even more of a conflict, since you can literally see every side of the equation. Gather feedback from a well-curated list of advisors (rather than opinion-polling everyone, which will only leave you more confused). Turn to folks who are compassionate but also tell it like they see it. Has someone been giving you mixed messages? Ask pointed questions to cut through the fog, but know that they may still be extra evasive. The truth may continue to elude you.

11

DECEMBER *Moon Phases*

SUN	MON	TUE	WED	THU	FRI	SAT
					1 ♋ 11:00AM	**2** ♌
3 ♌ ♍ 10:50PM	**4** ♍	**5** ♍ Third Quarter	**6** ♍ ♎ 11:35AM	**7** ♎	**8** ♎ ♏ 10:35PM	**9** ♏
10 ♏	**11** ♏ ♐ 6:11AM	**12** ♐ New Moon 6:32PM	**13** ♐ ♑ 10:31AM	**14** ♑	**15** ♑ ♒ 12:56PM	**16** ♒
17 ♒ ♓ 2:58PM	**18** ♓	**19** ♓ First Quarter ♈ 5:47PM	**20** ♈	**21** ♈ ♉ 9:50PM	**22** ♉	**23** ♉
24 ♉ ♊ 3:15AM	**25** ♊	**26** ♊ ♋ 10:15AM ♋ FM 7:33PM	**27** ♋	**28** ♋ ♌ 7:23PM	**29** ♌	**30** ♌
31 ♌ ♍ 6:53AM						

Times listed are Eastern US Time Zone

♈ ARIES	♊ GEMINI	♌ LEO	♎ LIBRA	♐ SAGITTARIUS	♒ AQUARIUS	
♉ TAURUS	♋ CANCER	♍ VIRGO	♏ SCORPIO	♑ CAPRICORN	♓ PISCES	

FM FULL MOON   **NM** NEW MOON   **LE** LUNAR ECLIPSE   **SE** SOLAR ECLIPSE

12

MERCURY IN CAPRICORN

**1-23
DEC**

Stack up the cash and enter 2024 with a confident hold on your career! Master strategist Mercury sails into Capricorn, helping you put a plan in action for your final act of 2023. Set your sights on success, but follow due process when it comes to making decisions. (Mercury will be turning retrograde from December 13 to January 1. Cutting corners then could create an epic meltdown...so just don't.) Ambitious Capricorn is all about forward thinking and setting goals, making this the ideal time to get a head start on any resolutions. Just keep them down-to-earth and doable so you don't get discouraged. Take advantage of holiday parties by using them as an opportunity to tastefully network. No need to seal any deals at the open bar but QR contact info and set up a meeting early next year!

VENUS-PLUTO SQUARE

**3
DEC**

Power struggles could pervade your love life today, as seductress Venus locks horns with manipulative Pluto. Controlling, dominating or avoidant behavior will only heap fuel on the fire and deepen the divisive dynamic. Get to the root of what's really driving this tension. Obsessing? Hard as it is to stop your brain from fixating (and your fingers from Googling or texting), try to keep things above board.

12

VENUS ENTERS SCORPIO

4-29 DEC

When Venus sashays into seductive Scorpio for a month, there's no telling what might transpire! Get in touch with eroticism through dance, sensual movement or good old-fashioned bedroom gymnastics. Dive deep into emotional exploration to move past any blocks. A transformative and intimate holiday season awaits! Venus in Scorpio turns up the mystery, but too much secretiveness could devolve into jealousy or stir up unnecessary trust issues.

VENUS-SATURN TRINE

5 DEC

As romantic Venus connects with mature Saturn, love could take a turn for the serious. Single? Don't rule out a slightly older prospect or a stable person you might have written off as "boring." (Those secure attachments have their benefits, too!) For couples, it's a great day to talk about the future and to make concrete plans for some holiday activities you can enjoy as a duo.

WANING QUARTER MOON IN VIRGO

5 DEC

Look—and look again—before you leap. The quarter moon in responsible, thorough Virgo is by your side to dot those i's and cross those t's, nudging you to give that presentation or important email one last glance before sending it off into the world. (Watch your texts and DMs, too!) Resist the urge to lean too hard into Virgo's perfectionist tendencies and check yourself if you're putting too much pressure on those around you. If you're not seeing the results you want, perhaps it's time to call in a pro to suit your high standards — or adjust your expectations entirely.

12

NEPTUNE DIRECT IN PISCES

6 DEC

What's next? That question has required deep contemplation for the past few months, and even that hasn't necessarily yielded much clarity. But after today, answers start coming into focus as tuned-in Neptune ends a long retrograde in its home turf of compassionate, dreamy Pisces. During this period of soul-searching, you may have come to enlightening realizations about yourself, your desires and your relationships. Now, you can start putting those divine downloads into action. Pro tip: That doesn't mean you should stop the daydreams. Quite the opposite! Neptune is a master at manifestation

MERCURY-JUPITER TRINE #1

7 DEC

With messenger Mercury in Capricorn and outspoken Jupiter in Taurus teaming up in stabilizing earth signs, it's time to put your money where your mouth AND your mind are. Pitch a visionary idea—and set your asking price a little higher than you're comfortable requesting. Just make sure you've got a rock-solid plan backed up by facts and experience. Under these stars you'll have to really show that you can walk your talk. This is the first in a trio of Mercury-Jupiter trines, since Mercury will go retrograde later this month. Prepare for a conversation that happens in several acts, perhaps because you have to procure paperwork or answer some discovery questions. The next two trines are on December 18 and then a third will arrive in January. It might take until the New Year for your final-*final* answer to come through.

12

9 DEC

VENUS-JUPITER OPPOSITION

Never satisfied? The grass looks greener over every fence as indulgent Jupiter and romantic Venus drum up dueling desires. With Venus in intense Scorpio, someone's minor misstep could spiral into a dealbreaker, leading you to dismiss someone who might have actual promise. Do your best to stay grounded in realistic expectations. Couples could make mountains out of microdramas, and things might get ugly. Call a time-out before it goes too far. Not attached? Don't tie yourself down to anyone yet. Sample the bountiful buffet before you settle on a favorite dish.

12 DEC

NEW MOON IN SAGITTARIUS 6:32PM EST

Are you thinking big enough? The year's only new moon in visionary Sagittarius nudges you out of the safety zone. Get ready for a bold entry into uncharted terrain or to take a supersized leap of faith. Got the urge to travel? Even if your journey happens next year, don't shy away from pressing "book now" on a great bucket-list destination deal. With courageous Mars mashing up with la luna, you're feeling especially bold and ready to risk big. Multiply your adventurous and horizon-expanding ideas by (at least) ten. But make sure you've got a backup plan, since you could be tempted to gamble. Need some extra motivation? Think about the people you'll help and inspire as a role model. As healing Chiron breezes by the new moon in a supportive trine, do it for the people who didn't get a chance—or those who might believe they can when you lead by example. Just keep one toe planted on terra firma, as a square from dreamy Neptune doesn't exactly scream "practical" when it comes to your exciting plans.

12

MERCURY RETROGRADE

13 DEC

-

1 JAN, 2024

Do you hear what I hear? Absolutely not. Blame it on the static of Mercury retrograde, which—we're sorry to report—begins today and jams up the signals until New Year's Day. With chaos and miscommunications rippling through the rest of 2023, leave absolutely nothing up to chance with holiday plans. While Mercury's backing up through Capricorn until the 23rd, set up an online hub with addresses, timelines and dishes and drinks everyone should bring to the celebration. (And plan on sending about five follow-up texts.) If you're jetting off to ring in the occasion, double check your luggage to make sure you've got the essentials—not to mention an extra phone charger and a Kindle. Delays will be likely, especially when Mercury backs into travel sign Sagittarius on the 23rd. Choose your fellow partygoers carefully. One divisive debater can ruin everything.

12

16 DEC

SUN-NEPTUNE SQUARE

Reflect before you project! Hazy Neptune in Pisces is at loggerheads with the Sagittarius Sun, which could leave everyone in a swirl of sticky rumors and questionable data. Finding that nugget of truth could take an entire search party...but then again, is it you that's obscuring the facts? As you scour the surface for details, look inward. Out of self-protection, you may be muddying the waters by being evasive, elusive—or avoiding conversations because they feel "difficult." Unfortunately, these deflections will only arouse more suspicion. Brewing trust issues may be at play. Perhaps this is a red flag that you aren't as certain about someone as you thought. While you're soul searching, be on alert for creative inspiration. (Or just escape to a live show or exhibit!) Let that spark flow freely, no rules or feedback allowed.

18 DEC

MERCURY-JUPITER TRINE #2

The second of three Mercury-Jupiter trines (the first was on December 7) puts another burst of momentum behind your big ideas. This time, however, Mercury is retrograde in cautious Capricorn, so you'll need to tread carefully. Getting cocky or making assumptions could cost you a promising opportunity. Rather than trying to knock one out of the park before the New Year, use this energy burst to tighten your game plan. You may have to go back to the drawing board to get more information, or perhaps the person you're trying to convince has a few tough but essential questions. Do the harder work now and you could emerge victorious in January when this duo meets again for a final rendezvous.

12

<table>
<tr><td>

**19
DEC**

</td></tr>
</table>

WAXING QUARTER MOON IN PISCES

Coincidence or divine intervention? At today's Pisces quarter moon, manifesting powers are dialed up to eleven. While it's great to be smart and self-reliant, remember that the universe WANTS to support your desires. Are you allowing that to happen? Look at where you might be blocking miracles or ignoring key signals. That includes your gut feelings, especially if you suspect someone's intentions could be less than noble. Interrogating them might not yield much, but paying attention to their body language and reading their energy could reveal whose side they're really on.

<table>
<tr><td>

**21
DEC**

</td></tr>
</table>

VENUS-URANUS OPPOSITION

Mood swing alert! Strong emotions might erupt like molten lava under today's explosive and unpredictable face-off of romantic Venus and volatile Uranus. Try not to interact with someone who's behaving like a ticking time bomb. Feeling the urge for more freedom? It's totally possible to create more space in a relationship without calling the whole thing off. Avoid making rash moves, as this energy will leave as quickly as it starts.

12

21 DEC - 20 JAN

SUN IN CAPRICORN

The shortest day of the year belongs to the longest-suffering sign of Capricorn, the tireless Sea Goat who persists against all odds! At the winter solstice, we welcome the start of Capricorn season. For the next four weeks, take a pragmatic and humble approach to all you do. Goal-setter Capricorn loves an ambitious plan (emphasis on the "plan" part). Write down where you'd like to be a year from now and reverse-engineer a master map that will get you there, one discerning step at a time. Could someone in your life use a not-so-secret Santa? Capricorn is the provider sign, reminding us that 'tis better to give. (Fortunately, it's also ruled by boundary-hound Saturn, so generosity doesn't have to turn into a sacrifice.) Look for ways you can pass on your expertise, like taking a younger relative or a greener coworker under your wing. What goes around comes around!

12

MERCURY IN SAGITTARIUS

23 DEC - 13 JAN, 2024

Mouthy Mercury, which is retrograde until January 1, backs into outspoken Sagittarius for the rest of the year. Cheeky comments that are normally entertaining could come across as rude, tactless or inappropriate under these signal-scrambling skies. Save the adult humor and off-the-cuff remarks for 2024, because they'll surely disrupt the holiday cheer, especially if you tread past "family friendly" terrain. Who needs to heap more fire on that Yule log? Visiting loved ones might require extra precautions during this argumentative time. If you need to cut a trip short or stay at a hotel to preserve the peace, err on the side of "personal space." You might want to rethink that out-of-town invitation for NYE, especially if plans have already started to get complicated. Sharing an Airbnb with ten of your closest friends might mean starting 2024 with ten brand-new frenemies. Not worth the risk!

VENUS-NEPTUNE TRINE

25 DEC

On Cupid, on Vixen! Romance reigns as these two enchanting planets unite in sensitive and sensual water signs Scorpio and Pisces. Compassion and creativity are also off the charts, making it a beautiful day to start a project as a duo or to listen generously to each other's POV. Under these healing skies, you can repair a rift. But use caution, as you may get a little too wrapped up in trying to solve someone's problems. This cosmic alignment makes everyone an emotional sponge.

12

FULL MOON IN CANCER 7:33PM EST

<table>
<tr><td>26
DEC</td></tr>
</table>

As the holiday season starts to wind down, the quiet and comfort of the year's second Cancer full moon brings a much-need moment to chill. With the warm-fuzzies in high gear, use today to catch up with close friends and trade notes on your holiday celebrations. Emotions will be close to the surface, so don't be surprised if a sentimental exchange brings on the waterworks. Or maybe you just need a long winter's nap after all the holly jolly hooplah. Ease into your cozy space or spend some time feathering your nest to turn it back into a sanctuary (not a gift-wrapping station). Since this full moon gets a boost from systematic Saturn, get ready to make some adult decisions in your personal life. A relative might need extra support in the weeks ahead or you may need to fund some repair work. And if you're feeling taxed, don't forget that the "lean on me" thing goes both ways.

CHIRON DIRECT IN ARIES

<table>
<tr><td>26
DEC</td></tr>
</table>

Stop playing martyr and stand up for yourself! You'll get a confidence boost as healing comet Chiron rockets forward into firestarter Aries, ending a retrograde that started July 23. Just beware the temptation to blow up in anger if you get a surge of suppressed resentment. While Chiron wheeled backwards through Aries, passive aggressive barbs and sneering put-downs may have been people's best defense. Now that Chiron's back in forward motion, be wary of the fine line between assertiveness and aggression. Chiron also has incredible healing powers, so unlock its key potential (seriously, the symbol for this asteroid is a key) and turn anger into purpose and passion.

12

MERCURY-NEPTUNE SQUARE

27 DEC

Your left and right brain hemispheres battle for supremacy as tough-talking Mercury in Sagittarius squares off with softhearted Neptune in Pisces. Half of you wants to lay down the law with strict orders. The other half is melting into a giant pile of mush. And with both planets in mutable signs, every option may seem as valid as the next. Although you're conflicted about the right course of action, there is a middle ground. Try expert Suzy Welch's 10-10-10 rule for decision-making. Reflect on how the results of your choice could unfold in ten minutes, ten months and ten years. You'll be surprised by the insight! Beyond that, are you having too many "conversations" in your head? Get into dialogue with the so-called offending party. By asking a few open-ended questions, you could unpack their not-so-hidden motives and get to the bottom of the miscommunication. Sweet relief!

SUN-JUPITER TRINE

27 DEC

Adopt an experimental and open-minded attitude today. As the trailblazing Sun and adventurous Jupiter unite in earth signs Capricorn and Taurus, thinking outside the box can lead to a financial breakthrough or something that builds a secure nest egg. Stuck in a mental rut? Go for a walk (or drive) in nature, preferably off your beaten path. Reach out to a mentor or an expert you admire for advice. Upload a video of yourself sharing your expertise—when you have to impart your wisdom to others, it forces you to think about it with a beginner's mind. Cultivate that under these optimistic and openhearted moonbeams.

12

MERCURY-MARS MEETUP

27 DEC

Contentious much? As aggressive Mars and retrograde Mercury merge in outspoken Sagittarius, you're likely to fire off a comeback before having a chance to cool down and think it through—much less separate fact from fiction. And that could be unfortunate indeed, as the truth that emerges could look very different from the distorted drama in your head.

MARS-NEPTUNE SQUARE

28 DEC

It may seem fun to take a gamble today, but that's a slippery slope. Unless you have the facts in front of you, hedge your bets! With the most active planet (Mars) at loggerheads with the most passive one (Neptune), you could take yourself on a wild ride of impulsivity and skewed intuition. Go back to the drawing board and do some quality research. Don't assume that a "maybe" is a "yes" until you've 100 percent confirmed it. Moreover, don't let anyone sweet talk you into making decisions, especially if they involve a financial transaction.

12

29 DEC
-
23 JAN, 2024

VENUS IN SAGITTARIUS

Mercury might be retrograde this NYE, but it's not going to rain on Venus' parade! Just in the nick of time, the planet of love and romance bounds into fun-loving, optimistic Sagittarius, helping us turn the calendar with hope in our hearts. Thought you'd stay home with sparkling cider and a 12:01 bedtime? Try again. Venus in Sagittarius has better plans, like hopping on a standby flight to watch the fireworks burst in a new city. Can't quite pull it off in time for the 31st? This Venus cycle opens minds and hearts until January 23. Stay in ambassador mode post-celebrations. Keep your personal borders open to all high-vibe people who come your way, even (and especially) if they arrive in a package unlike your own.

30 DEC

JUPITER DIRECT IN TAURUS

Forward, ho! Auspicious Jupiter ends a retrograde slowdown that began on September 4. As the planet of expansion powers forward in tactile and tenacious Taurus, a sustainable and profitable idea could pick up speed. If a work project has drifted from its original mission or purpose, you'll be able to come together again. It will be easy to prioritize without getting scattered or limiting the potential of an idea now. That's something worth popping the bubbly for. And with hedonistic Jupiter in luxe-loving Taurus, spring for a vintage bottle!

12

MORE BOOKS BY THE ASTROTWINS

HOW TO GET ALONG WITH ANYONE (*YES, EVEN THAT PERSON)

Any two zodiac signs CAN be compatible, as long as they understand what makes the other one tick. The AstroTwins simplify the secrets of synastry—the 7 unique energies encoded in the distance between your signs. Take your relationships from difficult to dynamic and start bringing out your best.

SUPERCOUPLE

Unlock the astrology secrets to sizzling attraction and deep connection, and get through the hard stuff fast! Did you know that your relationship has a zodiac sign and chart? The Supercouple system is the ultimate guide to finding true compatibility—by understanding why you came together and what your divine destiny could be!

MOMSTROLOGY

Parenting DOES come with instructions! This ultimate guide to raising your kids AND flourishing as a mom takes you through every season of parenthood, from birth to toddler to school years and leaving the nest. A favorite baby shower gift, featured by *Good Morning America* and a #1 Amazon bestseller.

START READING NOW AT **ASTROSTYLE.COM/BOOKS**

2023

NUMEROLOGY

UNIVERSAL YEAR 7

In Numerology, each calendar year adds up to a single-digit number, which holds a unique energetic influence & imprint.

BY FELICIA BENDER, NUMEROLOGIST

Welcome to 2023, a 7 Universal Year

$(2 + 0 + 2 + 3 = 7)$

We all feel this energy, and it's called the Universal Year.

During a Universal Year, everyone on the planet experiences the energy of its particular number, from January 1 to December 31.

Whether or not you make New Year's resolutions, most of us

intuitively feel a profound energy shift whenever the calendar turns. In Numerology, that transition is a pivot point, marking the passage into a new Universal Year—the collective atmosphere of the world for a 12-month period.

Each number comes with its own unique resonance or theme. The energy of the 7 is all about diving inward. Its focus is on **spiritual and personal growth and evolution.**

We're bridging from 2022's nurturing, relationship-focused 6 Universal Year energy into a time of reflection and inner focus.

This is a vital year to take a collective pause as we prepare for a massive reset.

The diffuse energy of 7 beckons us to go inward, quiet down, slow down, and sit with ourselves. To study, analyze, ask questions, and peel our personal "onions." As we contemplate bigger questions, deep shadows rise to the surface—both collectively and individually.

The 7 Universal Year is both spiritual *and* scientific. Along with tapping our intuition, there's a drive to research, find and analyze the data and quantify knowledge and information.

Financial gain, however, is *not* the core focus during a 7 Universal Year. No, we can't just go along with "business as usual" or place a Band-Aid (or a tourniquet!) on our fractured economic systems. However, putting a focus on money above all else will bring a harder lesson or a "fail" in 2023.

Starting in 2024, we will enter a three-year "push" time of global transition and transformation. Next year is an 8 Universal Year, where money and power take a front seat. Before then, the 7 Universal Year readies us to make wise and spiritually mature decisions.

HOW TO MAKE THE MOST OUT OF THE 7 UNIVERSAL YEAR

1. Slow down.

The energy of the 7 is slow, deep, soul-shifting, and needs time for gradual digestion and integration. Blazing forward "business as usual" is a recipe for some harder lessons to come into play. Think of 2023 as a sabbatical or a retreat. Like academics, we may take time away from our usual duties to study, research and work on a project that will ultimately pay off.

After giving so generously during 2022's 6 Universal Year, we may enter 2023 feeling slightly fatigued and energetically spent. We may be less inclined to socialize or make sacrifices for loved ones. Take time for rest. Reconnect with the natural world and turn inward. Plan, organize, set a wise trajectory and prepare for the major transition cycle starting in 2024 and completing at the end of 2026.

2. Ask the hard questions, dig deep — and be open to the answers.

Have you been avoiding certain pain points and triggers? Brace yourself. They're likely to arise during the 7 Universal Year, begging to be examined. The golden insights of a 7 Universal Year arise when we reflect on our inner workings—then revise and organize as needed.

Despite the call to dive deeper, some of us may surf along superficially during a 7 Universal Year. We may adhere to narrow-minded dogma instead of opening our minds to expanded realms of potentiality. As we butt up against our own edges, feelings of victimization can be heightened. We may cling to outmoded structures that are holding us back from a more evolved existence.

As a global community, it's obvious that we're undergoing massive changes. We are in the midst of a breakdown, which hasn't brought out the best in the human species. While infrastructures crumble (economic, environmental, health care, etc.), the choice appears to be this: Cling to old paradigms or open up to a reinvention of how our entire global community engages and operates.

During the Universal 7 Year, we are *readying* ourselves for a period of major transition. In 2023, we must reevaluate our deepest wants, needs, and values—both individually and as a global community. 2024 will be all about bringing new discoveries and a revised trajectory into the material world. But for now, we have to reflect on the ways we manage our resources and the long-term effect this has on the world at large.

3. *Merging science & intuition.*

The 7 Universal Year accelerates scientific developments. In its skeptical moments, the 7 wants proof. This is a powerful year for discoveries that can be quantified and measured. Ideally, the 7 also brings a beautiful balance between intellect and spirit—the seen and the unseen. The power of the 7 is its ability to bridge the analytic left brain and the intuitive right brain.

4. *Take time for healing — whatever that means to you.*

Numerologist Dr. Juno Jordan suggests that the invitation from the number 7 is for us to develop the "right state of mind." The 7 Universal Year is a Petri dish of opportunity to do some deep, soul-evolving healing. How can we resolve long-held grudges, wounds and affronts? How can we make amends? How can we forgive (without condoning egregious behavior) and move forward? As we heal ourselves individually it impacts the "whole" in a powerful way.

5. Go with the flow.

The highest expression of the energy of the 7 is its uncanny sense of flow and serendipity. In 2023, we are called to surrender to the unknown and embrace that which is out of our control. Developing trust is a worthy challenge in a 7 Universal Year—trust in the Universe, trust in flow, trust in self. We will make missteps, but we are here to learn from them.

Steven Spielberg once said, "Your intuition never shouts. It always whispers." During the 7 Universal Year, create practices that allow you to hear your inner voice. Haul out the meditation pillow and the yoga mat. Get out into nature. Plant your garden and watch it grow. Quiet down. Read a book. Take a class. Unplug from your devices every now and again.

CONCLUSION

The 7 Universal Year supports us in taking a deep dive inward. In the process, we can take leaps in our spiritual growth and evolution—ones that will benefit humankind in the years ahead. ✸

Learn more at astrostyle.com/numerology and feliciabender.com

2023

LUNAR YEAR
OF THE
WATER RABBIT

YEAR OF THE WATER RABBIT

The Year of the Water Rabbit

January 22, 2023 to February 9, 2024

Farewell, fierce Water Tiger! "Soft and fluffy" is 2023's mood when the gentle, emo Water Rabbit hops to the helm as our new lunar ruler.

Top tip for 2023: Try a little tenderness. (Make that a lot of it!) After clawing our way through the cold, competitive energy of 2022's Water Tiger, it's time to change our stripes. Not a moment too soon, the ethereal Water Rabbit arrives to restore us to serenity.

THEMES OF A RABBIT YEAR:

- SERENITY
- ABUNDANCE
- SPIRITUALITY
- CREATIVITY
- HEIGHTENED SENSITIVITY
- EXPRESSING AFFECTION
- DESIRE FOR INTIMATE BONDING
- ESCAPISM
- ADDICTIVE TENDENCIES
- VICTIM MINDSET

The Lunar Calendar & the Year of the Water Rabbit

Rabbit takes the wheel! This galactic changing of guard always takes place on the Chinese (Lunar) New Year. Lunar NYE is celebrated during the annual Aquarius new moon, which is the final day of each year. Note: The timing is based on the lunisolar calendar, not the Gregorian calendar, which is why Lunar New Year's shifts dates annually. In 2023, Lunar NYE—and the Aquarius new moon—arrive on January 21 and New Year's Day is January 22.

The Water Element

In Chinese astrology, any year ending in 2 or 3 is ruled by the water element. Yin in its expression, water brings the energy of deep emotion, creativity, fluidity and fluctuation. Ideally, these are years meant for diving deep, examining feelings and shapeshifting. However, depending on the ruling animal, water can flow hot, cold, icy or steamy.

From Predator to Prey?

Last year's Water Tiger aroused feelings that were reactive and revolutionary. It was anything *but* calm! Conflicts centered around extreme convictions, from the Russia-Ukraine war to the hijab-burnings in Iran to the fight for reproductive rights and fraught U.S. Midterm elections. In our personal lives, many of us bear battle scars from standing up for our principles with neighbors, family and once-close friends. It was indeed the Tiger's jungle out there.

While these ideological wars aren't going to dissipate overnight, the shift on January 22 will be palpable. Think about it: We are flipping from the ultimate predator (Tiger) to the ultimate prey (Rabbit). Suddenly, our sense of safety will be tantamount. Survival instincts: activated!

While Tiger is solitary, Rabbit is social and communal. The emotional dam may break in 2023, bringing an outpouring of empathy. We could drown in feelings of sorrow or victimhood. Or we may just get so overwhelmed that we need trusted allies to pull us out of a hole. That's good reason to huddle with a support network—or to actively go develop one.

Calling all Cuddlebunnies

The affectionate Rabbit loves to cuddle and bond. This is the year to wrap our arms around each other...literally! Studies show that a hug lasting for 20-30 seconds triggers the body to release soothing neurochemicals like oxytocin.

Funny bunny fact: When rabbits are happy, they literally do a full-bodied leap into the air called a "binky." If you've ever witnessed one, we bet it sparked instant joy for you. Go watch one on YouTube and we dare you not to smile!

During this touchy-feely year, we'd all be wise to consider the phenomenon of emotional contagion observed by neuroscientists. Feelings can, er, bunny hop, from person to person, even if we're simply witnessing a facial gesture. Yes, your smile could literally turn someone's frown upside down—or vice versa. So check that RBF!

The Rabbit's Ruling Planet Is Neptune

The Rabbit is ruled by spiritual Neptune and shares traits to the Western zodiac sign of Pisces, the sign that rules illusions, escape, boundlessness and profound visualization. Reality may be a fluid concept in 2023, one we may wish to scurry away from as often as possible.

But this desire comes with a bright red warning label!

Rabbit years are times when our fears are easily triggered. And there are plenty of scary things happening in this fast-changing world, from the climate crisis to inflation to autocrats with nuclear weapons forming alliances. (All when we are still grappling with new strains of COVID and monkeypox...) In 1963, the last Water Rabbit year on the books, JFK was assassinated—and Lee Harvey Oswald shot and killed—stirring up global fears, conspiracy theories and unrest.

To mitigate our overwhelming feelings, we run a high risk of escaping into addictive vices during Water Rabbit years. Yet these Band-Aids only send us plummeting further down the wrong kind of rabbit holes. There's nothing wrong with self-soothing but opt for healthy means of release.

A wise use of Rabbit's Piscean-style energy would be to work on your subconscious mind. Think: guided meditation, binaural beats, hypnotherapy and sleep sanctification. Keep those blue-light-emitting devices out of the bedroom, turn on the soothing music (instead of an agitating streaming series) and pipe in calming scents from an aromatherapy diffuser. Try natural supplements like magnesium or various adaptogenic mushrooms before tucking in. Dreams will be vivid during the Water Rabbit Year, so do what you can to make them sweet.

Follow The Leader?

Because rabbits are skittish, they can be docile and easily manipulated by treats. Metaphorically, Water Rabbit years are times to be extra careful of the carrots being dangled in our path. It's almost too easy to turn to a so-called enlightened master who is actually a master manipulator—or a full-on cult leader. (Three words: Follow the money.) Careful what you get yourself wrapped up in when you're feeling lonely, isolated or in need of a community.

Of course, maybe it's time to amass a metaphoric cult following? For artists, 2023 is prime time for attracting fans. Beatlemania broke out in 1963, the last time we had a Water Rabbit year, with frenzied teens going wild for those four Brits with funny bowl haircuts and boppy ditties about holding hands.

Water, Water Everywhere...

The Water Rabbit can open up more flow: financially, creatively and spiritually. Rabbits are abundant creatures, capable of bearing seven "kits" in five litters every year. Metaphorically, 2023 is a year that's fertile in possibility. Creative financing could afford us opportunities via bartering or shared economic models.

Neptune, the Rabbit's galactic guardian, rules the seas, which are currently in crisis. As we enter 2023, there is much work to be done. Oceans are warming to the tipping point. The watery devastations were massive in 2022: Florida's west coast was ravaged by Hurricane Ian, parts of China's Yangtze River dried up, monsoons flooded India and droughts in the western U.S. brought a surge of forest fires, water shortages and other alarming shifts to weather patterns.

While we hoped that 2022's Water Tiger would spur innovations, solutions remain at large. Perhaps the Rabbit will apply its creativity the process.

Dream A Little (or Not-So-Little) Dream

Rather than fall prey to fear, Rabbit years are powerful times for healing and visualization. In 1963, the prior Water Rabbit Year, Dr. Martin Luther King, Jr. delivered his legendary *I Have a Dream* speech—a Neptunian/Piscean ideal if ever there were.

While addressing deeply rooted racial injustice, King painted a picture of the world he envisaged where "...my four little children will one day live in a nation where they will not be judged by the color of their skin but by the content of their character."

As we enter 2023, we are ready for another dream that, ironically, wakes us up. As much as we might want to tune out, ignore the news and focus on what's convenient, that sort of escapism could be detrimental to our existence as a species.

Manifestation is a powerful tool during the Water Rabbit year, but not if we confuse it with blithe "positive thinking." Problems must be addressed while we hold the vision of a better, brighter future. It's a paradox, but our future as a species might just depend on it. Fortunately, Rabbit years give us great survival instincts. Let's hop to it!

Read more at astrostyle.com/chinese-astrology

2023

EPHEMERIS

JANUARY 2023

January 2023

Longitude & Retrograde Ephemeris [00:00 UT]

Day	Sid.time	☉	☽	+12h☽	☿	♀	♂	♃	♄	♅	♆	♇	☊	☊	⚸	⚷	Day
1 Su	06:41:33	♑10°17'02	♉03°38'57	♉09°58'26	℞ 23°42	♑27°22	℞ 09°03	♈01°11	♒22°25	℞ 15°08	♓22°52	♑27°39	℞ 10°12	♉11°45	♋29°09	♈11°58	1 Su
2 Mo	06:45:30	♑11°18'10	♉16°14'16	♉22°26'36	♑23°05	♑28°38	♊08°54	♈01°18	♒22°31	♉15°07	♓22°53	♑27°41	♉10°09	℞ 11°45	♋29°15	♈11°58	2 Mo
3 Tu	06:49:26	♑12°19'19	♉28°36'12	♊04°43'08	♑22°18	♑29°53	♊08°46	♈01°26	♒22°37	♉15°06	♓22°54	♑27°43	♉10°05	♉11°43	♋29°22	♈11°59	3 Tu
4 We	06:53:23	♑13°20'27	♊10°48'05	♊16°51'02	♑21°19	♒01°08	♊08°38	♈01°34	♒22°43	♉15°05	♓22°55	♑27°45	♉10°02	♉11°39	♋29°29	♈11°59	4 We
5 Th	06:57:20	♑14°21'35	♊22°52'36	♊28°52'43	♑20°12	♒02°23	♊08°32	♈01°41	♒22°49	♉15°04	♓22°56	♑27°47	♉09°59	♉11°32	♋29°35	♈12°00	5 Th
6 Fr	07:01:16	♑15°22'43	♋04°51'53	♋10°50'01	♑18°58	♒03°38	♊08°26	♈01°49	♒22°55	♉15°03	♓22°57	♑27°49	♉09°56	♉11°23	♋29°42	♈12°01	6 Fr
7 Sa	07:05:13	♑16°23'51	♋16°47'33	♋22°44'21	♑17°40	♒04°53	♊08°21	♈01°57	♒23°01	♉15°03	♓22°58	♑27°50	♉09°53	♉11°11	♋29°49	♈12°01	7 Sa
8 Su	07:09:09	♑17°24'59	♋28°40'53	♌04°37'00	♑16°19	♒06°08	♊08°17	♈02°06	♒23°08	♉15°02	♓22°59	♑27°52	♉09°49	♉10°58	♋29°56	♈12°02	8 Su
9 Mo	07:13:06	♑18°26'06	♌10°33'11	♌16°29'19	♑14°59	♒07°23	♊08°13	♈02°14	♒23°14	♉15°01	♓23°00	♑27°54	♉09°46	♉10°44	♌00°02	♈12°03	9 Mo
10 Tu	07:17:02	♑19°27'14	♌22°25'57	♌28°23'01	♑13°42	♒08°38	♊08°10	♈02°22	♒23°21	♉15°00	♓23°02	♑27°56	♉09°43	♉10°32	♌00°09	♈12°04	10 Tu
11 We	07:20:59	♑20°28'21	♍04°21'08	♍10°20'22	♑12°30	♒09°53	♊08°09	♈02°31	♒23°27	♉15°00	♓23°03	♑27°58	♉09°40	♉10°21	♌00°16	♈12°05	11 We
12 Th	07:24:55	♑21°29'29	♍16°21'23	♍22°24'20	♑11°25	♒11°08	♊08°08	♈02°40	♒23°34	♉14°59	♓23°04	♑28°00	♉09°37	♉10°13	♌00°23	♈12°06	12 Th
13 Fr	07:28:52	♑22°30'35	♍28°30'00	♎04°38'36	♑10°29	♒12°23	D 08°07	♈02°49	♒23°40	♉14°59	♓23°05	♑28°02	♉09°34	♉10°07	♌00°29	♈12°07	13 Fr
14 Sa	07:32:49	♑23°31'43	♎10°50'59	♎17°07'27	♑09°42	♒13°38	♊08°08	♈02°58	♒23°47	♉14°58	♓23°07	♑28°04	♉09°30	♉10°05	♌00°36	♈12°08	14 Sa
15 Su	07:36:45	♑24°32'50	♎23°28'51	♎29°55'29	♑09°04	♒14°53	♊08°09	♈03°07	♒23°53	♉14°58	♓23°08	♑28°06	♉09°27	♉10°04	♌00°43	♈12°10	15 Su
16 Mo	07:40:42	♑25°33'56	♏06°28'13	♏13°07'15	♑08°36	♒16°08	♊08°11	♈03°17	♒24°00	♉14°57	♓23°10	♑28°08	♉09°24	D 10°04	♌00°49	♈12°11	16 Mo
17 Tu	07:44:38	♑26°35'03	♏19°53'19	♏26°46'26	♑08°18	♒17°23	♊08°14	♈03°26	♒24°07	♉14°57	♓23°11	♑28°10	♉09°21	℞ 10°04	♌00°56	♈12°12	17 Tu
18 We	07:48:35	♑27°36'10	♐03°47'05	♐10°54'59	♑08°09	♒18°38	♊08°17	♈03°36	♒24°13	♉14°57	♓23°12	♑28°12	♉09°18	♉10°02	♌01°03	♈12°14	18 We
19 Th	07:52:31	♑28°37'17	♐18°10'16	♐25°32'09	D♑08°08	♒19°53	♊08°21	♈03°45	♒24°20	♉14°56	♓23°14	♑28°14	♉09°15	♉09°58	♌01°10	♈12°15	19 Th
20 Fr	07:56:28	♑29°38'23	♑03°00'20	♑10°33'32	♑08°16	♒21°08	♊08°26	♈03°55	♒24°27	♉14°56	♓23°15	♑28°16	♉09°11	♉09°51	♌01°16	♈12°16	20 Fr
21 Sa	08:00:24	♒00°39'28	♑18°10'59	♑25°50'59	♑08°31	♒22°23	♊08°32	♈04°05	♒24°34	♉14°56	♓23°17	♑28°18	♉09°08	♉09°41	♌01°23	♈12°18	21 Sa
22 Su	08:04:21	♒01°40'33	♒03°32'26	♒11°13'26	♑08°53	♒23°38	♊08°38	♈04°15	♒24°41	♉14°56	♓23°18	♑28°20	♉09°05	♉09°29	♌01°30	♈12°19	22 Su
23 Mo	08:08:18	♒02°41'38	♒18°52'49	♒26°28'48	♑09°21	♒24°52	♊08°45	♈04°26	♒24°47	D 14°56	♓23°20	♑28°22	♉09°02	♉09°18	♌01°37	♈12°21	23 Mo
24 Tu	08:12:14	♒03°42'42	♓04°00'28	♓11°26'20	♑09°55	♒26°07	♊08°53	♈04°36	♒24°54	♉14°56	♓23°22	♑28°24	♉08°59	♉09°07	♌01°43	♈12°23	24 Tu
25 We	08:16:11	♒04°43'44	♓18°45'56	♓25°58'17	♑10°34	♒27°22	♊09°01	♈04°46	♒25°01	♉14°56	♓23°23	♑28°26	♉08°55	♉08°59	♌01°50	♈12°24	25 We
26 Th	08:20:07	♒05°44'45	♈03°03'25	♈10°00'50	♑11°18	♒28°37	♊09°10	♈04°57	♒25°08	♉14°56	♓23°25	♑28°28	♉08°52	♉08°53	♌01°57	♈12°26	26 Th
27 Fr	08:24:04	♒06°45'46	♈16°50'56	♈23°33'39	♑12°06	♒29°52	♊09°19	♈05°08	♒25°15	♉14°56	♓23°27	♑28°30	♉08°49	♉08°50	♌02°03	♈12°28	27 Fr
28 Sa	08:28:00	♒07°46'45	♉00°09'41	♉06°39'10	♑12°58	♓01°06	♊09°30	♈05°18	♒25°22	♉14°57	♓23°28	♑28°32	♉08°46	♉08°49	♌02°10	♈12°30	28 Sa
29 Su	08:31:57	♒08°47'44	♉13°02'58	♉19°21'23	♑13°53	♓02°21	♊09°40	♈05°29	♒25°29	♉14°57	♓23°30	♑28°34	♉08°43	♉08°49	♌02°17	♈12°32	29 Su
30 Mo	08:35:53	♒09°48'41	♉25°35'18	♊01°45'03	♑14°52	♓03°36	♊09°52	♈05°40	♒25°36	♉14°57	♓23°32	♑28°35	♉08°40	♉08°49	♌02°24	♈12°34	30 Mo
31 Tu	08:39:50	♒10°49'36	♊07°51'32	♊13°55'00	♑15°53	♓04°50	♊10°04	♈05°52	♒25°43	♉14°58	♓23°34	♑28°37	♉08°36	♉08°47	♌02°30	♈12°36	31 Tu
Δ Delta	01:58:17	30°32'34"	394°12'34"	393°56'34"	-7°48'	37°27'	1°00'	4°40'	3°18'	-0°10'	0°41'	0°58'	-1°35'	-2°58'	3°21'	0°38'	Delta

Ephemeris tables and data provided by **Astro-Seek.com**. All times in UTC.

FEBRUARY 2023

February 2023

Longitude & Retrograde Ephemeris [00:00 UT]

Day	Sid.time	☉	☽	+12h☽	☿	♀	♂	♃	♄	♅	♆	♇	☊	☊	⚸	⚷	Day
1 We	08:43:47	♒11°50'31	♊19°56'16	♊25°55'34	DS 16°57	♓06°05	♊10°16	♈06°03	♒25°51	♉14°58	♓23°35	♑28°39	℞ 08°33	℞ 08°42	♌02°37	♈12°38	1 We
2 Th	08:47:43	♒12°51'25	♋01°53'37	♋07°50'31	♑18°03	♓07°19	♊10°29	♈06°14	♒25°58	♉14°59	♓23°37	♑28°41	♉08°30	♉08°34	♌02°44	♈12°40	2 Th
3 Fr	08:51:40	♒13°52'17	♋13°46'56	♋19°42'50	♑19°11	♓08°34	♊10°43	♈06°26	♒26°05	♉14°59	♓23°39	♑28°43	♉08°27	♉08°24	♌02°50	♈12°42	3 Fr
4 Sa	08:55:36	♒14°53'08	♋25°38'48	♌01°34'46	♑20°22	♓09°48	♊10°57	♈06°37	♒26°12	♉15°00	♓23°41	♑28°45	♉08°24	♉08°10	♌02°57	♈12°44	4 Sa
5 Su	08:59:33	♒15°53'58	♌07°31'11	♌13°27'56	♑21°34	♓11°03	♊11°11	♈06°49	♒26°19	♉15°00	♓23°43	♑28°47	♉08°21	♉07°56	♌03°04	♈12°46	5 Su
6 Mo	09:03:29	♒16°54'46	♌19°25'29	♌25°23'40	♑22°48	♓12°17	♊11°26	♈07°00	♒26°26	♉15°01	♓23°45	♑28°49	♉08°17	♉07°41	♌03°11	♈12°48	6 Mo
7 Tu	09:07:26	♒17°55'33	♍01°22'54	♍07°23'04	♑24°04	♓13°32	♊11°42	♈07°12	♒26°34	♉15°02	♓23°47	♑28°51	♉08°14	♉07°27	♌03°17	♈12°51	7 Tu
8 We	09:11:22	♒18°56'20	♍13°24'38	♍19°27'30	D 25°21	♓14°46	♊11°58	♈07°24	♒26°41	♉15°03	♓23°49	♑28°53	♉08°11	♉07°15	♌03°24	♈12°53	8 We
9 Th	09:15:19	♒19°57'05	♍25°32'12	♎01°38'41	♑26°40	♓16°00	♊12°15	♈07°36	♒26°48	♉15°04	♓23°50	♑28°55	♉08°08	♉07°05	♌03°31	♈12°55	9 Th
10 Fr	09:19:16	♒20°57'49	♎07°47'36	♎13°58'58	♑27°59	♓17°15	♊12°31	♈07°48	♒26°55	♉15°04	♓23°52	♑28°56	♉08°05	♉06°59	♌03°38	♈12°58	10 Fr
11 Sa	09:23:12	♒21°58'32	♎20°13'30	♎26°31'19	♑29°21	♓18°29	♊12°49	♈08°00	♒27°02	♉15°05	♓23°54	♑28°58	♉08°01	♉06°56	♌03°44	♈13°00	11 Sa
12 Su	09:27:09	♒22°59'13	♏02°53'12	♏09°19'17	♒00°43	♓19°43	♊13°07	♈08°12	♒27°10	♉15°06	♓23°56	♑29°00	♉07°58	♉06°55	♌03°51	♈13°03	12 Su
13 Mo	09:31:05	♒23°59'54	♏15°50'22	♏22°26'36	♒02°07	♓20°57	♊13°25	♈08°25	♒27°17	♉15°08	♓23°58	♑29°02	♉07°55	D 06°55	♌03°58	♈13°05	13 Mo
14 Tu	09:35:02	♒25°00'34	♏29°08'45	♐05°56'50	♒03°31	♓22°11	♊13°43	♈08°37	♒27°24	♉15°09	♓24°00	♑29°04	♉07°52	℞ 06°55	♌04°04	♈13°08	14 Tu
15 We	09:38:58	♒26°01'13	♐12°51'28	♐19°52'29	♒04°57	♓23°25	♊14°02	♈08°50	♒27°31	♉15°10	♓24°03	♑29°05	♉07°49	♉06°54	♌04°11	♈13°10	15 We
16 Th	09:42:55	♒27°01'50	♐27°00'13	♑04°14'08	♒06°24	♓24°39	♊14°22	♈09°02	♒27°39	♉15°11	♓24°05	♑29°07	♉07°46	♉06°50	♌04°18	♈13°13	16 Th
17 Fr	09:46:51	♒28°02'27	♑11°34'14	♑18°59'34	♒07°52	♓25°53	♊14°42	♈09°15	♒27°46	♉15°12	♓24°07	♑29°09	♉07°42	♉06°45	♌04°25	♈13°16	17 Fr
18 Sa	09:50:48	♒29°03'02	♑26°29'39	♒04°03'07	♒09°20	♓27°07	♊15°02	♈09°28	♒27°53	♉15°14	♓24°09	♑29°11	♉07°39	♉06°36	♌04°31	♈13°18	18 Sa
19 Su	09:54:45	♓00°03'36	♒11°39'09	♒19°16'03	♒10°50	♓28°21	♊15°22	♈09°40	♒28°00	♉15°15	♓24°11	♑29°13	♉07°36	♉06°26	♌04°38	♈13°21	19 Su
20 Mo	09:58:41	♓01°04'09	♒26°52'47	♓04°27'35	♒12°21	♓29°35	♊15°43	♈09°53	♒28°08	♉15°16	♓24°13	♑29°14	♉07°33	♉06°16	♌04°45	♈13°24	20 Mo
21 Tu	10:02:38	♓02°04'39	♓11°59'30	♓19°26'56	♒13°53	♈00°49	♊16°04	♈10°06	♒28°15	♉15°18	♓24°15	♑29°16	♉07°30	♉06°07	♌04°51	♈13°27	21 Tu
22 We	10:06:34	♓03°05'08	♓26°49'14	♈04°05'10	♒15°26	♈02°03	♊16°26	♈10°19	♒28°22	♉15°19	♓24°17	♑29°18	♉07°27	♉05°59	♌04°58	♈13°30	22 We
23 Th	10:10:31	♓04°05'36	♈11°14'30	♈18°16'29	♒16°59	♈03°16	♊16°48	♈10°32	♒28°29	♉15°21	♓24°19	♑29°19	♉07°23	♉05°54	♌05°05	♈13°32	23 Th
24 Fr	10:14:27	♓05°06'01	♈25°11'17	♉01°58'36	♒18°34	♈04°30	♊17°10	♈10°45	♒28°37	♉15°23	♓24°22	♑29°21	♉07°20	♉05°51	♌05°12	♈13°35	24 Fr
25 Sa	10:18:24	♓06°06'25	♉08°38'57	♉15°12'19	♒20°10	♈05°44	♊17°33	♈10°58	♒28°44	♉15°24	♓24°24	♑29°23	♉07°17	D 05°51	♌05°18	♈13°38	25 Sa
26 Su	10:22:20	♓07°06'47	♉21°39'28	♉28°00'36	♒21°46	♈06°57	♊17°56	♈11°12	♒28°51	♉15°26	♓24°26	♑29°24	♉07°14	♉05°52	♌05°25	♈13°41	26 Su
27 Mo	10:26:17	♓08°07'06	♊04°16'38	♊10°27'50	♒23°24	♈08°11	♊18°19	♈11°25	♒28°58	♉15°28	♓24°28	♑29°26	♉07°11	♉05°52	♌05°32	♈13°44	27 Mo
28 Tu	10:30:14	♓09°07'24	♊16°35'09	♊22°38'56	♒25°02	♈09°24	♊18°42	♈11°38	♒29°06	♉15°29	♓24°30	♑29°28	♉07°07	℞ 05°52	♌05°39	♈13°47	28 Tu
Δ Delta	01:46:27	27°16'53"	-356°38'53"	-356°43'21"	38°05'	-33°19'	8°26'	5°35'	3°14'	0°31'	0°55'	0°48'	-1°25'	-2°49'	3°01'	1°09'	Delta

March 2023

Longitude & Retrograde Ephemeris [00:00 UT]

Day	Sid.time	☉	☽	+12h☽	☿	♀	♂	♃	♄	♅	♆	♇	☊	☊	⚸	⚷	Day
1 We	10:34:10	♓10°07'40	♊28°40'04	♋04°38'53	♒26°42	♈10°38	♊19°06	♈11°52	♒29°13	♉15°31	♓24°33	♑29°29	℞ 07°04	℞ 05°50	♌05°45	♈13°50	1 We
2 Th	10:38:07	♓11°07'54	♋10°36'13	♋16°32'20	♒28°23	♈11°51	♊19°30	♈12°05	♒29°20	♉15°33	♓24°35	♑29°31	♉07°01	♉05°46	♌05°52	♈13°53	2 Th
3 Fr	10:42:03	♓12°08'06	♋22°27'59	♋28°23'21	♓00°04	♈13°04	♊19°54	♈12°19	♒29°27	♉15°35	♓24°37	♑29°32	♉06°58	♉05°39	♌05°59	♈13°56	3 Fr
4 Sa	10:45:60	♓13°08'16	♌04°19'06	♌10°15'17	♓01°47	♈14°18	♊20°19	♈12°32	♒29°34	♉15°37	♓24°39	♑29°34	♉06°55	♉05°30	♌06°05	♈14°00	4 Sa
5 Su	10:49:56	♓14°08'24	♌16°12'32	♌22°10'48	♓03°31	♈15°31	♊20°44	♈12°46	♒29°41	♉15°39	♓24°42	♑29°35	♉06°52	♉05°21	♌06°12	♈14°03	5 Su
6 Mo	10:53:53	♓15°08'30	♌28°10'36	♍04°11'49	♓05°16	♈16°44	♊21°09	♈12°59	♒29°48	♉15°41	♓24°44	♑29°37	♉06°48	♉05°11	♌06°19	♈14°06	6 Mo
7 Tu	10:57:49	♓16°08'34	♍10°14'56	♍16°19'45	♓07°01	♈17°57	♊21°34	♈13°13	♒29°56	♉15°43	♓24°46	♑29°38	♉06°45	♉05°01	♌06°26	♈14°09	7 Tu
8 We	11:01:46	♓17°08'36	♍22°26'44	♍28°35'40	♓08°48	♈19°10	♊22°00	♈13°27	♓00°03	♉15°45	♓24°48	♑29°40	♉06°42	♉04°53	♌06°32	♈14°12	8 We
9 Th	11:05:43	♓18°08'36	♎04°46'59	♎11°00'30	♓10°37	♈20°23	♊22°25	♈13°41	♓00°10	♉15°47	♓24°51	♑29°41	♉06°39	♉04°47	♌06°39	♈14°15	9 Th
10 Fr	11:09:39	♓19°08'35	♎17°16'41	♎23°35'22	♓12°26	♈21°36	♊22°51	♈13°54	♓00°17	♉15°50	♓24°53	♑29°43	♉06°36	♉04°43	♌06°46	♈14°19	10 Fr
11 Sa	11:13:36	♓20°08'31	♎29°57'02	♏06°21'36	♓14°16	♈22°49	♊23°18	♈14°08	♓00°24	♉15°52	♓24°55	♑29°44	♉06°32	♉04°41	♌06°53	♈14°22	11 Sa
12 Su	11:17:32	♓21°08'26	♏12°49'35	♏19°20'56	♓16°08	♈24°01	♊23°44	♈14°22	♓00°31	♉15°54	♓24°57	♑29°45	♉06°29	D 04°41	♌06°59	♈14°25	12 Su
13 Mo	11:21:29	♓22°08'20	♏25°56'12	♐02°35'20	♓18°00	♈25°14	♊24°11	♈14°36	♓00°38	♉15°57	♓25°00	♑29°47	♉06°26	♉04°43	♌07°06	♈14°29	13 Mo
14 Tu	11:25:25	♓23°08'11	♐09°18'53	♐16°06'45	♓19°54	♈26°26	♊24°38	♈14°50	♓00°44	♉15°59	♓25°02	♑29°48	♉06°23	♉04°44	♌07°13	♈14°32	14 Tu
15 We	11:29:22	♓24°08'02	♐22°59'26	♐29°56'41	♓21°49	♈27°39	♊25°05	♈15°04	♓00°51	♉16°01	♓25°04	♑29°49	♉06°20	♉04°45	♌07°19	♈14°35	15 We
16 Th	11:33:18	♓25°07'50	♑06°58'51	♑14°05'30	♓23°44	♈28°51	♊25°32	♈15°18	♓00°58	♉16°04	♓25°06	♑29°51	♉06°17	℞ 04°44	♌07°26	♈14°39	16 Th
17 Fr	11:37:15	♓26°07'37	♑21°16'46	♑28°31'55	♓25°41	♉00°04	♊25°59	♈15°32	♓01°05	♉16°06	♓25°09	♑29°52	♉06°13	♉04°42	♌07°33	♈14°42	17 Fr
18 Sa	11:41:12	♓27°07'22	♒05°50'48	♒13°12'25	♓27°39	♉01°16	♊26°27	♈15°46	♓01°12	♉16°09	♓25°11	♑29°53	♉06°10	♉04°38	♌07°40	♈14°45	18 Sa
19 Su	11:45:08	♓28°07'05	♒20°36'19	♒28°01'15	♓29°38	♉02°28	♊26°55	♈16°01	♓01°19	♉16°11	♓25°13	♑29°54	♉06°07	♉04°33	♌07°46	♈14°49	19 Su
20 Mo	11:49:05	♓29°06'47	♓05°26'36	♓12°50'58	♈01°37	♉03°41	♊27°23	♈16°15	♓01°25	♉16°14	♓25°16	♑29°56	♉06°04	♉04°27	♌07°53	♈14°52	20 Mo
21 Tu	11:53:01	♈00°06'27	♓20°13'42	♓27°33'25	♈03°37	♉04°53	♊27°51	♈16°29	♓01°32	♉16°17	♓25°18	♑29°57	♉06°01	♉04°22	♌08°00	♈14°56	21 Tu
22 We	11:56:58	♈01°06'04	♈04°49'34	♈12°01'00	♈05°38	♉06°05	♊28°19	♈16°43	♓01°39	♉16°19	♓25°20	♑29°58	♉05°58	♉04°18	♌08°06	♈14°59	22 We
23 Th	12:00:54	♈02°05'40	♈19°07'23	♈26°07'51	♈07°39	♉07°17	♊28°48	♈16°58	♓01°45	♉16°22	♓25°22	♑29°59	♉05°54	♉04°16	♌08°13	♈15°03	23 Th
24 Fr	12:04:51	♈03°05'13	♉03°02'26	♉09°50'33	♈09°40	♉08°28	♊29°16	♈17°12	♓01°52	♉16°25	♓25°25	♒00°00	♉05°51	♉04°15	♌08°20	♈15°06	24 Fr
25 Sa	12:08:47	♈04°04'45	♉16°32'30	♉23°08'04	♈11°40	♉09°40	♊29°45	♈17°26	♓01°58	♉16°27	♓25°27	♒00°01	♉05°48	D 04°15	♌08°27	♈15°09	25 Sa
26 Su	12:12:44	♈05°04'14	♉29°37'47	♊06°01'39	♈13°41	♉10°52	♋00°14	♈17°40	♓02°05	♉16°30	♓25°29	♒00°02	♉05°45	♉04°17	♌08°33	♈15°13	26 Su
27 Mo	12:16:41	♈06°03'41	♊12°20'23	♊18°34'09	♈15°41	♉12°03	♋00°43	♈17°55	♓02°11	♉16°33	♓25°31	♒00°03	♉05°42	♉04°18	♌08°40	♈15°16	27 Mo
28 Tu	12:20:37	♈07°03'05	♊24°43'48	♋00°49'35	♈17°40	♉13°15	♋01°13	♈18°09	♓02°18	♉16°36	♓25°34	♒00°04	♉05°38	♉04°20	♌08°47	♈15°20	28 Tu
29 We	12:24:34	♈08°02'28	♋06°52'24	♋12°52'31	♈19°37	♉14°26	♋01°42	♈18°24	♓02°24	♉16°39	♓25°36	♒00°05	♉05°35	♉04°20	♌08°54	♈15°23	29 We
30 Th	12:28:30	♈09°01'48	♋18°50'52	♋24°47'44	♈21°33	♉15°38	♋02°12	♈18°38	♓02°31	♉16°42	♓25°38	♒00°06	♉05°32	℞ 04°20	♌09°00	♈15°27	30 Th
31 Fr	12:32:27	♈10°01'05	♌00°43'58	♌06°39'51	♈23°26	♉16°49	♋02°42	♈18°52	♓02°37	♉16°44	♓25°40	♒00°07	♉05°29	♉04°18	♌09°07	♈15°31	31 Fr
Δ Delta	01:58:16	-29°53'25"	392°03'53"	392°00'58"	-56°44'	36°11'	13°35'	7°00'	3°24'	1°13'	1°07'	0°37'	-1°35'	-1°31'	3°21'	1°40'	Delta

APRIL 2023

April 2023

Longitude & Retrograde Ephemeris [00:00 UT]

Day	Sid.time	☉	☽	+12h ☽	☿	♀	♂	♃	♄	♅	♆	♇	☊	☊	⚸	⚷	Day
1 Sa	12:36:23	♈11°00'21	♌12°36'11	♌18°33'10	♈25°17	♉18°00	♋03°12	♈19°07	♓02°43	♉16°47	♓25°43	♒00°08	℞ 05°26	℞ 04°16	♌09°14	♈15°34	1 Sa
2 Su	12:40:20	♈11°59'34	♌24°31'32	♍00°31'24	♈27°05	♉19°11	♋03°42	♈19°21	♓02°49	♉16°50	♓25°45	♒00°09	♉05°23	♉04°12	♌09°20	♈15°38	2 Su
3 Mo	12:44:16	♈12°58'45	♍06°33'26	♍12°37'38	♈28°50	♉20°22	♋04°12	♈19°36	♓02°55	♉16°53	♓25°47	♒00°10	♉05°19	♉04°09	♌09°27	♈15°41	3 Mo
4 Tu	12:48:13	♈13°57'53	♍18°44'36	♍24°54'14	♉00°31	♉21°33	♋04°42	♈19°50	♓03°01	♉16°56	♓25°49	♒00°10	♉05°16	♉04°06	♌09°34	♈15°45	4 Tu
5 We	12:52:09	♈14°57'00	♎01°07'02	♎07°22'49	♉02°08	♉22°44	♋05°12	♈20°05	♓03°08	♉16°59	♓25°51	♒00°11	♉05°13	♉04°03	♌09°41	♈15°48	5 We
6 Th	12:56:06	♈15°56'04	♎13°42'00	♎20°04'19	♉03°41	♉23°54	♋05°43	♈20°19	♓03°14	♉17°02	♓25°54	♒00°12	♉05°10	♉04°01	♌09°47	♈15°52	6 Th
7 Fr	13:00:03	♈16°55'07	♎26°30'08	♏02°59'07	♉05°08	♉25°05	♋06°14	♈20°33	♓03°19	♉17°06	♓25°56	♒00°13	♉05°07	♉04°00	♌09°54	♈15°55	7 Fr
8 Sa	13:03:59	♈17°54'07	♏09°31'36	♏16°07'12	℞s 06°31	♉26°15	♋06°44	♈20°48	♓03°25	♉17°09	♓25°58	♒00°13	♉05°04	D 04°00	♌10°01	♈15°59	8 Sa
9 Su	13:07:56	♈18°53'06	♏22°46'13	♏29°28'15	♉07°49	♉27°25	♋07°15	♈21°02	♓03°31	♉17°12	♓26°00	♒00°14	♉05°00	♉04°00	♌10°07	♈16°02	9 Su
10 Mo	13:11:52	♈19°52'02	♐06°13'36	♐13°01'51	♉09°01	♉28°35	♋07°46	♈21°17	♓03°37	♉17°15	♓26°02	♒00°15	♉04°57	♉04°01	♌10°14	♈16°06	10 Mo
11 Tu	13:15:49	♈20°50'57	♐19°53'16	♐26°47'24	♉10°07	♉29°46	♋08°17	♈21°31	♓03°43	♉17°18	♓26°04	♒00°15	♉04°54	♉04°03	♌10°21	♈16°09	11 Tu
12 We	13:19:45	♈21°49'50	♑03°44'31	♑10°44'07	♉11°08	♊00°55	♋08°48	♈21°46	♓03°48	♉17°21	♓26°06	♒00°16	♉04°51	♉04°03	♌10°28	♈16°13	12 We
13 Th	13:23:42	♈22°48'42	♑17°46'24	♑24°50'50	♉12°02	♊02°05	♋09°20	♈22°00	♓03°54	♉17°25	♓26°08	♒00°16	♉04°48	♉04°04	♌10°34	♈16°16	13 Th
14 Fr	13:27:38	♈23°47'32	♒01°57'31	♒09°05'48	♉12°51	♊03°15	♋09°51	♈22°15	♓04°00	♉17°28	♓26°11	♒00°17	♉04°44	℞ 04°04	♌10°41	♈16°20	14 Fr
15 Sa	13:31:35	♈24°46'20	♒16°15'42	♒23°26'27	♉13°33	♊04°25	♋10°23	♈22°29	♓04°05	♉17°31	♓26°13	♒00°17	♉04°41	♉04°03	♌10°48	♈16°23	15 Sa
16 Su	13:35:32	♈25°45'06	♓00°37'59	♓07°49'24	♉14°09	♊05°34	♋10°54	♈22°44	♓04°10	♉17°34	♓26°15	♒00°18	♉04°38	♉04°03	♌10°55	♈16°27	16 Su
17 Mo	13:39:28	♈26°43'51	♓15°00'33	♓22°10'30	♉14°39	♊06°43	♋11°26	♈22°58	♓04°16	♉17°38	♓26°17	♒00°18	♉04°35	♉04°02	♌11°01	♈16°30	17 Mo
18 Tu	13:43:25	♈27°42'34	♓29°18'59	♈06°25'06	♉15°03	♊07°53	♋11°58	♈23°13	♓04°21	♉17°41	♓26°19	♒00°19	♉04°32	♉04°01	♌11°08	♈16°34	18 Tu
19 We	13:47:21	♈28°41'15	♈13°28'39	♈20°28'43	♉15°20	♊09°02	♋12°30	♈23°27	♓04°26	♉17°44	♓26°21	♒00°19	♉04°29	♉04°00	♌11°15	♈16°37	19 We
20 Th	13:51:18	♈29°39'54	♈27°25'12	♉04°17'20	♉15°31	♊10°11	♋13°02	♈23°42	♓04°31	♉17°48	♓26°23	♒00°19	♉04°25	♉04°00	♌11°21	♈16°41	20 Th
21 Fr	13:55:14	♉00°38'31	♉11°05'08	♉17°48'01	♉15°36	♊11°20	♋13°34	♈23°56	♓04°37	♉17°51	♓26°25	♒00°20	♉04°22	D 04°00	♌11°28	♈16°44	21 Fr
22 Sa	13:59:11	♉01°37'06	♉24°26'11	♊00°59'14	℞ 15°36	♊12°28	♋14°06	♈24°10	♓04°42	♉17°54	♓26°27	♒00°20	♉04°19	♉04°00	♌11°35	♈16°48	22 Sa
23 Su	14:03:07	♉02°35'40	♊07°27'31	♊13°50'51	♉15°29	♊13°37	♋14°38	♈24°25	♓04°47	♉17°58	♓26°29	♒00°20	♉04°16	♉04°00	♌11°42	♈16°51	23 Su
24 Mo	14:07:04	♉03°34'12	♊20°09'45	♊26°24'11	♉15°17	♊14°45	♋15°11	♈24°39	♓04°52	♉18°01	♓26°30	♒00°20	♉04°13	♉04°01	♌11°48	♈16°55	24 Mo
25 Tu	14:11:01	♉04°32'41	♋02°34'49	♋08°41'44	♉15°00	♊15°54	♋15°43	♈24°54	♓04°56	♉18°04	♓26°32	♒00°21	♉04°10	℞ 04°01	♌11°55	♈16°58	25 Tu
26 We	14:14:57	♉05°31'08	♋14°45'42	♋20°46'56	♉14°38	♊17°02	♋16°16	♈25°08	♓05°01	♉18°08	♓26°34	♒00°21	♉04°06	♉04°00	♌12°02	♈17°01	26 We
27 Th	14:18:54	♉06°29'33	♋26°46'15	♌02°43'55	♉14°12	♊18°10	♋16°48	♈25°22	♓05°06	♉18°11	♓26°36	♒00°21	♉04°03	♉04°00	♌12°09	♈17°05	27 Th
28 Fr	14:22:50	♉07°27'56	♌08°40'47	♌14°37'09	♉13°42	♊19°18	♋17°21	♈25°37	♓05°10	♉18°15	♓26°38	♒00°21	♉04°00	D 04°00	♌12°15	♈17°08	28 Fr
29 Sa	14:26:47	♉08°26'17	♌20°33'54	♌26°31'17	♉13°09	♊20°25	♋17°54	♈25°51	♓05°15	♉18°18	♓26°40	♒00°21	♉03°57	♉04°00	♌12°22	♈17°11	29 Sa
30 Su	14:30:43	♉09°24'35	♍02°30'11	♍08°30'50	♉12°34	♊21°33	♋18°26	♈26°05	♓05°19	♉18°22	♓26°42	♒00°21	♉03°54	♉04°01	♌12°29	♈17°15	30 Su
Δ Delta	01:54:19	28°24'14"	379°54'00"	379°57'40"	17°16'	33°32'	15°14'	6°58'	2°36'	1°34'	0°58'	0°13'	-1°32'	-0°15'	3°14'	1°40'	Delta

MAY 2023

May 2023

Longitude & Retrograde Ephemeris [00:00 UT]

Day	Sid.time	☉	☽	+12h☽	☿	♀	♂	♃	♄	♅	♆	♇	☊	☊	⚸	⚷	Day
1 Mo	14:34:40	♉10°22'52	♍14°34'03	♍20°39'59	℞ 11°57	♊22°40	♋18°59	♈26°19	♓05°24	♉18°25	♓26°43	♒00°21	℞ 03°50	♉04°01	♌12°35	♈17°18	1 Mo
2 Tu	14:38:36	♉11°21'07	♍26°49'24	♎03°02'20	♉11°18	♊23°47	♋19°32	♈26°34	♓05°28	♉18°29	♓26°45	℞ 00°21	♉03°47	♉04°02	♌12°42	♈17°21	2 Tu
3 We	14:42:33	♉12°19'19	♎09°19'28	♎15°40'42	♉10°40	♊24°54	♋20°05	♈26°48	♓05°32	♉18°32	♓26°47	♒00°21	♉03°44	♉04°03	♌12°49	♈17°25	3 We
4 Th	14:46:30	♉13°17'30	♎22°06'33	♎28°36'50	♉10°01	♊26°01	♋20°39	♈27°02	♓05°36	♉18°35	♓26°49	♒00°21	♉03°41	♉04°03	♌12°56	♈17°28	4 Th
5 Fr	14:50:26	♉14°15'39	♏05°11'52	♏11°51'19	♉09°23	♊27°07	♋21°12	♈27°16	♓05°41	♉18°39	♓26°50	♒00°21	♉03°38	℞ 04°03	♌13°02	♈17°31	5 Fr
6 Sa	14:54:23	♉15°13'46	♏18°35'21	♏25°23'27	♉08°47	♊28°14	♋21°45	♈27°30	♓05°45	♉18°42	♓26°52	♒00°21	♉03°35	♉04°03	♌13°09	♈17°34	6 Sa
7 Su	14:58:19	♉16°11'52	♐02°15'40	♐09°11'19	♉08°13	♊29°20	♋22°18	♈27°44	♓05°48	♉18°46	♓26°54	♒00°21	♉03°31	♉04°02	♌13°16	♈17°38	7 Su
8 Mo	15:02:16	♉17°09'56	♐16°10'21	♐23°11'58	♉07°42	♋00°26	♋22°52	♈27°58	♓05°52	♉18°49	♓26°55	♒00°21	♉03°28	♉04°01	♌13°22	♈17°41	8 Mo
9 Tu	15:06:12	♉18°07'59	♑00°16'04	♑07°21'48	♉07°14	♋01°32	♋23°25	♈28°12	♓05°56	♉18°53	♓26°57	♒00°21	♉03°25	♉03°59	♌13°29	♈17°44	9 Tu
10 We	15:10:09	♉19°06'00	♑14°29'03	♑21°36'59	♉06°50	♋02°37	♋23°59	♈28°26	♓06°00	♉18°56	♓26°58	♒00°20	♉03°22	♉03°57	♌13°36	♈17°47	10 We
11 Th	15:14:05	♉20°04'00	♑28°45'29	♒05°53'48	♉06°29	♋03°43	♋24°32	♈28°40	♓06°03	♉19°00	♓27°00	♒00°20	♉03°19	♉03°56	♌13°43	♈17°50	11 Th
12 Fr	15:18:02	♉21°01'58	♒13°01'53	♒20°09'02	♉06°13	♋04°48	♋25°06	♈28°54	♓06°07	♉19°03	♓27°01	♒00°20	♉03°16	♉03°55	♌13°49	♈17°53	12 Fr
13 Sa	15:21:59	♉21°59'55	♒27°15'18	♓04°20'03	♉06°01	♋05°53	♋25°40	♈29°08	♓06°10	♉19°07	♓27°03	♒00°20	♉03°12	D 03°55	♌13°56	♈17°56	13 Sa
14 Su	15:25:55	♉22°57'51	♓11°23'22	♓18°24'42	♉05°53	♋06°57	♋26°13	♈29°22	♓06°14	♉19°10	♓27°04	♒00°19	♉03°09	♉03°56	♌14°03	♈17°59	14 Su
15 Mo	15:29:52	♉23°55'46	♓25°24'12	♈02°21'19	♉05°51	♋08°02	♋26°47	♈29°36	♓06°17	♉19°14	♓27°06	♒00°19	♉03°06	♉03°57	♌14°10	♈18°02	15 Mo
16 Tu	15:33:48	♉24°53'39	♈09°16'13	♈16°08'22	D 05°52	♋09°06	♋27°21	♈29°50	♓06°20	♉19°17	♓27°07	♒00°19	♉03°03	♉03°58	♌14°16	♈18°05	16 Tu
17 We	15:37:45	♉25°51'31	♈22°57'58	♈29°44'29	♉05°59	♋10°10	♋27°55	♉00°03	♓06°23	♉19°21	♓27°09	♒00°18	♉03°00	♉03°59	♌14°23	♈18°08	17 We
18 Th	15:41:41	♉26°49'22	♉06°28'06	♉13°08'20	♉06°09	♋11°14	♋28°29	♉00°17	♓06°26	♉19°24	♓27°10	♒00°18	♉02°56	℞ 04°00	♌14°30	♈18°11	18 Th
19 Fr	15:45:38	♉27°47'12	♉19°45'22	♉26°18'45	♉06°25	♋12°17	♋29°03	♉00°31	♓06°29	♉19°27	♓27°11	♒00°17	♉02°53	♉03°59	♌14°36	♈18°14	19 Fr
20 Sa	15:49:34	♉28°45'00	♊02°48'43	♊09°14'53	♉06°45	♋13°20	♋29°37	♉00°44	♓06°32	♉19°31	♓27°13	♒00°17	♉02°50	♉03°57	♌14°43	♈18°17	20 Sa
21 Su	15:53:31	♉29°42'47	♊15°37'35	♊21°56'29	♉07°09	♋14°23	♌00°12	♉00°58	♓06°35	♉19°34	♓27°14	♒00°16	♉02°47	♉03°54	♌14°50	♈18°20	21 Su
22 Mo	15:57:28	♊00°40'32	♊28°12'00	♋04°23'57	♉07°37	♋15°26	♌00°46	♉01°11	♓06°37	♉19°38	♓27°15	♒00°16	♉02°44	♉03°49	♌14°57	♈18°23	22 Mo
23 Tu	16:01:24	♊01°38'16	♋10°32'52	♋16°38'38	♉08°10	♋16°28	♌01°20	♉01°25	♓06°40	♉19°41	♓27°16	♒00°15	♉02°41	♉03°45	♌15°03	♈18°25	23 Tu
24 We	16:05:21	♊02°35'59	♋22°41'54	♋28°42'43	♉08°46	♋17°30	♌01°55	♉01°38	♓06°42	♉19°45	♓27°18	♒00°15	♉02°37	♉03°40	♌15°10	♈18°28	24 We
25 Th	16:09:17	♊03°33'40	♌04°41'47	♌10°39'14	♉09°26	♋18°32	♌02°29	♉01°51	♓06°45	♉19°48	♓27°19	♒00°14	♉02°34	♉03°36	♌15°17	♈18°31	25 Th
26 Fr	16:13:14	♊04°31'19	♌16°35'54	♌22°32'00	♉10°11	♋19°33	♌03°03	♉02°05	♓06°47	♉19°51	♓27°20	♒00°13	♉02°31	♉03°34	♌15°23	♈18°34	26 Fr
27 Sa	16:17:10	♊05°28'57	♌28°28'23	♍04°25'20	♉10°58	♋20°34	♌03°38	♉02°18	♓06°49	♉19°55	♓27°21	♒00°13	♉02°28	♉03°32	♌15°30	♈18°36	27 Sa
28 Su	16:21:07	♊06°26'34	♍10°23'45	♍16°23'58	♉11°50	♋21°35	♌04°13	♉02°31	♓06°51	♉19°58	♓27°22	♒00°12	♉02°25	D 03°32	♌15°37	♈18°39	28 Su
29 Mo	16:25:04	♊07°24'09	♍22°26'52	♍28°32'44	♉12°45	♋22°35	♌04°47	♉02°44	♓06°53	♉20°02	♓27°23	♒00°11	♉02°21	♉03°33	♌15°44	♈18°41	29 Mo
30 Tu	16:29:00	♊08°21'42	♎04°42'29	♎10°56'18	♉13°43	♋23°35	♌05°22	♉02°57	♓06°55	♉20°05	♓27°24	♒00°10	♉02°18	♉03°34	♌15°50	♈18°44	30 Tu
31 We	16:32:57	♊09°19'14	♎17°15'02	♎23°38'47	♉14°44	♋24°35	♌05°57	♉03°10	♓06°57	♉20°08	♓27°25	♒00°10	♉02°15	♉03°36	♌15°57	♈18°46	31 We
Δ Delta	01:58:17	28°56'22"	392°40'59"	392°58'47"	2°47'	31°54'	16°57'	6°50'	1°32'	1°43'	0°41'	-0°11'	-1°35'	-0°25'	3°21'	1°28'	Delta

Ephemeris tables and data provided by **Astro-Seek.com**. All times in UTC.

JUNE 2023

June 2023

Longitude & Retrograde Ephemeris [00:00 UT]

Day	Sid.time	☉	☽	+12h ☽	☿	♀	♂	♃	♄	♅	♆	♇	☊	☊	⚸	⚷	Day
1 Th	16:36:53	♊10°16'45	♏00°08'13	♏06°43'16	♉15°49	♋25°34	♌06°31	♉03°23	♓06°58	♉20°12	♓27°26	℞ 00°09	℞ 02°12	♉03°37	♌16°04	♈18°49	1 Th
2 Fr	16:40:50	♊11°14'15	♏13°24'26	♏20°11'23	♉16°56	♋26°33	♌07°06	♉03°36	♓07°00	♉20°15	♓27°27	♒00°08	♉02°09	℞ 03°37	♌16°10	♈18°51	2 Fr
3 Sa	16:44:46	♊12°11'43	♏27°04'23	♐04°02'49	♉18°07	♋27°31	♌07°41	♉03°49	♓07°01	♉20°18	♓27°28	♒00°07	♉02°06	♉03°35	♌16°17	♈18°54	3 Sa
4 Su	16:48:43	♊13°09'11	♐11°06'39	♐18°14'59	♉19°21	♋28°29	♌08°16	♉04°02	♓07°03	♉20°21	♓27°29	♒00°06	♉02°02	♉03°31	♌16°24	♈18°56	4 Su
5 Mo	16:52:39	♊14°06'37	♐25°27'32	♑02°43'10	♉20°38	♋29°27	♌08°51	♉04°14	♓07°04	♉20°25	♓27°30	♒00°06	♉01°59	♉03°26	♌16°31	♈18°58	5 Mo
6 Tu	16:56:36	♊15°04'03	♑10°01'23	♑17°20'56	♉21°57	♌00°24	♌09°26	♉04°27	♓07°05	♉20°28	♓27°31	♒00°05	♉01°56	♉03°19	♌16°37	♈19°01	6 Tu
7 We	17:00:33	♊16°01'28	♑24°41'17	♒02°01'11	♉23°20	♌01°20	♌10°01	♉04°40	♓07°06	♉20°31	♓27°31	♒00°04	♉01°53	♉03°13	♌16°44	♈19°03	7 We
8 Th	17:04:29	♊16°58'52	♒09°20'10	♒16°37'08	♉24°45	♌02°16	♌10°36	♉04°52	♓07°07	♉20°34	♓27°32	♒00°03	♉01°50	♉03°08	♌16°51	♈19°05	8 Th
9 Fr	17:08:26	♊17°56'16	♒23°51'48	♓01°03'18	♉26°13	♌03°12	♌11°11	♉05°04	♓07°08	♉20°38	♓27°33	♒00°02	♉01°47	♉03°04	♌16°58	♈19°07	9 Fr
10 Sa	17:12:22	♊18°53'38	♓08°11'36	♓15°16'05	♉27°44	♌04°07	♌11°46	♉05°17	♓07°09	♉20°41	♓27°34	♒00°01	♉01°43	♉03°02	♌17°04	♈19°10	10 Sa
11 Su	17:16:19	♊19°51'01	♓22°16'55	♓29°13'40	♉29°18	♌05°02	♌12°22	♉05°29	♓07°10	♉20°44	♓27°34	♒00°00	♉01°40	D 03°01	♌17°11	♈19°12	11 Su
12 Mo	17:20:15	♊20°48'22	♈06°06'44	♈12°55'47	♊00°54	♌05°56	♌12°57	♉05°41	♓07°11	♉20°47	♓27°35	♑29°59	♉01°37	♉03°02	♌17°18	♈19°14	12 Mo
13 Tu	17:24:12	♊21°45'43	♈19°41'19	♈26°23'06	♊02°34	♌06°49	♌13°32	♉05°53	♓07°11	♉20°50	♓27°36	♑29°58	♉01°34	♉03°03	♌17°24	♈19°16	13 Tu
14 We	17:28:08	♊22°43'04	♉03°01'37	♉09°36'41	♊04°15	♌07°42	♌14°07	♉06°05	♓07°11	♉20°53	♓27°36	♑29°57	♉01°31	♉03°04	♌17°31	♈19°18	14 We
15 Th	17:32:05	♊23°40'25	♉16°08'45	♉22°37'37	♊06°00	♌08°34	♌14°43	♉06°17	♓07°12	♉20°56	♓27°37	♑29°56	♉01°27	℞ 03°03	♌17°38	♈19°20	15 Th
16 Fr	17:36:02	♊24°37'45	♉29°03'43	♊05°26'47	♊07°47	♌09°26	♌15°18	♉06°29	♓07°12	♉20°59	♓27°37	♑29°55	♉01°24	♉03°00	♌17°45	♈19°21	16 Fr
17 Sa	17:39:58	♊25°35'04	♊11°47'15	♊18°04'49	♊09°37	♌10°17	♌15°54	♉06°41	♓07°12	♉21°02	♓27°38	♑29°54	♉01°21	♉02°55	♌17°51	♈19°23	17 Sa
18 Su	17:43:55	♊26°32'24	♊24°19'52	♋00°32'08	♊11°30	♌11°07	♌16°29	♉06°53	℞ 07°12	♉21°05	♓27°38	♑29°52	♉01°18	♉02°47	♌17°58	♈19°25	18 Su
19 Mo	17:47:51	♊27°29'42	♋06°42'01	♋12°49'18	♊13°25	♌11°57	♌17°05	♉07°04	♓07°12	♉21°08	♓27°38	♑29°51	♉01°15	♉02°38	♌18°05	♈19°27	19 Mo
20 Tu	17:51:48	♊28°27'00	♋18°54'23	♋24°57'07	♊15°22	♌12°46	♌17°41	♉07°16	♓07°12	♉21°11	♓27°39	♑29°50	♉01°12	♉02°28	♌18°11	♈19°28	20 Tu
21 We	17:55:44	♊29°24'17	♌00°58'00	♌06°56'58	♊17°21	♌13°34	♌18°16	♉07°27	♓07°12	♉21°14	♓27°39	♑29°49	♉01°08	♉02°17	♌18°18	♈19°30	21 We
22 Th	17:59:41	♋00°21'34	♌12°54'37	♌18°50'57	♊19°23	♌14°21	♌18°52	♉07°39	♓07°11	♉21°17	♓27°39	♑29°48	♉01°05	♉02°08	♌18°25	♈19°32	22 Th
23 Fr	18:03:37	♋01°18'50	♌24°46'40	♍00°41'55	♊21°27	♌15°08	♌19°28	♉07°50	♓07°11	♉21°20	♓27°40	♑29°47	♉01°02	♉02°00	♌18°32	♈19°33	23 Fr
24 Sa	18:07:34	♋02°16'05	♍06°37'27	♍12°33'30	♊23°32	♌15°53	♌20°04	♉08°01	♓07°10	♉21°23	♓27°40	♑29°45	♉00°59	♉01°55	♌18°38	♈19°35	24 Sa
25 Su	18:11:31	♋03°13'20	♍18°30'56	♍24°30'03	♊25°39	♌16°38	♌20°39	♉08°12	♓07°10	♉21°25	♓27°40	♑29°44	♉00°56	♉01°52	♌18°45	♈19°36	25 Su
26 Mo	18:15:27	♋04°10'34	♎00°31'45	♎06°36'24	♊27°48	♌17°22	♌21°15	♉08°23	♓07°09	♉21°28	♓27°40	♑29°43	♉00°53	♉01°50	♌18°52	♈19°38	26 Mo
27 Tu	18:19:24	♋05°07'47	♎12°44'55	♎18°57'39	♊29°57	♌18°05	♌21°51	♉08°34	♓07°08	♉21°31	♓27°40	♑29°42	♉00°49	D 01°50	♌18°58	♈19°39	27 Tu
28 We	18:23:20	♋06°05'00	♎25°15'32	♏01°38'48	♋02°08	♌18°47	♌22°27	♉08°45	♓07°07	♉21°34	♓27°41	♑29°40	♉00°46	♉01°51	♌19°05	♈19°40	28 We
29 Th	18:27:17	♋07°02'12	♏08°08'19	♏14°44'10	♋04°18	♌19°28	♌23°03	♉08°55	♓07°06	♉21°36	♓27°41	♑29°39	♉00°43	℞ 01°51	♌19°12	♈19°42	29 Th
30 Fr	18:31:13	♋07°59'25	♏21°27'02	♏28°16'45	♋06°29	♌20°07	♌23°39	♉09°06	♓07°05	♉21°39	♓27°41	♑29°38	♉00°40	♉01°49	♌19°19	♈19°43	30 Fr
Δ Delta	01:54:19	27°42'39"	381°18'48"	381°33'29"	50°40'	24°33'	17°07'	5°42'	0°06'	1°27'	0°14'	-0°31'	-1°32'	-1°47'	3°14'	0°53'	Delta

Ephemeris tables and data provided by **Astro-Seek.com**. All times in UTC.

JULY 2023

July 2023

Longitude & Retrograde Ephemeris [00:00 UT]

Day	Sid.time	☉	☽	+12h ☽	☿	♀	♂	♃	♄	♅	♆	♇	☊	☊	⚸	⚷	Day
1 Sa	18:35:10	♋08°56'36	♐05°13'42	♐12°17'25	♋08°40	♌20°46	♌24°15	♉09°16	℞ 07°03	♉21°42	℞ 27°41	℞ 29°36	℞ 00°37	℞ 01°46	♌19°25	♈19°44	**1** Sa
2 Su	18:39:06	♋09°53'48	♐19°27'53	♐26°44'12	♋10°51	♌21°24	♌24°51	♉09°27	♓07°02	♉21°44	♓27°41	♑29°35	♉00°33	♉01°39	♌19°32	♈19°45	**2** Su
3 Mo	18:43:03	♋10°50'59	♑04°06'00	♑11°31'59	♋13°01	♌22°00	♌25°28	♉09°37	♓07°01	♉21°47	♓27°41	♑29°34	♉00°30	♉01°31	♌19°39	♈19°46	**3** Mo
4 Tu	18:46:60	♋11°48'10	♑19°01'25	♑26°32'45	♋15°11	♌22°35	♌26°04	♉09°47	♓06°59	♉21°49	♓27°41	♑29°32	♉00°27	♉01°21	♌19°45	♈19°47	**4** Tu
5 We	18:50:56	♋12°45'21	♒04°05'07	♒11°36'51	♋17°19	♌23°09	♌26°40	♉09°57	♓06°58	♉21°52	♓27°40	♑29°31	♉00°24	♉01°11	♌19°52	♈19°48	**5** We
6 Th	18:54:53	♋13°42'32	♒19°07'09	♒26°34'33	♋19°26	♌23°41	♌27°16	♉10°07	♓06°56	♉21°54	♓27°40	♑29°30	♉00°21	♉01°02	♌19°59	♈19°49	**6** Th
7 Fr	18:58:49	♋14°39'43	♓03°58'29	♓11°17'47	♋21°32	♌24°12	♌27°53	♉10°17	♓06°54	♉21°57	♓27°40	♑29°28	♉00°18	♉00°55	♌20°06	♈19°50	**7** Fr
8 Sa	19:02:46	♋15°36'54	♓18°32'16	♓25°41'09	♋23°36	♌24°42	♌28°29	♉10°27	♓06°52	♉21°59	♓27°40	♑29°27	♉00°14	♉00°51	♌20°12	♈19°51	**8** Sa
9 Su	19:06:42	♋16°34'06	♈02°44'37	♈09°42'13	♋25°39	♌25°10	♌29°05	♉10°36	♓06°50	♉22°01	♓27°40	♑29°26	♉00°11	♉00°48	♌20°19	♈19°52	**9** Su
10 Mo	19:10:39	♋17°31'18	♈16°34'24	♈23°20'59	♋27°40	♌25°37	♌29°42	♉10°46	♓06°48	♉22°04	♓27°39	♑29°24	♉00°08	♉00°48	♌20°26	♈19°52	**10** Mo
11 Tu	19:14:36	♋18°28'31	♉00°02'35	♉06°39'11	♋29°39	♌26°02	♍00°18	♉10°55	♓06°46	♉22°06	♓27°39	♑29°23	♉00°05	D 00°48	♌20°32	♈19°53	**11** Tu
12 We	19:18:32	♋19°25'44	♉13°11'27	♉19°39'26	♌01°36	♌26°25	♍00°55	♉11°04	♓06°44	♉22°08	♓27°39	♑29°21	♉00°02	℞ 00°47	♌20°39	♈19°54	**12** We
13 Th	19:22:29	♋20°22'58	♉26°03'48	♊02°24'35	♌03°32	♌26°47	♍01°31	♉11°13	♓06°41	♉22°10	♓27°38	♑29°20	♈29°59	♉00°45	♌20°46	♈19°54	**13** Th
14 Fr	19:26:25	♋21°20'12	♊08°42'25	♊14°57'16	♌05°26	♌27°06	♍02°08	♉11°22	♓06°39	♉22°13	♓27°38	♑29°19	♈29°55	♉00°41	♌20°53	♈19°55	**14** Fr
15 Sa	19:30:22	♋22°17'26	♊21°09'42	♊27°19'38	♌07°18	♌27°24	♍02°45	♉11°31	♓06°36	♉22°15	♓27°38	♑29°17	♈29°52	♉00°33	♌20°59	♈19°55	**15** Sa
16 Su	19:34:18	♋23°14'41	♋03°27'34	♋09°33'20	♌09°08	♌27°41	♍03°21	♉11°40	♓06°34	♉22°17	♓27°37	♑29°16	♈29°49	♉00°23	♌21°06	♈19°56	**16** Su
17 Mo	19:38:15	♋24°11'57	♋15°37'26	♋21°39'39	♌10°56	♌27°55	♍03°58	♉11°49	♓06°31	♉22°19	♓27°37	♑29°14	♈29°46	♉00°11	♌21°13	♈19°56	**17** Mo
18 Tu	19:42:11	♋25°09'12	♋27°40'27	♌03°39'40	♌12°42	♌28°07	♍04°35	♉11°57	♓06°28	♉22°21	♓27°36	♑29°13	♈29°43	♈29°57	♌21°19	♈19°56	**18** Tu
19 We	19:46:08	♋26°06'29	♌09°37'45	♌15°34'33	♌14°27	♌28°17	♍05°12	♉12°05	♓06°26	♉22°23	♓27°35	♑29°12	♈29°40	♈29°43	♌21°26	♈19°57	**19** We
20 Th	19:50:05	♋27°03'45	♌21°30'37	♌27°25'51	♌16°09	♌28°25	♍05°48	♉12°14	♓06°23	♉22°25	♓27°35	♑29°10	♈29°36	♈29°31	♌21°33	♈19°57	**20** Th
21 Fr	19:54:01	♋28°01'02	♍03°20'50	♍09°15'37	♌17°50	♌28°31	♍06°25	♉12°22	♓06°20	♉22°27	♓27°34	♑29°09	♈29°33	♈29°20	♌21°40	♈19°57	**21** Fr
22 Sa	19:57:58	♋28°58'19	♍15°10'51	♍21°06'40	♌19°29	♌28°34	♍07°02	♉12°29	♓06°17	♉22°28	♓27°34	♑29°07	♈29°30	♈29°12	♌21°46	♈19°57	**22** Sa
23 Su	20:01:54	♋29°55'36	♍27°03'49	♎03°02'32	♌21°06	♌28°36	♍07°39	♉12°37	♓06°14	♉22°30	♓27°33	♑29°06	♈29°27	♈29°06	♌21°53	♈19°57	**23** Su
24 Mo	20:05:51	♌00°52'54	♎09°03'39	♎15°07'28	♌22°41	℞ 28°35	♍08°16	♉12°45	♓06°10	♉22°32	♓27°32	♑29°04	♈29°24	♈29°03	♌22°00	℞ 19°57	**24** Mo
25 Tu	20:09:47	♌01°50'12	♎21°14'55	♎27°26'17	♌24°14	♌28°31	♍08°53	♉12°52	♓06°07	♉22°34	♓27°31	♑29°03	♈29°20	♈29°03	♌22°06	♈19°57	**25** Tu
26 We	20:13:44	♌02°47'30	♏03°42'34	♏10°04'02	♌25°46	♌28°26	♍09°30	♉13°00	♓06°04	♉22°35	♓27°31	♑29°02	♈29°17	♈29°02	♌22°13	♈19°57	**26** We
27 Th	20:17:40	♌03°44'49	♏16°31'39	♏23°05'34	♌27°15	♌28°17	♍10°07	♉13°07	♓06°00	♉22°37	♓27°30	♑29°00	♈29°14	♈29°02	♌22°20	♈19°57	**27** Th
28 Fr	20:21:37	♌04°42'09	♏29°46'36	♐06°34'46	♌28°43	♌28°07	♍10°45	♉13°14	♓05°57	♉22°39	♓27°29	♑28°59	♈29°11	♈29°00	♌22°27	♈19°57	**28** Fr
29 Sa	20:25:34	♌05°39'28	♐13°30'37	♐20°33'49	♍00°08	♌27°54	♍11°22	♉13°21	♓05°53	♉22°40	♓27°28	♑28°57	♈29°08	♈28°57	♌22°33	♈19°57	**29** Sa
30 Su	20:29:30	♌06°36'48	♐27°44'34	♑05°02'05	♍01°32	♌27°39	♍11°59	♉13°27	♓05°50	♉22°42	♓27°27	♑28°56	♈29°05	♈28°50	♌22°40	♈19°56	**30** Su
31 Mo	20:33:27	♌07°34'09	♑12°26'08	♑19°55'29	♍02°54	♌27°21	♍12°36	♉13°34	♓05°46	♉22°43	♓27°26	♑28°55	♈29°01	♈28°42	♌22°47	♈19°56	**31** Mo
Δ Delta	01:58:17	28°37'33"	397°12'25"	397°38'04"	54°13'	6°34'	18°20'	4°17'	-1°17'	1°01'	-0°14'	-0°41'	-1°35'	-3°04'	3°21'	0°11'	**Delta**

Ephemeris tables and data provided by **Astro-Seek.com.** All times in UTC.

August 2023

Longitude & Retrograde Ephemeris [00:00 UT]

Day	Sid.time	☉	☽	+12h☽	☿	♀	♂	♃	♄	♅	♆	♇	☊	☊	⚸	⚷	Day
1 Tu	20:37:23	♌08°31'31	♑27°29'26	♒05°06'21	♍04°13	℞ 27°01	♍13°14	♉13°40	℞ 05°42	♉22°44	℞ 27°26	℞ 28°53	℞ 28°58	℞ 28°31	♌22°53	℞ 19°55	1 Tu
2 We	20:41:20	♌09°28'53	♒12°45'15	♒20°24'18	♍05°31	♌26°39	♍13°51	♉13°47	♓05°38	♉22°46	♓27°25	♑28°52	♈28°55	♈28°21	♌23°00	♈19°55	2 We
3 Th	20:45:16	♌10°26'16	♒28°02'27	♓05°37'58	♍06°46	♌26°14	♍14°28	♉13°53	♓05°35	♉22°47	♓27°24	♑28°50	♈28°52	♈28°11	♌23°07	♈19°54	3 Th
4 Fr	20:49:13	♌11°23'40	♓13°10'00	♓20°37'08	♍08°00	♌25°48	♍15°06	♉13°59	♓05°31	♉22°48	♓27°23	♑28°49	♈28°49	♈28°03	♌23°14	♈19°54	4 Fr
5 Sa	20:53:09	♌12°21'05	♓27°58'54	♈05°14'18	℞s 09°11	♌25°20	♍15°43	♉14°05	♓05°27	♉22°50	♓27°22	♑28°48	♈28°45	♈27°58	♌23°20	♈19°53	5 Sa
6 Su	20:57:06	♌13°18'31	♈12°23'21	♈19°25'27	♍10°19	♌24°50	♍16°21	♉14°10	♓05°23	♉22°51	♓27°21	♑28°46	♈28°42	♈27°56	♌23°27	♈19°53	6 Su
7 Mo	21:01:03	♌14°15'59	♈26°20'58	♉03°09'42	♍11°26	♌24°18	♍16°58	♉14°16	♓05°19	♉22°52	♓27°19	♑28°45	♈28°39	♈27°55	♌23°34	♈19°52	7 Mo
8 Tu	21:04:59	♌15°13'27	♉09°52'15	♉16°28'39	♍12°29	♌23°45	♍17°36	♉14°21	♓05°15	♉22°53	♓27°18	♑28°43	♈28°36	D 27°55	♌23°40	♈19°51	8 Tu
9 We	21:08:56	♌16°10'58	♉22°59'39	♉29°25'23	♍13°31	♌23°11	♍18°13	♉14°26	♓05°11	♉22°54	♓27°17	♑28°42	♈28°33	℞ 27°55	♌23°47	♈19°50	9 We
10 Th	21:12:52	♌17°08'29	♊05°46'39	♊12°03'37	♍14°29	♌22°35	♍18°51	♉14°31	♓05°06	♉22°55	♓27°16	♑28°41	♈28°30	♈27°53	♌23°54	♈19°49	10 Th
11 Fr	21:16:49	♌18°06'02	♊18°17'05	♊24°27'11	♍15°25	♌21°59	♍19°29	♉14°36	♓05°02	♉22°56	♓27°15	♑28°39	♈28°26	♈27°50	♌24°01	♈19°49	11 Fr
12 Sa	21:20:45	♌19°03'36	♋00°34'38	♋06°39'31	♍16°18	♌21°22	♍20°07	♉14°40	♓04°58	♉22°57	♓27°14	♑28°38	♈28°23	♈27°43	♌24°07	♈19°48	12 Sa
13 Su	21:24:42	♌20°01'12	♋12°42'29	♋18°43'33	♍17°07	♌20°45	♍20°44	♉14°45	♓04°54	♉22°58	♓27°12	♑28°37	♈28°20	♈27°35	♌24°14	♈19°47	13 Su
14 Mo	21:28:38	♌20°58'49	♋24°43'18	♌00°41'39	♍17°53	♌20°08	♍21°22	♉14°49	♓04°49	♉22°58	♓27°11	♑28°35	♈28°17	♈27°24	♌24°21	♈19°45	14 Mo
15 Tu	21:32:35	♌21°56'27	♌06°39'09	♌12°35'42	♍18°36	♌19°31	♍22°00	♉14°53	♓04°45	♉22°59	♓27°10	♑28°34	♈28°14	♈27°12	♌24°27	♈19°44	15 Tu
16 We	21:36:32	♌22°54'06	♌18°31'46	♌24°27'16	♍19°15	♌18°54	♍22°38	♉14°57	♓04°41	♉23°00	♓27°09	♑28°33	♈28°11	♈27°00	♌24°34	♈19°43	16 We
17 Th	21:40:28	♌23°51'47	♍00°22'40	♍06°17'52	♍19°51	♌18°18	♍23°16	♉15°01	♓04°36	♉23°00	♓27°07	♑28°32	♈28°07	♈26°48	♌24°41	♈19°42	17 Th
18 Fr	21:44:25	♌24°49'29	♍12°13'24	♍18°09'12	♍20°22	♌17°42	♍23°54	♉15°04	♓04°32	♉23°01	♓27°06	♑28°30	♈28°04	♈26°39	♌24°48	♈19°41	18 Fr
19 Sa	21:48:21	♌25°47'12	♍24°05'49	♎00°03'18	♍20°49	♌17°08	♍24°32	♉15°07	♓04°27	♉23°01	♓27°05	♑28°29	♈28°01	♈26°32	♌24°54	♈19°39	19 Sa
20 Su	21:52:18	♌26°44'56	♎06°02'16	♎12°02'48	♍21°11	♌16°34	♍25°10	♉15°10	♓04°23	♉23°02	♓27°03	♑28°28	♈27°58	♈26°27	♌25°01	♈19°38	20 Su
21 Mo	21:56:14	♌27°42'42	♎18°05'38	♎24°10'56	♍21°29	♌16°03	♍25°48	♉15°13	♓04°18	♉23°02	♓27°02	♑28°27	♈27°55	♈26°25	♌25°08	♈19°37	21 Mo
22 Tu	22:00:11	♌28°40'28	♏00°19'31	♏06°31'33	♍21°41	♌15°32	♍26°27	♉15°16	♓04°14	♉23°03	♓27°01	♑28°26	♈27°51	D 26°25	♌25°14	♈19°35	22 Tu
23 We	22:04:07	♌29°38'16	♏12°47'57	♏19°08'55	♍21°49	♌15°04	♍27°05	♉15°19	♓04°09	♉23°03	♓26°59	♑28°24	♈27°48	♈26°25	♌25°21	♈19°34	23 We
24 Th	22:08:04	♍00°36'05	♏25°35'19	♐02°07'21	℞ 21°51	♌14°37	♍27°43	♉15°21	♓04°05	♉23°03	♓26°58	♑28°23	♈27°45	♈26°26	♌25°28	♈19°32	24 Th
25 Fr	22:12:01	♍01°33'55	♐08°45'48	♐15°30'43	♍21°47	♌14°12	♍28°21	♉15°23	♓04°00	♉23°04	♓26°56	♑28°22	♈27°42	℞ 26°26	♌25°34	♈19°31	25 Fr
26 Sa	22:15:57	♍02°31'47	♐22°22'44	♐29°21'40	♍21°37	♌13°50	♍29°00	♉15°25	♓03°56	♉23°04	♓26°55	♑28°21	♈27°39	♈26°24	♌25°41	♈19°29	26 Sa
27 Su	22:19:54	♍03°29'39	♑06°27'52	♑13°40'45	♍21°22	♌13°30	♍29°38	♉15°27	♓03°51	♉23°04	♓26°53	♑28°20	♈27°36	♈26°20	♌25°48	♈19°27	27 Su
28 Mo	22:23:50	♍04°27'33	♑21°00'18	♑28°25'31	♍21°00	♌13°12	♎00°17	♉15°29	♓03°47	♉23°04	♓26°52	♑28°19	♈27°32	♈26°15	♌25°55	♈19°26	28 Mo
29 Tu	22:27:47	♍05°25'29	♒05°55'57	♒13°30'10	♍20°32	♌12°56	♎00°55	♉15°30	♓03°42	♉23°04	♓26°50	♑28°18	♈27°29	♈26°08	♌26°01	♈19°24	29 Tu
30 We	22:31:43	♍06°23'25	♒21°07'21	♒28°45'47	♍19°59	♌12°42	♎01°34	♉15°31	♓03°38	℞ 23°04	♓26°49	♑28°17	♈27°26	♈26°00	♌26°08	♈19°22	30 We
31 Th	22:35:40	♍07°21'23	♓06°24'30	♓14°01'41	♍19°20	♌12°31	♎02°12	♉15°32	♓03°33	♉23°04	♓26°47	♑28°16	♈27°23	♈25°53	♌26°15	♈19°20	31 Th
Δ Delta	01:58:16	28°49'52"	398°55'03"	398°55'19"	15°06'	-14°29'	18°58'	1°51'	-2°09'	0°19'	-0°38'	-0°37'	-1°35'	-2°38'	3°21'	-0°35'	Delta

Ephemeris tables and data provided by **Astro-Seek.com**. All times in UTC.

December 2023

Longitude & Retrograde Ephemeris [00:00 UT]

Day	Sid.time	☉	☽	+12h ☽	☿	♀	♂	♃	♄	♅	♆	♇	☊	☊	⚸	⚷	Day
1 Fr	04:38:23	♐08°30'40	♋21°45'14	♋27°56'45	℞s 29°16	♎25°34	♐04°41	℞ 07°06	♓01°07	℞ 20°21	℞ 24°53	♑28°30	℞ 22°31	℞ 23°54	♍06°31	℞ 15°45	1 Fr
2 Sa	04:42:20	♐09°31'28	♌04°04'39	♌10°08'56	♑00°27	♎26°44	♐05°24	♉07°00	♓01°10	♉20°19	♓24°53	♑28°31	♈22°27	♈23°47	♍06°37	♈15°44	2 Sa
3 Su	04:46:16	♐10°32'16	♌16°10'24	♌22°09'13	♑01°36	♎27°54	♐06°07	♉06°54	♓01°13	♉20°16	♓24°53	♑28°33	♈22°24	♈23°42	♍06°44	♈15°43	3 Su
4 Mo	04:50:13	♐11°33'07	♌28°06'15	♍04°01'46	♑02°41	♎29°04	♐06°50	♉06°49	♓01°16	♉20°14	♓24°53	♑28°34	♈22°21	♈23°39	♍06°51	♈15°41	4 Mo
5 Tu	04:54:09	♐12°33'59	♍09°56'44	♍15°51'28	♑03°43	♏00°15	♐07°34	♉06°44	♓01°19	♉20°12	♓24°53	♑28°35	♈22°18	♈23°38	♍06°57	♈15°40	5 Tu
6 We	04:58:06	♐13°34'51	♍21°46'56	♍27°43'30	♑04°41	♏01°25	♐08°17	♉06°39	♓01°22	♉20°10	♓24°53	♑28°37	♈22°15	D 23°38	♍07°04	♈15°39	6 We
7 Th	05:02:02	♐14°35'45	♎03°42'09	♎09°43'12	♑05°33	♏02°36	♐09°00	♉06°34	♓01°25	♉20°07	D 24°53	♑28°38	♈22°12	♈23°39	♍07°11	♈15°38	7 Th
8 Fr	05:05:59	♐15°36'41	♎15°47'36	♎21°55'37	♑06°21	♏03°47	♐09°44	♉06°29	♓01°29	♉20°05	♓24°53	♑28°40	♈22°08	♈23°40	♍07°18	♈15°37	8 Fr
9 Sa	05:09:55	♐16°37'38	♎28°08'05	♏04°25'09	♑07°02	♏04°58	♐10°27	♉06°25	♓01°32	♉20°03	♓24°53	♑28°41	♈22°05	℞ 23°40	♍07°24	♈15°36	9 Sa
10 Su	05:13:52	♐17°38'36	♏10°47'31	♏17°15'07	♑07°36	♏06°09	♐11°10	♉06°20	♓01°36	♉20°01	♓24°53	♑28°43	♈22°02	♈23°39	♍07°31	♈15°35	10 Su
11 Mo	05:17:49	♐18°39'35	♏23°48'30	♐00°27'22	♑08°03	♏07°20	♐11°54	♉06°16	♓01°39	♉19°59	♓24°53	♑28°45	♈21°59	♈23°35	♍07°38	♈15°34	11 Mo
12 Tu	05:21:45	♐19°40'35	♐07°11'58	♐14°01'45	♑08°20	♏08°31	♐12°37	♉06°12	♓01°43	♉19°57	♓24°53	♑28°46	♈21°56	♈23°28	♍07°44	♈15°33	12 Tu
13 We	05:25:42	♐20°41'36	♐20°56'43	♐27°56'03	♑08°28	♏09°43	♐13°21	♉06°08	♓01°47	♉19°55	♓24°54	♑28°48	♈21°52	♈23°20	♍07°51	♈15°32	13 We
14 Th	05:29:38	♐21°42'39	♑04°59'33	♑12°06'09	℞ 08°26	♏10°54	♐14°05	♉06°05	♓01°51	♉19°53	♓24°54	♑28°49	♈21°49	♈23°10	♍07°58	♈15°31	14 Th
15 Fr	05:33:35	♐22°43'41	♑19°15'30	♑26°26'28	♑08°13	♏12°06	♐14°48	♉06°01	♓01°55	♉19°51	♓24°54	♑28°51	♈21°46	♈23°00	♍08°04	♈15°31	15 Fr
16 Sa	05:37:31	♐23°44'45	♒03°38'41	♒10°51'02	♑07°48	♏13°18	♐15°32	♉05°58	♓01°59	♉19°49	♓24°54	♑28°53	♈21°43	♈22°50	♍08°11	♈15°30	16 Sa
17 Su	05:41:28	♐24°45'49	♒18°03'14	♒25°14'20	♑07°12	♏14°30	♐16°16	♉05°55	♓02°03	♉19°47	♓24°55	♑28°54	♈21°40	♈22°43	♍08°18	♈15°29	17 Su
18 Mo	05:45:24	♐25°46'53	♓02°24'12	♓09°32'05	♑06°24	♏15°42	♐17°00	♉05°52	♓02°07	♉19°45	♓24°55	♑28°56	♈21°37	♈22°38	♍08°24	♈15°29	18 Mo
19 Tu	05:49:21	♐26°47'57	♓16°38'04	♓23°41'34	♑05°26	♏16°54	♐17°44	♉05°50	♓02°11	♉19°43	♓24°56	♑28°58	♈21°33	♈22°36	♍08°31	♈15°28	19 Tu
20 We	05:53:18	♐27°49'02	♈00°42'52	♈07°41'31	♑04°19	♏18°06	♐18°27	♉05°47	♓02°16	♉19°41	♓24°56	♑28°59	♈21°30	D 22°36	♍08°38	♈15°28	20 We
21 Th	05:57:14	♐28°50'07	♈14°37'55	♈21°31'41	♑03°04	♏19°18	♐19°11	♉05°45	♓02°20	♉19°40	♓24°56	♑29°01	♈21°27	♈22°36	♍08°44	♈15°28	21 Th
22 Fr	06:01:11	♐29°51'12	♈28°23'14	♉05°12'14	♑01°44	♏20°30	♐19°55	♉05°43	♓02°25	♉19°38	♓24°57	♑29°03	♈21°24	℞ 22°36	♍08°51	♈15°27	22 Fr
23 Sa	06:05:07	♑00°52'18	♉11°59'03	♉18°43'19	♑00°21	♏21°42	♐20°39	♉05°41	♓02°29	♉19°36	♓24°58	♑29°05	♈21°21	♈22°35	♍08°58	♈15°27	23 Sa
24 Su	06:09:04	♑01°53'23	♉25°25'21	♊02°04'42	♐28°59	♏22°55	♐21°24	♉05°40	♓02°34	♉19°34	♓24°58	♑29°06	♈21°18	♈22°30	♍09°04	♈15°27	24 Su
25 Mo	06:13:00	♑02°54'29	♊08°41'39	♊15°15'42	♐27°40	♏24°07	♐22°08	♉05°38	♓02°39	♉19°33	♓24°59	♑29°08	♈21°14	♈22°23	♍09°11	♈15°27	25 Mo
26 Tu	06:16:57	♑03°55'36	♊21°47'05	♊28°15'16	♐26°26	♏25°20	♐22°52	♉05°37	♓02°44	♉19°31	♓24°59	♑29°10	♈21°11	♈22°13	♍09°18	♈15°27	26 Tu
27 We	06:20:53	♑04°56'43	♋04°40'31	♋11°02'21	♐25°20	♏26°32	♐23°36	♉05°36	♓02°48	♉19°30	♓25°00	♑29°12	♈21°08	♈22°01	♍09°24	♈15°27	27 We
28 Th	06:24:50	♑05°57'50	♋17°21'02	♋23°36'11	♐24°23	♏27°45	♐24°20	♉05°35	♓02°53	♉19°28	♓25°01	♑29°14	♈21°05	♈21°48	♍09°31	D 15°27	28 Th
29 Fr	06:28:47	♑06°58'57	♋29°48'12	♌05°56'49	♐23°35	♏28°58	♐25°05	♉05°35	♓02°58	♉19°27	♓25°02	♑29°15	♈21°02	♈21°34	♍09°38	♈15°27	29 Fr
30 Sa	06:32:43	♑08°00'04	♌12°02'31	♌18°05'11	♐22°58	♐00°10	♐25°49	♉05°34	♓03°04	♉19°25	♓25°02	♑29°17	♈20°58	♈21°22	♍09°45	♈15°27	30 Sa
31 Su	06:36:40	♑09°01'12	♌24°05'27	♍00°03'20	♐22°32	♐01°23	♐26°34	♉05°34	♓03°09	♉19°24	♓25°03	♑29°19	♈20°55	♈21°12	♍09°51	♈15°27	31 Su
Δ Delta	01:58:16	30°30'32"	392°20'12"	392°06'35"	-6°43'	35°49'	21°52'	-1°31'	2°01'	-0°57'	0°09'	0°49'	-1°35'	-2°42'	3°20'	-0°18'	Delta

Ephemeris tables and data provided by **Astro-Seek.com.** All times in UTC.

SEPTEMBER 2023

September 2023

Longitude & Retrograde Ephemeris [00:00 UT]

Day	Sid.time	☉	☽	+12h ☽	☿	♀	♂	♃	♄	♅	♆	♇	☊	☊	⚸	⚷	Day
1 Fr	22:39:36	♍08°19'23	♓21°36'27	♓29°07'10	℞ 18°36	℞ 12°23	♎02°51	♉15°33	℞ 03°29	℞ 23°04	℞ 26°46	℞ 28°15	℞ 27°20	℞ 25°48	♌26°21	℞ 19°18	**1** Fr
2 Sa	22:43:33	♍09°17'24	♈06°33'14	♈13°53'23	♍17°47	♌12°17	♎03°29	♉15°34	♓03°24	♉23°04	♓26°44	♑28°14	♈27°17	♈25°44	♌26°28	♈19°17	**2** Sa
3 Su	22:47:30	♍10°15'27	♈21°07'23	♈28°14'26	♍16°55	♌12°13	♎04°08	♉15°34	♓03°20	♉23°03	♓26°43	♑28°13	♈27°13	♈25°43	♌26°35	♈19°15	**3** Su
4 Mo	22:51:26	♍11°13'32	♉05°14'42	♉12°07'45	♍15°59	♌12°12	♎04°47	♉15°34	♓03°15	♉23°03	♓26°41	♑28°12	♈27°10	D 25°43	♌26°42	♈19°13	**4** Mo
5 Tu	22:55:23	♍12°11'39	♉18°54'04	♉25°33'33	♍15°02	D 12°13	♎05°26	℞ 15°34	♓03°11	♉23°03	♓26°39	♑28°11	♈27°07	♈25°44	♌26°48	♈19°11	**5** Tu
6 We	22:59:19	♍13°09'48	♊02°06'54	♊08°34'11	♍14°03	♌12°16	♎06°04	♉15°34	♓03°06	♉23°02	♓26°38	♑28°10	♈27°04	♈25°46	♌26°55	♈19°09	**6** We
7 Th	23:03:16	♍14°07'59	♊14°56'14	♊21°13'14	♍13°05	♌12°22	♎06°43	♉15°34	♓03°02	♉23°02	♓26°36	♑28°09	♈27°01	℞ 25°46	♌27°02	♈19°06	**7** Th
8 Fr	23:07:12	♍15°06'12	♊27°26'04	♋03°34'54	♍12°09	♌12°30	♎07°22	♉15°33	♓02°57	♉23°02	♓26°35	♑28°08	♈26°57	♈25°45	♌27°08	♈19°04	**8** Fr
9 Sa	23:11:09	♍16°04'27	♋09°40'38	♋15°43'26	♍11°16	♌12°40	♎08°01	♉15°32	♓02°53	♉23°01	♓26°33	♑28°07	♈26°54	♈25°43	♌27°15	♈19°02	**9** Sa
10 Su	23:15:05	♍17°02'44	♋21°44'07	♋27°42'48	♍10°27	♌12°52	♎08°40	♉15°31	♓02°49	♉23°00	♓26°31	♑28°06	♈26°51	♈25°38	♌27°22	♈19°00	**10** Su
11 Mo	23:19:02	♍18°01'03	♌03°40'15	♌09°36'32	♍09°43	♌13°06	♎09°19	♉15°30	♓02°44	♉23°00	♓26°30	♑28°05	♈26°48	♈25°33	♌27°28	♈18°58	**11** Mo
12 Tu	23:22:59	♍18°59'24	♌15°32'20	♌21°27'37	♍09°06	♌13°22	♎09°58	♉15°29	♓02°40	♉22°59	♓26°28	♑28°05	♈26°45	♈25°26	♌27°35	♈18°56	**12** Tu
13 We	23:26:55	♍19°57'47	♌27°23'03	♍03°18'32	♍08°37	♌13°41	♎10°37	♉15°27	♓02°36	♉22°58	♓26°27	♑28°04	♈26°42	♈25°19	♌27°42	♈18°53	**13** We
14 Th	23:30:52	♍20°56'12	♍09°14'40	♍15°11'21	♍08°16	♌14°01	♎11°17	♉15°26	♓02°32	♉22°58	♓26°25	♑28°03	♈26°38	♈25°13	♌27°49	♈18°51	**14** Th
15 Fr	23:34:48	♍21°54'38	♍21°09'06	♍27°07'50	♍08°03	♌14°23	♎11°56	♉15°24	♓02°27	♉22°57	♓26°23	♑28°02	♈26°35	♈25°08	♌27°55	♈18°49	**15** Fr
16 Sa	23:38:45	♍22°53'07	♎03°08'05	♎09°09'46	Ds 08°00	♌14°46	♎12°35	♉15°21	♓02°23	♉22°56	♓26°22	♑28°02	♈26°32	♈25°04	♌28°02	♈18°46	**16** Sa
17 Su	23:42:41	♍23°51'37	♎15°13'24	♎21°18'55	♍08°06	♌15°12	♎13°14	♉15°19	♓02°19	♉22°55	♓26°20	♑28°01	♈26°29	♈25°02	♌28°09	♈18°44	**17** Su
18 Mo	23:46:38	♍24°50'09	♎27°26'57	♏03°37'25	♍08°22	♌15°38	♎13°54	♉15°16	♓02°15	♉22°54	♓26°18	♑28°00	♈26°26	D 25°02	♌28°15	♈18°41	**18** Mo
19 Tu	23:50:34	♍25°48'43	♏09°50'59	♏16°07'38	♍08°47	♌16°07	♎14°33	♉15°14	♓02°11	♉22°53	♓26°17	♑28°00	♈26°23	♈25°03	♌28°22	♈18°39	**19** Tu
20 We	23:54:31	♍26°47'20	♏22°28'05	♏28°52'19	♍09°21	♌16°37	♎15°13	♉15°11	♓02°07	♉22°52	♓26°15	♑27°59	♈26°19	♈25°04	♌28°29	♈18°36	**20** We
21 Th	23:58:28	♍27°45'57	♐05°21'03	♐11°54'18	♍10°03	♌17°09	♎15°52	♉15°07	♓02°03	♉22°51	♓26°13	♑27°59	♈26°16	♈25°06	♌28°35	♈18°34	**21** Th
22 Fr	00:02:24	♍28°44'36	♐18°32'44	♐25°16'16	♍10°54	♌17°42	♎16°32	♉15°04	♓02°00	♉22°50	♓26°12	♑27°58	♈26°13	♈25°07	♌28°42	♈18°31	**22** Fr
23 Sa	00:06:21	♍29°43'17	♑02°05'31	♑09°00'14	♍11°53	♌18°16	♎17°11	♉15°00	♓01°56	♉22°49	♓26°10	♑27°58	♈26°10	℞ 25°07	♌28°49	♈18°29	**23** Sa
24 Su	00:10:17	♎00°42'00	♑16°00'50	♑23°06'52	♍12°59	♌18°52	♎17°51	♉14°57	♓01°52	♉22°48	♓26°08	♑27°57	♈26°07	♈25°07	♌28°56	♈18°26	**24** Su
25 Mo	00:14:14	♎01°40'44	♒00°18'29	♒07°34'57	♍14°12	♌19°28	♎18°31	♉14°53	♓01°48	♉22°46	♓26°07	♑27°57	♈26°03	♈25°05	♌29°02	♈18°24	**25** Mo
26 Tu	00:18:10	♎02°39'30	♒14°56'07	♒22°20'52	♍15°30	♌20°07	♎19°10	♉14°49	♓01°45	♉22°45	♓26°05	♑27°56	♈26°00	♈25°02	♌29°09	♈18°21	**26** Tu
27 We	00:22:07	♎03°38'17	♒29°48'48	♓07°18'32	♍16°54	♌20°46	♎19°50	♉14°44	♓01°41	♉22°44	♓26°03	♑27°56	♈25°57	♈24°59	♌29°16	♈18°19	**27** We
28 Th	00:26:03	♎04°37'07	♓14°49'24	♓22°19'55	♍18°22	♌21°26	♎20°30	♉14°40	♓01°38	♉22°42	♓26°02	♑27°55	♈25°54	♈24°57	♌29°22	♈18°16	**28** Th
29 Fr	00:29:60	♎05°35'58	♓29°49'21	♈07°16'12	♍19°54	♌22°08	♎21°10	♉14°35	♓01°35	♉22°41	♓26°00	♑27°55	♈25°51	♈24°55	♌29°29	♈18°13	**29** Fr
30 Sa	00:33:57	♎06°34'51	♈14°39'52	♈21°59'03	♍21°29	♌22°51	♎21°50	♉14°31	♓01°31	♉22°39	♓25°58	♑27°55	♈25°48	♈24°53	♌29°36	♈18°11	**30** Sa
Δ Delta	01:54:21	28°15'28"	-383°03'25"	-382°51'52"	2°53'	10°27'	18°59'	-1°02'	-1°57'	-0°24'	-0°47'	-0°19'	-1°32'	-0°54'	3°14'	-1°07'	**Delta**

Ephemeris tables and data provided by **Astro-Seek.com.** All times in UTC.

THE ASTROTWINS

Identical twin sisters Ophira and Tali Edut, known as the AstroTwins, are professional astrologers who reach millions worldwide. As the official astrologers for *ELLE* magazine and the matchmakers on Amazon Prime Video's *Cosmic Love* they bring the stars down to earth with their empowering approach to horoscopes.

Bestselling authors, they've written a collection of books, including *Love Zodiac*, *Supercouple* and *Momstrology* (their #1 Amazon parenting guide) and their own brand imprint annual horoscope guides.

With a mission to "empower astrology lovers how to create lives of passion and purpose using the stars as a guide," the AstroTwins have created a suite of courses applying astrology to love, career and home design. Their signature program, Astropreneurs, teaches aspiring and current business owners how to tap into their unique astrological strengths to build careers they love.

Daily, weekly & monthly horoscopes by The AstroTwins

astrostyle.com | @astrotwins